Frommer's

Nashville & Memphis

6th Edition

by Linda Romine

WILEY

Wiley Publishing, Inc.

About the Author

Linda Romine has been a professional writer for nearly 2 decades. With a background in music, she has worked on the editorial staffs of various newspapers and magazines as a reporter, music critic, travel editor, and restaurant reviewer.

Published by:

Wiley Publishing, Inc.

111 River St.
Hoboken, NJ 07030-5774

ISBN 0-7645-4443-8

Editors: David Allen & Myka Carroll
Production Editor: Ian Skinnari
Cartographer: Elizabeth Puhl
Photo Editor: Richard Fox
Production by Wiley Indianapolis Composition Services

For information on our other products and services or to obtain technical support, please contact our Customer Care Department within the U.S. at 800-762-2974, outside the U.S. at 317-572-3993 or fax 317-572-4002.

Wiley also publishes its books in a variety of electronic formats. Some content that appears in print may not be available in electronic formats.

Manufactured in the United States of America

5   4   3   2   1

Contents

List of Maps

An Invitation to the Reader

In researching this book, we discovered many wonderful places — hotels, restaurants, shops, and more. We're sure you'll find others. Please tell us about them, so we can share the information with your fellow travelers in upcoming editions. If you were disappointed with a recommendation, we'd love to know that, too. Please write to:

Frommer's Nashville & Memphis, 6th Edition
Wiley Publishing, Inc. • 111 River St. • Hoboken, NJ 07030-5774

An Additional Note

Please be advised that travel information is subject to change at any time — and this is especially true of prices. We therefore suggest that you write or call ahead for confirmation when making your travel plans. The authors, editors, and publisher cannot be held responsible for the experiences of readers while traveling. Your safety is important to us, however, so we encourage you to stay alert and be aware of your surroundings. Keep a close eye on cameras, purses, and wallets, all favorite targets of thieves and pickpockets.

Other Great Guides for Your Trip:

Frommer's Atlanta
Frommer's The Carolinas & Georgia
Frommer's Family Vacations in the National Parks
Frommer's Portable Savannah
Frommer's USA
Frommer's Virginia
Unofficial Guide to the Great Smoky & Blue Ridge Region

Frommer's Star Ratings, Icons & Abbreviations

Every hotel, restaurant, and attraction listing in this guide has been ranked for quality, value, service, amenities, and special features using a **star-rating system**. In country, state, and regional guides, we also rate towns and regions to help you narrow down your choices and budget your time accordingly. Hotels and restaurants are rated on a scale of zero (recommended) to three stars (exceptional). Attractions, shopping, nightlife, towns, and regions are rated according to the following scale: zero stars (recommended), one star (highly recommended), two stars (very highly recommended), and three stars (must-see).

In addition to the star-rating system, we also use **seven feature icons** that point you to the great deals, in-the-know advice and unique experiences that separate travelers from tourists. Throughout the book, look for:

Finds	Special finds — those places only insiders know about
Fun Fact	Fun facts — details that make travelers more informed and their trips more fun
Kids	Best bets for kids, and advice for the whole family
Moments	Special moments–those experiences that memories are made of
Overrated	Places or experiences not worth your time or money
Tips	Insider tips — great ways to save time and money
Value	Great values — where to get the best deals

The following **abbreviations** are used for credit cards:

AE	American Express	DISC	Discover	V	Visa
DC	Diners Club	MC	MasterCard		

Frommers.com

Now that you have the guidebook to a great trip, visit our website at **www.frommers.com** for travel information on more than 3,000 destinations. With features updated regularly, we give you instant access to the most current trip-planning information available. At Frommers.com, you'll also find the best prices on airfares, accommodations, and car rentals — and you can even book travel online through our travel booking partners. At Frommers.com, you'll also find the following:

- Online updates to our most popular guidebooks
- Vacation sweepstakes and contest giveaways
- Newsletter highlighting the hottest travel trends
- Online travel message boards with featured travel discussions

What's New in Nashville & Memphis

If you haven't been to Nashville or Memphis in a few years, you're in for a pleasant surprise. Tennessee's two largest cities continue to evolve into reenergized metropolitan communities that manage to pay loving homage to their storied musical pasts while offering an increasing array of new cultural attractions, professional sports, and dining and lodging options to please travelers with varied tastes and interests.

NASHVILLE

Nashville is basking in a resurgence of popularity unmatched since the mid-1940s, when singer/songwriters such as Hank Williams first came to town and helped launch American country music. Today his grandson, Hank III, takes the stage for his own brand of "HellBilly" music. Among the up-and-coming acts on the Nashville rock-and-alternative scene are the Kings of Leon, as well as Venus Hum, which has been touring as an opening act for Blue Man Group.

PLANNING YOUR TRIP Due to construction, the 2004 **Southern Festival of Books** will be held in Memphis. It is expected to return to War Memorial Plaza in 2005.

WHERE TO STAY The city's finest historic hotel, the **Hermitage,** is now open following a $15 million renovation. The landmark property is better than ever, a 123-room haven of refinement and elegance. Its flagship restaurant, **Capitol Grille,** is the epitome of civility and charm—a gourmet restaurant with a club-like atmosphere that remains locals' top choice for power lunches or pre-theater dinner.

One of the newest additions on the lodging scene is in the West End, where the **Nashville Marriott at Vanderbilt University,** 2555 West End Ave. (© 615/321-1300) is drawing raves from business and leisure travelers alike for its spacious rooms, superior service, and bird's-eye views of the nearby Vandy football stadium and the Parthenon in Centennial Park. Latitude seafood restaurant has become a happening nightspot, too.

WHERE TO DINE When it comes to new restaurants, Nashville has a tempting array of choices. In the artsy, bohemian 12th Avenue South district, which is evolving into one of Music City's coolest neighborhoods, look into **Mirror,** 2317 12th Ave. S. (© 615/383-8330). "Eat, drink, reflect" is the motto of this chic bar that serves killer martinis, delicious salads and grilled fish, and terrific tapas with your choice of Spanish sherries. If you're in a pizza state of mind, make your way across the street to **Mafiaoza's,** 2400 12th Ave. S. (© 615/269-4646), a friendly Italian eatery where you can get it by the slice or whole pie, and munch on some calamari while you're waiting for the pizza to toast in the wood-fired ovens.

In the West End, **Acorn,** 114 28th Ave. N. (© 615/320-4399) is one of the most promising new restaurants to

From Elvis Sights to Goo Goo Clusters: How Do Memphis & Nashville Compare?

Tennessee's two largest cities have much in common, but that doesn't necessarily mean they're equal. Here's an off-the-cuff primer on what's what:

- **Barbecue:** The cities tie in this category. The slow-cooked, pulled-pork sandwiches served up at **Corky's Bar-B-Q**, 5259 Poplar Ave. (© 901/ 685-9744), a Memphis-based barbecue landmark, are just as good at the newer location in Nashville (100 Franklin Rd., Brentwood; © 615/ 373-1020). If you have an aversion to coleslaw sharing bun space with the pig meat, remember to order yours without the customary cabbage topping.

- **Brew Pubs:** The oven-roasted gourmet pizzas and specialty-brewed beers of **Boscos,** a Tennessee-based chain that originated in suburban Germantown (outside Memphis), are also great in either city. Both boast prime locations: In Memphis, there's a Boscos in midtown's Overton Square, 2120 Madison Ave. (© 901/432-2222); while Nashville's is not far from Vanderbilt University in the West End, 1805 21st Ave. S. (© 615/385-0050).

- **Elvis:** If a home is a man's castle, **Graceland**, 3734 Elvis Presley Blvd. (© 800/238-2000), was the King's. Memphis may have the best Elvis Presley sights, from the infamous Jungle Room at Graceland to the slick souvenir shops that enshrine the late entertainer. Nashville, however, offers a lesser-known and less-exploited facet of Elvis's career in the **RCA Studio B** (30 Music Square West), a small, nondescript studio on Music Row where he recorded albums.

- **Football:** Yes, the **Tennessee Titans** (© 615/565-4200; www.titans online.com), the pride of Nashville and the city's first NFL team, have an embarrassing past. When the former Houston Oilers moved to Tennessee and awaited Nashville to build a new stadium, the future Superbowl competitors played their first season in Memphis.

open in Nashville in many years. This place has buzz like you wouldn't believe. The strikingly modern two-story eatery is set inside a gracious old mansion shaded by towering oak trees. Abstract paintings, decorative sculptural pieces, and dramatic lighting set the mood inside, where well-heeled diners can opt for entrees such as grilled lamb or wasabi-crusted, sushi-grade seared tuna; plus tapas and quiche. A heated, outdoor patio upstairs makes a romantic spot for a late-night drink.

EXPLORING NASHVILLE Don't look now, but Fan Fair has a new name. The annual bonding celebration between country music stars and their fans is now known as the CMA (Country Music Association) Music Festival. It's still being held in early June at The Coliseum downtown.

Meanwhile, several worthy exhibitions are set to open in 2004. At the **Country Music Hall of Fame and Museum,** *Night Train to Nashville: Music City Rhythm & Blues 1945-1970* will explore the link between country and R&B. It opened in March 2004

Snubbed at not landing the team, Memphians stayed away from the games in droves.

- **Goo Goo Clusters:** You can buy Goo Goo Clusters in both cities, but they might taste gooier in Nashville, where the nutty, chocolate-covered marshmallow-crème candies rose to fame as a one-time sponsor of the *Grand Ole Opry.*
- **Music:** Sometimes stereotypes are true. While both cities offer more than one musical genre, when boiled down to basics, their musical personalities stack up like this: Memphis is low-down, greasy **blues** played in smoky juke joints or along neon-studded Beale Street. Nashville is plaintive **bluegrass** performed in concert halls or rowdy, boot-scootin' **country** blaring away in barn-sized clubs.
- **Parks:** **Overton Park** in Memphis is a lush oasis in an urban setting. Ditto for **Centennial Park** in Nashville; however, Music City's green space is also home to an impressive replica of Greece's Parthenon.
- **Rivers:** Nashville has the **Cumberland,** a bucolic tributary that wends through one edge of town, while Memphis has become synonymous with **Old Man River,** the broad and muddy Mississippi River that slices between Tennessee and Arkansas.
- **Statues of Famous Sons:** Guitar slung over one shoulder, the bronze **Elvis** statue on Memphis's Beale Street is a favorite place for a photo op, as are the larger-than-life likenesses of the two kings—**Elvis and B.B. King**—at that city's Tennessee State Welcome Center. But Nashville, with all its august state capital buildings, has **Sgt. Alvin York,** a beloved Tennessee war hero and Quaker (immortalized in the movies by Gary Cooper). Trivia-loving shutterbugs take note that this stately statue bears a flaw: The rifle the World War I soldier is holding is from World War II.

and will run through December 2005. The museum is located at 225 5th Ave. S. (© **615/416-2001**). In summer 2004, the **Frist Center for the Visual Arts,** 919 Broadway (© **615/ 244-3340**), will present *Migration Series from the Philips Collection,* an exhibition of works by 20th-century African-American artist Jacob Lawrence. Included are works tracing the movement of blacks from the rural South to the industrial North between the first and second world wars. Running concurrently will be an exhibition of European masterworks from the same collection, showcasing such superstar artists as Cézanne, Monet, Degas, Picasso, and Gauguin.

On the outskirts of town, expect big doings from the **Hermitage,** the plantation home of former U.S. President Andrew Jackson. In 2004, a series of events is planned in observance of the mansion's bicentennial. A side note for those who love good home cooking: **Monell's,** a Nashville meat-and-three eatery famous for its fried chicken and turnip greens, has opened a cafe at the Hermitage, 4580 Rachel's Lane (© **615/889-2941**).

AFTER DARK A handful of new nightspots keep Nashville jumping after dark. **Easy's in the Village,** 1910 Belcourt Ave. (© **615/292-7575**) has become a welcome West End addition, where college kids and the laid-back singles crowd mingle over Cajun-inspired munchies, mini-hamburgers, and plenty of beer. Closer to downtown, partyers can join the mixed (gay and straight) crowd at **Tribe,** 1517 Church St. (© **615/329-2912**), a hip urban club and video-music bar that offers a full menu, too.

If it's an authentic Delta blues juke joint you're after, look no farther than **B.B. King's Blues Club,** 152 Second Ave. (© **615/256-2727**). The best in live blues, rock and gospel music are frequently booked here, though B. B. and his legendary guitar, Lucille, are expected to do at least a couple of shows each year, as with the original B. B. King's Blues Club in Memphis.

MEMPHIS

What's new in Memphis? "What's not?" might be the better question. This lazy Southern city that languished in the decades following the 1968 assassination of the Rev. Martin Luther King, Jr. has been reborn. Unprecedented development over the past few years has transformed downtown into the vibrant heartbeat of a newly energized city that proudly trumpets its musical heritage as Home of the Blues and Birthplace of Rock 'n' Roll.

One of the biggest current construction projects is the new 18,200-seat **FedEx Forum** arena, which is being built for the NBA's Memphis Grizzlies. The targeted completion date is August 2004, just in time for the 2004–05 basketball season.

Not a hoops nut? Well, music fans should also take note of that date, too, because the Smithsonian's nearby **Memphis Rock 'n' Soul Museum** recently announced plans to relocate inside the new arena, allowing greater access and expanded viewing hours for this cultural treasure trove of American music.

Also, book lovers should plan to visit Memphis—not Nashville—for the **2004 Southern Festival of Books.** The festival will be held at the Cook Convention Center and outdoors on Civic Plaza.

WHERE TO STAY Hands down the most sophisticated hotel in Memphis, **The Madison,** 79 Madison Ave. (© **901/333-1200**) is a jewel in downtown's bustling landscape. Converted from a historic 1905 building (a former bank), the property has 110 rooms, including 44 suites. The independently owned member of the prestigious Small Luxury Hotels of the World offers 24-hour room service, valet parking and doormen, and twice-daily maid service. Rooftop views of the Mississippi River are sublime. And here's another one for the camera: the modern exercise room is in the old bank vault.

A more inexpensive alternative to the pricey Madison is the immaculate **SpringHill Suites by Marriott,** 21 N. Main St. (© **901/522-2100**). Spacious suites are well equipped for business travelers but are comfortable enough for leisure tourists as well. There's a small outdoor pool and a cheery breakfast area. Free parking is a value-added plus.

WHERE TO DINE Located in the Cooper Young Historic District of Midtown, one of the hot new restaurants in town is called the **Beauty Shop,** 966 S. Cooper (© **901/272-7111**). Just for fun, this upscale bar and restaurant is located in a former 1940s-era beauty parlor. While noshing on gourmet fare with a New American/global flare, guests may sit in refurbished hair dryer chairs—or at tables and banquettes. It's the current place in Memphis to see and to be seen.

In the heart of downtown, next door to the landmark Automatic Slim's Tonga Club (and right across the street from The Peabody) sits **Café 61,** 85 S. Second St. (© **901/523-9351**). This funky, laid-back eatery—a cross between Highway 61 and Route 66—serves up an eclectic menu of Cajun, American, and even Asian dishes. It's a one-of-a-kind place where you can choose an egg roll or satay of the day, or a thick Creole pork chop served with spicy crawfish macaroni and cheese.

EXPLORING MEMPHIS   Rising from the proverbial ashes in South Memphis is the new **Soulsville USA: Stax Museum of American Music,** 926 E. McLemore (© **901/946-2535**). This state-of-the-art museum and youth academy for the performing arts opened in 2003 on the grounds of the former Stax recording studio, which was razed in 1989. In the 1960s and early 70s, Stax produced more than 500 hit songs by the likes of Otis Redding, Sam & Dave, Wilson Pickett, the Staple Singers, and many more. The museum pays homage to these and other stars of American popular music. Don't miss the revolving display showcasing Isaac Hayes's blinding "Superfly," a gold-trimmed, peacock-blue 1972 Cadillac Eldorado with thick shag carpeting inside.

After much hoopla and anticipation, the **pandas** have finally landed at the **Memphis Zoo,** 2000 Prentiss Place (© **901/276-WILD**). The adorable black-and-white giant pandas, named Ya Ya and Le Le, are the main attraction at the zoo's new China exhibition that opened last spring. Keeping Ya Ya and Le Le company here are graceful swans, cranes, otter, goldfish, hog deer, and monkeys. A Chinese sculpture garden, tearoom, pagoda, and dragon-shaped walkways are among the architectural elements of the exhibition.

AFTER DARK   Beale Street is still the life of the party when it comes to Memphis nightlife. Joining the crowd recently is **Pat O'Brien's Memphis,** 310 Beale St. (© **901/529-0900**), a long-awaited outpost of the famed New Orleans original. The huge, two-story bar has an outdoor patio as well as a quiet piano lounge. On any given weekend, the big beer hall is where you'll find the rowdiest of the rowdy, however.

Meanwhile, everybody's talking about **ten** at the **Plaza Club,** the hippest private late-night club in Memphis. Owned by business and civic leaders Dean and Kristi Jernigan (who spearheaded the birth of the Memphis Redbirds' baseball team a few years ago), the club was launched in late October 2003 as an adjunct to the existing Plaza Club in the Toyota Center at AutoZone Park, 175 Toyota Plaza, Suite 200 (© **901/405-0700**). The posh Plaza Club is transformed into a tapas bar and nightclub with deejay-spun tunes at 10pm Thursday through Saturday. Annual memberships for the late-night club only start at $150.

A few blocks away, **Isaac Hayes** is giving his relatively new namesake club at 150 Peabody Place (© **901/529-9222**) another try. The restaurant, bar, and live-entertainment venue closed briefly in fall 2003, then reopened with new management, but with Hayes's ongoing involvement.

On that note, visitors should be aware that Elvis Presley's Memphis, the Beale Street nightclub operated by the same folks who run Graceland (and all The King's ventures), unceremoniously closed in late summer 2003, after several years in business. At press time, the glitzy, Graceland-esque property was still vacant, with no plans for another tenant to move in.

1

The Best of Nashville

Nashville may be the capital of Tennessee, but it's better known as Music City USA, the country music mecca. Yet it is so much more. Combining small-town warmth with an unexpected urban sophistication, Nashville is an increasingly popular tourist destination that boasts world-class museums and major-league sports teams; an eclectic dining and after-hours scene; and an eye-catching skyline ringed by a beautiful countryside of rolling hills, rivers and lakes, and wide open green spaces.

Ultimately, though, Nashville is the heart and soul of country music, that uniquely American blend of humble gospel, blues, and mountain music that has evolved into a $2-billion-a-year industry. At its epicenter, Nashville is still the city where unknown musicians can become overnight sensations, where the major record deals are cut and music-publishing fortunes made, and where the *Grand Ole Opry* still takes center stage.

Symbolic of Nashville's vitality is downtown, an exciting place that is finally breathing new life. Once tired and abandoned warehouses now bustle in the entertainment area known as The District. This historic neighborhood teems with tourist-oriented nightclubs and restaurants, including a new B.B. King's Blues Club, the ubiquitous Hard Rock Cafe that's become a staple of most large cities, and the one-and-only Wildhorse Saloon (the most famous boot-scootin' dance hall in the land). Luckily, The District isn't yet all glitz and tour-bus nightclubs. Along lower Broadway there are still half a dozen or more dive bars where the air reeks of stale beer and cigarettes and live music plays day and night. In these bars, aspiring country bands lay down their riffs and sing their hearts out in hopes of becoming tomorrow's superstars. With so many clubs, restaurants, shops, and historic landmarks, The District is one of the South's most vibrant nightlife areas.

Folks looking for tamer entertainment head out to the Music Valley area, home to the *Grand Ole Opry*, the radio show that started the whole country music ball rolling back in 1925. Clustered in this land the locals sometimes refer to as "Nashvegas" are other music-related attractions, including the epic Opryland Hotel, the nostalgic *General Jackson* showboat, several modest souvenir shops posing as museums, and theaters featuring family entertainment, with the majority showcasing performers from the *Grand Ole Opry*. Dozens of other clubs and theaters around the city also feature live music of various genres.

Country isn't the only music you'll hear in this city. Mainstream rock stars are also being lured by the city's intangible vibe. (Sheryl Crow is one of the high-profile stars to have recently moved here.) They come here for inspiration, to record new material, or for cross-over collaborations with local music pros. No matter the genre, the city seems to attract more musicians each year. Which means there's enough live music here in Nashville to keep your toes tappin' even long after you hit the highway home.

1 Frommer's Favorite Nashville Experiences

- **Attending the *Grand Ole Opry.*** This live radio broadcast is an American institution and is as entertaining today as it was when it went on the air nearly 80 years ago. Luckily, the current Grand Ole Opry House, 2804 Opryland Dr. (℃ 615/889-6611), is quite a bit more comfortable than the old Ryman Auditorium where the *Opry* used to be held. See p. 117.

- **Checking Out Up-and-Comers at the Bluebird Cafe.** With its excellent acoustics and two shows a night, the Bluebird Cafe, 4104 Hillsboro Rd. (℃ 615/383-1461), is Nashville's most famous venue for country songwriters. Only the best make it here, and many of the people who play the Bluebird wind up getting "discovered." See p. 124.

- **Line Dancing at the Wildhorse Saloon.** What Gilley's once did for country music, the Wildhorse Saloon, 120 Second Ave. N. (℃ 615/251-1000), is doing again. The country line dancing craze that swept the nation reached its zenith in this massive saloon. It continues today. See p. 124.

- **Catching a Show at the Ryman Auditorium.** Known as the "Mother Church of Country Music," the Ryman Auditorium, 116 Fifth Ave. N. (℃ 615/254-1445 for information, 615/889-6611 for tickets; or call Ticketmaster at 615/737-4849), was the home of the *Grand Ole Opry* for more than 30 years. Now restored, it once again has country music coming from its historic stage. And, yes, the old church pews are still there and just as uncomfortable as they always were. See p. 121.

- **Spotting the Next Hot Band at Robert's Western World.** Robert's Western World, 416 Broadway (℃ 615/256-7937), a former Western-wear store now transformed into a bar, helped launch the career of BR5-49. Since BR5-49 hit the big time, a band called Brazilbilly has been trying to fill their boots; though by the time you reach town, Brazilbilly may have hit it big and moved on, and this bar is sure to have another great band to take its place. Check it out. See p. 121.

- **Downing a Cold Long-Neck and Listening to Hot Country Tunes at Tootsie's.** Sure, Tootsie's Orchid Lounge, 422 Broadway (℃ 615/726-0463), is a dive, but it's a dive with so much history and so many country music ghosts haunting its stage that a person can get drunk on atmosphere alone. No matter what time of night or day, if Tootsie's is open, you can bet there's a band on stage. See p. 121.

- **Spending the Better Part of a Day at the Country Music Hall of Fame and Museum.** Lots of interesting displays chronicling the history of country music make the new Country Music Hall of Fame and Museum, 222 Fifth Ave. S. (℃ 800/852-6437), one of the most fascinating attractions in Nashville. Even if you never thought you were a fan of country music, you may learn differently here. See p. 85.

- **Cruising on the Cumberland.** Cruising the Cumberland River on a paddle-wheeler gives you a totally different perspective on Nashville. Add food and entertainment, provided on the *General Jackson* showboat, 2812 Opryland Dr. (℃ 615/889-6611), and you have the makings of a memorable excursion. See p. 120.

- **Slurping a Chocolate Shake at the Elliston Place Soda Shop.** Sure, every city has its retro diner these days, but the Elliston Place Soda Shop, 2111 Elliston Place (© **615/327-1090**), is the real thing. It's been in business since 1939 and makes the best chocolate shakes in Nashville. See p. 75.

- **Listening to Tales of the Life and Times of Belmont Mansion's Illustrious Owner.** Antebellum Nashville had more than its fair share of wealthy citizens, but you usually only hear about the men. However, at the Belmont Mansion, 1900 Belmont Blvd. (© **615/460-5459**), guides will tell you all about Adelicia Acklen, a woman of means who meant business. Prenuptial agreements, hobnobbing with royalty in Europe, smuggling cotton, and double-crossing both the Union and Confederate armies are just a few of the fascinating tales told about this liberated woman of the mid–19th century. See p. 91.

- **Hanging Out in the Opryland Hotel Atriums.** If you thought Orlando and Las Vegas had exclusive rights to fantasy hotels, think again. With three huge atriums, the Opryland Hotel, 2800 Opryland Dr. (© **615/889-1000**), creates tropical fantasy gardens under its acres of glass roof. You can wander around, oohing and ahhing at the massive waterfalls, the quarter-mile-long river—complete with boats—and the fountains, streams, and ponds. See p. 88.

- **Guitar Shopping at Gruhn Guitars.** There aren't too many stores where you can test-drive a $25,000 guitar, but you can here. If you want to be able to say that you've played a 1938 Martin D-38, drop in at Gruhn, 400 Broadway (© **615/256-2033**), convince them you've got the money, and start pickin'. See p. 115.

- **Pretending You're a Star Shopping for New Clothes at Manuel's.** Manuel Exclusive Clothier, 1922 Broadway (© **615/321-5444**), sells work clothes—work clothes for country music stars, that is. You know, the rhinestone cowboy sort of ensembles that look great under stage lights. Maybe these aren't the kind of duds your boss would approve of, but, hey, maybe one day you'll be able to quit your day job. See p. 115.

- **Spending an Afternoon in Lynchburg, Home of Jack Daniel's.** Whether you drink Jack Daniel's or not, you've probably seen the magazine ads that evoke the people and processes of the Jack Daniel's distillery in Lynchburg. For once, it's just like in the ads. A tour of the distillery, lunch at Miss Mary Bobo's Boarding House (if you can get reservations), and a stroll around the town square will have you wishing there were more places like Lynchburg. See p. 134.

2 Best Nashville Hotel Bets

- **Best Historic Hotel:** Built in 1910 in the beaux-arts style, the **Hermitage Hotel,** 231 Sixth Ave. N. (© **800/251-1908** or 615/244-3121), boasts the most elegant lobby in the city. The marble columns, gilded plasterwork, and stained-glass ceiling recapture the luxuries of a bygone era. This is a classic grand hotel. See p. 48.

- **Best for Business Travelers:** Not only does the **Nashville Airport Marriott,** 600 Marriott Dr. (© **800/228-9290** or 615/889-9300), have rooms designed specifically with business travelers

Nashville & Memphis

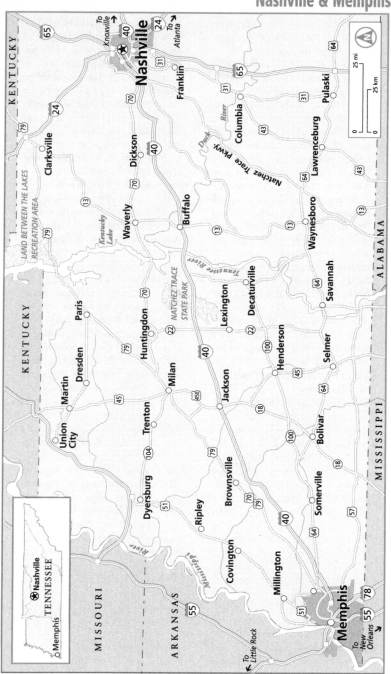

in mind, but it also has plenty of athletic facilities to help those same travelers unwind. Perhaps best of all, it's close to the airport and easy to find. See p. 59.

- **Best Hotel Lobby for Pretending that You're Loaded:** Although the **Opryland Hotel,** 2800 Opryland Dr. (© **615/883-2211** or 615/889-1000), is a major Nashville attraction and draws all types of tourists and travelers, it will set you back a bundle to stay here. So, just do as everyone else does and pretend that you're a guest as you stroll the atriums and elegant lobbies. See p. 56.

- **Best for Families:** With an indoor pool, a game room, and a tropical atrium complete with a stream running through it, the **Embassy Suites Nashville,** 10 Century Blvd. (© **800/EMBASSY [362-2779]** or 615/871-0033), is a good place to bring the kids. Parents might also appreciate having a bedroom (and TV) all to themselves. The free buffet breakfast and in-room refrigerators also help cut expenses. See p. 58.

- **Best Moderately Priced Hotel:** With its mountain-lodge lobby, the **Holiday Inn Express–Airport,** 1111 Airport Center Dr. (© **800/HOLIDAY [465-4329]** or 615/883-1366), features style beyond its modest rates. It's also in an attractively landscaped office park that's great for jogging. See p. 60.

- **Best Budget Hotel:** Located in the airport area convenient to Opry Mills and Briley Parkway, the **SpringHill Suites by Marriott,** 1100 Airport Center Dr., (© **888/287-9400** or 615/884-6111), is a good and economical choice for tourists. See p. 60.

- **Best Service:** Whether you're here on business or to do the country music thing, you won't find better

service than at the **Loews Vanderbilt Plaza Hotel,** 2100 West End Ave. (© **800/23-LOEWS** or 615/885-2200). See p. 54.

- **Best Location:** If you're here on business or for a night on the town in The District, the **Renaissance Nashville Hotel,** 611 Commerce St. (© **800/HOTELS-1 [468-3571]** or 615/255-8400), is your best downtown choice. It's connected to the convention center and is only a block from the Ryman Auditorium. See p. 49.

- **Best Health Club:** Where else in Music City can you ice-skate, go swimming, and play tennis year-round? The **Thomas F. Frist Centennial Sportsplex,** 25th Ave. N. at Brandau Ave. (© **615/862-8480**), offers all this as well as outdoor swimming and extensive fitness facilities. Several area hotels offer passes to the health club.

- **Best Hotel Pool:** The main pool at the **Sheraton Music City,** 777 McGavock Pike (© **800/325-3535** or 615/885-2200), is fairly large and is situated in the hotel's quiet central courtyard. There's also plenty of patio space where you can spend time lounging. A smaller indoor pool is available for the cooler months of the year. See p. 59.

- **Best Views:** The new high-rise **Nashville Marriott at Vanderbilt,** 2555 West End Ave., (© **800/228-9290**), offers birds-eye views of the Vanderbilt University football stadium as well as the Parthenon in Centennial Park. See p. 54.

- **Best for a Romantic Getaway:** With its opulent beaux-arts lobby, dark and romantic basement bar and restaurant, and comfortable, newly redecorated rooms, the **Hermitage Hotel,** 231 Sixth Ave. N. (© **800/251-1908** or 615/244-3121), is Nashville's most romantic hotel. Plus, it's only a couple of blocks from The District. See p. 48.

- **Best for Country Music Fans:** With the *Grand Ole Opry* and numerous theaters showcasing live country music nearby, the **Opryland Hotel,** 2800 Opryland Dr. (© 615/883-2211 or 615/889-1000), should be the first choice of country music fans (provided they can swallow the bill). See p. 56.

3 Best Nashville Dining Bets

- **Best Spot for a Romantic Dinner:** If you've got plenty of money to burn and want to treat your special someone to a very romantic evening out, make a reservation at **Arthur's,** Union Station hotel, 1001 Broadway (© 615/255-1494). You can count on such dishes as rack of lamb, chateaubriand (large grilled or broiled beef tenderloin), and *tournedos* (small filet of beef) to make regular appearances. Best of all, the setting, in the old Union Station, will have you thinking you've stepped into an old black-and-white movie. See p. 63.
- **Best Spot for a Business Lunch:** **Capitol Grille,** 231 Sixth Ave. N. (© 615/244-3121), at the Hermitage Hotel, is very popular with the downtown business set. Why? It could be the prime spot next to the state capitol, or the traditional ambience, or perhaps the secret is in dishes such as Jack Daniel's-marinated steak with roasted garlic mashed potatoes and rosemary fried cabbage. See p. 66.
- **Best Spot for a Celebration:** With its wild and colorful decor and adventurous cuisine, **Bound-'ry,** 911 20th Ave. S. (© 615/321-3043), even has some circular booths—perfect for a festive celebratory gathering. See p. 72.
- **Best Decor:** Burnished hues and coppery wall sconces offset the contemporary artwork that fills the West End's newest upscale restaurant and bar. **Acorn,** 114 28th Ave. N. (© 615/320-4399) is easily one of Nashville's most visually sumptuous restaurants. See p. 70.
- **Best Value: Zola,** 3001 West End Ave. (© 615/320-7778), serves some of the best globally inspired fusion cuisine in Nashville. Plentiful portions, attentive service, and delicious gourmet food make it a great value for the money. Try the paella, and you'll taste what I mean. See p. 73.
- **Best for Kids:** It's not everywhere that you get to eat in a restaurant next to a full-size trolley car, and anyway, isn't spaghetti one of the major food groups? For less than most restaurants charge for a round of drinks, the whole family can eat at **The Old Spaghetti Factory,** 160 Second Ave. N. (© 615/254-9010), in the heart of The District. See p. 69.
- **Best Wine List:** With an inventory of more than 15,000 bottles, **The Wild Boar,** 2014 Broadway (© 615/329-1313), offers the most extensive wine list in Nashville. The well-stocked cellar at this exclusive restaurant, considered one of the finest wine cellars in the nation, has garnered numerous awards over the years. See p. 71.
- **Best Japanese Cuisine:** While there is cheaper Japanese food to be had around town, you won't find better food than at **Goten,** 110 21st Ave. S. (© 615/321-4537), which combines modern

ashville Websites

ore about what's happening in Music City USA, check out
websites:

- **www.musiccityusa.com (and/or nashvillecvb.com):** The Nashville
Convention and Visitors Bureau's encyclopedic site is award-winning
and crammed with nearly everything you ever wanted to know
about Nashville. Info on lodging, restaurants, nightlife, attractions,
and group travel is concise and user-friendly. A personalized itinerary feature allows you to glean and compile info based on your
preferences, such as family options or African-American history.
- **www.nashscene.com:** The alternative weekly newspaper, *Nashville
Scene* is an incisive, highly entertaining read packed with the latest
news and reviews on the city's art galleries, restaurants, politics, and
nightlife. Click on the annual "Best of Nashville" issue or laugh out
loud at their annual Boner Awards.
- **www.tennessean.com:** The daily newspaper where Al Gore got his
start as a reporter, the *Tennessean* serves up one of the most extensive sites about Nashville and the region. In-depth guides on everything from the NFL's Tennessee Titans to downtown architecture
(what's the deal with that Batman-esque skyscraper, anyway?) are
fodder for this fun site.
- **www.tennesseebackroads.org:** A visitors' guide, Tennessee Back-
roads takes an off-the-beaten-path approach to the state's scenic
small towns and less-traveled roads, and the non-touristy sites to be
found there.
- **www.tnstateparks.com:** Tennessee State Parks features helpful
maps and info about camping, lodging, and outdoor recreation.
- **www.tnvacation.com:** The state's official tourist guidebook divides
the Volunteer State by geographic region—Western (Memphis),
Middle (Nashville), and the mountainous Eastern region including
the Smoky Mountains. This site gives practical info about road rules
and other regulations, and a good general overview of what Tennessee has to offer.

minimalist decor, elegantly prepared food, and an excellent sushi
bar. See p. 72.
- **Best New American Cuisine:** The
long menu at the **Sunset Grill,**
2001 Belcourt Ave. (© **615/
386-FOOD**), highlights contemporary combinations (such as
blackberry duck with roasted
sweet potatoes) and has a great
wine list. For years now, this has
been one of the trendiest restaurants in town. See p. 73.

- **Best Traditional Southern Cuisine:** Country ham with red-eye
gravy and homemade biscuits
with fruit jams are perennially
popular at the **Loveless Café,**
8400 Tenn. 100 (© **615/646-
9700**). See p. 79.
- **Best Soul Food:** Crispy fried
chicken, mashed potatoes, and
slow-simmered turnip greens are
simply delicious at **Harper's,**
2610 Jefferson St. (© **615/329-
1909**). Eaten with cornbread,

sweet iced tea, and warm banana pudding for dessert, they're sublime.

- **Best Barbecue:** I narrowed my search to the pulled-pork-shoulder sandwich, and agree that **Whitt's Barbecue,** 5310 Harding Rd. (© **615/356-3435**), does the best job. Drizzle some barbecue sauce on the pile of juicy, flavorful pork in this sandwich and you too will become a true believer. See p. 82.

- **Best Burgers and Beer:** Tennessee's homegrown **Bosco's,** 1805 21st Ave. S. (© **615/385-0050**) with locations in Nashville and Memphis, serves great wood-fired pizzas, burgers, and its sig-nature Flaming Stone Beer. See p. 127.

- **Best Catfish:** At **Cock of the Walk,** 2624 Music Valley Dr. (© **615/889-1930**), just up the road from the Opryland Hotel, you can discover just why the South is so enamored of fried catfish. See p. 80.

- **Best Pizza: DaVinci's Gourmet Pizza,** 1812 Hayes St. at 19th Ave., 1 block off West End Ave. (© **615/329-8098**), serves Nashville's favorite pizza. Step through the door of this funky neighborhood pizza joint, which is located in a renovated brick house near Vanderbilt University, and your salivary glands will immediately plunge into overdrive. See p. 74.

- **Best Desserts:** If you subscribe to the belief that, life being uncertain, you should eat dessert first, then on the way to dinner drop by **Provence Breads & Café,** 1705 21st Ave. S. (© **615/386-0363**), and indulge in one of the classic and decadently rich pastries here. See p. 82.

- **Best Late-Night Dining:** It has to be a toss-up between **Sunset Grill,** 2001 Belcourt Ave. (© **615/ 386-FOOD**), and **Bound'ry,** 911 20th Ave. S. (© **615/321-3043**), both of which serve New American and New Southern cuisine and stay open until after 1am. See p. 73 and 72.

- **Best Fast Food:** Try **Calypso,** 2424 Elliston Place (© **615/321-3878**), and other area locations, for some fast and healthful Caribbean food. The rotisserie chicken is the favorite, but the salads are scrumptious too. See p. 74.

2

Planning Your Trip to Nashville

It's the country music capital of the world, and Nashville is a major tourist destination. As the city's popularity has grown, so too has the need for pre-visit planning. Before leaving home, you should try to make hotel and car reservations. Not only will these reservations save you money, but also you won't have to struggle with trying to find accommodations after you arrive. If you are hoping to attend the *Grand Ole Opry* or are coming to town specifically for the city's biggest event, the Country Music Association's Music Festival (formerly known as International Country Music Fan Fair), you should purchase your tickets well in advance.

Summer is the peak tourist season in Nashville, and from June to September downtown hotels are often fully booked for days or even weeks at a time. Consequently, reservations—for hotel rooms, for rental cars, for a table at a restaurant—are imperative.

When to go? How far in advance to plan? How to get there? These are some of questions this chapter addresses, and here you'll find the essentials you'll need to plan a trip to Nashville.

1 Visitor Information

Before heading to Music City, you can get more information on the city by contacting the **Nashville Convention & Visitors Bureau,** 211 Commerce St. (© **615/259-4700**) In the United Kingdom, call © **44/1462-40784.** In Germany, call © **49/521-9860415.**

For information on the state of Tennessee, contact the **Tennessee Department of Tourism Development,** P.O. Box 23170, Nashville, TN 37202 (© **800/836-6200** or 615/741-2158).

You can also find information about Nashville at the following websites:

- Nashville Convention & Visitors Bureau: **www.musiccityusa.com**
- The *Nashville Scene,* Nashville's main arts and entertainment weekly: **www.nashvillescene.com**
- The *Tennessean,* Nashville's morning daily newspaper: **www.tennessean.com**

2 Money

Tourism is big business here and, for the most part, people visiting Nashville don't intend to spend a lot of money. If you are willing to budget, you can get by on about $100 a day per person for inexpensive food and accommodations. However, if you want to splurge, you'll certainly have the opportunity.

A credit card is the most convenient way to pay for hotel rooms and meals in restaurants; if you plan to rent a car, you'll need a credit card for the deposit. Most hotels, restaurants, and many shops also accept traveler's checks and personal checks. ATMs are readily available and use the Cirrus, PLUS, Most, and Honor networks.

Impressions

Most of the country music seems to have such a good story . . . so we blues people kind of feel that we're cousins.

—B.B. King

ATMS

The easiest and best way to get cash while you're away from home is from an ATM. The **Cirrus** (℃ **800/424-7787;** www.mastercard.com) and **PLUS** (℃ **800/843-7587;** www.visa.com) networks span the globe; look at the back of your bank card to see which network you're on, then call or check online for ATM locations at your destination. Be sure you know your personal identification number (PIN) before you leave home and be sure to find out your daily withdrawal limit before you depart. Also keep in mind that many banks impose a fee every time a card is used at a different bank's ATM. On top of this, the bank from which you withdraw cash may charge its own fee.

TRAVELER'S CHECKS

Traveler's checks are something of an anachronism from the days before the ATM made cash accessible at any time. However, keep in mind that you will likely be charged an ATM withdrawal fee if the bank is not your own, so if you're withdrawing money every day, you might be better off with traveler's checks—provided you don't mind showing identification every time you want to cash one.

You can get traveler's checks at almost any bank. **American Express** offers denominations of $20, $50, $100, $500, and (for cardholders only) $1,000. You'll pay a service charge ranging from 1% to 4%. You can also get American Express traveler's checks over the phone by calling ℃ **800/221-7282;** Amex gold and platinum cardholders who use this number are exempt from the 1% fee.

Visa offers traveler's checks at Citibank locations nationwide, as well as at several other banks. The service charge ranges between 1.5% and 2%; checks come in denominations of $20, $50, $100, $500, and $1,000. Call ℃ **800/732-1322** for information. AAA members can obtain Visa checks without a fee at most AAA offices or by calling ℃ **866/339-3378. MasterCard** also offers traveler's checks. Call ℃ **800/223-9920** for a location near you.

CREDIT CARDS

Credit cards are a safe way to carry money and they provide a convenient record of all your expenses. You can also withdraw cash advances from your credit cards at banks or ATMs, provided you know your PIN. If you've forgotten yours, or didn't even know you had one, call the number on the back of your credit card and ask the bank to send it to you—it usually takes 5 to 7 business days.

WHAT TO DO IF YOUR WALLET IS LOST OR STOLEN

Be sure to tell all of your credit card companies the minute you discover your wallet has been lost or stolen and file a report at the nearest police precinct. Your credit card company or insurer may require a police report number or record of the loss. Most credit card companies have an emergency toll-free number to call if your card is lost or stolen; they may be able to wire you a cash advance immediately or deliver an emergency credit card in a day or two. Visa's U.S. emergency number is ℃ **800/847-2911** or 410/581-9994. American Express cardholders and traveler's check holders should

What Things Cost in Nashville	US$
Taxi from the airport to the city center	20
Bus ride between any two downtown points	1.45
Local telephone call	.35
Double room at the Opryland Hotel (very expensive)	99–279
Double room at Doubletree Hotel (expensive)	89–169
Double room at the Shoney's Inn–Music Valley (moderate)	81–111
Lunch for one at the Mad Platter (moderate)	24
Lunch for one at Harper's (inexpensive)	5
Dinner for one, without wine, at the Wild Boar (expensive)	65
Dinner for one, without wine, at Bound'ry (moderate)	25
Dinner for one at Uncle Bud's Catfish (inexpensive)	11
Bottle of beer	2.50–3
Coca-Cola	1.25–1.50
Cup of coffee or iced tea	1.25–1.50
Roll of ASA 100 Kodacolor film, 36 exposures	6
Movie ticket	7.50
Theater ticket for the Tennessee Repertory Theatre	10–35

call © **800/221-7282.** MasterCard holders should call © **800/307-7309** or 636/722-7111. For other credit cards, call the toll-free number directory at © **800/555-1212.** If you need emergency cash over the weekend when all banks and American Express offices are closed, you can have money wired to you via **Western Union** (© **800/325-6000;** www.western union.com).

Identity theft and fraud are potential complications of losing your wallet, especially if you've lost your driver's license along with your cash and credit cards. Notify the major credit-reporting bureaus immediately; placing a fraud alert on your records may protect you against liability for criminal activity. The three major U.S. credit-reporting agencies are **Equifax** (© **800/766-0008;** www.equifax.com), **Experian** (© **888/397-3742;** www.experian.com), and **TransUnion** (© **800/680-7289;** www.transunion.com).

3 When to Go

CLIMATE

Summer is the peak tourist season in Nashville but is also when the city experiences its worst weather. During July and August, and often in September as well, temperatures can hover around 100°F, with humidity of close to 100%. Can you say "muggy"? Spring and fall, however, last for several months and are both quite pleasant.

Days are often warm and nights cool, though during these two seasons the weather changes, so bring a variety of clothes. Heavy rains can hit any time of year, and if you spend more than 3 or 4 days in town, you can almost bet on seeing some rain. Winters can be cold, with daytime temperatures staying below freezing, and snow is not unknown.

Nashville's Average Monthly Temperatures & Rainfall

	Jan	Feb	Mar	Apr	May	June	July	Aug	Sept	Oct	Nov	Dec
Temp (°F)	37	41	49	59	68	76	80	79	72	60	48	40
Temp (°C)	3	5	9	15	20	25	27	26	22	15	9	4
Days of rain	11	11	12	11	11	9	10	9	8	7	10	11

NASHVILLE CALENDAR OF EVENTS

In addition to those special events listed below, you can catch live national musical acts throughout the summer months. On Wednesday nights (July–Sept) **Uptown Mix** has showcased such acts as the North Mississippi Allstars and The Mavericks at Riverfront Park. Admission $5. For more information, call ℂ **615/321-3043**. Thursday nights (May–August) **Dancin' in The District** is held at The Coliseum downtown. Admission is $3. Performances (by bands such as Hootie and the Blowfish and the Indigo Girls in 2003) take place between 5 and 10pm. For more information, call ℂ **615/329-2556**.

For free culture of another ilk, the Frist Museum offers **Frist Fridays** on the last Friday of every month (May–September). Free admission includes live music and appetizers outside on the courtyard, along with entry into the Frist's galleries. 5:30 to 9pm. For more information, call ℂ **615/244-3340**.

February

Americana Spring Sampler Craft, Folk Art & Antique Show, Tennessee State Fairgrounds. About 125 craft and antique professionals from more than 20 states display their wares (ℂ **615/227-2080**). Early February.

April

Tin Pan South, various venues, sometimes including the Ryman Auditorium. Sponsored by the 4,000-member Nashville Songwriters Association, this five-day festival showcases some of the best new and established songwriters in the country (ℂ **615/256-3354**). Early to mid-April.

May

Tennessee Renaissance Festival, in Triune (20 miles/32km south of downtown Nashville). Maidens, knights, gypsies, jugglers, jousting, games, and food—think whole turkey legs that you can eat like a barbarian—are some of the people and activities you'll find at this medieval fair held on the grounds of the **Castle Gwynn** (ℂ **615/395-9950**). Weekends in May, including Memorial Day.

Tennessee Crafts Fair, Centennial Park. With the largest display of Tennessee crafts, this fair opens the summer season. Food, demonstrations, and children's craft activities (ℂ **615/385-1904**). Early May.

Running of the Iroquois Steeplechase, Percy Warner Park. This horse race has been a Nashville ritual for more than 50 years. A benefit for Vanderbilt Children's Hospital, the event is accompanied by tailgate picnics (ℂ **615/322-7284** or 615/343-4231). Second Saturday in May.

June

Country Music Association (CMA) Music Festival, (formerly known as Fan Fair) The Coliseum. A chance for country artists and their fans to meet and greet each other in a weeklong music celebration. Glitzy stage shows and picture/autograph sessions with country music stars are all part of the action. A Texas barbecue and tickets for sightseeing are included in the price of a ticket, along with a bluegrass concert and the Grand Masters Fiddling Championship. This is the biggest country music event of the year in Nashville, so book your tickets far in advance. Contact the CMA Office (ℂ **615/244-2840**) for ticket information. Mid-June.

American Artisan Festival, Centennial Park. Artisans from 35 states present a wide range of crafts from blown glass to leather and quilts. Children's art booth and music, too (© 615/298-4691). Mid-June.

Independence Day Celebration, Riverfront Park. Family-oriented, alcohol-free event attracts 100,000 people for entertainment, food, and fireworks (© 615/862-8400). July 4.

Uncle Dave Macon Days, Cannonsburg Village. Murfreesboro (30 miles/48km southeast of downtown Nashville). Named for one of the founders of the *Grand Ole Opry,* this festival features old-time dancing with lots of fiddle and banjo music, as well as a gospel showcase on Sunday during the festival. (© 800/716-7560). Second weekend in July.

August

Annual Americana Summer Sampler Craft, Folk Art & Antique Show, Tennessee State Fairgrounds. Retail and wholesale art fair with more than 125 craftspeople and antiques dealers. There are also lectures, demonstrations, and exhibits (© 615/227-2080). First weekend in August.

Annual Tennessee Walking-Horse National Celebration, Celebration Grounds, Shelbyville (40 miles/ 64km southeast of downtown Nashville). The World Grand Championship of the much-loved Tennessee walking horse, plus trade fairs and dog shows (© 931/684-5915). Late August.

September

Music City Jazz & Heritage Festival, Riverfront Park. The festival coincides with the John Merritt Classic football game (and battle of the marching bands) at Tennessee State University (© 800/791-8368 or 615/506-5114). Labor Day weekend.

Franklin Jazz Festival, in Franklin (15 miles/24km south of downtown Nashville). Jazz and blues music are performed on the historic town square in downtown Franklin (© 615/256-9596). Early September.

Belle Meade Plantation Fall Fest, Belle Meade Plantation. Antiques, crafts, children's festival, garage treasures sale, and food from local restaurants (© 800/270-3991 or 615/356-0501). Mid-September.

African Street Festival, Tennessee State University, main campus. Featured entertainment includes gospel, R&B, jazz, reggae music, and children's storytelling (© 615/329-3540). Mid-September.

Tennessee State Fair, Tennessee State Fairgrounds. Sprawling livestock and agriculture fair, with 4-H Club members and Future Farmers well represented. And a midway, of course (© 615/862-8980). Early to mid-September.

TACA Fall Crafts Fair, Centennial Park. This upscale fine-crafts market features artisans from throughout Tennessee. (© 615/385-1904). Late September.

October

Southern Festival of Books, War Memorial Plaza. Readings, panel discussions, and book signings by authors from around the United States, with an emphasis on Southern writers (© 615/320-7001, ext. 73; www.tn-humanities.org). Early October 2005. (The 2004 festival will be held in Memphis; see chapter 11.)

Annual Oktoberfest, Historic Germantown, at the corner of 8th Ave. North and Monroe St. Tours of

Germantown, polka dancing, accordion players, and lots of authentic German food (© 615/256-2729). Early to mid-October.

Annual NAIA Pow Wow, place to be determined. Native Americans from the United States and Canada gather for this powwow sponsored by the Native American Indian Association (© 615/232-9179). Mid-October.

Birthday of the *Grand Ole Opry,* Grand Ole Opry House. Three-day party with performances, autographs, and picture sessions with *Opry* stars. In recent years, the all-star lineup has run the gamut from Ralph Stanley to Alan Jackson (© 615/889-3060; www.gaylord opryland.com). Mid-October.

November

Americana Christmas Sampler Craft, Folk Art & Antique Show, Tennessee State Fairgrounds. Shop for Christmas treasures and handicraft arts (© 615/227-2080). Early November.

Longhorn World Championship Rodeo, Tennessee Miller Coliseum, outside of Murfreesboro. Professional cowboys and cowgirls participate in this rodeo to win championship points (© 800/357-6336 or 615/876-1016; www.longhornrodeo.com). Third weekend in November.

Christmas at Belmont, Belmont Mansion, Belmont University Campus. The opulent antebellum mansion is decked out in Victorian Christmas finery, and the gift shop is a great place to shop for Christmas-y Victorian reproductions. In 2003, Belmont's annual Christmas concert, starring Nashville legend Brenda Lee, was broadcast on PBS on Christmas night. Taped in early December at the Massey Performing Arts Center, the annual program also features carols and classical favorites by Belmont students and faculty (© 615/460-5459). Late November to late December.

A Country Christmas, Opryland Hotel. More than two million Christmas lights are used to decorate the grounds of the hotel. A musical revue featuring the "Dancing Waters" fountain show, holiday dinner, and crafts fair round out the holiday activities here (© 615/871-7637). November 1 to December 25.

December

Rudolph's Red Nose Run & Nashville Gas Christmas Parade, downtown Nashville. After a 5K race that begins at 1pm, the Christmas parade of 100 floats, bands, and clowns starts at 2pm at 9th and Broadway (© 615/734-1754). For information on the race, call © 615/871-7637. First Sunday in December.

4 Health & Insurance

STAYING HEALTHY
BEFORE YOU GO

In most cases, your existing health plan will provide the coverage you need. But double-check; you may want to buy **travel medical insurance** instead. (See the section on insurance below.) Bring your insurance ID card with you when you travel.

If you suffer from a chronic illness, consult your doctor before your departure. For conditions like epilepsy, diabetes, or heart problems, wear a **Medic Alert identification tag** (© 800/825-3785; www.medicalert. org), which will immediately alert doctors to your condition and give them access to your records through Medic Alert's 24-hour hotline.

Pack **prescription medications** in your carry-on luggage, and carry prescription medications in their original containers, with pharmacy labels—otherwise they won't make it through airport security. Also bring along copies of your prescriptions in case you lose your pills or run out. Don't forget an extra pair of contact lenses or prescription glasses.

WHAT TO DO IF YOU GET SICK AWAY FROM HOME

If you need a doctor, call **Tri-Star Medline** at © **800/265-8624** or **615/342-1919,** available Monday through Friday from 8am to 5pm; or contact the **Vanderbilt Medical Group Physician Referral Service** at © **615/322-3000.** If you have dental problems, a nationwide referral service known as **1-800-DENTIST** (© **800/336-8478**) will provide the name of a nearby dentist or clinic.

You may want to ask the concierge at your hotel to recommend a local doctor—even his or her own. This will probably yield a better recommendation than any 800-number would.

TRAVEL INSURANCE

Check your existing insurance policies and credit-card coverage before you buy travel insurance. You may already be covered for lost luggage, cancelled tickets, or medical expenses. The cost of travel insurance varies widely, depending on the cost and length of your trip, your age, health, and the type of trip you're taking.

TRIP-CANCELLATION INSUR-ANCE Trip-cancellation insurance helps you get your money back if you have to back out of a trip, if you have to go home early, or if your travel supplier goes bankrupt. Allowed reasons for cancellation can range from sickness to natural disasters to the State Department declaring your destination unsafe for travel. (Insurers usually won't cover vague fears, though, as many travelers discovered who tried to cancel their trips in October 2001 because they were wary of flying.) In this unstable world, trip-cancellation insurance is a good buy if you're getting tickets well in advance—who knows what the state of the world, or of your airline, will be in 9 months? Insurance policy details vary, so read the fine print—and especially make sure that your airline or cruise line is on the list of carriers covered in case of bankruptcy. For information, contact one of the following insurers: **Access America** (© 866/807-3982; www.accessamerica.com); **Travel Guard International** (© 800/826-4919; www.travelguard.com); **Travel Insured International** (© 800/243-3174; www.travelinsured.com); and **Travelex Insurance Services** (© 888/457-4602; www.travelex-insurance.com).

MEDICAL INSURANCE Most health insurance policies cover you if you get sick away from home—but check, particularly if you're insured by an HMO. If you require additional medical insurance, try **MEDEX International** (© **800/527-0218** or 410/453-6300; www.medexassist. com) or **Travel Assistance International** (© **800/821-2828;** www.travel assistance.com; for general information on services, call the company's

Worldwide Assistance Services, Inc., at © **800/777-8710**).

LOST-LUGGAGE INSURANCE On domestic flights, checked baggage is covered up to $2,500 per ticketed passenger. If you plan to check items more valuable than the standard liability, see if your valuables are covered by your homeowner's policy, get baggage insurance as part of your comprehensive travel-insurance package, or buy Travel Guard's "BagTrak" product. Don't buy insurance at the airport, as it's usually overpriced. Be sure to take any valuables or irreplaceable items with you in your carry-on luggage, as many valuables (including books, money, and electronics) aren't covered by airline policies.

If your luggage is lost, immediately file a lost-luggage claim at the airport, detailing the luggage contents. For most airlines, you must report delayed, damaged, or lost baggage within 4 hours of arrival. The airlines are required to deliver luggage, once found, directly to your house or destination free of charge.

CAR RENTAL INSURANCE For information on car renter's insurance, see "Getting Around Nashville," in chapter 3.

5 Specialized Travel Resources

FOR TRAVELERS WITH DISABILITIES

Almost all hotels and motels in Nashville offer wheelchair-accessible accommodations, but when making reservations be sure to ask. Additionally, the MTA public bus system in Nashville has either wheelchair-accessible regular vehicles or offers special transportation services for travelers with disabilities. To find out more about special services, call **Access Ride** (© **615/880-3970**).

The **Disability Information Office,** 25 Middleton St. (© **615/862-6492**), provides a referral and information service for visitors with disabilities. The *Nashville City Vacation Guide,* available either through this office or the Nashville Convention & Visitors Bureau, includes information on accessibility of restaurants, hotels, attractions, shops, and nightlife around Nashville.

In addition, both **Amtrak** (© **800/USA-RAIL** [872-7245]; www.amtrak.com) and **Greyhound** (© **800/752-4841**; www.greyhound.com) offer special fares and services for the disabled. Call at least a week in advance of your trip for details.

Organizations that offer assistance to disabled travelers include **Moss-Rehab** (www.mossresourcenet.org), which provides a library of accessible-travel resources online; the **Society for Accessible Travel and Hospitality** (© **212/447-7284**; www.sath.org; annual membership fees: $45 adults, $30 seniors and students), which offers a wealth of travel resources for all types of disabilities and informed recommendations on destinations, access guides, travel agents, tour operators, vehicle rentals, and companion services; and the **American Foundation for the Blind** (© **800/232-5463**; www.afb.org), which provides information on traveling with Seeing Eye dogs.

CAR RENTALS Many of the major car rental companies now offer hand-controlled cars for disabled drivers. **Avis** can provide such a vehicle at any of its locations in the United States with 48-hour advance notice; **Hertz** requires between 24 and 72 hours of advance reservation at most of its locations. **Wheelchair Getaways of Tennessee** (© **888/245-9944**; www.wheelchair-getaways.com) rents specialized vans with wheelchair lifts and other features for the disabled.

FOR GAY & LESBIAN TRAVELERS

To find out more about the Nashville gay and lesbian community, contact the **Rainbow Community Center,** 961 Woodland St. (© 615/297-0008; www.rainbowcommunitycenter.org). Another helpful resource is **The International Gay & Lesbian Travel Association (IGLTA)** (© 800/448-8550 or 954/776-2626; www.iglta.org), the trade association for the gay and lesbian travel industry, which offers an online directory of gay- and lesbian-friendly travel businesses. Go to their website and click on "Members."

Many agencies offer tours and travel itineraries specifically for gay and lesbian travelers. **Above and Beyond Tours** (© 800/397-2681; www.abovebeyondtours.com) is the exclusive gay and lesbian tour operator for United Airlines. **Now, Voyager** (© 800/255-6951; www.nowvoyager. com) is a well-known San Francisco–based, gay-owned and operated travel service.

FOR SENIORS

Don't be shy about asking for discounts, but always carry some kind of identification, such as a driver's license, that shows your date of birth. Many hotels, museums, and theaters offer discounts to senior citizens. Also, mention the fact that you're a senior citizen when you first make your travel reservations. For example, both **Amtrak** (© 800/USA-RAIL [872-7245]; www.amtrak.com) and **Greyhound** (© 800/752-4841; www. greyhound.com) offer discounts to persons over 62.

Members of **AARP,** 601 E St. NW, Washington, DC 20049 (© 800/424-3410 or 202/434-2277; www. aarp.org), get discounts on hotels, airfares, and car rentals. AARP offers members a wide range of benefits, including *AARP: The Magazine* and a monthly newsletter. Anyone over 50 can join.

Many reliable agencies and organizations target the 50-plus market. One that offers trips to Nashville and Memphis is **Elderhostel** (© 877/426-8056; www.elderhostel.org), which arranges study programs for those aged 55 and over (and a spouse or companion of any age) in the U.S. and in more than 80 countries around the world. Most courses last 5 to 7 days in the U.S., and many include airfare, accommodations in university dormitories or modest inns, meals, and tuition.

Recommended publications offering travel resources and discounts for seniors include: the quarterly magazine *Travel 50 & Beyond* (www. travel50andbeyond.com); *Travel Unlimited: Uncommon Adventures for the Mature Traveler* (Avalon); *101 Tips for Mature Travelers,* available from Grand Circle Travel (© 800/221-2610 or 617/350-7500; www.gct.com); *The 50+ Traveler's Guidebook* (St. Martin's Press); and *Unbelievably Good Deals and Great Adventures That You Absolutely Can't Get Unless You're Over 50* (McGraw-Hill).

FOR FAMILIES

Nashville is a great place for a family vacation. There are children's museums, miniature-golf courses, and a water amusement park to keep the kids entertained. Always be sure to ask about special family rates or parents' passes to various attractions.

At many hotels and motels, children stay free in their parents' room if no additional bed is required. Always be sure to ask about a lodging's policy regarding children when making a reservation or booking a room. Children's menus are also available at many restaurants.

You can find good family-oriented vacation advice on the Internet from sites like the **Family Travel Network** (www.familytravelnetwork.com); **Traveling Internationally with Your Kids** (www.travelwithyourkids.com), a comprehensive site offering sound advice for long-distance and international travel with children; and **Family Travel Files** (www.thefamilytravelfiles.com), which offers an online magazine and a directory of off-the-beaten-path tours and tour operators for families.

FOR STUDENTS

Arm yourself with your student ID and consider getting an **International Student Identity Card (ISIC),** which offers substantial savings on rail passes, plane tickets, and entrance fees. It also provides you with basic health and life insurance and a 24-hour help line. The card is available for $22 from **STA Travel** (② **800/781-4040;** www.statravel.com), the biggest student travel agency in the world. If you're no longer a student but are still under 26, you can get a **International Youth Travel Card (IYTC)** for the same price from the same people, which entitles you to some discounts (but not on museum admissions). (*Note:* In 2002, STA Travel bought competitors **Council Travel** and **USIT Campus** after they went bankrupt. It's still operating some offices under the Council name, but it's owned by STA.)

Travel CUTS (② **800/667-2887** or 416/614-2887; www.travelcuts.com) offers similar services for both Canadians and U.S. residents.

There are many universities and colleges in the Nashville area, but the main ones are **Vanderbilt University,** on West End Ave. (② **615/322-7311**), a private four-year research-oriented university; **Tennessee State University,** 3500 John A. Merritt Blvd. (② **615/963-5000**), a public four-year university; **Belmont University,** 1900 Belmont Blvd. (② **615/460-6000**), a Baptist liberal arts university; and **Fisk University,** 1000 17th Ave. N. (② **615/329-8500**), a private four-year African-American university.

West End Avenue around Vanderbilt University is full of restaurants, cafés, and shops. The area around Belmont University also has some college-type hangouts.

FOR BLACK TRAVELERS

The best resource for heritage attractions in Nashville is **www.musiccity usa.com**, the Nashville visitor bureau website.

The Internet also offers a number of other helpful travel sites. **Black Travel Online** (www.blacktravel online.com) posts news on upcoming events and includes links to articles and travel-booking sites. **Soul of America** (www.soulofamerica.com) is a more comprehensive website, with travel tips, event and family reunion postings, and sections on historically black beach resorts and active vacations.

For more information, check out the following collections and guides: *Go Girl: The Black Woman's Guide to Travel & Adventure* (Eighth Mountain Press), a compilation of travel essays by writers including Jill Nelson and Audre Lorde, with some practical information and trip-planning advice; *Travel and Enjoy Magazine* (② **866/266-6211;** www.travel andenjoy.com; subscription: $24 per year), which focuses on discounts and destination reviews; and the more narrative *Pathfinders Magazine* (② **877/ 977-PATH;** www.pathfinderstravel. com; subscription: $15 per year), which includes articles on everything from Rio de Janeiro to Ghana.

FOR SINGLE TRAVELERS

Many people prefer traveling alone, and for independent travelers, solo journeys offer infinite opportunities to make friends and meet locals. Unfortunately, if you like resorts, tours or cruises, you're likely to get hit with a "single supplement" to the base price. Single travelers can avoid these supplements, of course, by agreeing to room with other single travelers on the trip. An even better idea is to find a compatible roommate before you go from one of the many roommate locator agencies.

Travel Companion Exchange (TCE) (© 631/454-0880; www.travel companions.com) is one of the nation's oldest roommate finders for single travelers. At press time, however, service was suspended; check the website for updates. **Travel Buddies Singles Travel Club** (© 800/998-9099; www.travelbuddiesworldwide. com), based in Canada, runs small, intimate, single-friendly group trips and will match you with a roommate free of charge and save you the cost of single supplements. **TravelChums** (© 212/787-2621; www.travelchums. com) is an Internet-only travel-companion matching service with elements of an online personals-type site,

hosted by the respected New York–based Shaw Guides travel service. **The Single Gourmet Club** (www. singlegourmet.com/chapters.php) is an international social, dining, and travel club for singles of all ages, with offices in 21 cities in the U.S. and Canada. Annual membership fees vary from city to city.

For more information, check out Eleanor Berman's *Traveling Solo: Advice and Ideas for More Than 250 Great Vacations* (Globe Pequot), a guide with advice on traveling alone, whether on your own or on a group tour. Or turn to the **Travel Alone and Love It** website (www.travel aloneandloveit.com), designed by former flight attendant Sharon Wingler, the author of the book of the same name. Her site is full of tips for single travelers.

6 Planning Your Trip Online

SURFING FOR AIRFARES

The "big three" online travel agencies, **Expedia.com, Travelocity.com,** and **Orbitz.com** sell most of the air tickets on the Internet. (Canadian travelers should try expedia.ca and Travelocity.ca; U.K. residents can go for expedia.co.uk and opodo.co.uk.) Each has different business deals with the airlines and may offer different fares on the same flights, so it's wise to shop around. Expedia and Travelocity will also send you **e-mail notification** when a cheap fare becomes available to your favorite destination. Of the smaller travel agency websites, **SideStep** (www.sidestep.com) has gotten the best reviews from Frommer's authors. It's a browser add-on that purports to "search 140 sites at once," but in reality only beats competitors' fares as often as other sites do.

Also remember to check **airline websites,** especially those for low-fare

carriers such as Southwest, JetBlue, AirTran, WestJet, or Ryanair, whose fares are often misreported or simply missing from travel agency websites. Even with major airlines, you can often shave a few bucks from a fare by booking directly through the airline and avoiding a travel agency's transaction fee. But you'll get these discounts only by **booking online:** Most airlines now offer online-only fares that even their phone agents know nothing about. For the websites of airlines that fly to and from your destination, see appendix D.

Great **last-minute deals** are available through free weekly e-mail services provided directly by the airlines. Most of these are announced on Tuesday or Wednesday and must be purchased online. Most are only valid for travel that weekend, but some (such as Southwest's) can be booked weeks or months in advance. Sign up for

Frommers.com: The Complete Travel Resource

For an excellent travel-planning resource, we highly recommend **Frommers.com** (www.frommers.com). We're a little biased, of course, but we guarantee you'll find the travel tips, reviews, monthly vacation giveaways, and online-booking capabilities thoroughly indispensable. Among the special features are our popular **Message Boards,** where Frommer's readers post queries and share advice (sometimes even our authors show up to answer questions); **Frommers.com Newsletter,** for the latest travel bargains and insider travel secrets; and our Frommer's **Destinations** section, where you'll get expert travel tips, hotel and dining recommendations, and advice on the sights to see for more than 3,000 destinations around the globe. When your research is done, the **Online Reservations System** (www.frommers.com/book_a_trip) takes you to Frommer's preferred online partners for booking your vacation at affordable prices.

kayak.com

weekly e-mail alerts at airline websites or check mega-sites that compile comprehensive lists of last-minute specials, such as **Smarter Living** (www.smarterliving.com). For last-minute trips, **www.site59.com** often has better deals than the major-label sites.

If you're willing to give up some control over your flight details, use an **opaque fare service** like **Priceline** (www.priceline.com; www.priceline.co.uk for Europeans) or **Hotwire** (www.hotwire.com). Both offer rock-bottom prices in exchange for travel on a "mystery airline" at a mysterious time of day, often with a mysterious change of planes en route. The mystery airlines are all major, well-known carriers—and the possibility of being sent from Philadelphia to Chicago via Tampa is remote; the airlines' routing computers have gotten a lot better than they used to be. But your chances of getting a 6am or 11pm flight are pretty high. Hotwire tells you flight prices before you buy; Priceline usually has better deals than Hotwire, but you have to play their "name our price" game. If you're new at this, the helpful folks at **BiddingForTravel** (www.biddingfortravel.com) do a

good job of demystifying Priceline's prices. Priceline and Hotwire are great for flights within North America and between the U.S. and Europe.

SURFING FOR HOTELS

Shopping online for hotels is much easier in the U.S., Canada, and certain parts of Europe than it is in the rest of the world. But many smaller hotels and B&Bs—especially outside the U.S.—don't show up on websites at all. Of the "big three" sites, **Expedia** may be the best choice, thanks to its long list of special deals. **Travelocity** runs a close second. Hotel specialist sites **hotels.com** and **hoteldiscounts.com** are also reliable. An excellent free program, **TravelAxe** (www.travelaxe.net), can help you search multiple hotel sites at once, even ones you may never have heard of.

Priceline and Hotwire are even better for hotels than for airfares; with both, you're allowed to pick the neighborhood and quality level of your hotel before offering up your money. Priceline's hotel product even covers Europe and Asia, though it's much better at getting luxury lodging for moderate prices than at finding anything at the bottom of the scale. *Note:* Hotwire overrates its hotels by one star—what Hotwire calls a four-star is a three-star anywhere else.

SURFING FOR RENTAL CARS

For booking rental cars online, the best deals are usually found at rental car company websites, although all the major online travel agencies also offer rental-car reservations services. Priceline and Hotwire work well for rental cars, too; the only "mystery" is which major rental company you get, and for most travelers the difference between Hertz, Avis, and Budget is negligible.

7 The 21st-Century Traveler

INTERNET ACCESS AWAY FROM HOME

Travelers have any number of ways to check their e-mail and access the Internet on the road. Of course, using your own laptop—or even a PDA or electronic organizer with a modem—gives you the most flexibility. But even if you don't have a computer, you can still access your e-mail and even your office computer from cybercafes.

WITHOUT YOUR OWN COMPUTER

It's hard nowadays to find a city that doesn't have a few cybercafes. Although there's no definitive directory for cybercafes—these are independent businesses, after all—two places to start looking are at **www. cybercaptive.com** and **www.cyber cafe.com**.

Aside from formal cybercafes, most **youth hostels** nowadays have at least one computer you can get to the Internet on. And most **public libraries** in both Nashville and Memphis offer Internet access free or for a small charge. Avoid **hotel business centers,** which often charge exorbitant rates.

Tennessee's airports now have **Internet kiosks** scattered throughout their gates. These kiosks, which you'll also see in hotel lobbies, and some coffee shops, give you basic Web access for a per-minute fee that's usually higher than cybercafe prices. The kiosks' clunkiness and high price means they should be avoided whenever possible.

To retrieve your e-mail, ask your **Internet Service Provider (ISP)** if it has a Web-based interface tied to your existing e-mail account. If your ISP doesn't have such an interface, you can use the free **mail2web** service (www. mail2web.com) to view and reply to your home e-mail. For more flexibility, you may want to open a free, Web-based e-mail account with **Yahoo! Mail** (http://mail.yahoo.com) or Fastmail (www.fastmail.fm). (Microsoft's Hotmail is another popular option, but Hotmail has severe spam problems.) Your home ISP may be able to forward your e-mail to the Web-based account automatically.

If you need to access files on your office computer, look into a service called **GoToMyPC** (www.gotomypc. com). The service provides a Web-based interface for you to access and manipulate a distant PC from anywhere—even a cybercafe—provided your "target" PC is on and has an always-on connection to the Internet (such as with Road Runner cable). The service offers top-quality security, but if you're worried about hackers, use your own laptop rather than a cybercafe to access the GoToMyPC system.

WITH YOUR OWN COMPUTER

Major ISPs have **local access numbers** around the world, allowing you to go online by simply placing a local call. Check your ISP's website or call its toll-free number and ask how you can use your current account away from home, and how much it will cost.

If you're traveling outside the reach of your ISP, the **iPass** network has dial-up numbers in most of the world's countries. You'll have to sign up with an iPass provider, who will then tell you how to set up your computer for your destination(s). For a list of iPass providers, go to www.ipass.com and click on "Individual Purchase." One solid provider is **i2roam** (*©* **866/ 811-6209** or 920/235-0475; www. i2roam.com).

Most business-class hotels throughout the world offer dataports for laptop modems, and a few thousand hotels in the U.S. and Europe now offer high-speed Internet access using an Ethernet network cable. You'll have to bring your own cables either way, so call your hotel in advance to find out what the options are.

If you have an 802.11b/**wi-fi** card for your computer, several commercial companies have made wireless service available in airports, hotel lobbies, and coffee shops, primarily in the U.S. **T-Mobile Hotspot** (www.t-mobile. com/hotspot) serves up wireless connections at more than 1,000 Starbucks coffee shops nationwide. **Boingo**

(www.boingo.com) and **Wayport** (www.wayport.com) have set up networks in airports and high-class hotel lobbies. IPass providers (see above) also give you access to a few hundred wireless hotel lobby setups. Best of all, you don't need to be staying at the Four Seasons to use the hotel's network; just set yourself up on a nice couch in the lobby. Unfortunately, the companies' pricing policies are byzantine, with a variety of monthly, per-connection, and per-minute plans.

Community-minded individuals have also set up **free wireless networks** in major cities around the world. These networks are spotty, but you get what you (don't) pay for. Each network has a home page explaining how to set up your computer for their particular system; start your explorations at www. personaltelco.net/index.cgi/Wireless Communities.

USING A CELLPHONE

Just because your cellphone works at home doesn't mean it'll work elsewhere in the country (thanks to our nation's fragmented cellphone system). It's a good bet that your phone will work in major cities. But take a look at your wireless company's coverage map on its website before heading

---

Online Traveler's Toolbox

Veteran travelers usually carry some essential items to make their trips easier. The following is a selection of online tools to bookmark and use.

- **Visa ATM Locator** (www.visa.com), for locations of PLUS ATMs worldwide, or **MasterCard ATM Locator** (www.mastercard.com), for locations of Cirrus ATMs worldwide.
- **Intellicast** (www.intellicast.com) and **Weather.com** (www.weather. com) give weather forecasts for all 50 states and for cities around the world.
- **Mapquest** (www.mapquest.com). This best of the mapping sites lets you choose a specific address or destination, and in seconds, will return a map and detailed directions.

out—T-Mobile, Sprint, and Nextel are particularly weak in rural areas. If you need to stay in touch at a destination where you know your phone won't work, **rent** a phone that does from **InTouch USA** (© **800/872-7626;** www.intouchglobal.com) or at a rental car location, but be aware that you'll pay $1 a minute or more for airtime.

If you're not from the U.S., you'll be appalled at the poor reach of our **GSM (Global System for Mobiles) wireless network,** which is used by much of the rest of the world (see below). Your phone will probably work in most major U.S. cities; it definitely won't work in many rural areas. (To see where GSM phones work in the U.S., check out www.tmobile.com/coverage/national_popup.asp) And you may or may not be able to send SMS (text messaging) home—something Americans tend not to do anyway, for various cultural and technological reasons. (International budget travelers like to send text messages home because it's much cheaper than making international calls.) Assume nothing—call your wireless provider and get the full scoop. In a worst-case scenario, you can always rent a phone; InTouch USA delivers to hotels.

8 Getting There

BY PLANE

For information on flights to the United States from other countries, see "Getting to the U.S." in appendix A.

THE MAJOR AIRLINES

Nashville is served by the following major airlines: **American Airlines** (© 800/433-7300); **Continental** (© 800/525-0280); **Delta** (© 800/221-1212); **Northwest-KLM** (© 800/225-2525); **Southwest** (© 800/435-9792); **United Airlines** (© 800/241-6522); and **US Airways** (© 800/428-4322).

Southwest is the city's largest carrier, with some 87 daily flights out of the city. Most Southwest flights will depart and arrive from the airport's Concourse C. Southwest Airlines also offers air/hotel packages. For details, visit **Southwest Airlines Vacations** online at **www.swavacations.com**, or call © **800/423-5683.**

GETTING INTO TOWN FROM THE AIRPORT

Nashville International Airport (© **615/275-1675**) is located about 8 miles east of downtown Nashville and is just south of I-40. It takes about 15 minutes to reach downtown Nashville from the airport. See "Getting Around Nashville," in chapter 3 for information on car-rental facilities at the Nashville airport. Many hotels near the airport offer a complimentary shuttle service, while others slightly farther away have their own fee shuttles; check with your hotel when you make your reservation.

The **Gray Line Airport Express** (© **615/275-1180**) operates shuttles between the airport and downtown and West End hotels. These shuttles operate from the airport every 15 to 20 minutes daily between 6am and 11pm; in addition to the hotels listed below, a few other hotels are on call. The downtown shuttle stops at the following hotels: Hilton, Union Station, Courtyard by Marriott (Fourth and Church), Holiday Inn Express, Renaissance Nashville Hotel, Nashville Sheraton, Westin Hermitage, and Doubletree Hotel Nashville. The West End shuttle stops at the following hotels: Loews Vanderbilt Plaza Hotel, Embassy Suites-West End, Holiday Inn Select, Courtyard by Marriott, Marriott–Vanderbilt,

> ### Tips Airport Shuttles
>
> Airport shuttle schedules vary according to the number of passengers at any given time. If you are the first one on or the last one off, your travel time may be doubled. If there are two or three people in your party, it's usually cheaper and faster to take a cab.

Guest House Inn, Hampton Inn–Vanderbilt, Hampton Inn and Suites–Elliston Place, and Days Inn–Vanderbilt. Rates are $11 one-way and $17 round-trip.

Metropolitan Transit Authority **buses** connect the airport and downtown Nashville. The no. 18 Elm Hill Pike bus runs between 8:13am and 5:33pm Monday to Friday (shorter hours and fewer departures on Saturday and Sunday). The adult, base fare is $1.45 each way, with exact change required, and the ride takes approximately 40 minutes. Buses from the airport leave at the ground-level curbside. Buses for the airport leave from Shelter C at Deaderick St. and 4th Ave. For the most current schedule information, call ✆ **615/862-5950** Monday to Friday between 6:30am and 6pm and Saturday 8am to 1pm.

Metered **taxi fare** from the airport into downtown Nashville will cost you a $20 flat rate, or a few dollars more from the airport to West End hotels. Taxis are available on the ground level of the airport terminal. For information, call the Transportation Licensing Commission (TLC) at ✆ **615/862-6777.**

GETTING THROUGH THE AIRPORT

With the federalization of airport security, security procedures at U.S. airports are more stable and consistent than ever. Generally, you'll be fine if you arrive at the airport **1 hour** before a domestic flight; if you show up late, tell an airline employee and she'll probably whisk you to the front of the line.

Bring a **current, government-issued photo ID** such as a driver's license or passport. Keep your ID at the ready to show at check-in, the security checkpoint, and sometimes even the gate. (Children under 18 do not need photo IDs for domestic flights, but the adults checking in with them should have them.)

The TSA has phased out **gate check-in** at all U.S. airports. Passengers with e-tickets can still beat the ticket-counter lines by using **electronic kiosks** or even **online check-in.** Ask your airline which alternatives are available, and if you're using a kiosk, bring the credit card you used to book the ticket or your frequent-flier card. If you're checking bags or looking to snag an exit-row seat, you will be able to do so using most airlines' kiosks; again, call your airline for up-to-date information. **Curbside check-in** is also a good way to avoid lines, although a few airlines still ban curbside check-in; call before you go.

Security checkpoint lines are getting shorter, but some doozies remain. If you have trouble standing for long periods of time, tell an airline employee; the airline will provide a wheelchair. Speed up security by **not wearing metal objects** such as big belt buckles. If you've got metallic body parts, a note from your doctor can prevent a long chat with the security screeners. Keep in mind that only **ticketed passengers** are allowed past security, except for folks escorting disabled passengers or children.

Federalization has stabilized **what you can carry on** and **what you can't.**

Flying with Film & Video

Never pack film—developed or undeveloped—in checked bags, as the new, more powerful scanners in U.S. airports can fog film. The film you carry with you can be damaged by scanners as well. X-ray damage is cumulative; the faster the film, and the more times you put it through a scanner, the more likely the damage. Film under 800 ASA is usually safe for up to five scans. If you're taking your film through additional scans, U.S. regulations permit you to demand hand inspections. In international airports, you're at the mercy of airport officials. Keep in mind that airports are not the only places where your camera may be scanned: Highly trafficked attractions are X-raying visitors' bags with increasing frequency.

Most photo supply stores sell protective pouches designed to block damaging X-rays. The pouches fit both film and loaded cameras. They should protect your film in checked baggage, but they also may raise alarms and result in a hand inspection.

An organization called **Film Safety for Traveling on Planes, FSTOP** (© **888/301-2665;** www.f-stop.org), can provide additional tips for traveling with film and equipment.

Carry-on scanners will not damage **videotape** in video cameras, but the magnetic fields emitted by the walk-through security gateways and handheld inspection wands will. Always place your loaded camcorder on the screening conveyor belt or have it hand-inspected. Be sure your batteries are charged, as you will probably be required to turn the device on to ensure that it's what it appears to be.

The general rule is that sharp things are out, nail clippers are okay, and food and beverages must be passed through the X-ray machine—but that security screeners can't make you drink from your coffee cup. Bring food in your carry-on rather than checking it, as explosive-detection machines used on checked luggage have been known to mistake food (especially chocolate, for some reason) for bombs. Travelers in the U.S. are allowed one carry-on bag, plus a "personal item" such as a purse, briefcase, or laptop bag. Carry-on hoarders can stuff all sorts of things into a laptop bag; as long as it has a laptop in it, it's still considered a personal item. The Transportation Security Administration (TSA) has issued a list of restricted items; check its website (**www.tsa.gov**) for details.

At press time, the TSA is also recommending that you **not lock your checked luggage** so screeners can search it by hand if necessary. The agency says to use plastic "zip ties" instead, which can be bought at hardware stores and can be easily cut off.

FLYING FOR LESS: TIPS FOR GETTING THE BEST AIRFARE

Passengers sharing the same airplane cabin rarely pay the same fare. Travelers who need to purchase tickets at the last minute, change their itinerary at a moment's notice, or fly one-way often get stuck paying the premium rate. Here are some ways to keep your airfare costs down.

- Passengers who can book their ticket **long in advance,** who can **stay over Saturday night,** or who **fly midweek** or **at less-trafficked hours** will pay a fraction of the full fare. If your schedule is flexible, say so, and ask if you can secure a cheaper fare by changing your flight plans.
- You can also save on airfares by keeping an eye out in local newspapers for **promotional specials** or **fare wars,** when airlines lower prices on their most popular routes. You rarely see fare wars offered for peak travel times, but if you can travel in the off-months, you may snag a bargain.
- Search **the Internet** for cheap fares (see "Planning Your Trip Online," earlier in this chapter).
- **Consolidators,** also known as bucket shops, are great sources for international tickets, although they usually can't beat the Internet on fares within North America. Start by looking in Sunday newspaper travel sections; U.S. travelers should focus on the *New York Times, Los Angeles Times,* and *Miami Herald. Beware:* Bucket shop tickets are usually nonrefundable or rigged with stiff cancellation penalties, often as high as 50% to 75% of the ticket price, and some put you on charter

airlines with questionable safety records.

Several reliable consolidators are worldwide and available on the Net. **STA Travel** (www.sta travel.com) is now the world's leader in student travel, thanks to their purchase of Council Travel. It also offers good fares for travelers of all ages. **FlyCheap** (© **800/ FLY-CHEAP;** www.1800flycheap. com) is owned by package-holiday megalith MyTravel.

- Join **frequent-flier clubs.** Accrue enough miles, and you'll be rewarded with free flights and elite status. It's free, and you'll get the best choice of seats, faster response to phone inquiries, and prompter service if your luggage is stolen, your flight is canceled or delayed, or if you want to change your seat. You don't need to fly to build frequent-flier miles—**frequent-flier credit cards** can provide thousands of miles for doing your everyday shopping.

BY CAR

Nashville is a hub city intersected by three interstate highways. **I-65** runs north to Louisville, Kentucky, and south to Birmingham, Alabama. **I-40** runs west to Memphis and east to Knoxville, Tennessee. **I-24** runs northwest toward St. Louis and southeast

---

Travel in the Age of Bankruptcy

Airlines go bankrupt, so protect yourself by purchasing **your tickets with a credit card,** as the Fair Credit Billing Act guarantees that you can get your money back from the credit card company if a travel supplier goes under (and if you request the refund within 60 days of the bankruptcy.) **Travel insurance** can also help, but make sure it covers against "carrier default" for your specific travel provider. And be aware that if a U.S. airline goes bust mid-trip, a 2001 federal law requires other carriers to take you to your destination (albeit on a space-available basis) for a fee of no more than $25, provided you rebook within 60 days of the cancellation.

toward Atlanta. Downtown Nashville is the center of the hub, encircled by Interstates 40, 65, and 265. Briley Parkway on the east, north, and west and I-440 on the south form a larger "wheel" around this hub.

If you're heading into downtown Nashville, follow the signs for I-65/24 and take either Exit 84 or Exit 85. If you're headed to Music Valley (Opryland Hotel), take I-40 east to the Briley Parkway exit and head north. If your destination is the West End/Music Row area, take I-40 around the south side of downtown and get off at the Broadway exit.

Here are some driving distances from selected cities: Atlanta, 250 miles; Chicago, 442 miles; Cincinnati, 291 miles; Memphis, 210 miles; New Orleans, 549 miles; and St. Louis, 327 miles.

If you are a member of the **American Automobile Association** (AAA) and your car breaks down, call ©️ **800/222-4357** for 24-hour emergency road service. The **local AAA office** in Nashville is at 2501 Hillsboro Rd., Suite 1 (©️ **615/297-7700**), and is open Monday to Friday 1:30am to 5:30pm.

BY BUS

Greyhound Lines (©️ **800/231-2222**) offers service to Nashville from around the country. These buses operate along interstate corridors or local routes. The fare between New York and Nashville is about $95 one-way and $159 round-trip; the fare between Chicago and Nashville is about $65 one-way and $119 round-trip. The Greyhound bus station is on the south side of downtown Nashville at 200 Eighth Ave. S.

9 Packages for the Independent Traveler

Before you start your search for the lowest airfare, you may want to consider booking your flight as part of a travel package. Package tours are not the same thing as escorted tours. Package tours are simply a way to buy the airfare, accommodations, and other elements of your trip (such as car rentals, airport transfers, and sometimes even activities) at the same time and often at discounted prices—kind of like one-stop shopping. Packages are sold in bulk to tour operators—who resell them to the public at a cost that usually undercuts standard rates.

Package tours can vary by leaps and bounds. Some offer a better class of hotels than others. Some offer the same hotels for lower prices. Some offer flights on scheduled airlines, while others book charters. Some limit your choice of accommodations and travel days. You are often required to make a large payment up front. On the plus side, packages can save you money, offering group prices but allowing for independent travel. Some even let you add on a few guided excursions or escorted day trips (also at prices lower than if you booked them yourself) without booking an entirely escorted tour.

Before you invest in a package tour, get some answers. Ask about the **accommodations choices** and prices for each. Then look up the hotels' reviews in a Frommer's guide and check their rates for your specific dates of travel online. You'll also want to find out what **type of room** you get. If you need a certain type of room, ask for it; don't take whatever is thrown your way. Request a nonsmoking room, a quiet room, a room with a view, or whatever you fancy.

Finally, look for **hidden expenses.** Ask whether airport departure fees and taxes, for example, are included in the total cost.

HOW TO FIND A PACKAGE DEAL

One good source of package deals is the airlines themselves. Most major airlines offer air/land packages, including **Southwest Airlines Vacations** (✆ 800/423-5683; www.swavacations. com), **American Airlines Vacations** (✆ 800/321-2121; www.aavacations. com), **Delta Vacations** (✆ 800/221-6666; www.deltavacations.com), **Continental Airlines Vacations** (✆ 800/301-3800; www.coolvacations.com), and **United Vacations** (✆ 888/854-3899; www.unitedvacations.com). Several big **online travel agencies**—Expedia, Travelocity, Orbitz, Site59, and Lastminute.com—also do a brisk business in packages. If you're unsure about the pedigree of a smaller packager, check with the Better Business Bureau in the city where the company is based, or go online at www.bbb.org. If a packager won't tell you where it's based, don't fly with them.

Travel packages are also listed in the travel section of your local Sunday newspaper. Or check ads in the national travel magazines such as *Arthur Frommer's Budget Travel Magazine, Travel & Leisure, National Geographic Traveler,* and *Condé Nast Traveler.*

The **Delta Queen Steamboat Company,** Robin Street Wharf, 1380 Port of New Orleans Place, New Orleans, LA 70130-1890 (✆ **800/543-1949**), offers paddle-wheel steamboat tours that include Nashville (as well as other Tennessee cities like Memphis and Chattanooga) in its itineraries. For more information, go to www.deltaqueen.com.

Quite a few tour companies in Nashville arrange 2- and 3-night tours of the city. These tours usually include lodging and tickets to various attractions and performances, with tickets to the *Grand Ole Opry* tops among these. Transportation around the city is sometimes an additional charge. If you don't like planning, these tours can be a good value. You usually have a range of hotel choices in different price categories. Some of these tour companies include **Gray Line Tours,** 2416 Music Valley Dr., Nashville, TN 37214 (✆ **800/251-1864** or 615/227-2270; www.graylinenashville. com); and **Johnny Walker Tours,** 2416 Music Valley Dr., Nashville, TN 37214 (✆ **800/722-1524** or 615/834-8585).

10 Tips on Accommodations

SAVING ON YOUR HOTEL ROOM

The **rack rate** is the maximum rate that a hotel charges for a room. Hardly anybody pays this price, however. To lower the cost of your room:

- **Ask about special rates or other discounts.** Always ask whether a room less expensive than the first one quoted is available, or whether any special rates apply to you. You may qualify for corporate, student, military, senior, or other discounts. Mention membership in AAA, AARP, frequent-flier programs, or trade unions, which may entitle you to special deals as well. Find out the hotel policy on children—do kids stay free in the room or is there a special rate?

- **Dial direct.** When booking a room in a chain hotel, you'll often get a better deal by calling the individual hotel's reservation desk than at the chain's main number.

- **Book online.** Many hotels offer Internet-only discounts, or supply rooms to Priceline, Hotwire, or Expedia at rates much lower than the ones you can get through the hotel itself.

- **Remember the law of supply and demand.** Resort hotels are most crowded and therefore most expensive on weekends, so discounts are usually available for midweek stays. Business hotels in downtown locations are busiest during the week, so you can expect big discounts over the weekend. Many hotels have high-season and low-season prices, and booking the day after "high season" ends can mean big discounts.
- **Look into group or long-stay discounts.** If you come as part of a large group, you should be able to negotiate a bargain rate, since the hotel can then guarantee occupancy in a number of rooms. Likewise, if you're planning a long stay (at least 5 days), you might qualify for a discount. As a general rule, expect 1 night free after a 7-night stay.
- **Avoid excess charges and hidden costs.** When you book a room, ask whether the hotel charges for parking. Use your own cellphone, pay phones, or prepaid phone cards instead of dialing direct from hotel phones, which usually have exorbitant rates. And don't be tempted by the room's minibar offerings: Most hotels charge through the nose for water, soda, and snacks. Finally, ask about local taxes and service charges, which can increase the cost of a room by 15% or more. If a hotel insists upon tacking on a surprise "energy surcharge" that wasn't mentioned at check-in or a "resort fee" for amenities you didn't use, you can often make a case for getting it removed.
- **Book an efficiency.** A room with a kitchenette allows you to shop for groceries and cook your own meals. This is a big money saver, especially for families on long stays.

LANDING THE BEST ROOM

Somebody has to get the best room in the house. It might as well be you. You can start by joining the hotel's frequent-guest program, which may make you eligible for upgrades. A hotel-branded credit card usually gives it owner "silver" or "gold" status in frequent-guest programs for free. Always ask about a corner room. They're often larger and quieter, with more windows and light, and they often cost the same as standard rooms. When you make your reservation, ask if the hotel is renovating; if it is, request a room away from the construction. Ask about nonsmoking rooms, rooms with views, rooms with twin, queen-, or king-size beds. If you're a light sleeper, request a quiet room away from vending machines, elevators, restaurants, bars, and discos. Ask for one of the rooms that have been most recently renovated or redecorated.

If you aren't happy with your room when you arrive, say so. If another room is available, most lodgings will be willing to accommodate you.

11 Recommended Books & Films

BOOKS

GENERAL   If you'd like to learn more about Nashville history, you'll find some in *Paths of the Past* (University of Tennessee Press, 1988), by Paul H. Bergeron. This brief history of Tennessee between the years 1770 and 1970 includes quite a bit on Nashville itself. For a more thorough look at Tennessee and Nashville history, read *Tennessee, A Short History* (University of Tennessee Press, 1990), by Stanley J. Folmsbee, Robert E. Corlew, and Enoch L. Mitchell; or *Tennessee: A History* (W. W. Norton and Co., 1984), by Wilma Dykeman.

COUNTRY MUSIC There are scores of books about the country music industry and country stars, and you'll find good selections of these books at most of the bookstores in Nashville. For a very thorough history of country music, read the scholarly *Country Music* (University of Texas Press, 1985), by Bill Malone. *Finding Her Voice: The Saga of Women in Country Music* (Crown Publishers, 1993), by Mary A. Bufwack and Robert K. Oermann, is the essential history of women country singers and covers the topic up to 1991. The book is organized by both genre and time periods. *Grand Ole Opry* (Henry Holt, 1989), by Chet Hagan, is the official Opryland USA history of this country music tradition. The book includes lots of great old photos.

If you want to know what it's really like in the country music business, there are plenty of books that will give you an insider's perspective. One of the latest of these is *Nashville's Unwritten Rules* (Overlook, 1998), by Dan Daley. This book looks at the producers, the songwriters, and the musicians to paint a picture of how the music really gets made in Music City. For profiles of a wide range of country acts from around the country, read *In the Country of Country* (Pantheon, 1997), by Nicholas Dawidoff. With its evocative old photos, this book ventures out into the country to try to understand the roots of country music. Another indispensable resource is *The Encyclopedia of Country Music: The Ultimate Guide to the Music* (Oxford Press, 1998), edited by Paul Kingsbury and others.

For evocative portraiture of past and present Nashville regulars, including Bela Fleck, Alan Jackson, and Peter Frampton, pore over photographer Michel Arnaud's *Nashville: The Pilgrims of Guitar Town* (Stewart, Tabori & Chang, 2000). Focused predominantly on the 1950s through the 1970s, *Temples of Sound: Inside the Great Recording Studios* (Chronicle Books, 2003), by Jim Cogan, offers a behind-the-scenes look at all the major American studios, including RCA in Nashville, where Elvis and many others recorded.

FICTION Peter Taylor, a winner of the Pulitzer Prize, is one of the few Nashville writers to garner a national reputation. His works of Southern fiction have been well received both in the South and elsewhere. In *A Summons to Memphis* (Ballantine Books, 1986), he tells a story of a Southerner haunted by an unhappy childhood in Nashville and Memphis who returns to the South from New York City. *In the Miro District* (Ballantine Books, 1990), *The Oracle at Stoneleigh Court* (Alfred Knopf, 1993), and *The Old Forest and Other Stories* (The Modern Library, 1995) are three recent collections of Taylor's short stories, many of which are set around Tennessee.

For young school-aged children, check out *Goin' Someplace Special* (Atheneum, 2001), by Nashville native and Newberry winner Pat C. McKissack, with watercolor illustrations by Jerry Pinkney. It tells the story of a young black girl growing up in the segregated South in the 1950s.

FILMS

A modern-day classic, *Coal Miner's Daughter* (1980), starring Sissy Spacek, is the story of country star Loretta Lynn and is considered one of the best films to use the country music industry as its background. It and *Sweet Dreams,* a 1985 movie starring Jessica Lange as Patsy Cline, evoke a sense of what downtown Nashville was like in the early years of country music during the late 1940s and 1950s.

Back in 1975, director Robert Altman trained his baleful and ironic eye on the city in another classic film, *Nashville,* which covered a day in the life of the city and several typically

Nashvillian characters. A few decades later, River Phoenix portrayed a struggling Music City songwriter in *The Thing Called Love* (1993). Sadly, it was the young actor's last on-screen appearance. He died of a drug overdose a few months after the film was released.

Brief but memorable Music City scenes can also be spotted in Spike Lee's *Get on the Bus* (1996) and the satirical *Wag the Dog* (1997). Perhaps best known of all, *The Green Mile* (1999), starring Tom Hanks, was filmed at the abandoned Tennessee State Penitentiary outside Nashville. Robert Redford and James Gandolfini followed suit, filming their prison drama *The Last Castle* (2001) at the former prison.

3

Getting to Know
Music City USA

Getting your bearings in a new city is often the hardest part of taking a trip, but in the following pages you'll find everything you'll need to know to get settled in after you arrive in town. This is the sort of nuts-and-bolts information that will help you familiarize yourself with Nashville.

1 Nashville Orientation

VISITOR INFORMATION
On the baggage-claim level of Nashville International Airport, you'll find the **Airport Welcome Center** (℃ 615/275-1675), where you can pick up brochures, maps, and bus information, and get answers to any questions you may have about touring the city. This center is open daily from 6:30am to midnight. In downtown Nashville, you'll find the **Nashville Convention & Visitors Bureau Visitors Center,** Fifth Avenue and Broadway (℃ 615/259-4747), the main source of information on the city and surrounding areas. The information center is located at the base of the radio tower of the Nashville Arena and is open daily during daylight hours. Signs on interstate highways around the downtown area will direct you to the Arena. Information is also available from the main office of the **Chamber of Commerce/Nashville Convention & Visitors Bureau,** 211 Commerce St., Nashville, TN 37219 (℃ 615/259-4700). The office is open Monday to Friday 8am to 5pm.

For information on the state of Tennessee, contact the **Tennessee Department of Tourism Development,** P.O. Box 23170, Nashville, TN 37202 (℃ 615/741-2158).

CITY LAYOUT
Nashville was built on a bend in the Cumberland River; this and other bends in the river have defined the city's expansion over the years. The area referred to as **downtown** is located on the west side of the Cumberland and is built in a grid pattern. Numbered avenues run parallel to the river on a northwest–southeast axis. Streets perpendicular to the river are named. Though the grid pattern is interrupted by I-40, it remains fairly regular until you get to Vanderbilt University in the **West End** area.

For the most part, Nashville is a sprawling modern city. Though there are some areas of downtown that are frequented by pedestrians, the city is primarily oriented toward automobiles. With fairly rapid growth in recent years, the city's streets and highways have been approaching their carrying capacity, and rush hours see plenty of long backups all around the city. The most important things to watch out for when driving around Nashville are the numerous divisions of the interstate highways that encircle the city. If you don't pay very close attention to which lane you're supposed to be in, you can easily wind up heading in the wrong direction.

MAIN ARTERIES & STREETS   The main arteries in Nashville radiate from downtown like spokes on a wheel. **Broadway** is the main artery through downtown Nashville and leads southwest from the river. Just after crossing I-40, Broadway forks, with the right fork becoming **West End Avenue.** West End Avenue eventually becomes Harding Road out in the Belle Meade area. If you stay on Broadway (the left fork), the road curves around to the south, becoming 21st Avenue and then Hillsboro Pike.

Eighth Avenue is downtown's other main artery and runs roughly north–south. To the north, Eighth Avenue becomes **MetroCenter Boulevard** and to the south it forks, with the right fork becoming **Franklin Pike** and the left fork becoming **Lafayette Road** and then Murfreesboro Pike.

There are also several roads that you should become familiar with out in the suburbs. **Briley Parkway** describes a large loop that begins just south of the airport, runs up the east side of the city through the area known as Music Valley, and then curves around to the west, passing well north of downtown. On the south side of the city, **Harding Place** connects I-24 on the east with Belle Meade on the west. Don't confuse Harding Place with Harding Road.

FINDING AN ADDRESS   Nashville's address-numbering system begins in downtown at Broadway and the Cumberland River and increases as you move away from this point. In the downtown area, and out as far as there are numbered avenues, avenues include either a north or south designation. The dividing line between north and south is the Broadway and West End Avenue corridor.

STREET MAPS   You can get a map of the city from the **Nashville Convention & Visitors Bureau Visitors Center,** Fifth Avenue and Broadway (© 615/259-4747), which is located below the radio tower of the Nashville Arena. Maps can also be obtained in many hotel lobbies and at the **Airport Welcome Center** (© 615/275-1675) on the baggage-claim level at the Nashville International Airport.

If you happen to be a member of **AAA,** you can get free maps of Nashville and Tennessee from your local AAA office or from the Nashville office at 2501 Hillsboro Rd., Suite 1 (© **615/297-7700**). They're open Monday to Friday 8:30am to 5:30pm and Saturday 9am to 1pm.

THE NEIGHBORHOODS IN BRIEF

While there are plenty of neighborhoods throughout the city, few are of real interest to most visitors. There are, however, named areas of the city that you'll want to be familiar with. There are also several outlying bedroom communities that may be of interest.

Downtown   With the state capitol, the Tennessee State Museum, the Tennessee Center for the Performing Arts, the Tennessee Convention Center, and the Ryman Auditorium, downtown Nashville is a surprisingly vibrant area for a small Southern city. However, this is still almost exclusively a business and government district, and after dark the streets empty out, with the exception of the area known as The District.

The District   With restored buildings housing interesting shops, tourist restaurants, nightclubs, and bars, this downtown historic district (along Second Ave. and Broadway) is the center of Nashville's nightlife scene. With each passing year, it becomes a livelier spot; pickup trucks and limousines jockey for space at night along Second Avenue. On Friday and Saturday nights, the sidewalks are packed with partyers

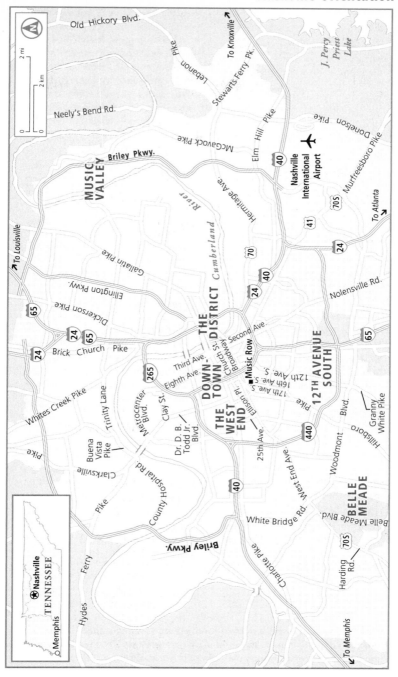

who roam from dive bar to retro-disco to line-dance hootenanny.

The West End While tourists and barflies congregate in The District, the moneymakers and musicians of the Nashville scene gather in the West End, referred to by locals as the intellectual side of town. Located adjacent to Vanderbilt University, this upscale neighborhood is home to many small shops, lots of excellent (and often expensive) restaurants, and several hotels. The presence of many college students in the area adds yet another dimension to the West End scene.

Music Row Recording studios and record companies make this neighborhood, located around the corner of 16th Avenue South and Demonbreun Street (pronounced "De-mon-bree-in"), the center of the country music recording industry. The old Country Music Hall of Fame and Museum moved out of this neighborhood in the spring of 2001, leaving many of the country music souvenir shops vacant. However, if driving down the tree-lined boulevards to see stately homes converted into the offices of country music publishers, public relations agents, and the occasional gated recording studio excites you, by all means take a spin through the neighborhood.

12th Ave. S. What would have been unthinkable only a few years ago has come to pass. A once-blighted area south of downtown is poised for a renaissance. Idealists,

entrepreneurs, and young adults with dreams have been buying up and restoring old houses to set up shop. As a result, an interesting, off-the-beaten-path array of quirky boutiques and happening restaurants and night spots now dot the area roughly bordered by Linden and Kirkwood avenues.

Belle Meade This community, located 7 miles (11km) southwest of downtown Nashville (take West End Ave.), is one of the wealthiest in the Nashville area and is home to several excellent restaurants and upscale shops. Mansions abound in Belle Meade, and country stars own many of them. Two such historic mansions—Belle Meade Plantation and Cheekwood—are open to the public.

Music Valley This area on the east side of Nashville is where you'll find the Opryland Hotel, the Grand Ole Opry House, Opry Mills shopping center, and numerous other country-theme tourist attractions. There are very few decent restaurants in the area (except within Opry Mills and the Opryland Hotel itself).

Green Hills & South Nashville Upscale shopping, trendy restaurants, affluent residential areas, and shiny new SUVs help define the suburban enclave of Green Hills. Among Nashvillians, Green Hills is considered to be a lively, happening neighborhood. Tourists might visit the vast Green Hills Mall that anchors the area.

(*Fun Fact* **The King**

Elvis Presley may be more closely identified with Memphis than Nashville, but the King did, indeed, make his mark on the Music City. Elvis recorded more than 200 of his songs, including Christmas carols, at RCA's historic Studio B on Music Row.

Impressions

*Take of London fog 30 parts; malaria 10 parts; gas leaks 20 parts; dew-
drops gathered in a brickyard at sunrise 25 parts; odor of honeysuckle 15
parts. Mix. The mixture will give you an approximate conception of a
Nashville drizzle.*

—O. Henry, "A Municipal Report," in *Strictly Business,* 1910

2 Getting Around Nashville

BY PUBLIC TRANSPORTATION

BY BUS Nashville is served by the extensive and efficient **Metropolitan Transit Authority (MTA)** bus system. For information on routes or schedules, call the Customer Service Center (✆ **615/862-5950**), which is open Monday to Friday 6:30am until 6pm. The MTA information center and ticket booth, located on Deaderick Street at Fifth Avenue, is open Monday to Friday 6:30am to 8pm and on Saturday 8am to 1pm. MTA bus stops are marked with blue-and-white signs; in the downtown area, signs include names and numbers of all the routes using that stop. All express buses are marked with an X following the route number.

Adult **bus fares** are $1.45 ($1.75 for express buses); children under 4 ride free. Exact change is required. You can ride for 25¢ on any MTA bus within the downtown area bordered by James Robertson Parkway, Franklin Street, the Cumberland River, and I-40; just ask the bus driver for a **RUSH card** and return it when you leave.

You can purchase a weekly pass good for unlimited local rides from Sunday to Saturday for $15 per adult or $9 per youth age 19 and under; a picture ID is required. Seniors and riders with disabilities qualify for a 70¢ fare with an MTA Golden Age, Medicare, Tennesenior, or Special Service card. Call ✆ **615/862-5950** to register for this discount.

BY TROLLEY For a quick way to get around downtown during weekdays, look for the LunchLINE shuttles. As a convenience to downtown workers, the Central Business Improvement District and Nashville Downtown Partnership offers a free trolley that loops through the heart of downtown weekdays from 11am to 1:30pm. Riders may hop on or off at any of the 15 stops. No tickets are required.

The **downtown route** passes by many points of interest in downtown Nashville and is a good way to get acquainted with the city. For more information, look at this website: www.nashvilledowntown.com.

BY CAR

Because the city and its many attractions are quite spread out, the best way to get around Nashville is by car. It's surprisingly easy to find your way around the city and to find parking, even downtown. But bring plenty of cash. Parking can cost a few coins in the meter or upwards of $10 during special events. The only time driving is a problem is during morning and evening rush hours. At these times, streets leading south and west out of downtown can get quite congested.

RENTAL CARS

All the major rental car companies and several independent ones have offices in Nashville. Fortunately, most of the companies have desks conveniently located on the lower level at the Nashville International Airport. Major car-rental companies in Nashville include: **Alamo Rent-A-Car,** at the airport (© 800/327-9633 or 615/275-1050); **Avis Rent-A-Car,** at the airport (© 800/831-2847 or 615/361-1212); **Budget Rent-A-Car,** at 1816 Church St., 1525 N. Gallatin Pike, and at the airport (© 800/763-2999 or 615/366-0822); **Dollar Rent-A-Car,** at the airport (© 800/800-4000 or 615/376-0503); **Enterprise Rent-a-Car,** at the airport (© 800/325-8007 or 615/872-7722); **Hertz,** at the airport (© 800/654-3131 or 615/361-3131); **National Car Rental,** at the airport (© 800/227-7368 or 615/361-7467); and **Thrifty Car Rental,** 1201 Briley Parkway at Vultee Blvd.), and at the airport (© 800/367-2277 or 615/361-6050).

SAVING MONEY ON A RENTAL CAR   Car rental rates vary even more than airline fares. The price you pay will depend on the size of the car, where and when you pick it up and drop it off, the length of the rental period, where and how far you drive it, whether you purchase insurance, and a host of other factors. A few key questions could save you hundreds of dollars:

- Are weekend rates lower than weekday rates? Ask if the rate is the same for pickup Friday morning, for instance, as it is for Thursday night.
- Is a weekly rate cheaper than the daily rate? Even if you only need the car for 4 days, it may be cheaper to keep it for 5.
- Does the agency assess a drop-off charge if you don't return the car to the same location where you picked it up? Is it cheaper to pick up the car at the airport compared to a downtown location?
- Are special promotional rates available? If you see an advertised price in your local newspaper, be sure to ask for that specific rate; otherwise you may be charged the standard cost. Terms change constantly.
- Are discounts available for members of AARP, AAA, frequent flyer programs, or trade unions? If you belong to any of these organizations, you may be entitled to discounts of up to 30%.
- How much tax will be added to the rental bill? Local tax? State use tax?
- What is the cost of adding an additional driver's name to the contract?
- How many free miles are included in the price? Free mileage is often negotiable, depending on the length of your rental.
- How much does the rental company charge to refill your gas tank if you return with the tank less than full? Though most rental companies claim these prices are "competitive," fuel is almost always cheaper in town. Try to allow enough time to refuel the car yourself before returning it.

   Some companies offer "refueling packages," in which you pay for an entire tank of gas up front. The price is usually fairly competitive with local gas prices, but you don't get credit for any gas remaining in the tank. If a stop at a gas station on the way to the airport will make you miss your plane, then by all means take advantage of the fuel purchase option. Otherwise, skip it.

⌜Tips⌝ Comparing Car Rental Costs

Be sure to compare the cost of renting a car downtown as opposed to at the airport. Often times, downtown rates will be lower. It may be cheaper to take a shuttle or taxi downtown to your hotel, and then book your car from there.

DEMYSTIFYING RENTER'S INSURANCE   Before you drive off in a rental car, be sure you're insured. Hasty assumptions about your personal auto insurance or a rental agency's additional coverage could end up costing you tens of thousands of dollars—even if you are involved in an accident that was clearly the fault of another driver.

If you already hold a **private auto insurance** policy, you are most likely covered in the United States for loss of or damage to a rental car, and liability in case of injury to any other party involved in an accident. Be sure to find out whether you are covered in the area you are visiting, whether your policy extends to all persons who will be driving the rental car, how much liability is covered in case an outside party is injured in an accident, and whether the type of vehicle you are renting is included under your contract. (Rental trucks, sports utility vehicles, and luxury vehicles such as a Jaguar may not be covered.)

Most **major credit cards** provide some degree of coverage as well, provided they were used to pay for the rental. Terms vary widely, however, so be sure to call your credit card company directly before you rent.

If you are **uninsured,** your credit card provides primary coverage as long as you decline the rental agency's insurance. This means the credit card will cover damage or theft of a rental car for the full cost of the vehicle. (In a few states, however, theft is not covered; ask specifically about the state law where you will be renting and driving.) If you already have insurance, your credit card will provide secondary coverage—which basically covers your deductible.

Credit cards **will not cover liability,** or the cost of injury to an outside party and/or damage to an outside party's vehicle. If you do not hold an insurance policy, you may seriously want to consider purchasing additional liability insurance from your rental company. Be sure to check the terms carefully. Also, bear in mind that each credit card company has its own peculiarities. Call your own credit card company for details.

The basic insurance coverage offered by most car rental companies, known as the **Loss/Damage Waiver (LDW)** or **Collision Damage Waiver (CDW),** can cost as much as $20 per day. It usually covers the full value of the vehicle with no deductible if an outside party causes an accident or other damage to the rental car. You will probably be covered in case of theft as well. If you are at fault in an accident, however, you will be covered for the full replacement value of the car but not for liability. Most rental companies will require a police report in order to process any claims you file, but your private insurer will not be notified of the accident.

PACKAGE DEALS   Many packages are available that include airfare, accommodations, and a rental car with unlimited mileage. Compare these prices with the cost of booking airline tickets, accommodations, and renting a car separately to see if these offers are good deals.

PARKING

In downtown Nashville, there are a variety of parking lots, ranging from $4 to $10 per day. Drop your money into the self-service machine at the end of the parking lot. Downtown parking is also available in other municipal and private lots and parking garages.

When parking on the street, be sure to check the time limit on parking meters. Also be sure to check whether or not you can park in a parking space during rush hour (4–5:30pm) or your car may be ticketed and towed. On-street parking meters are free after 6pm on weekdays, after noon on Saturday and all day Sunday.

DRIVING RULES

A right turn at a red light is permitted after coming to a full stop, unless posted otherwise, but drivers must first yield to vehicles that have a green light or pedestrians in the walkway. Children under 4 years of age must be in a children's car seat or other approved restraint when in the car.

Tennessee has a very strict DUI (driving under the influence of alcohol) law, and has a law that states a person driving under the influence with a child under 12 years of age in the vehicle may be charged with a felony.

BY TAXI

For quick cab service, call American **Music City Taxi** (© **615/262-0451**), **Checker Cab** (© **615/256-7000**), or **Allied Taxi** (© **615/244-7433**). The flag-drop rate is $3; after that it's $1.90 per mile.

ON FOOT

Downtown Nashville is the only area where you're likely to do much walking around. In this area, you can visit numerous attractions, do some shopping, have a good meal, and go to a club, all without having to get in your car. The suburban strips can't make that claim.

FAST FACTS: **Nashville**

Airport See "Getting There," in chapter 2.

American Express In the airport area, the American Express Travel Service office is at 402 BNA Dr., Building 100, Suite 303 (© **800/528-4800** or 615/367-4900), and is open Monday to Friday 8:30am to 5pm.

Area Code The telephone area code in Nashville is **615.**

Business Hours Banks are generally open Monday to Thursday 9am to 4pm, on Friday 9am to 5 or 6pm, and on Saturday morning. Office hours in Nashville are usually Monday to Friday 8:30am to 5pm. In general, stores in downtown Nashville are open Monday to Saturday 10am to 6pm. Shops in suburban Nashville malls are generally open Monday to Saturday 10am to 9pm and on Sunday 1 to 6pm. Bars in Nashville are frequently open all day long and are allowed to stay open daily until 3am, but might close between 1 and 3am.

Camera Repair Because camera repairs usually take several weeks, your best bet is to take your camera home with you. You can buy a few disposable cameras so you at least have some photos of your trip to Nashville.

Car Rentals See "Getting Around Nashville," earlier in this chapter.

Climate See "When to Go to Nashville," in chapter 2.

Dentists If you should need a dentist while you're in Nashville, contact **Dental Referral Service** (© **800/243-4444**).

Doctors If you need a doctor, call **Medline** (© **615/342-1919**), available Monday to Friday 8am to 5pm; or contact the **Vanderbilt Medical Group**

Physician Referral Service (℡ 615/322-3000), or **Columbia Medline** (℡ 800/265-8624).

Drugstores See "Pharmacies," below.

Embassies/Consulates See appendix A, "For International Visitors."

Emergencies Phone ℡ **911** for fire, police, emergency, or ambulance. If you get into desperate straits, call **Travelers' Aid** of the Nashville Union Mission, 639 Lafayette St. (℡ **615/780-9471**). It's primarily a mission that helps destitute people, but if you need help in making phone calls or getting home, they might be able to help.

Eyeglass Repair If you have problems with your glasses, call **Horner Rausch**, which has 1-hour service. They have several locations. One is downtown at 968 Main St. (℡ **615/226-0251**), and is open Monday to Friday 9am to 6pm and on Saturday 8am to 3pm. Another store is at 2135 N. Gallatin Road near Rivergate Mall (℡ **615/859-7888**), where hours are Monday to Friday 9:30am to 7pm and Saturday 9:30am to 5pm.

Hospitals The following hospitals offer emergency medical treatment: **St. Thomas Hospital,** 4220 Harding Rd. (℡ **615/222-2111**); and **Vanderbilt University Medical Center,** 1211 22nd Ave. S., in the downtown/Vanderbilt area (℡ **615/322-5000**).

Hotlines The **Suicide Crisis Intervention** hotline number is ℡ **615/244-7444.**

Information See "Visitor Information," earlier in this chapter.

Libraries The new Main Library of Nashville and Davidson County is at 615 Church St. (℡ **615/862-5800**). It's open Monday to Thursday 9am to 8pm, Friday 9am to 6pm, Saturday 9am to 5pm, and Sunday 2 to 5pm.

Liquor Laws The legal drinking age in Tennessee is 21. Bars are allowed to stay open until 3am every day. Beer can be purchased at drug, grocery, or package stores, but wine and liquor are sold through package stores only.

Lost Property If you left something at the airport, call the **Airport Authority** at ℡ **615/275-1675;** if you left something on an **MTA** bus, call ℡ **615/862-5969.**

Luggage Storage/Lockers Hotels will usually store your bags for several hours or sometimes even several days. There is also a luggage-storage facility at the Greyhound Lines bus station at 200 Eighth Ave. S., although these are ostensibly for Greyhound passengers only.

Maps See "City Layout," earlier in this chapter.

Newspapers/Magazines The *Tennessean* is Nashville's morning daily and Sunday newspaper. The alternative weekly is the *Nashville Scene.*

Pharmacies (late-night) The following **Walgreen's Pharmacies** are open 24 hours a day: 518 Donelson Pike (℡ **615/883-5108**); 5600 Charlotte Pike (℡ **615/356-5161**); and 627 Gallatin Rd. (℡ **615/865-0010**); or call ℡ **800/925-4733** for the Walgreen's nearest you.

Police For police emergencies, phone ℡ **911.**

Post Office The post office located at 901 Broadway (℡ **800/275-8777**) is convenient to downtown and the West End, and will accept mail addressed to General Delivery. It's open Monday to Friday 8am to 5pm and on Saturday 8am to 2pm. There's also a post office in the downtown arcade at 16 Arcade (© **615/248-2287**), which is open Monday to Friday 8:30am to 5pm.

Radio Nashville has more than 30 AM and FM radio stations. Some specialize in a particular style of music, including gospel, soul, big band, and jazz. Of course, there are several country music stations, including WSM (650 AM and 95.5 FM), the station that first broadcast the *Grand Ole Opry,* and the popular WSIX (97.9 FM). WPLN (90.3 FM) is Nashville's National Public Radio station, and WRLT (100.1 FM) plays adult alternative music. For eclectic college radio, tune to Vanderbilt University's WRVU (91.1 FM).

Restrooms Public restrooms can be found at the parking lot on First Avenue South in downtown Nashville and also at hotels, restaurants, and shopping malls.

Safety Even though Nashville is not a huge city, it has its share of crime. Take extra precaution with your wallet or purse when you're in a crush of people (such as a weekend night in The District)—pickpockets take advantage of crowds. Whenever possible at night, try to park your car in a garage, not on the street. When walking around town at night, stick to the busier streets of The District. The lower Broadway area, though popular with visitors, also attracts a rather unruly crowd to its many bars. See also "Safety," in appendix A, "For International Visitors."

Taxes In Tennessee, the state sales tax is 9.25%. This tax applies to goods as well as all recreation, entertainment, and amusements. However, in the case of services, the tax is often already included in the admission price or cost of a ticket. The Nashville hotel and motel room tax is 5%, which when added to the 9.25% makes for a total hotel-room tax of 14.25%. There is a 2% car-rental tax plus an additional car-rental surcharge.

Taxis See "Getting Around Nashville," earlier in this chapter.

Television Local television channels include 2 (ABC), 4 (NBC), 5 (CBS), 8 (PBS), 17 (FOX), 30 (UPN), 39 (independent), and 58 (WB).

Time Zone Tennessee is in the central time zone—Central Standard Time (CST) or Central Daylight Time, depending on the time of year—making it 2 hours ahead of the West Coast and 1 hour behind the East Coast.

Transit Info Call © **615/862-5950** for information on the MTA bus system or trolleys.

Weather For the local forecast, call the **National Weather Service** (© **615/ 754-4633**).

4

Where to Stay in Nashville

Nashville caters to tens of thousands of country music fans each year and so has an abundance of inexpensive and moderately priced hotels. Whatever your reason for being in Nashville, you'll likely find a hotel that's both convenient and fits your budget. If you're used to exorbitant downtown hotels, you'll be pleasantly surprised to learn that rooms in downtown Nashville are for the most part very reasonably priced. They face increasing competition from a mushrooming cluster of new moderately priced hotels in the airport area along Elm Hill Pike, easily reached by heading east out of the city on I-40. If you want to be close to the city's best restaurants and wealthiest neighborhoods, book a room in a West End hotel. The majority of the hotel and motel rooms in the city are in the $75 to $120 range (and on most weekends $100 might buy you a room at one of the downtown high-rise hotels).

However, if you do want to splurge, you certainly can. There are several good luxury hotels, including two in historic buildings in downtown Nashville, and several out near the airport. One of downtown's newest, the 330-suite Hilton Suites Nashville, was completed in August 2000. However, for sheer visual impact, you can't beat the massive Opryland Hotel, where Southern opulence and Disney-esque tropical fantasies merge to create a hotel that is as much a destination as it is a place to stay. A night here will run you $200 on average.

The rates quoted below are, for the most part, the published rates, sometimes called "rack rates" in hotel-industry jargon. At expensive business and resort hotels, rack rates are what you are most likely to be quoted if you walk in off the street and ask what a room will cost for that night. However, it's often not necessary to pay this high rate if you plan ahead or ask for a discount. It's often possible to get low corporate rates even if you aren't visiting on business. Frequently, there are also special discount rates available, especially on weekends. Also, many hotel and motel chains now have frequent-guest and other special programs that you can join. These programs often provide savings off the regular rates.

Virtually all hotels now offer nonsmoking rooms and rooms equipped for guests with disabilities. When making a reservation, be sure to request the type of room you need. While TVs and telephones are the norm, charges for telephone calls vary widely. Some offer free local calls, while others do not. Many hotels are also enhancing their electronic in-room amenities with such perks as video games. Increasingly, many are also adding free in-room high-speed Internet access.

If you'll be traveling with children, always check into policies on children staying for free. Some hotels let children under 12 stay free, while others set the cutoff age at 18. Still others charge you for the kids, but let them eat for free in the hotel's restaurant.

The rates quoted here don't include the Tennessee sales tax (9.25%) or the Nashville room tax (5%), which together will add 14.25% onto your room bill. Keep this in mind if you're on a tight budget. I have used the following rate definitions for price categories in this chapter (rates are for double rooms): **very expensive,** more than $175; **expensive,** $125 to $175; **moderate,** $75 to $125; **inexpensive,** under $75.

1 Downtown & North Nashville

VERY EXPENSIVE

The Hermitage Hotel ★★★ *Moments*   This historic downtown hotel, built in 1910 in the classic beaux-arts style, is Nashville's grand hotel. Reopened in 2003 after an $18 million restoration, this is the city's top choice if you crave both space and elegance. The lobby, with its marble columns, gilded plasterwork, and stained-glass ceiling, is the most magnificent in the city. Afternoon tea is served here Thursdays through Saturdays. Guest rooms (all of which are suites) are recently upgraded, spacious, and comfortable, with down-filled duvets and pillows on the beds. All rooms feature large windows and marble-floored bathrooms with double vanities. Before you settle in for a long soak in the tub, ask the staff to draw you a warm bath with a sprinkling of rose petals. North-side rooms have good views of the capitol.

Down in the lower level you'll find the Capitol Grille, which, with its vaulted ceiling, has the feel of a wine cellar. Also in the basement is a dark and woody lounge with an ornate plasterwork ceiling. Every floor has handicapped-accessible rooms.

231 6th Ave. N., Nashville, TN 37219. ℂ 888/888-9414 or 615/244-3121. Fax 615/254-6909. www.the hermitagehotel.com. 123 suites. $199–$265 suite, $289 2-bedroom suite. AE, DC, DISC, MC, V. Valet parking $16 plus tax. Pets allowed (no deposit required). **Amenities:** Restaurant and lounge; 24-hour concierge and room service; massage; babysitting; dry cleaning. *In room:* A/C, TV w/pay movies, dataport, hair dryer, iron, umbrella, DVD-CD player.

EXPENSIVE

Doubletree Hotel Nashville ★★   Of the three modern high-rise hotels in downtown Nashville, this is one of the best choices if you're here on vacation. It has a less hectic atmosphere than the Sheraton or the Renaissance, and extensive renovations completed in 2002 have given the Doubletree a very contemporary look. (But the fresh-baked cookies delivered to your room upon check-in are strictly a down-home touch.) Located a few blocks from The District, this hotel is also convenient for anyone in town on state government business. The corner rooms, with their sharply angled walls of glass, are the most appealing units in the hotel. Also, be sure to ask for a room facing the street as these get more sunlight. An executive level offers additional amenities including a buffet breakfast and vouchers for drinks in the lobby lounge.

315 4th Ave. N., Nashville, TN 37219-1693. ℂ 800/222-TREE or 615/244-8200. Fax 615/747-4894. www. doubletree.com. 338 units. $89–$169 double; $230–$400 suite. AE, DC, DISC, MC, V. Valet parking $12; self-parking $18. **Amenities:** Restaurant and quiet lounge; indoor pool; exercise room; concierge; business center; limited room service; same-day dry cleaning; concierge-level rooms. *In room:* A/C, TV w/pay movies, dataport, coffeemaker, hair dryer, iron.

Hilton Suites Nashville Downtown ★★   One of Nashville's newest hotels boasts a bustling downtown location, palm-lined atrium lobby, and one of the city's hottest watering holes–Eddie George's Sports Grill, named for the Tennessee Titans' star running back. Booking a room here is a good bet if you plan to spend time at the Coliseum or the Country Music Hall of Fame and Museum, both of which are within short walking distance of the Hilton. Each suite comes equipped with a pullout sofa couch, two TVs, in-room movies and video games, microwave, refrigerator, coffeemaker and more, making the Hilton a comfy but sophisticated place to hang your hat while in Music City.

121 4th Ave. S., Nashville, TN 37201. (C) **800/HILTONS** or 615/620-1000. Fax 615/620-1001. www.nashville hilton.com. 330 units. $139–$219 double. Rates include breakfast. AE, DC, DISC, MC, V. Valet parking $17; self-parking $12. **Amenities:** 2 restaurants; lounge; indoor pool; fitness center; car-rental desk; business center; laundry/valet. *In room:* A/C, TV w/pay movies, fridge, coffeemaker, video games, microwave.

Holiday Inn Express ⭐   Looks can be deceiving. Catty-cornered from the Union Station Hotel, this rather nondescript property (formerly known as the Ramada Inn Conference Center) offers a budget-pleasing choice for business travelers who want to stay downtown. Value-added perks include free wi/fi (wireless Internet connection) in all public areas, and free continental breakfast. The location is convenient–it's only about 5 blocks straight down Broadway to The District. Rooms are recently renovated and reasonably spacious, and if you ask for an upper-floor room on the west side of the short hall, you'll get a view of the impressive Union Station.

920 Broadway, Nashville, TN 37203. (C) **800/258-2466** or 615/244-0150. Fax 615/244-0445. www.holiday-inn.com. 287 units. $129 double; $179 suite. AE, DISC, MC, V. Free parking. **Amenities:** Outdoor pool; exercise room; business center. *In room:* A/C, TV, dataport with high-speed Internet access, fridges in suites, coffeemaker, hair dryer, iron.

The Millennium Maxwell House Hotel ⭐   So just why is a hotel named for a brand of coffee? The original Maxwell House, where President Theodore Roosevelt stayed, was in downtown Nashville. This modern-day successor is a 10-story hotel that sits just off I-265 about 1½ miles (2.5km) north of downtown and is convenient to downtown. The rooms are decorated in muted/earth tones, with your choice of full-size or king-size beds. Rather basic but relaxing and pleasant. South-side rooms on the upper floors of the hotel have a commanding view of the Nashville skyline and are well worth requesting. Glass elevators on the outside of the building also take full advantage of the unobstructed views.

2025 Metro Center Blvd., Nashville, TN 37228-1505. (C) **800/457-4460** or 615/259-4343. Fax 615/313-1327. www.millennium-hotels.com. 289 units. $80–$140 double; $175–$400 suite. AE, DC, DISC, MC, V. Free self-parking. **Amenities:** Restaurant; outdoor pool; nearby golf course; 2 lighted tennis courts; exercise room; concierge; tour desk; business center; coin-op laundry; dry cleaning. *In room:* A/C, TV w/pay movies, dataport, coffeemaker, hair dryer, iron.

Renaissance Nashville Hotel ⭐⭐   Because it's directly connected to the Nashville Convention Center, this large, modern hotel is often filled with conventioneers and consequently can feel crowded and chaotic. However, it does offer all the expected luxuries. The king rooms (especially the corner kings, which have huge bathrooms) are a better choice than rooms with two beds, which are a bit cramped. However, whichever style room you choose, you'll at least have a comfortable wingback chair in which to relax, and walls of glass let in plenty of light. The upper floors offer additional amenities, including a

---

Impressions

Good to the last drop.

    –Teddy Roosevelt, discussing the coffee at Nashville's Maxwell House
        Hotel (now known as The Millennium Maxwell House Hotel)

Nashville Accommodations: Downtown, Music Row & the West End

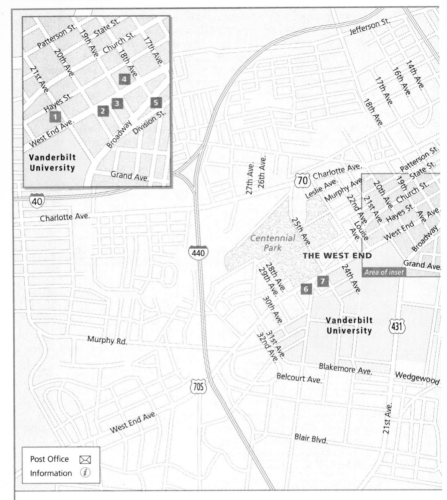

Post Office ⊠
Information ⓘ

Best Western Downtown
  Convention Center **11**
Best Western Hotel
  Downtown/Music Row **8**
Courtyard by Marriott **2**
Days Inn Vanderbilt/Music Row **4**
Doubletree Hotel Nashville **15**
Embassy Suites Hotel **5**
Hampton Inn Vanderbilt **3**
The Hermitage Hotel **14**
Hilton Inn Express **17**

Hilton Suites Nashville Downtown **18**
Holiday Inn Select Vanderbilt **6**
Loews Vanderbilt Plaza Hotel **1**
The Millennium Maxwell House Hotel **13**
Nashville Marriott at Vanderbilt **7**
Renaissance Nashville Hotel **16**
Sheraton Nashville Downtown **12**
Shoney's Inn–Nashville Music Row **9**
Wyndham Union Station **10**

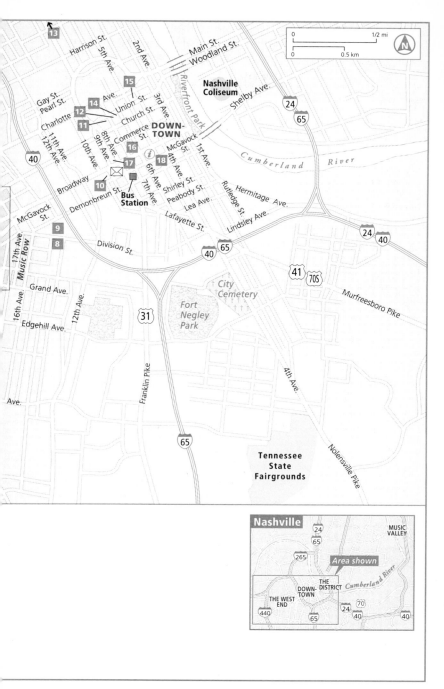

concierge, private lounge, bathrobes, express checkout, complimentary continental breakfast and evening hors d'oeuvres, and evening turndown service. The Commerce Street Grille, located off the lobby, serves American fare in a sort of Southern-plantation setting. In the greenhouse-like sky bridge you'll find a lounge deli, where Krispy Kreme donuts and Starbucks coffee are available each morning.

611 Commerce St., Nashville, TN 37203. © **800/HOTELS-1** or 615/255-8400. Fax 615/255-8202. www. renaissancehotels.com. 673 units. $169–$210 double; $295–$895 suite. AE, DC, DISC, MC, V. Valet parking $16; self-parking $5–$9. **Amenities:** 2 restaurants and 2 bars; indoor pool; exercise room; indoor hot tub; sauna; concierge; business center; sundries shop; 24-hour room service; massage; valet/laundry service; sundeck. *In room:* A/C, TV w/pay movies, dataport, coffeemaker, hair dryer, iron.

Sheraton Nashville Downtown ⭐   Popular with business travelers and legislators, the Sheraton provides the widest variety of amenities among Nashville's downtown high-rise hotels. The former rooftop restaurant no longer revolves, but the hotel boasts an atrium lobby with glass elevators to shuttle guests up and down the hotel's 28 floors, making for great views of the nearby Tennessee State Capitol. It's also within blocks of both The District, the city's main evening-entertainment area, and the Nashville Convention Center. Guests here have plenty of dining and drinking options and won't have to deal with the crowds and chaos that are found at the nearby Renaissance Nashville Hotel. The northside rooms overlooking the capitol have the best views and there are club-level rooms with extra amenities for an additional charge. On the mezzanine level, there's a casual restaurant; the lobby has a sunken lounge area.

623 Union St., Nashville, TN 37219. © **800/447-9825** or 615/259-2000. Fax 615/742-6056. www.sheraton. com or www.sheratonnashville.net. 476 units. $109–$209 double; $225–$800 suite. AE, DC, DISC, MC, V. Valet parking $14; self-parking $12. **Amenities:** Restaurant; lounge; indoor pool; fitness center; sauna; concierge; limited room service; valet/laundry service. *In room:* A/C, TV w/pay movies, some rooms with faxes, all dataport, coffeemaker, hair dryer, iron.

Wyndham Union Station ⭐⭐ *(Moments*   Housed in the Romanesque Gothic former Union Station railway terminal, built in 1900, this hotel is a grandly restored National Historic Landmark. The lobby is the former main hall of the railway station and has a vaulted ceiling of Tiffany stained glass. Everywhere you look, there's exquisite gilded plasterwork. The hotel's best accommodations are the gallery deluxe rooms, which have 22-foot-high ceilings and huge arched walls of glass that overlook the lobby. A few other rooms also have high ceilings and large windows, and though unique, can get quite hot in the afternoon. Although all rooms offer exterior views, some also have the disadvantage of overlooking the railroad tracks, a plus for railroad buffs but perhaps less endearing to others. If you're looking for a unique and atmospheric accommodation in Nashville, this is it. Arthur's, the former train station's women's smoking room, is the hotel's premier restaurant and one of city's finest (see p. 63 for details). For breakfast, there's the gallery, a raised area in the main lobby. The vaultlike

---

Tips   Boots Made for Walking

If you're staying at either the Opryland Hotel or the Sheraton Music City, comfortable walking shoes are a must. Even if you opt for the valet parking, the distances between drop-off points and your room can be daunting within these huge properties.

> ## (Kids) Family-Friendly Hotels
>
> **Embassy Suites Nashville** (*p. 58*)   With an indoor pool and a garden atrium, there is plenty to keep the kids distracted here. The two-room suites also provide lots of space and kitchenettes.
>
> **Nashville Airport Marriott** (*p. 59*)   Set on spacious grounds, this hotel gives the kids plenty of room to roam. There's an indoor/outdoor pool and even a basketball court.
>
> **Opryland Hotel** (*p. 56*)   The kids can wander all over this huge hotel's three tropical atriums, exploring waterfalls, hidden gardens, fountains, whatever, and then head for one of the pools. There are also enough restaurants under this one roof to keep everyone in the family happy.

McKinley Room, with its arched windows, stone walls, and Spanish floor tiles has been converted to a conference room.

1001 Broadway, Nashville, TN 37203. ℂ **800/996-3426** or 615/726-1001. Fax 615/248-3554. www. wyndham.com. 124 units. $149–$179 double; $50 additional per suite. AE, DC, DISC, MC, V. Valet parking $13. Pets less than 20 pounds accepted for $25 non-refundable deposit per visit. **Amenities:** 2 restaurants and a lounge; access to adjacent fitness center; limited room service; same-day dry cleaning. *In room:* A/C, TV w/pay movies, dataport, coffeemaker, hair dryer, iron, video games.

MODERATE

Best Western Downtown Convention Center   Perks such as free valet parking (one car per room) and continental breakfast make this motel a frugal choice if you're on a budget but want the convenience of being downtown. The District, the Ryman Auditorium, and the Tennessee Performing Arts Center are all within a few blocks. The guest rooms are basic, but all bathrooms and soft goods in the rooms were renovated recently. If you're looking for a room with a view, ask for one on an upper-floor on the north side.

711 Union St., Nashville, TN 37219. ℂ **800/627-3297** or 615/242-4311. Fax 615/242-1654. www.best western.com. 101 units. $69–$118 double. AE, DC, DISC, MC, V. Free valet parking. **Amenities:** Exercise room; coin-op laundry. *In room:* A/C, TV, dataport, hair dryer, iron, safe.

2 Music Row & the West End

For locations of hotels in this section, see the "Nashville Accommodations: Downtown, Music Row & the West End" map on p. 50.

EXPENSIVE

Embassy Suites Hotel ★★ *(Finds)*   Among the newest hotels in the city's trendy West End/Vanderbilt University district, this property combines gracious service and impeccable decor. A sunny garden atrium features lush plants, cascading waterfalls, and overstuffed furniture arranged in cozy nooks. The spacious, tastefully appointed suites have comfy sleeper sofas, easy chairs, work desks, and lamps. With value-added touches including a generous, cooked-to-order breakfast (included in the room rate) and free shuttle service to downtown and other locales within a 2-mile radius of the hotel, this is a good choice for those who want to feel pampered without paying an arm and a leg. Downstairs, a new Omaha Steak House opened in 2003.

Fun Fact **Nashville Notables**

Music stars such as Sheryl Crow and Vince Gill aren't the only celebrities who hang their hats in Nashville. Other past and present locals include Al Gore, Reese Witherspoon, Ashley Judd, Annie Potts, Oprah Winfrey, Donna Summer, and Fred Thompson, a former senator turned actor (*Law and Order*).

1811 Broadway, Nashville, TN 37203. © **800/362-2779** or 615/320-8881. www.embassysuites.com. 208 units. $119–$209 double. Rates include cooked-to-order breakfast. AE, DC, DISC, MC, V. Valet parking $15; self-parking $11. **Amenities:** Restaurant; lounge; complimentary access to nearby health club; exercise room; spa; sauna; limited room service; coin-op laundry; same-day dry cleaning. *In room:* A/C, TV w/pay movies, dataport, kitchenette (microwave, minibar, and sink), coffeemaker, hair dryer.

Loews Vanderbilt Plaza Hotel ★★★   This posh high-rise across the street from Vanderbilt University maintains an air of quiet sophistication, which makes it the most luxurious West End hotel. European tapestries and original works of art adorn the travertine-floored lobby. In addition, the hotel houses the upscale Kraus commercial art gallery. The lower guest rooms, with angled walls that slope inward, are among the hotel's most charming, with a wall of curtains lending a romantic coziness. Service is gracious and attentive. Concierge-level rooms are more spacious and upscale and include complimentary breakfast and evening hors d'oeuvres in an elegant lounge with a view of the city. One level below the lobby, you'll find a Ruth's Chris Steakhouse.

2100 West End Ave., Nashville, TN 37203. © **800/23-LOEWS** or 615/320-1700. Fax 615/320-5019. www.loewsvanderbilt.com. 340 units. $99–$199 double; $375–$900 suite. AE, DC, DISC, MC, V. Valet parking $17; self-parking $14. Pets allowed; no deposit required if paying by credit card, although guests are liable for damage caused by pets. **Amenities:** 2 restaurants; exercise room; spa; concierge; business center; 24-hr. room service; massage; babysitting; valet/laundry service; concierge-level rooms; shoe-shine service. *In room:* A/C, TV and CD player, fax, dataport, minibar, coffeemaker, hair dryer, iron, safe, umbrella.

Nashville Marriott at Vanderbilt ★★ *Kids*   Nashville's newest high-rise hotel is a rose-colored class act that rivals the nearby Loews in terms of elegance and sophistication. Upper rooms at the 11-story property offer birds-eye views of both the Vanderbilt football stadium and the Parthenon in nearby Centennial Park. The location is also ideal for those who want to be in the thick of things: it's within a corner of an upscale shopping complex (P.F. Chang's China Bistro is among the tenants) and close to all the West End action. (The down side is that during peak dinner hours and weekends, the hotel parking lot and garage can become a tangled traffic jam.) Guests visiting here on business will appreciate the spacious rooms, which are decorated in soothing cream colors and include well-lighted work desks and multi-line phones. The hotel's new restaurant, Latitude, is drawing raves as a chic spot for cocktails and seafood.

2555 West End Ave. Nashville, TN 37203. © **800/228-9290** or 615/321-1300. Fax 615/321-1400. www.marriott.com. 307 units. $99–$159 double; $189–$209 suite. AE, DC, DISC, MC, V. Valet parking $15. **Amenities:** Restaurant and lounge; indoor pool; tennis health club; concierge; 24-hr. room service; babysitting; valet/laundry service. *In room:* A/C, TV w/pay movies and video games, fax, dataport with high-speed Internet access, coffeemaker, hair dryer, iron. Safe deposit boxes available at front desk.

MODERATE

Courtyard by Marriott ★   This seven-story hotel on West End Avenue fills the price and service gap between the Loews Vanderbilt Plaza and the less-expensive motels listed below. Guest rooms are none too large, but those with king beds were conceived with the business traveler in mind. Rooms in Building A were completely refurnished in 2003. All the rooms have coffeemakers, and the medium-size bathrooms have a moderate amount of counter space. For the most part, what you get here is a good location close to Music Row at prices only slightly higher than those at area motels. A breakfast buffet is available daily (at an additional charge of $6.95 plus tax), and the hotel offers a whirlpool and an exercise room.

1901 West End Ave., Nashville, TN 37203. ℂ 800/245-1959 or 615/327-9900. Fax 615/327-8127. www. courtyard.com. 223 units. $85–$135 double; $125–$150 suite. AE, DC, DISC, MC, V. Free parking garage. **Amenities:** Restaurant and bar; outdoor pool; exercise room; business center; coin-op laundry; laundry service; same-day dry cleaning. *In room:* A/C, TV, fax, dataport, coffeemaker, hair dryer, iron.

Hampton Inn Vanderbilt *(Value)*   This reliable chain motel is located just 1 block from Vanderbilt University and 6 blocks from both Music Row and the Parthenon. Guest rooms are modern and comfortable. You'll find the king rooms particularly spacious. There are quite a few good restaurants within walking distance.

1919 West End Ave., Nashville, TN 37203. ℂ **800/HAMPTON** or 615/329-1144. Fax 615/320-7112. www. hampton-inn.com. 171 units. $94–$149 double. Rates include continental breakfast. AE, DC, DISC, MC, V. Free parking. **Amenities:** Outdoor pool; exercise room; valet laundry; same-day dry cleaning. *In room:* A/C, TV, dataport, coffeemaker, hair dryer, iron.

Holiday Inn Select Vanderbilt   With the Vanderbilt University football stadium right outside this 12-story hotel's back door, it isn't surprising that this is a favorite with Vanderbilt alumni and football fans. However, if you stay here, you're also right across the street from Centennial Park and the Parthenon. Couples and business travelers will do well to ask for a king room. These are considerably more comfortable than rooms with two beds in them, and have work desks. If you ask for a room on the park side of the hotel, you may be able to see the Parthenon from your room. All the rooms here have small private balconies.

2613 West End Ave., Nashville, TN 37203. ℂ **800/HOLIDAY** or 615/327-4707. Fax 615/327-8034. www. holiday-inn.com. 300 units. $109–$119 double; $199–$249 suite. AE, DC, DISC, MC, V. Valet parking $3; free self-parking. **Amenities:** Restaurant; lounge; outdoor pool; exercise room; concierge; tour desk; business center; coin-op laundry; laundry service; same-day dry cleaning. *In room:* A/C, TV w/pay movies, dataport, coffeemaker, hair dryer, iron.

INEXPENSIVE

Best Western Hotel Downtown/Music Row *(★)*   Remodeled in 2001, this is a casual place (formerly a Quality Inn) that has seen a drop in business since the Country Music Hall of Fame moved out of the neighborhood. Bargain-priced rooms are standard, although the suites offer significantly more space for just a few extra dollars. Live music is performed nightly in the lounge, but it won't disturb your sleep.

1407 Division St., Nashville, TN 37203. ℂ **800/228-5151** or 615/242-1631. Fax 615/244-9519. www.best western.com. 102 units. $49–$59 double; $59–$69 suite. Rates include continental breakfast. Free local calls. AE, DC, DISC, MC, V. Free self-parking. Pets $5 per day. **Amenities:** Lounge; outdoor pool. *In room:* A/C, TV, dataport, unstocked fridge and microwave in 20 units, coffeemaker, hair dryer, iron, safe.

Days Inn Vanderbilt/Music Row   Though this motel dates back to the 1960s, the rooms have been refurbished since then. Local calls are free, making it a good choice if you're on a budget. A free shuttle to the nearby medical center offers another perk for guests who need it. In addition, Music Row and Vanderbilt University are both within walking distance.

1800 West End Ave., Nashville, TN 37203. ℂ **800/325-2525** or 615/327-0922. Fax 615/327-0102. www.days inn.com. 151 units. $72–$102 double. Rates include continental breakfast. AE, DC, DISC, MC, V. Free parking. **Amenities:** Restaurant; outdoor pool; exercise room; complimentary shuttle to nearby medical center; laundry service; dry cleaning. *In room:* A/C, TV, dataport, coffeemaker, hair dryer, iron on request.

Shoney's Inn–Nashville Music Row ⭐ If you want to stay right in the heart of Music Row and possibly spot a few country music stars while you're in town, try this sort of modern antebellum-style motel. In the lobby, you'll find walls covered with dozens of autographed photos of country music stars who have stayed here. The rooms are fairly standard, though they are all quite clean and comfortable. Free local calls and faxes are a plus. The suites are large and one has a whirlpool tub.

1501 Demonbreun St., Nashville, TN 37203. ℂ **800/552-4667** or 615/255-9977. Fax 615/242-6127. www. shoneysinn.com. 154 units. $65–$79 double; $109–$119 suite. Rates include free continental breakfast. AE, DC, DISC, MC, V. Free self-parking, with mobile-home and bus spaces available. Pet deposit $100. **Amenities:** Outdoor pool; nearby golf course; nearby lighted tennis courts; business center; in-room massage; dry cleaning. *In room:* A/C, TV, dataport, coffeemaker, hair dryer and iron on request.

3 The Music Valley Area

If you plan to spend any amount of time at either the Opryland Hotel or the Opry Mills mall, staying in the Music Valley area will be your best bet. It will also be much more convenient if you plan to attend the Grand Ole Opry, where the second of two nightly shows can sometimes extend past midnight. After a night of all that barn-raising music, who wants to get in their car and drive across town to get to their hotel?

VERY EXPENSIVE

Opryland Hotel ⭐⭐⭐ *(Kids* What Graceland is to Memphis, Opryland is to Nashville. In other words, whether you're an Elvis fan or not, you owe it to yourself to visit the mansion at least once. Ditto for Opryland. Whether you're into country music or not, a tour of this palatial property with its 85-foot water fountains, tropical foliage, and winding "rivers," has become almost obligatory. The Opryland has the look and feel of a massive theme park and it does attract thousands of visitors daily (on top of the numbers who are actually staying at this massive hotel). The most impressive of the hotel's numerous areas is the Cascade Conservatory, which consists of two linked atriums. Waterfalls splash across rocky outcroppings, and fountains dance with colored lights and lasers. Bridges and meandering paths and a revolving gazebo bar add a certain quaint charm. Elsewhere at Opryland, the Magnolia lobby resembles an elegant antebellum mansion, with its classically proportioned double staircase worthy of Tara itself. Escalators were recently added in the Delta area (one of the three atriums) of the hotel.

Guest rooms, while modern and comfortable, don't quite live up to the promise of the public areas. Though colonial American decor and tasteful floral wallpaper give them a touch of class, they are still of average size and not overly plush. Wingback chairs, however, provide an extra measure of comfort. The more expensive rooms are those overlooking the three atriums. While offering a nice view, these rooms are not quiet when musical events are occurring in the lobby below. Food and shops are dotted throughout the Opryland Hotel. From coffee and *beignets* on the go to a full, sit-down seafood feast, there's something here for all tastes and budgets.

2800 Opryland Dr., Nashville, TN 37214-1297. ℂ **615/883-2211** or 615/889-1000. Fax 615/871-5728. www. gaylordhotels.com. 2,883 units. $99–$279 double; $319–$3,500 suite. AE, DC, DISC, MC, V. Valet parking $16,

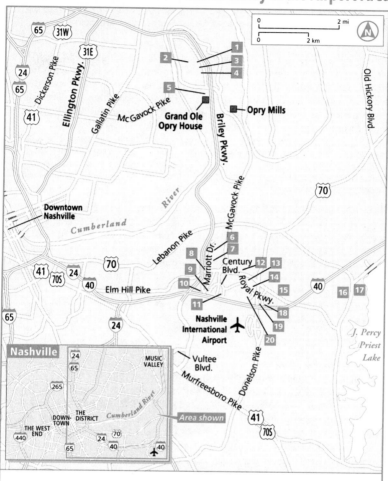

AmeriSuites Opryland **2**

Best Western Calumet Inn **17**

Comfort Inn Express **1**

Days Inn–Nashville East **16**

Doubletree Guest Suites **6**

Embassy Suites Nashville **9**

Holiday Inn Express Airport **18**

Holiday Inn Select
Opryland/Airport **8**

Homewood Suites **13**

La Quinta Inn Airport **7**

Nashville Airport Marriott **10**

Opryland Hotel **5**

Quality Inn & Suites **12**

Red Roof Inn **3**

Red Roof Inn–Nashville East **20**

Sheraton Music City **11**

Shoney's Inn–Music Valley **4**

SpringHill Suites by Marriott **15**

Super 8 Motel–
Nashville/Airport/Music City **14**

Wyndham Garden Hotel–
Nashville Airport **19**

plus tax; self-parking $7, plus tax. **Amenities:** 14 restaurants and lounges; 3 outdoor pools; golf club; exercise room; children's daycare; game/video room; concierge; tour desk; car-rental desk; business center; 30 retail shops; salon; 24-hr. room service; laundry service; dry cleaning. *In room:* A/C, TV w/pay movies, fax, dataport, kitchen or kitchenette, minibar, or unstocked fridge in some units, coffeemaker, hair dryer, iron, safe.

MODERATE

AmeriSuites Opryland ⭐   This mid-rise hotel is located just off Music Valley Drive and is your most comfortable choice in the area if you aren't willing to splurge on the Opryland Hotel. The biggest drawback here is that there is no restaurant on the premises. Guest rooms are larger than most, and a wall-to-wall refurbishment of the property began in late 2003. Rooms can even be a bit cramped unless you opt for a single king bed.

220 Rudy's Circle, Nashville, TN 37214. ✆ **800/833-1516** or 615/872-0422. Fax 615/872-9283. www. amerisuites.com. 125 units. $89–$119 double. Rates include continental breakfast. AE, DISC, MC, V. Free parking. **Amenities:** Small outdoor pool; exercise room; business center; limited room service; coin-op laundry; laundry service; same-day dry cleaning. *In room:* A/C, TV, dataport, kitchenette, unstocked fridge, coffeemaker, hair dryer, iron, safe.

Shoney's Inn–Music Valley   This modern hotel is one of the first lodgings along Music Valley Drive and is within walking distance of the Opryland Hotel. Recent renovations include a new continental breakfast bar and refurbished lobby and lounge. An indoor pool makes this a good choice for an off-season vacation. Five of the 13 suites feature two sleeper-sofas in addition to a king-sized bed, which makes these convenient for families. Small kitchenettes are another bonus. A complimentary airport shuttle is also available.

2420 Music Valley Dr., Nashville, TN 37214. ✆ **800/552-4667** or 615/885-4030. Fax 615/391-0632. www. shoneysinn.com 185 units. $81–$111 double. Rates include continental breakfast. AE, DC, DISC, MC, V. Free self-parking, including covered garage. Pet deposit $100. **Amenities:** Lounge; indoor pool; outdoor hot tub. *In room:* A/C, TV, dataport, coffeemaker.

INEXPENSIVE

A number of national and regional chain motels, generic but dependable, can be found in the area (see appendix D for toll-free reservation numbers), including: **Red Roof Inn,** 2460 Music Valley Dr. (✆ **615/889-0090**), charging $50 to $90 double (with an outdoor pool and an adjacent miniature-golf course); and **Comfort Inn Express,** 2516 Music Valley Dr. (✆ **615/889-0086**), charging $66 to $82 for a double.

4 The Airport Area

Business travelers may find the plethora of airport hotels most conveniently located to their needs. But even leisure travelers including those with families may find many of these resort-style properties appealing for their broad array of amenities.

EXPENSIVE

Embassy Suites Nashville ⭐ *Kids*   This all-suite hotel makes a great choice and a good value for families, as well as business travelers. Not only do you get a two-room suite, but breakfast and evening cocktails are also included in the rates. These rooms are spacious, modern, and tastefully decorated in warm colors. The centerpiece of the hotel is its large atrium, which is full of tropical plants, including palm trees. A rocky stream runs through the atrium and there are caged tropical songbirds adding their cheery notes to the pleasant atmosphere. The casual restaurant is located amid the tropical plants in the atrium and serves moderately priced meals. Also in the atrium are the lounge where the evening manager's reception is held and a dining area where complimentary breakfast is served.

10 Century Blvd., Nashville, TN 37214. (C) 800/EMBASSY or 615/871-0033. Fax 615/883-9245. www. embassy-suites.com. 296 units. $99–$179 suite. Rates include cooked-to-order breakfast. AE, DC, DISC, MC, V. Free parking. **Amenities:** Restaurant and bar; indoor pool; exercise room; hot tub; sauna; game room; concierge; limited room service; complimentary airport shuttle; complimentary evening manager's reception; gift shop. *In room:* A/C, TV w/pay movies, dataport, wet bar with fridge, coffeemaker, hair dryer, iron.

Holiday Inn Select Opryland/Airport   If you're looking for someplace convenient to the airport, this Holiday Inn just off the Briley Parkway is a good bet. The lobby features two back-to-back atriums, one of which houses the reception desk, a car-rental desk, and a couple of seating areas, while the other contains the swimming pool, a lobby lounge area, and a terraced restaurant. Guest rooms are fairly standard but feature big TVs and plenty of counter space in the bathrooms. The king rooms have a bit more space and are designed with business travelers in mind. On the 14th-floor executive level, you'll receive a complimentary breakfast and other upgraded amenities.

2200 Elm Hill Pike, Nashville, TN 37214. (C) 800/HOLIDAY or 615/883-9770. Fax 615/391-4521. www. holiday-inn.com. 382 units. $109–$140 double. AE, DC, DISC, MC, V. Free parking. **Amenities:** Restaurant; 2 lounges; indoor pool; exercise room; indoor hot tub; sauna; video-game room; car-rental desk; business center; limited room service; coin-op laundry; valet/laundry service; airport shuttle. *In room:* A/C, TV w/pay movies, dataport, fridges and microwaves (available for $10 each), coffeemaker, hair dryer, iron, safe.

Nashville Airport Marriott ★★ *Kids*   This is one of Nashville's most resortlike hotels, featuring lots of recreational facilities, not the least of which is an indoor/outdoor pool that is being renovated in 2004. If you want to stay in shape while you're away from home, this is an excellent choice. The hotel grounds cover 17 landscaped and wooded acres, though the proximity to the highway keeps the grounds rather noisy. Traffic sounds are not a problem if you book an upper-level floor. All the guest rooms feature elegant, classically styled furnishings and come with irons and ironing boards, as well as hair dryers. For business travelers, there are large work desks and a concierge level. Families will do well to ask for a lower-level poolside room; for extra space, try one of the corner rooms, which are 30% larger than standard rooms. The casual restaurant serves a wide range of pasta, poultry dishes and generous salads, and has a pleasant view of the woods outside. A quiet lounge sometimes has live music.

600 Marriott Dr., Nashville, TN 37214-5010. (C) 800/228-9290 or 615/889-9300. Fax 615/889-9315. www. marriott.com. 405 units. $99–$149 double; $199–$299 suite. AE, DC, DISC, MC, V. Free parking. **Amenities:** Restaurant and lounge; indoor/outdoor pool; tennis courts; health club; whirlpool; sauna; concierge; tour desk; room service; babysitting; valet/laundry service; complimentary airport shuttle; picnic area; basketball court; volleyball court. *In room:* A/C, TV w/pay movies, fax, dataport, coffeemaker, hair dryer, iron.

Sheraton Music City ★★   Big, elegant, and set on 23 acres in a modern business park near the airport, this large convention hotel has a commanding vista of the surrounding area. Classic Georgian styling sets the tone and conjures up the feel of an antebellum mansion. In the elegant lobby, you'll find marble floors and burnished cherrywood paneling, and off to one side, a lounge with the feel of a conservatory. Following a recent $8 million renovation, all guest rooms have been updated with new carpeting, furnishings, and bedding. With the business traveler in mind, each room has three phones, large work desks, and plenty of closet space, as well as a couple of comfortable chairs. In the bathrooms, you'll find a coffeemaker and a phone.

777 McGavock Pike, Nashville, TN 37214-3175. ℂ **800/325-3535** or 615/885-2200. Fax 615/231-1134. www.sheratonmusiccity.com. 410 units. $120–$165 double; $150–$600 suite. AE, DC, DISC, MC, V. Valet parking $7; free self-parking. **Amenities:** Restaurant; lounge; outdoor pool in quiet central courtyard; indoor pool; tennis courts; health club with whirlpool, sauna, and exercise equipment; concierge; 24-hr. room service; valet/laundry service; complimentary airport shuttle. *In room:* A/C, TV, dataport, free high-speed Internet access, stocked minibar in suites, coffeemaker, hair dryer, iron.

MODERATE

Holiday Inn Express Airport ⭐ *Value*   Though you might expect from the name that this is a basic motel, in truth it is quite removed from the generic mainstream. From the minute you pull up to the grand entry portico, you'll recognize that this is a great value. Step through the door and you'll find yourself in the lobby of a remote mountain lodge. There are moose-antler chandeliers hanging from exposed roof beams, a stone floor, and a river-rock fireplace. The guest rooms are all fairly spacious, with country-pine furniture and extra-large bathrooms. Many rooms have little balconies overlooking the courtyard gardens or the rolling hills of the surrounding office park.

1111 Airport Center Dr., Nashville, TN 37214. ℂ **800/HOLIDAY** or 615/883-1366. Fax 615/889-6867. www. holiday-inn.com. 202 units. $69–$99 double. Rates include continental breakfast. Free local calls. AE, DC, DISC, MC, V. Free parking. **Amenities:** Outdoor pool. *In room:* A/C, TV w/movies, dataport, coffeemaker, hair dryer, iron.

Wyndham Garden Hotel–Nashville Airport   Recently renovated, this hotel has a refreshingly peaceful ambience. Just inside the front door, you'll find a seating area with a living-room feel beckoning you to sit down and relax a while. Behind this space is a lounge done up to look like a library. The guest rooms all feature classic cherrywood furniture. Spacious bathrooms include plenty of counter space.

1112 Airport Center Dr., Nashville, TN 37214. ℂ **800/822-4200** or 615/889-9090. Fax 615/885-1564. www. wyndham.com. 204 units. $79–$115 double; $99–$125 suite. AE, DC, DISC, MC, V. Free parking. **Amenities:** Restaurant; indoor pool; exercise room; hot tub; room service; laundry/valet service; complimentary airport shuttle. *In room:* A/C, TV w/movies, dataport, coffeemaker, hair dryer, iron.

INEXPENSIVE TO MODERATE

National and regional chain motels in the area are increasing exponentially. Some of the newest properties include the following (see appendix D for toll-free reservation numbers): **Doubletree Guest Suites,** 2424 Atrium Way (ℂ **615/889-8889**), charging $79 to $179 for a double; **Homewood Suites,** 2640 Elm Hill Pike ℂ **615/884-8111**), charging $89 to $119; **Quality Inn and Suites,** 2521 Elm Hill Pike (ℂ **615/391-3919**), charging $89 to $95 for a double; **La Quinta Inn Airport,** 2345 Atrium Way (ℂ **615/885-3000**), charging $71 to $78 for a double; and **SpringHill Suites by Marriott,** 1100 Airport Center Dr. (ℂ **615/884-6111**), charging $69 to $89 for a double.

Other good budget bets include such old standbys as **Best Western Calumet Inn,** 701 Stewart's Ferry Pike (ℂ **615/889-9199;** www.bestwestern.com), charging $53 to $63 for a double (adjacent to Uncle Bud's restaurant); **Days Inn–Nashville East,** 3445 Percy Priest Dr. (ℂ **615/889-8881;** www.daysinn. com), charging $49 to $69 for a double (also adjacent to Uncle Bud's); **Red Roof Inn–Nashville East,** 510 Claridge Dr. (ℂ **615/872-0735;** www.redroof. com), charging $50 to $64 for a double; and **Super 8 Motel–Nashville/ Airport/Music City,** 720 Royal Pkwy. (ℂ **615/889-8887**), charging $54 to $65 for a double.

5

Where to Dine in Nashville

The rest of the country may make fun of Southern cooking, with its fatback and chitlins, collard greens, and fried everything, but there is much more to Southern food than these tired stereotypes. You'll find that Southern fare, in all its diversity, is a way of life here in Nashville. This is not to say that you can't get good Italian, French, German, Japanese, Chinese, or even Thai—you can. However, as long as you're below the Mason–Dixon line, you owe it to yourself to try a bit of country cookin'. Barbecue and fried catfish are two inexpensive staples well worth trying (see "Barbecue" and "The Music Valley & Airport Areas" sections later in this chapter for restaurants serving these foods). If you enjoy good old-fashioned American food, try a "meat-and-three" restaurant, where you get your choice of three vegetables with your meal. However, to find out what Southern cooking is truly capable of, try someplace serving New Southern or New American cuisine. This is the equivalent of California cuisine, but made with traditional, and not-so-traditional, Southern ingredients.

As Nashville has grown more popular as a tourist destination, it has also begun to attract some big chain restaurants. Down in The District you'll find **Hard Rock Cafe,** 100 Broadway (© **615/742-9900**), and **Morton's of Chicago,** 641 Church St. (© **615/259-4558**).

Out in the West End you'll find **P.F. Chang's China Bistro** (2535 West End Ave., © **615/329-8901**), and **Ruth's Chris Steakhouse,** 2100 West End Ave. (© **615/320-0163**).

I have divided the following restaurant listings into five different general locations: **Downtown, the District & 12th Avenue South,** which is roughly the area within 12 blocks of the Cumberland River between Broadway and Jefferson Street; **Music Row & the West End,** which refers to the area along West End Avenue and Broadway beginning about 20 blocks from the river; **Green Hills & South Nashville,** which refers to the large area of the city's southern suburbs, with many of the restaurants clustered around the Mall at Green Hills; **Belle Meade & Environs,** which is roughly along Harding Road (a western extension of West End Ave.); and **Music Valley & the Airport,** which is the area between the airport and the Opryland Hotel.

For these listings, I have classified restaurants in the following categories (estimates do not include beer, wine, or tip): **expensive,** if a complete dinner would cost $30 or more; **moderate,** where you can expect to pay between $15 and $30 for a complete dinner; and **inexpensive,** where a complete dinner can be had for less than $15.

1 Restaurants by Cuisine

AMERICAN

Elliston Place Soda Shop ✮ (Music Row & the West End, $, p. 75)

Green Hills Grille (Green Hills & South Nashville, $$, p. 76)

Monell's ✮ (Downtown, The District & 12th Avenue South, $, p. 68)

Harper's ✮✮ (Green Hills and South Nashville, $, p. 77)

Houston's (Music Row & the West End, $$, p. 72)

Pancake Pantry ✮ (Music Row & the West End, $, p. 75)

Rainforest Café (The Music Valley & Airport Areas, $$, p. 80)

Rotier's ✮ (Music Row & the West End, $, p. 75)

Satsuma Tea Room (Downtown, The District & 12th Avenue South, $, p. 69)

Sylvan Park Murphy Road ✮ (Green Hills & South Nashville, $, p. 77)

BARBECUE

Bar-B-Cutie ✮ (The Music Valley & Airport Areas, $, p. 80)

Corky's Bar-B-Q ✮✮ (Green Hills & South Nashville, $, p. 82)

Jack's Bar-B-Que ✮ (Downtown, The District & 12th Avenue South, $, p. 82)

Whitt's Barbecue ✮ (Belle Meade & Environs, $, p. 82)

BURGERS

Blackstone Restaurant & Brewery ✮ (Music Row & the West End, $$, p. 71)

Rotier's ✮ (Music Row & the West End, $, p. 75)

CARIBBEAN

Calypso ✮ (Music Row & the West End, $, p. 74)

Rainforest Café (The Music Valley & Airport Areas, $$, p. 80)

CONTINENTAL

Arthur's ✮✮✮ (Downtown, The District & 12th Avenue South, $$$, p. 63)

DELICATESSEN

Goldie's Deli ✮✮ (Belle Meade & Environs, $, p. 78)

Noshville ✮✮ (Music Row & the West End, $, p. 75)

FRENCH

The Wild Boar ✮✮ (Music Row & the West End, $$$, p. 71)

FUSION

Havana Lounge (Downtown, The District & 12th Avenue South, $$, p. 67)

Mirror ✮✮✮ (Downtown, The District & 12th Avenue South, $$, p. 68)

Zola ✮✮ (Music Row & the West End, $$, p. 73)

GERMAN

Gerst Haus ✮✮ (Downtown, The District & 12th Avenue South, $, p. 68)

ITALIAN

Mario's Ristorante ✮ (Music Row & the West End, $$$, p. 70)

The Old Spaghetti Factory (Downtown, The District & 12th Avenue South, $, p. 69)

JAPANESE

Benkay Japanese Restaurant ✮ (Belle Meade & Environs, $$, p. 78)

Goten ✮ (Music Row & the West End, $$, p. 72)

MEXICAN

La Hacienda Taqueria ✮ (Green Hills & South Nashville, $, p. 77)

La Paz Restaurante Cantina ✮ (Green Hills & South Nashville, $$, p. 77)

Key to Abbreviations: $$$$ = Very Expensive $$$ = Expensive $$ = Moderate $ = Inexpensive

Rosepepper Cantina & Mexican Grill (Green Hills and South Nashville, $, p. 77)

NEW AMERICAN/ NEW SOUTHERN

Acorn ⋆ (Music Row & the West End), $$$, p. 70)

Belle Meade Brasserie ⋆ (Belle Meade & Environs, $$$, p. 78)

Bound'ry ⋆⋆⋆ (Music Row & the West End, $$, p. 72)

Café One Two Three (Downtown, The District & 12th Avenue South, $$, p. 67)

Capitol Grille ⋆⋆⋆ (Downtown, The District & 12th Avenue South, $$$, p. 66)

F. Scott's Restaurant and Jazz Bar ⋆⋆⋆ (Green Hills & South Nashville, $$$, p. 76)

The Mad Platter ⋆ (Downtown, The District & 12th Avenue South, $$, p. 67)

The Merchants ⋆ (Downtown, The District & 12th Avenue South, $$$, p. 66)

Martha's at the Plantation ⋆⋆⋆ (Belle Meade & Environs, $$, p. 79)

Midtown Café ⋆ (Music Row & the West End, $$, p. 73)

Sunset Grill ⋆⋆ (Music Row & the West End, $$, p. 73)

12th & Porter ⋆ (Downtown, The District & 12th Avenue South, $, p. 70)

PIZZA

DaVinci's Gourmet Pizza ⋆ (Music Row & the West End, $, p. 74)

Mafiaoza's (Downtown, The District & 12th Avenue South, $, p. 68)

SEAFOOD

Atlantis ⋆ (Music Row & the West End, $$, p. 71)

Jimmy Kelly's ⋆ (Music Row & the West End, $$, p. 72)

SOUTHERN

Cock of the Walk ⋆ (The Music Valley & Airport Areas, $, p. 80)

Easy's in the Village (Music Row & the West End, $, p. 74)

Loveless Café ⋆⋆ (Belle Meade & Environs, $, p. 79)

Harper's ⋆⋆ (Green Hills and South Nashville, $, p. 77)

South Street ⋆ (Music Row & the West End, $$, p. 73)

Uncle Bud's Catfish ⋆ (The Music Valley & Airport Areas, $, p. 80)

SOUTHWESTERN

Green Hills Grille (Green Hills & South Nashville, $$, p. 76)

La Paz Restaurante Cantina ⋆ (Green Hills & South Nashville, $$, p. 77)

STEAKS

Fleming's Prime Steakhouse ⋆ (Music Row & the West End, $$$, p. 70)

Jimmy Kelly's ⋆ (Music Row & the West End, $$, p. 72)

Nick & Rudy's ⋆ (Music Row & the West End, $$$, p. 71)

The Palm Restaurant (Downtown, The District & 12th Avenue South, $$$, p.66)

Stock-Yard Restaurant (Downtown, The District & 12th Avenue South, $$$, p. 67)

THAI

The Orchid ⋆ (Belle Meade & Environs, $$, p. 79)

2 Downtown, The District & 12th Avenue South

EXPENSIVE

Arthur's ⋆⋆⋆ *Moments* CONTINENTAL   One of Nashville's finest restaurants, Arthur's is located in the renovated train depot that houses the historic

Nashville Dining: Downtown, Music Row & the West End

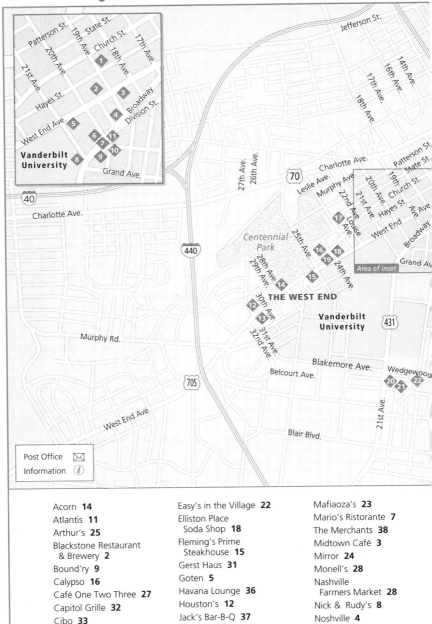

Acorn **14**
Atlantis **11**
Arthur's **25**
Blackstone Restaurant
 & Brewery **2**
Bound'ry **9**
Calypso **16**
Café One Two Three **27**
Capitol Grille **32**
Cibo **33**
DaVinci's Gourmet
 Pizza **1**

Easy's in the Village **22**
Elliston Place
 Soda Shop **18**
Fleming's Prime
 Steakhouse **15**
Gerst Haus **31**
Goten **5**
Havana Lounge **36**
Houston's **12**
Jack's Bar-B-Q **37**
Jimmy Kelly's **17**
The Mad Platter **29**

Mafiaoza's **23**
Mario's Ristorante **7**
The Merchants **38**
Midtown Café **3**
Mirror **24**
Monell's **28**
Nashville
 Farmers Market **28**
Nick & Rudy's **8**
Noshville **4**
The Old Spaghetti
 Factory **35**

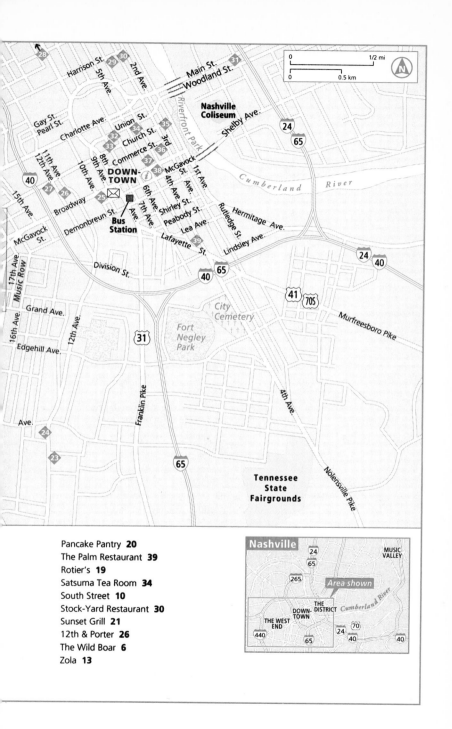

Pancake Pantry **20**
The Palm Restaurant **39**
Rotier's **19**
Satsuma Tea Room **34**
South Street **10**
Stock-Yard Restaurant **30**
Sunset Grill **21**
12th & Porter **26**
The Wild Boar **6**
Zola **13**

Union Station hotel. With its Venetian crystal chandeliers, walnut paneling, gilded plasterwork, and breathtaking stained-glass windows, Arthur's is a great place to impress a date. Fresh cream-colored roses adorn each table, and in the winter there's usually a fire crackling in the stone fireplace.

To savor every bite, set aside at least 2 or 3 hours for a meal here. The ever-changing menu is given vocally. Once you pick the entree, the chef selects all of its preceding courses. (Substitutions are allowed, however; just ask your waiter.) Main courses include succulent fresh fish prepared with light, flavorful sauces, as well as heavier fare. The rack of lamb is renowned, as are Arthur's wild game specialties. Flambéed desserts and liqueur-laced coffees are prepared tableside by expert servers who seem to relish this portion of the evening. (They'll even forewarn you to have your camera loaded and ready.)

In the Union Station hotel, 1001 Broadway. ✆ **615/255-1494.** www.arthursrestaurant.com. Reservations highly recommended. Jacket and tie preferred for men. 7-course fixed-price dinner $65. AE, DC, DISC, MC, V. Mon–Thurs 5:30–10pm; Fri–Sat 5:30–11pm; Sun 5:30–9pm. Free valet parking.

Capitol Grille ✦✦✦ NEW AMERICAN/NEW SOUTHERN Located in the lower level of the posh Hermitage hotel, the Capitol Grille is one of downtown Nashville's most elegant restaurants. Its clubby decor and polished service attracts politicians and power-lunchers as well as theater-goers from the nearby Tennessee Center for Performing Arts. Appetizers can go to extremes, ranging from a honey balsamic-glazed duck Napoleon to a champagne, Vidalia onion, and Brie cheese soup drizzled with blackberry coulis. More mainstream appetites may opt for generously-portioned entrees including filet mignon or sautéed grouper with fresh spinach. Desserts include a decadent caramelized apple cheesecake and a scrumptious chocolate mousse torte. On Sundays, a lavish brunch is served.

In the Hermitage, 231 Sixth Ave. N. ✆ **615/345-7116.** www.thehermitagehotel.com. Reservations recommended. Main courses $25–$35. AE, DC, DISC, MC, V. Daily 6:30–11am, 11:30am–2pm, and 5:30–10pm.

The Merchants ✦ NEW AMERICAN/NEW SOUTHERN Housed in a restored brick building amid the funky bars of lower Broadway, this classy restaurant is another favorite power-lunch spot and after-work hangout for the young executive set. The restaurant's first floor consists of a bar, a cafe, and an outdoor patio seating area. Upstairs is the more formal dining room. Dinner here might begin with lively tequila shrimp. From there, you could move on to beef tenderloin pan-seared with apples, Jack Daniel's, and maple syrup; or perhaps lamb chops with herbs, bourbon, and a cranberry demiglace. Merchants also boasts an extensive wine list.

401 Broadway. ✆ **615/254-1892.** www.merchantsrestaurant.com. Reservations recommended. Main courses $12–$35. AE, DC, DISC, MC, V. Mon–Thurs 11am–10pm; Fri–Sat 11am–11pm; Sun 3–9pm.

The Palm Restaurant STEAKS Currently the "in" place to see and to be seen, The Palm is an upscale enclave, located within the cushy confines of the Hilton Suites downtown. Conspicuous consumption is a hallmark here, where a 36 oz. New York Strip for two comes with a $60 price tag. Chops include thick cuts of lamb, pork, and veal, while beef eaters may opt for everything from prime rib to aged porterhouse. Salads, pasta, chicken, and fish dishes should appease diners who don't "do" beef. String beans, creamed spinach, mashed potatoes, and other sides are served family style. Celebs favor the private dining rooms, though if you keep your eyes peeled, you may see a Tennessee Titan or two, or the occasional country music star.

1140 5th Ave. S. ⓒ 615/742-7256. www.thepalm.com. Reservations recommended. Main courses $15 at lunch; $18–$38 dinner. AE, DC, DISC, MC, V. Mon–Fri 11am–11pm; Sat 5–11pm; Sun 5–10pm.

Stock-Yard Restaurant STEAKS   If The Palm seems too pretentious, head a few blocks uptown to the old Nashville Union Stockyard building where local old-money types have gathered to slice slabs of beef for decades. It's where Dad comes for Father's Day, or Son on his graduation. What you get is a very impressive foyer, complete with crystal chandelier, marble floor, and an alcove containing a wine display that includes what may be the oldest bottles of Madeira in the country (from 1776–92). A window off the foyer gives you a glimpse into the meat-storage room, so you can have a look at what you'll soon be served. For a steakhouse, this place actually has a pretty limited assortment of steaks, but most diners stop at the first offering—the prime rib. If you're not a steak eater but still would like to visit this Nashville tradition, you'll find several seafood, pork, and chicken dishes, as well as a few pasta plates. There's a nightclub downstairs from the restaurant in case you feel like dancing off some calories after dinner. The restaurant offers a free shuttle to hotels within a 15-mile radius. Call ahead for a space on the buses, which seat between 14 and 45 people.

901 2nd Ave. N. ⓒ 615/255-6464. www.stock-yardrestaurant.com. Reservations highly recommended. Main courses $21–$45. AE, DC, DISC, MC, V. Mon–Thurs 5–10pm; Fri–Sat 5–11pm; Sun 5–9pm.

MODERATE

Café One Two Three NEW SOUTHERN   If you're curious to discover what New Southern cooking is all about, seek out this surprisingly sophisticated spot in the middle of a warehouse district. Located across the street from the funky 12th & Porter restaurant/nightclub, and under the same management, this is a much more genteel establishment, with dark-wood paneling and conservative, traditional styling. However, the menu offerings are anything but conservative. How about some crawfish wontons with chipotle vinaigrette to start things off? You'll also find a good selection of salads; a recent selection was smoked shiitake, country ham, caramelized red onions, oranges, peppered pecans, and Gorgonzola cheese with a mustard-curry dressing. The entree list might include shrimp wrapped in apple-smoked bacon, a pecan-crusted lamb rack, or pork chops with a peanut-plum sauce. Another plus: Live jazz is offered periodically.

123 12th Ave. N. ⓒ 615/255-2233. www.faisons.com. Reservations recommended. Main courses $15–$30. AE, DC, DISC, MC, V. Mon–Thurs 5:30–midnight; Fri–Sat 5:30pm–1:30am.

Havana Lounge *Finds* FUSION   From the walk-in humidor to the wild zebra decor, this trendy spot above a billiards parlor will make you forget you're in Nashville. The innovative fusion of Caribbean and Asian culinary touches enlivens any choice from the menu. Case in point: the egg rolls are nori-wrapped pouches of black beans, saffron sticky rice, and vegetables, served with orange wasabi sauce, pickled ginger, and soy sauce. Even more bizarre is an Oriental-inspired paella that boldly melds saffron rice with mussels, shrimp, scallops, chicken, escargot, and chorizo in a tomato-garlic lemongrass broth. These dishes don't always succeed, but they are all daringly different.

154 2nd Ave. N. ⓒ 615/313-7665. Main courses $14–$20. AE, MC, V. Mon–Thurs 5–10pm; Fri–Sat 11am–1am.

The Mad Platter ✿ NEW AMERICAN/NEW SOUTHERN   For many years now, the Mad Platter has been one of Nashville's trendiest restaurants. Located in an old brick corner store in a historic neighborhood of restored Victorian houses, the Mad Platter feels like a cozy upscale library, with bookshelves crammed with knickknacks and old copies of *National Geographic*. The ambience is reserved, not pretentious, and service is personable, if a bit slow at times. The menu, including vegetarian options, changes daily. Appetizers might include a Gorgonzola-and-asparagus Napoleon, as well as a prosciutto roulade stuffed with truffle mousse. Recent entrees have included grilled duck breast basted with a pomegranate molasses and a rack of lamb moutarde. Don't you dare leave without trying the best-named dessert in all of Nashville: Chocolate Elvis is an obscenely rich, fudge-y cake that, put simply, takes the cake.

1239 6th Ave. N. (*C*) 615/242-2563. Reservations recommended. Main courses $20–$28. AE, DC, DISC, MC, V. Mon–Fri 11am–2pm; Tues–Sat 5:30–11pm; Sun 5–9pm.

Mirror ✦✦ FUSION   Mirror serves one of the best vodka cucumber martinis in town, a feat that befits this ultra hip bar and restaurant in the 12th Avenue South district. Metallic furniture, pale blue walls, and gauze curtains define the casual chic setting. Spanish sherry is a must when ordering from the extensive tapas menu, including olives, tuna ceviche (raw fish dish marinated in citrus juice and spices), and crispy prosciutto-wrapped cipollini onions. I highly recommend the warm goat cheesecake with mesclun greens, asparagus, tomatoes, and mushroom ragout. Entrees include light options (salmon spring rolls, carrot/ginger soufflé) and heartier seared duck or rosemary-marinated filet mignon with truffle mashed potatoes, spinach and sherry-spiked mushroom sauce.

2317 12th Ave. South (*C*) **615/383-8330**. www.eatdrinkreflect.com. Tapas $1–$3.50; main courses $13–$21. AE, MC, V. Mon–Sat 5–11pm.

INEXPENSIVE

In addition to the restaurants listed here, you can get quick, inexpensive meals at the **Nashville Farmers Market,** 900 Eighth Ave. N. ((*C*) **615/880-2001**), adjacent to the Bicentennial Capitol Mall State Park. It's open from 9am to 6pm 7 days a week, year-round.

Gerst Haus ✦✦ GERMAN   This beloved Nashville landmark is best known for its beer hall atmosphere, German food, and more recently, salads, catfish, and steaks. From its plum perch across the street from The Coliseum, chances are the Gerst Haus will be endearing new fans of hearty Bavarian fare for generations to come. Open for lunch and dinner.

301 Woodland St. (*C*) **615/244-8886**. Main courses $9–$16. AE, MC, V. Sun–Thurs 11am–10pm; Fri–Sat 11am–11pm.

Mafiaoza's PIZZA   With a toasty fire crackling in the pizza ovens and the dim roar of a lively cocktail crowd, this new pizzeria in the trendy 12th Avenue South district has quickly built a loyal following. An outdoor patio give patrons a great place to hang while throwing back a few beers or bottles of vino. Skip the soggy, tomato-laden bruschetta but try the meaty pasta dishes and thin-crust pizzas, sold by the slice or whole pie.

2400 12th Ave. S. (*C*) **615/269-4646**. Main courses $6.75–$22. AE, DISC, MC, V. Tues–Fri 4pm–3am; Sat–Sun 11am–3pm.

Monell's ✦ *Finds* AMERICAN   Dining out doesn't usually involve sitting at the same table with total strangers, but be prepared for just such a community experience at Monell's. Housed in a restored brick Victorian home, this very traditional boardinghouse-style lunch spot feels as if it has been around for ages, which is just what the proprietors want you to think. A meal at Monell's is

---

Kids **Family-Friendly Restaurants**

Elliston Place Soda Shop (p. 75)   Bring the kids by for a burger and a shake and tell them how their mom and dad or grandma and grandpa used to hang out in a place just like this one when they were love-struck teenagers.

Goldie's Deli (p. 78)   While grownups nosh on herring, chicken livers, and lox, keep the kids happy with a smiley-faced hotdog combo that comes with chips and a fountain drink.

The Old Spaghetti Factory (see below)   Kids love spaghetti and here, that's all there is to it. Adults will enjoy the Victorian decor. And kids will also love the old trolley car in the middle of the dining room.

Rainforest Café (p. 80)   Entertaining for the whole family, this theme cafe offers basic American sandwiches and entrees with a faint tropical flair—served in a jungle atmosphere complete with roaring elephants, chest-thumping gorillas, and thunderous, simulated rainstorms.

Uncle Bud's Catfish (p. 80)   The fun country decor and the all-you-can-eat catfish and fried chicken make this place a hit with families. Sure everything's fried, but this is a true Southern experience.

---

meant to conjure up family dinners at Grandma's house, so remember to say "please" when you ask for the mashed potatoes or peas. The food is good, old-fashioned home cookin' most of the year, and everything is all-you-can-eat. In December (the 1st through the 23rd), Monell's gets fancy and offers reservation-only Victorian dinners ($35).

1235 6th Ave. N. *C* **615/248-4747**. Main courses $9–$16. MC, V. Tues–Fri 10:30am–2pm; Fri 5–8:30pm; Sat 8:30am–1pm and 5–8:30pm; Sun 11am–3pm.

The Old Spaghetti Factory *Value* *Kids* ITALIAN   With its ornate Victorian elegance, you'd never guess that this restaurant was once a warehouse. Where boxes and bags were stacked, diners now sit surrounded by burnished wood. There's stained and beveled glass all around, antiques everywhere, and plush seating in the waiting area. The front of the restaurant is a large and very elegant bar. Now if they'd just do something about that trolley car someone parked in the middle of the dining room. A complete meal—including a salad, bread, spumoni ice cream, and a beverage—will cost you less than a cocktail in many restaurants. A great spot to bring the family, this is one of the cheapest places to get a meal in The District.

160 2nd Ave. N. *C* **615/254-9010**. www.osf.com. Main courses $4.60–$7.95. DISC, MC, V. Mon–Sat 11:30am–2pm; Mon–Thurs 5–10pm; Fri–Sat 5–11pm; Sun 4–10pm.

Satsuma Tea Room AMERICAN   The name is deceptive. While it sounds as if it could be a sushi bar, Satsuma is actually one of Nashville's classic pur-veyors of Southern home cooking. Occupying the ground floor of a small old building, the restaurant—open only for lunch—is popular with downtown office workers. The menu changes daily, but you might find chicken and dumplings, turkey a la king, baked pork chops, or roast leg of lamb available when you drop by. Before stepping through the door, be sure to check out the pie case in the front window. Loyal customers look forward to the seasonal Concord grape pie, available in the fall. Original artwork (which is for sale) is a surprising touch in such an inexpensive restaurant.

417 Union St. ✆ 615/256-0760. Main courses $6.25–$7.25. AE, DISC, MC, V. Mon–Fri 10:45am–2pm.

12th & Porter ✦ NEW AMERICAN   It's funky, it's retro, it's 12th & Porter. If you dig the turquoise-and-black checkerboard styling of the 1950s and like imaginative cooking, you should be sure to check out this place. Although primarily a nightclub that suffers some abuse at the hands (and feet) of weekend dance crowds, 12th & Porter serves up such interesting (and curiously named) dishes as Greek Unorthodox Pizza, Low-Death-Factor Pizza, Rasta Pasta, and Blue Hoe Cakes with boursin cheese and caviar. You'll find 12th & Porter in the warehouse district behind the offices of the *Tennessean* newspaper. There is valet parking, so you don't need to look for a parking space. An eclectic roster of musicians, from rock to country acts, takes the stage nightly around 9pm.

114 12th Ave. N. ✆ 615/254-7236. www.faisons.com. Reservations accepted only for parties of 6 or more. Main courses $6–$20; shows $5–$7 or more (call ahead). AE, DC, DISC, MC, V. Mon–Fri 11:30am–2pm; Mon–Thurs 5:30pm–midnight; Fri–Sat 5:30pm–1am.

3 Music Row & the West End

For locations of restaurants in this section, see the "Nashville Dining: Downtown, Music Row & the West End" map on p. 64.

EXPENSIVE

Acorn ✦ NEW AMERICAN   In a tree-shaded, gentrified neighborhood near Centennial Park, Acorn has been open since early 2003. With its evocative lighting, contemporary artwork, and burnished decor, the restaurant tries hard to mimic the stylish boldness of Bound'ry, another West End restaurant. Though a tad overpriced, the food is first-rate. I loved the wasabi-encrusted seared tuna with pureed sesame carrots and Japanese vegetables. Also popular are the acorn-squash-stuffed ravioli with cream sauce, chervil shrimp bisque, and pear and spinach salad studded with sugar-cinnamon walnuts. Tapas, quiche, and sandwiches make the late-night menu a notch above the typical bar food usually available at this hour.

114 28th Ave. N. ✆ 615/320-4399. www.theacornrestaurant.com. Reservations recommended. Main courses $16–$25. AE, DC, DISC, MC, V. Mon–Thurs 11am–midnight; Fri–Sat 11am–1am.

Fleming's Prime Steakhouse ✦ STEAKS   Here's an upscale but casual steakhouse offering prime bone-in steaks, meaty pork and lamb chops, and fresh seafood dishes. Loud and laid-back, this is a great place to kick back with friends and fellow carnivores. An excellent wine list features more than 100 premium vintages available by the glass. Another plus? The entire restaurant is nonsmoking.

2525 West End Ave. ✆ 615/342-0131. www.flemingssteakhouse.com. Reservations recommended. Main courses $25–$35. MC, V. Mon–Thurs 5–10pm; Fri–Sat 5–11pm; Sun 5–9pm.

Mario's Ristorante ✦ NORTHERN ITALIAN   With the exception of the baronial Wild Boar, which is located across the street, Mario's is the most exclusive and expensive restaurant in Nashville. In addition to the extensive wine list, you'll find vintages recommended in the margins of the main menu. Mario's is justly proud of its wine cellar, and rare wines and plenty of wine awards are on display in the restaurant's foyer. The menu is ostensibly northern Italian, so you might want to consider starting your meal with *carpaccio*. From there you can move on to the likes of duck breast with a plum sauce or perhaps Dover sole with pine nuts. However, traditionalists will likely opt for the rack of lamb in rosemary sauce. Should you wish to sample the atmosphere but can't afford dinner, you could have a drink in the bar (as long as you're appropriately attired). Jackets and ties are required for men.

2005 Broadway. ☎ **615/327-3232.** www.mariosfinedining.com. Reservations highly recommended. Jackets suggested for men. Main courses $22–$32. AE, DC, DISC, MC, V. Mon–Sat 5:30–11pm.

Nick & Rudy's ★ STEAK   One of the newest locally owned steakhouses to hit Nashville in the past few years (it opened in 2000), this upscale restaurant has the look and feel of a comfortable country club. However, Nick & Rudy's lacks the pretentiousness of The Palm, another of the city's ritzy steak places. Oysters and French onion soup have become favorites, along with generous steaks, chops, seafood, chicken, and pork dishes. There's no extra charge for the Old World charm, and tableside preparations of Caesar's salad and bananas Foster make mealtimes memorable here.

204 21st Ave. S. ☎ **615/329-8994.** www.nickandrudys.com. Reservations recommended. Main courses $16–$28. AE, DC, DISC, MC, V. Mon–Fri 11am–2pm, Mon–Sat 5–10pm.

The Wild Boar ★★ CONTEMPORARY FRENCH   If you're searching for the ritziest restaurant in Nashville, this is it. Palatial European surroundings imbued with rich colors and classical art create a refined atmosphere for the Wild Boar's high-dining experience. Service is impeccable, and the food is wonderful, yet the wine cellar is what truly sets this restaurant apart. If you happen to be an oenophile, you'll most certainly want to sample a bit of wine from the inventory of more than 15,000 bottles.

The menu changes daily, but you can almost always start out with Russian caviar. However, a potato Napoleon with seared foie gras in a red-port reduction will give you a better idea of why this restaurant is so highly acclaimed. From here you might move on to roasted pumpkin soup served in the shell and then a warm salad of pheasant breast and chestnut mousse with a smoked bacon vinaigrette. For a main course, you might be tempted by a beef Wellington. Extensive game specialties are featured in the fall and winter. There's live piano music on Friday and Saturday nights.

2014 Broadway. ☎ **615/329-1313.** www.wboar.com. Reservations highly recommended. Main courses $22–$36. AE, DC, DISC, MC, V. Mon–Thurs 6–10pm; Fri–Sat 6–10:30pm.

MODERATE

Atlantis ★ SEAFOOD   One of the few seafood restaurants in town, Atlantis is noted as much for its bright, jewel-toned decor as for its fresh culinary creations. Featuring fish flown in daily from throughout North and South America, dishes might include mustard-crusted Chilean sea bass with lobster mashed potatoes and lemon-basil vinaigrette, or a selection of raw oysters with horseradish slaw. With a dance floor, extensive wine list and bar menu, as well as valet parking, Atlantis aims to do it all.

1911 Broadway. ☎ **615/327-8001.** Reservations recommended. Main courses $20–$30. AE, DC, DISC, MC, V. Tues–Thurs 5–10pm; Fri–Sat 5–10pm; Sun 11:30am–2:30pm.

Blackstone Restaurant & Brewery ★ BURGERS/NEW AMERICAN   At this glitzy brew pub, brewing tanks in the front window silently crank out half a dozen different beers ranging from a pale ale to a dark porter. Whether you're looking for a quick bite of pub grub (pizzas, soups, pub-style burgers) or a more formal dinner (a meaty pork loin well complemented by apple chutney and a smidgen of rosemary, garlic, and juniper berries), you'll be satisfied with the food here, especially if you're into good microbrews. Fish and chips can't be beat, especially when washed down by a St. Charles Porter ale. This place is big, and you'll have the option of dining amid a pub atmosphere or in one of the sparsely elegant dining areas.

1918 West End Ave. ℂ 615/327-9969. Sandwiches, pizza, and main courses $8–$20. AE, DC, DISC, MC, V. Mon–Thurs 11am–midnight; Fri–Sat 11am–1am; Sun noon–10pm.

Bound'ry ⭐⭐⭐ NEW AMERICAN/NEW SOUTHERN   With its colorful murals and chaotic angles (seemingly inspired by Dr. Seuss), this Vanderbilt campus-area eatery is a fun yet sophisticated bastion of trendiness, popular with everyone from college students to families to businesspeople in suits. Add some jazz to the wild interior design and you have a very energetic atmosphere. From the tapas to the large plates, everything here seems to be good, but should they still be on the menu, don't miss the yin yang soup (a full-bodied melding of a white-bean–with-cheddar soup and a Cuban black-bean soup) or the stack of polenta, eggplant, portobello mushrooms, squash, roasted-red-pepper goat cheese, and smoked provolone with *puttanesca* sauce, pesto, and sun-dried tapenade. Wine and beer choices are quite extensive here.

911 20th Ave. S. ℂ 615/321-3043. Reservations recommended, except Fri–Sat after 6:30pm when it's first come, first served. Tapas $4.75–$11; main courses $20–$30. AE, DC, DISC, MC, V. Restaurant daily 5pm–1am. Bar daily 4pm–2:30am.

Goten ⭐ JAPANESE   Glass brick walls and a high-tech Zen-like elegance set the mood at this West End Japanese restaurant, situated across the street from Vanderbilt University. The valet parking is a clue that this restaurant is slightly more formal than other Japanese restaurants in Nashville. Don't come here expecting watery bowls of miso soup and a few noodles. Hibachi dinners are the specialty, with the menu leaning heavily toward steaks, which are just about as popular in Japan as they are in Texas. However, if you are more a sushi person, don't despair; the sushi bar here is Nashville's best, and you can get slices of the freshest fish in town. A sister restaurant, Goten 2, is at 209 10th Ave. S. (ℂ **615/251-4855**).

110 21st Ave. S. ℂ 615/321-4537. Reservations recommended. Main courses $15–$25. AE, DC, DISC, MC, V. Mon–Fri 11am–2pm; Sun–Thurs 5–10pm; Fri–Sat 5–11pm.

Houston's AMERICAN   West End Avenue is home to quite a few good restaurants, most of which are moderately priced and appeal to college students from nearby Vanderbilt University. Houston's is one of the more popular of such places, and you can be sure that it will be packed when you visit. Despite the fact that this is a new building, interior brick arches and exposed beams give the restaurant the feel of a renovated warehouse. There's even a dark oak bar with lots of brass and pine. The salads and burgers here are consistently voted the best in town, and they do a good job on prime rib and barbecue too. A few vegetarian dishes, such as a veggie burger and a vegetarian platter with brown rice, also find their way onto the menu.

3000 West End Ave. ℂ 615/269-3481. Reservations not accepted. Main courses $8–$24. AE, MC, V. Sun–Thurs 11am–10pm; Fri–Sat 11am–11pm.

Jimmy Kelly's ⭐ STEAKS/SEAFOOD   Tradition is the name of the game at Jimmy Kelly's, so if you long for the good old days of gracious Southern hospitality, be sure to schedule a dinner here. The restaurant is in a grand old home with neatly trimmed lawns and a valet-parking attendant (it's free) waiting out front. Inside you'll almost always find the dining rooms and bar bustling with activity as waiters in white jackets navigate from the kitchen to the tables and back. Though folks tend to dress up for dinner here, the several small dining rooms are surprisingly casual. The kitchen turns out well-prepared traditional dishes such as chateaubriand in a burgundy-and-mushroom sauce and blackened catfish (not too spicy, to accommodate the tastes of middle Tennessee). Whatever you have for dinner, don't miss the cornbread—it's the best in the city.

217 Louise Ave. ℭ 615/329-4349. www.jimmykellys.com. Reservations recommended. Main courses $13–$35. AE, DC, MC, V. Mon–Sat 5pm–midnight.

Midtown Café ✪ NEW AMERICAN/NEW SOUTHERN   Located just off West End Avenue, this small, upscale restaurant conjures up a very romantic atmosphere with indirect lighting and bold displays of art. The design has been pulling in Nashvillians for years. Rich and flavorful sauces are the rule here, with influences from all over the world. Be sure to start a meal here with the lemon-artichoke soup, which is as good as its reputation around town. From there, consider moving on to crab cakes served with cayenne hollandaise and available either as an appetizer or an entree. Lunches here are much simpler than dinners, with lots of sandwiches on the menu. However, a few of the same dishes from the dinner menu are available, including the crab cakes.

102 19th Ave. S. ℭ 615/320-7176. www.midtowncafe.com. Dinner reservations recommended. Main courses $12–$28. AE, DC, DISC, MC, V. Mon–Fri 11am–2:30pm; Sun–Sat 5–10pm.

South Street ✪ SOUTHERN   The flashing neon sign proclaiming "authentic dive bar," a blue-spotted pink cement pig, and an old tire swing out front should clue you in that this place doesn't take itself too seriously. In fact, this little wedge-shaped eatery is as tacky as an episode of *Hee Haw,* but with Harleys often parked out front. On the menu, you'll find everything from fried pickles to handmade nutty buddies (candy bars). However, the mainstays are crispy catfish, pulled pork barbecue, smoked chicken, ribs, and steaks with biscuits. If you're feeling flush, you can opt for the $43 crab-and-slab dinner for two (two kinds of crab and a "slab" of ribs).

907 20th Ave. S. ℭ 615/320-5555. Main courses $9–$13. AE, DC, DISC, MC, V. Mon–Sat 11am–2am; Sun 4pm–midnight.

Sunset Grill ✪✪ NEW AMERICAN/NEW SOUTHERN   In the West End neighborhood of Hillsboro Village, the Sunset Grill is that rare breed of restaurant that's both critically acclaimed in the national press and an enduring customer favorite with the locals. The decor is minimalist and monochromatic with original paintings to liven things up a bit. The menu changes daily, with an emphasis on seafood preparations. A favorite is the Szechuan duck (grilled breast meat served with fried confit egg roll, Asian veggies, and wild rice and finished with a spicy honey and bell-pepper sauce). The Sonoma Salad is a scrumptious combination of mixed field baby greens, tart apples, almonds, and blue cheese in a pink wine-garlic vinaigrette. The restaurant is also well known for its extensive selection of wines by the glass.

2001 Belcourt Ave. ℭ 615/386-FOOD (3663). www.sunsetgrill.com. Reservations recommended. Main courses $7–$42. AE, DC, DISC, MC, V. Tues–Fri 11am–4:45pm; Mon–Thurs 4:45–10pm; Fri–Sat 4:45–midnight; Sun 4:45–11pm.

Zola ✪✪ *Value* FUSION   Chef-owner Debra Paquette has been consistently named one of Nashville's best chefs, and Zola's wine list has received a *Wine*

Spectator Award of Excellence for the last few years. Rustic country-French decor lends warmth to the restaurant, where service is friendly and polished. The exotic menu is laced with Mediterranean appetizers such as Moroccan spiced scallops with sweet potato and pistachio griddle cakes, passion fruit sauce, and pomegranate glaze. The specialty of the house is Grandma Zola's Paella, steaming risotto studded with fresh fish, juicy scallops, ham, artichokes, shrimp, homemade Spanish sausage drizzled with a tangy green aioli. Zola's French Laundry is a deliciously different mélange of arugula, radicchio, diced green apples, toasted hazelnuts, Stilton cheese, and cured orange peel drenched in a champagne vinaigrette.

3001 West End Ave. © 615/320-7778. www.restaurantzola.com. Reservations highly recommended. Main courses $14–$25. AE, DC, DISC, MC, V. Mon–Thurs 5:30–10pm; Fri–Sat 5:30–11pm.

INEXPENSIVE

Calypso ⭐ *Value* CARIBBEAN If you're looking for a good, healthy, inexpensive meal in the West End, I can think of no better place to send you than Calypso. This casual restaurant is located in a small shopping plaza near the Parthenon and has the brightness of a fast-food outlet (though in the hot colors of the tropics). Rotisserie chicken, in a sauce made from more than 30 ingredients, is the most popular item on the menu, but there are also good vegetarian meals available such as Boca burgers, black bean salads, and pita sandwiches. The Caribbean salads—such as tropical chicken salad with pineapple and raisins, and black-bean salad topped with beef or chicken, cheddar cheese, green onions, and barbecue sauce—are among my favorites. Other Calypso locations are at 2279 N. Gallatin Pike (© **615/855-1680**), 700 Thompson (© **615/297-3888**), 5101 Harding Pike (© **615/356-1678**), and a new location to open in Cool Springs mall in 2004.

2424 Elliston Place. © 615/321-3878. Main courses $5.15–$7.85. AE, DISC, MC, V. Mon–Fri 11am–9pm; Sat–Sun 11:30am–8:30pm.

DaVinci's Gourmet Pizza ⭐ PIZZA Frequently voted the best pizza in Nashville, this casual neighborhood place is in a renovated brick house in a nondescript neighborhood. As you step through the front door, you'll likely be hit with the overpowering aromas of fragrant pizzas baking in the oven. The pizzas here are all made from scratch and include some very interesting creations. The oysters-Rockefeller pizza is made with smoked oysters, while the Southwestern comes with salsa, roasted chicken, and cilantro. With such offerings as potato pizza, vegetarians are catered to as well. To wash your pizza down, there are lots of imported and domestic beers. In the summer, there's outdoor seating in the flower-dotted front yard.

1812 Hayes St. (at 19th Ave., 1 block off West End Ave.). © 615/329-8098. Pizzas $6.50–$22. AE, DC, DISC, MC, V. Mon–Fri 11am–2pm; Sun–Thurs 4:30–9pm; Fri–Sat 4:30–10pm.

Easy's in the Village ⭐ SOUTHERN One of Nashville's best bets for late-night dining or Sunday brunch, Easy's is a quintessential college bar that serves up mouth-watering munchies with a New Orleans twist. Entrees and sandwiches lean toward such Southern favorites as fried catfish and red beans and rice. On Sundays, Bloody Marys go great with spicy gumbo, grits, eggs Benedict and beignets. Not everything has a Creole/Cajun flare, though. Easy's infamous "sliders," tiny cheeseburgers slathered in onions, are all-American—and addicting.

1910 Belcourt Ave. © 615/292-7575. Main courses $7.50–$16. AE, MC, V. Mon–Fri 11am–2:30am; Sat–Sun 10am–3pm.

> ## Tips Would You Like Fries With That?
>
> Desperately craving a chicken-salad sandwich on pumpernickel but don't see any parking spaces near the always jam-packed Noshville? Pull up at the door and leave your car running: The deli has free valet parking during the weekday lunch rush.

Elliston Place Soda Shop ✸ *Kids* AMERICAN   One of the oldest eating establishments in Nashville, the Elliston Place Soda Shop has been around since 1939, and it looks it. The lunch counter, black-topped stools, and signs advertising malted milks and banana splits all seem to have been here since the original opening. It's a treat to visit this time capsule of Americana, with its red-and-white tiled walls, old beat-up Formica tables, and individual booth jukeboxes. The soda shop serves plate lunches of an entree and veggies, with four different specials of the day. Of course, you can also get club sandwiches, steaks, and hamburgers, and the best chocolate shakes in town.

2111 Elliston Place. © 615/327-1090. Main courses $2–$5.50. AE, DC, MC, V. Mon–Fri 7am–7:30pm; Sat 7am–6pm.

Noshville ✸✸ DELICATESSEN   There's only so much fried chicken and barbecue you can eat before you just have to have a thick, juicy Reuben or a bagel with hand-sliced lox. When the deli craving strikes in Nashville, head for Noshville. The deli cases in this big, bright, and antiseptic place are filled to overflowing with everything from beef tongue to pickled herring to corned beef to chopped liver. Make mama happy: Start your meal with some good matzo-ball soup. Then satisfy the kid inside you by splurging on a hefty, two-fisted chocolate-and-vanilla-iced shortbread cookie.

1918 Broadway. © 615/329-NOSH (6674). www.noshville.citysearch.com. Main courses $6–$16. AE, DC, DISC, MC, V. Mon 6:30am–4pm; Tues–Thurs 6:30am–9pm; Fri 6:30am–11pm; Sat 7:30am–11pm; Sun 7:30am–9pm.

Pancake Pantry ✸ AMERICAN   The *New York Times, Bon Appetit,* and long lines even in all kinds of foul weather attest to the immense popularity of this satisfying but otherwise non-extraordinary eatery in Nashville's West End. College students, country-music stars, NFL players, tourists, and locals alike queue up outside the redbrick building for the chance to sit inside and sip a cup of coffee and cut into a stack of steamy flapjacks. With such varied wait times, it's worth noting that The Pancake Pantry also includes lunch items among its extensive breakfast menu.

1796 21st Ave. S. © 615/383-9333. Main courses $5–$15. AE, DC, DISC, MC, V. Mon–Fri 6am–3pm; Sat–Sun 6am–4pm.

Rotier's ✸ AMERICAN/BURGERS   If you're a fan of old-fashioned diners, don't miss Rotier's. This little stone cottage is surrounded by newer buildings, but has managed to remain a world unto itself. Sure, it looks like a dive from the outside, and the interior doesn't seem to have been upgraded in 40 years, but the food is good and the prices great. The cheeseburger here is said to be the best in the city, and the milk shakes are pretty good, too. For bigger appetites, there is that staple of Southern cooking—the "meat-and-three." You get a portion of meat (minute steak, pork chops, fried chicken, whatever) and three vegetables of your choice. They also do daily blue-plate specials and cheap breakfasts.

Tips Tired of Waiting?

The Pancake Pantry may be a breakfast-lover's first choice, but the daunting lines can aggravate appetites as well as patience. If so, you may want to ditch these hungry hordes and do brunch at **Jackson's Bar & Bistro**, which is across the street at 1800 21st Ave. S. at Belcourt Ave. (© **615/385-9968**). In nice weather, Jackson's has the added bonus of an outdoor patio. Another nearby option is the laid-back **Easy's in the Village** (p. 74), where brunch specialties like beignets, grits, and gumbo are served with New Orleans flair.

2413 Elliston Place. © 615/327-9892. www.rotiers.net. Sandwiches/main courses $4.25–$12. No credit cards. Mon–Thurs 10:30am–9:30pm; Fri 10:30am–10:30pm; Sat 9am–10:30pm.

4 Green Hills & South Nashville

EXPENSIVE

F. Scott's Restaurant and Jazz Bar ★★★ *Finds* NEW AMERICAN Chic and urbane, F. Scott's is an unexpected gem tucked amidst the shopping center hinterlands surrounding the Green Hills area. The classic movie-palace marquee out front announces in no uncertain terms that this place is different. Inside, everything is tastefully sophisticated yet comfortable and cozy. The restaurant's seasonally inspired menu is among the most creative in the city. Although the menu changes frequently, you might start with an appetizer of tender scallops, wild mushrooms, and spinach in a crispy phyllo cup with sun-dried tomatoes, bacon, and a white-truffle *beurre blanc* (warm butter sauce). The salad course of mesclun greens in a curried apple vinaigrette topped with goat cheese, cashews, and carrot shards, served in a crispy papadam cup, couldn't be tastier. Daring but universally delicious entrees vary from chile-braised short ribs with pineapple-plantain potato cakes, to pan-roasted Arctic char (a type of fish) with butternut squash spaetzle and green beans, and Singapore noodles with julienned beef, leeks, peppers, and onions. The wine list here is very good, although expensive. Live jazz in the lounge nightly provides another incentive to keep sophisticates coming back. There's also free valet parking.

2210 Crestmoor Rd. © 615/269-5861. www.fscotts.com. Reservations recommended. Main courses $17–$28. AE, DC, DISC, MC, V. Sun–Thurs 5:30–10pm; Fri–Sat 5:30–11pm.

MODERATE

Green Hills Grille AMERICAN/SOUTHWESTERN Located a few blocks past the Mall at Green Hills, this modern Santa Fe–style restaurant was an instant hit with Nashvillians when it opened several years ago. Although suburban strip malls surround it, both its interior decor and menu manage to do a decent job of conjuring up the new Southwest. While most dishes here tend to cater to spicy-food lovers, enough tamer offerings are available to satisfy those who aren't fire-eaters. For the former, there is "rattlesnake" pasta, and for the latter, there is mild tortilla soup. Spinach-and-artichoke dip makes a good starter. You can't go wrong with an overstuffed black-bean burrito or a juicy cheeseburger. The Green Hills Grille is popular both with businesspeople and families, so you can show up in either jeans or a suit.

2122 Hillsboro Dr. © 615/383-6444. www.greenhillsgrille.com. Reservations not accepted; call-ahead wait list. Main courses $8–$15. AE, DISC, MC, V. Sun–Thurs 10am–10pm; Fri–Sat 11am–11pm; Sat 10am–11pm.

La Paz Restaurante Cantina ⊛ MEXICAN/SOUTHWESTERN   From
the outside, this Green Hills Mexican restaurant is a surprisingly tasteful rendition of a Mexican or Southwestern villa. Inside, however, you'll find big dining
rooms and a bar that opens onto a deck, a concession to the Southern tradition
of the veranda. Rough-board floors and a partial-rock wall give the interior an
aged look that belies the restaurant's shopping-mall surroundings. The menu
features much more than the standard Mexican fare, and owes a lot to the modern cuisine of New Mexico. Santa Fe enchiladas, made from layered blue-corn
tortillas, broiled chicken, and cheese and baked with a green salsa, sour cream,
and avocado, are a good bet, as are the shrimp and pork-stuffed *poblano* chilies.
The restaurant also offers a private dining room.

3808 Cleghorn Ave. ⓒ **615/383-5200**. www.lapaz.com. Main courses $9–$13. AE, DC, DISC, MC, V.
Sun–Thurs 11am–10pm; Fri–Sat 11am–11pm.

INEXPENSIVE

Harper's ⊛⊛ *Finds* AMERICAN/SOUTHERN   If the thought of slow-simmered turnip greens, crispy fried chicken, tender sweet potatoes, and fluffy yeast
rolls makes your mouth water, wipe off your chin and immediately head to the
Jefferson Street district for Nashville's best soul food. Be sure to save room for a
slice of pie or a heaping bowl of banana pudding. Popular with white-collar professionals and blue-collar laborers alike, Harper's attracts a friendly, diverse clientele. Unlike seamier soul food haunts, this immaculate cafeteria accepts credit
cards but (thankfully) does not allow smoking.

2610 Jefferson St. ⓒ **615/329-1909**. Main courses $4–$7. AE, DISC, MC, V. Mon–Fri 10am–8pm; Sat–Sun
11am–6pm.

La Hacienda Taqueria ⊛ *Finds* MEXICAN   Although in a crummy neighborhood, sandwiched in a nondescript and easily missed spot, this is just about
the most authentic Mexican restaurant in Nashville (they even play Mexican
soap operas on the TV in the corner). It is incredibly popular with Nashvillians
starved for real Mexican food. The menu includes tasty little crisp tacos with a
long list of fillings, including *chorizo* and beef tongue. There are also fajitas with
chicken, beef, or shrimp. You can get Salvadoran *pupusas* (corn tortillas), and
just about everything comes with fresh house-made tortillas. Wash it all down
with a glass of *tamarindo*.

2615 Nolensville Rd. ⓒ **615/256-6142**. Main courses $5–$9. AE, DC, DISC, MC, V. Sun–Thurs 10am–9pm;
Fri–Sat 9am–10pm. Located next to a video store off the I-440 exit.

Rosepepper Cantina & Mexican Grill MEXICAN/SOUTHWESTERN
Fresh, Sonoran-style Mexican dishes fortified by homemade salsas and chunky
guacamole and tortilla chips are best bets at this festive hacienda in a working-
class neighborhood in southeastern Nashville. As compelling as the food is the
bar, which boasts more than 30 brands of tequila, and pours one of the tangiest
margaritas around.

1907 Eastland Ave. ⓒ **615/227-4777**. Main courses $6–$9. AE, DISC, MC, V. Mon–Thurs 11am–10pm;
Fri–at 11am–11pm; Sun 4–10pm.

Sylvan Park Murphy Road ⊛ AMERICAN   The Sylvan Park has been serving Nashville residents good old-fashioned Southern cooking for more than 50
years, and the restaurant's continuing popularity is demonstrated by the proliferation of Sylvan Park restaurants around the city. The "meat-and-three" concept is at the heart of the Sylvan Park experience—choose a meat serving such

as baked ham or fried chicken from the list of daily specials and add to it your choice of three vegetables. Vegetable choices might include turnip greens, lima beans, candied yams, and cranberry sauce. It's American food like Mom used to make. Don't forget a slice of homemade pie.

4502 Murphy Rd. © 615/292-9275. Main courses $6.25–$9. DISC, MC, V. Mon–Sat 10:30am–7:30pm.

5 Belle Meade & Environs

EXPENSIVE

Belle Meade Brasserie ⭐ NEW AMERICAN/NEW SOUTHERN This is the top restaurant in Belle Meade, the Nashville area's wealthiest community. Despite the decidedly residential and suburban feel of the surrounding neighborhoods, the Belle Meade Brasserie has managed to create a stylish urban sophistication. Pink tablecloths and black chairs set the tone, and changing art exhibits add plenty of color. You can dine in one of the intimate dining rooms, or, when the weather's good, out on the deck. The menu here roams the globe and brings it all back home to the South with such dishes as corn fritters with pepper jelly, a reworking of a couple of Southern classics that makes for an appetizer to wake up your mouth. While the menu changes every couple of months, you can expect to find the likes of double-thick Thai barbecue pork chops, a spicy tuna tower with roasted chili sauce, or a chicken roulade with spinach and sun-dried tomatoes. There are always several pasta dishes as well. To accompany your meal, you can choose from one of the finest wine lists in the city. Between 5pm and 7pm, you can get economical three-course, sun-downer dinners. You'll find the Brasserie just off Harding Road at the start of Harding Place (behind the Exxon station).

106 Harding Place. © 615/356-5450. Reservations recommended Fri and Sat. Main courses $16–$31. AE, DC, MC, V. Mon–Thurs 5–10pm; Fri–Sat 5–11pm.

MODERATE

Benkay Japanese Restaurant ⭐ JAPANESE Located in the Lion's Head Village shopping center, north of Harding Road near Belle Meade, Benkay is a casual and popular place. Though small, it manages to have a couple of *tatami* rooms, and, of course, a sushi bar. Plenty of natural wood throughout the restaurant sets an authentic Japanese flavor that is carried onto the menu. Appetizers include plenty of types of sushi and sashimi, as well as a variety of Japanese pickles. The bento lunch box is a good deal, as are the udon and soba noodle dishes. However, the restaurant is best known for its sushi, especially the creative house rolls. Among these, you'll find one made with fried soft-shell crab (the spider roll) and one made with smoked salmon and cream cheese (the bagel roll).

Lion's Head Village, 40 White Bridge Rd. © 615/356-6600. Reservations only for *tatami* rooms. Main courses $7–$15. DISC, MC, V. Mon–Thurs 5–10pm; Fri–Sat 5–10:30pm; (to-go orders-only hours are from Mon–Sat 2–5pm).

Goldie's Deli ⭐⭐ *Finds* *Kids* DELICATESSEN "Come to Goldie's, it's so fun. The Kosher food is Number 1!" Or so goes the motto of this often-overlooked gold mine. Tucked within a suburban shopping center, the deli draws regulars who lap up everything from chicken livers and latkes to knee-weakening chicken-noodle soup with matzo balls. New York-sized sandwiches come on a choice of pumpernickel or challah. Meats such as corned beef and pastrami, as well as chicken, tuna, and whitefish salads, are also sold by the pound. Though cramped and often crowded, a visit to this neighborhood deli is worth the trip.

It's kid-friendly, too: A smiley-faced hot dog (or peanut butter and jelly sandwich), chips, and fountain drink will please even the pickiest children.

4520 Harding Rd. ℂ **615/292-3589**. Main courses $3.57–$8.75. AE, MC, V. Sun–Thurs 7am–8pm; Fri–Sat 7am–9pm.

Martha's at the Plantation ★★★ NEW SOUTHERN   Fried green tomatoes with horseradish sauce, salmon and artichoke quiche, and herbed chicken-breast salad are indicative of the lunch menu at this delightful restaurant on the grounds of Belle Meade Plantation. The second-floor room is bright and airy; fresh flowers adorn the cloth-covered tables, and lots of windows frame the leafy treetops outside. Regional favorites include buttermilk-battered fried chicken with milk gravy, baked cheese grits, and savory cheddar olive spread. A summer favorite is the fresh fruit platter with pink poppyseed dressing and cheese straws. Wash it down with a crisp sauvignon blanc or tea-flavored punch. And save room for either sugar cookies with minty lemon sorbet, or the wicked fudge pie with vanilla-bean ice cream.

5025 Harding Rd. ℂ **615/353-2828**. www.bellemeadeplantation.com. Main courses $7–$10. AE, DISC, MC, V. Daily 11am–2pm.

The Orchid ★ THAI   You'll find this upscale Thai restaurant in a newer shopping plaza across White Bridge Road from the sprawling Lion's Head Village shopping center. You'll know you're in the right spot when you step out of your car and catch a whiff of the air, often redolent with exotic spices. Follow your nose into The Orchid and you'll have found the source of those tantalizing aromas. More elegant than its suburban strip-mall environs would suggest, The Orchid is a casually comfortable place to sample some authentic curry or pad thai, a Thai noodle dish. Order something with lots of garlic and you're sure to leave contented.

73 White Bridge Rd. ℂ **615/353-9411**. Reservations recommended on weekends. Main courses $6–$17. AE, DC, DISC, MC, V. Mon–Fri 11am–3pm; Mon–Sat 4–9:30pm; Sun 4–9pm.

INEXPENSIVE

Loveless Café ★★ *Moments* SOUTHERN   For some of the best country cooking in the Nashville area, take a trip out past the city's western suburbs to this old-fashioned roadhouse and popular Nashville institution. People rave about the cooking here—and with good reason. The country ham with red-eye gravy, Southern fried chicken, and homemade biscuits with homemade fruit jams are made just the way Granny used to make them back when the Loveless opened nearly 40 years ago. This restaurant may be a little out of the way, but it's well worth it if you like down-home cookin'—and if you're prepared to endure a long wait to get one of the few available tables inside.

8400 Tenn. 100, about 7½ miles (12km) south of Belle Meade and the turnoff from U.S. 70 S. ℂ **615/646-9700**. www.lovelesscafe.com. Reservations recommended. Breakfast $5.50–$9; dinner main courses $11–$21. AE, MC, V. Mon–Thurs 8am–8pm; Fri–Sun 8am–9pm.

6 Music Valley & the Airport Area

In addition to the restaurants listed here, you'll find several good, though somewhat overpriced, restaurants in the Opryland Hotel. For the most part, these restaurants serve steaks and Southern fare, though Cascades offers prime seafood, and the Italian-themed Ristorante Volare goes New American for its lavish brunch buffet on Sundays.

Opry Mills also boasts a plethora of eateries—from food-court buffet lines to sit-down chain restaurants—that provide a nice diversion if you're in the Music Valley area and crave something beyond barbecue or catfish.

MODERATE

Rainforest Café *(Kids* AMERICAN/CARIBBEAN   Lush waterfalls, live birds, and brilliantly colored fish in floor-to-ceiling aquariums provide a feast for the senses at this popular theme restaurant. Indulge in huge platters of oversized burgers, fish sandwiches, and rich entrees such as the creamy alfredo-based pasta, with pesto and chicken chunks. Then save room for the flaming chocolate volcano dessert, which is sure to turn heads when the safari-clad wait staff parades it to your table.

353 Opry Mills Dr. ✆ **615/514-3000.** www.rainforestcafe.com. Reservations recommended. Main courses $10–$30. AE, DC, DISC, MC, V. Mon–Thurs 11am–9:30pm; Fri–Sat 10:30am–10:30pm; Sun 10:30am–8:30pm.

INEXPENSIVE

Cock of the Walk ✦ SOUTHERN   This big, barnlike restaurant near the Opryland Hotel is well known around Nashville for having the best catfish in town. The restaurant critic Craig Claiborne even agreed when he ate here. Start your meal with that most bizarre of Southern appetizers, the fried dill pickle, then move on to the fried catfish filets with a pot o' greens. The restaurant takes its name from an old flatboatman's term for the top boatman.

2624 Music Valley Dr. ✆ **615/889-1930.** www.cockofthewalkrestaurant.com. Reservations accepted for groups of 20 or more. Main courses $9–$12. AE, DISC, MC, V. Mon–Thurs 5–9pm; Fri–Sat 5–10pm; Sun 11am–9pm.

Uncle Bud's Catfish ✦ *(Kids* SOUTHERN   Uncle Bud's, a Southern-themed family restaurant, has a country-kitchen atmosphere, with old farm tools and a covered wooden porch out front. Inside, red-and-white checked curtains and tablecloths, rough-hewn wood paneling, fishnets, and old signs on the walls set the down-home tone. Succulent fried catfish, served with crunchy hush puppies, is the main attraction here, and the all-you-can-eat dinner is the most popular option. They'll just keep bringing out all the catfish or fried chicken you can eat, along with as much as you want of the additional fixin's. The staff is friendly, and surroundings are informal and un-fussy. It's a loud, rowdy, family place where kids can be kids without drawing the ire of fellow diners. More adventurous diners can try the gator tail or frogs' legs. There's another convenient Uncle Bud's at 356 White Bridge Rd. (✆ **615/353-0016**).

714 Stewart's Ferry Pike. ✆ **615/872-7700.** Main courses $6–$15. AE, DC, DISC, MC, V. Sun–Thurs 10:45am–9pm; Fri–Sat 10:45am–10pm.

7 Barbecue

INEXPENSIVE

Bar-B-Cutie ✦ BARBECUE   If you're out by the airport and have an intense craving for barbecue, head to Bar-B-Cutie. Just watch for the sign with the barb-doll cowgirl in short shorts. Bar-B-Cutie has been in business since 1948 and, while there is mesquite-grilled chicken available, you'd be remiss if you didn't order the pork shoulder or baby-back ribs. There's another Bar-B-Cutie at 5221 Nolensville Rd. (✆ **615/834-6556**), on the south side of town.

501 Donelson Pike. ✆ **888/WE-BARBQ** or 615/872-0207. www.bar-b-cutie.com. Full meals $5–$10. AE, DC, MC, V. Sun–Thurs 10am–9pm; Fri–Sat 10am–10pm.

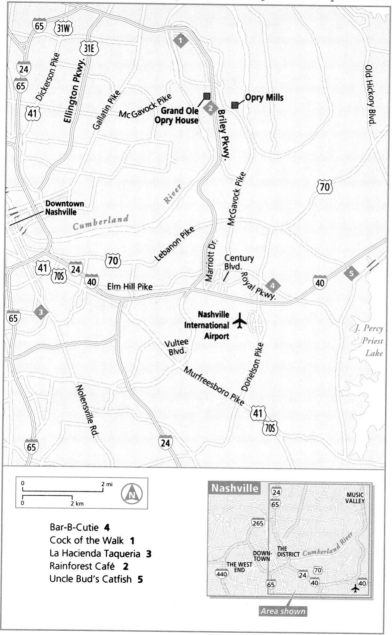

Bar-B-Cutie **4**
Cock of the Walk **1**
La Hacienda Taqueria **3**
Rainforest Café **2**
Uncle Bud's Catfish **5**

Corky's Bar-B-Q ★★ BARBECUE   While it seems logical that Nashville ought to have its own style of barbecue, the barbecue they make in Memphis seems so much better. That's why Corky's, a Memphis institution, serves its patented slow-smoked pulled pork, ribs, brisket, and chicken. Though this is a casual place, it's still Nashville's most upscale barbecue joint, serving both professionals with cellphones and day laborers in denim. Barbecued pork or beef sandwiches or dinners, which come with beans, coleslaw, and bread, are the primary attractions here.

100 Franklin Rd., Brentwood. ℂ 615/373-1020. www.corkysbbq.com. Main courses $9–$19. AE, DC, DISC, MC, V. Sun–Thurs 11am–9:30pm; Fri–Sat 11am–10:30pm.

Jack's Bar-B-Que ★ BARBECUE   When the barbecue urge strikes in The District, don't settle for cheap imitations; head to Jack's, where you can get pork shoulder, Texas beef brisket, St. Louis ribs, and smoked turkey, sausage, and chicken. There's another Jack's at 334 W. Trinity Lane (ℂ **615/228-9888**), in north Nashville.

416 Broadway. ℂ 615/254-5715. www.jacksbarbque.com. Main courses $3–$9.50. AE, DISC, MC, V. Summer Mon–Sat 10:30am–10pm; Winter Mon–Wed 10:30am–3pm; Thurs–Sat 10:30am–10pm. Open Sundays only for Tennessee Titans' home games.

Whitt's Barbecue ★ BARBECUE   Walk in, drive up, or get it delivered. Whitt's serves some of the best barbecue in Nashville. There's no seating here, so take it back to your hotel or plan a picnic. You can buy barbecued pork, beef, and even turkey by the pound, or order sandwiches and plates with the extra fixin's. The pork barbecue sandwiches, topped with zesty coleslaw, get my vote for best in town. Among the many other locations are those at 2535 Lebanon Rd. (ℂ **615/883-6907**), and 114 Old Hickory Blvd. E. (ℂ **615/868-1369**).

5310 Harding Rd. ℂ 615/356-3435. Meals $2.10–$6; barbecue $4.25–$6.30 per pound. AE, DC, DISC, MC, V. Mon–Sat 10:30am–8pm.

8 Cafes, Bakeries & Pastry Shops

When you just need a quick pick-me-up, a rich pastry, or some good rustic bread for a picnic, there are several good cafes, coffeehouses, and bakeries scattered around the city.

In hip Hillsboro Village, you'll find **Fido,** 1812 21st Ave. S. (ℂ **615/385-7959**), a big place with an artsy, urban feel. No, it's not one of those upscale dog bakeries. Though the space used to be a pet shop, it is the friendliest coffeehouse in Nashville. Across the street, you'll find **Provence Breads & Café** ★, 1705 21st Ave. S. (ℂ **615/386-0363;** www.provencebreads.com), which bakes the best breads and pastries in town and also serves sandwiches and salads. Provence also has a stylish bistro in the new downtown library, 601 Church St. (ℂ **615/644-1150**).

Becker's Bakery, 2600 12th Ave. S. (ℂ **615/383-5554**), a rather run-down storefront, has a propitious perch at the edge of the newly burgeoning 12th Ave. South neighborhood. A third-generation business dating back to the 1920s, the bakery covers the basics: pies, muffins, snickerdoodle cookies, and sugar-dusted cream horns. White, buttercream-frosted cakes line the old-fashioned display cases. Fresh biscuits and yeast rolls are sold by the sack.

Bongo Java, 2007 Belmont Blvd. (ℂ **615/385-JAVA;** www.bongojava.com), located just a couple of blocks from Belmont Mansion, caters primarily to Belmont University students and is located in an old house on a tree-lined street. It has good collegiate atmosphere, but parking during peak hours can pose a challenge.

In the downtown area, **Cibo,** 706 Church St. (🕿 **615/726-2426**), is a cozy European cafe renowned for its pastries and baked goods as well as salads, sandwiches, and take-home entrees such as manicotti and chocolate cake. Arrive early in the day if you want your pick of croissants and other goodies.

Over on the east side of the Cumberland River from downtown, you'll find the **Radio Cafe,** 1313 Woodland St. (🕿 **615/228-6045**), which has live music several nights a week but charges outrageous prices for espresso drinks.

In the Green Hills neighborhood, look for **Bread & Company,** 4105 Hillsboro Rd. (🕿 **615/29-BREAD**), an upscale bakery that specializes in European breads and pastries. They have wonderful focaccia, bagels, and breads that they can make up into sandwiches.

Out in the bucolic Sylvan Park neighborhood lies my favorite Nashville cafe: **Red Rooster,** 4501 Murphy Rd. (🕿 **615/279-8010**). Cheery yellow walls, the aroma of coffee (there's also an espresso bar), and NPR on the radio make it as inviting as your own kitchen. Their full breakfast menu, including specialties such as pancakes and Italian frittatas, are served all day. Thin-crust pizzas draw locals for lunch and early dinner.

6

Exploring Nashville

Nashville, Music City USA, the Country Music Capital of the World. There's no doubt why people visit Nashville. But you may be surprised to find that there's more to see and do here than just chase country stars. Sure, you can attend the *Grand Ole Opry,* linger over displays at the **Country Music Hall of Fame,** take a tour past the homes of the country legends, and hear the stars of the future at any number of clubs. However, the state capital of Tennessee also has plenty of museums and other attractions that have nothing to do with country music. Among the city's most enriching cultural attractions are the **Van Vechten Art Gallery at Fisk University,** the impressive **Frist Center for the Visual Arts,** and **Cheekwood Botanical Gardens**—not to mention Nashville's full-size reproduction of the **Parthenon.** So even if you've never heard of Marty Stuart or Martina McBride, you'll find something to keep you busy while you're in town. However, if you own every album ever released by George Jones or The Judds, you'll be in hog heaven on a visit to Nashville.

SUGGESTED ITINERARIES

If You Have 1 Day

Start your day downtown at the acclaimed new Country Music Hall of Fame and Museum. From here, walk a few blocks to tour the **Ryman Auditorium,** which for more than 30 years was the home of the *Grand Ole Opry.* Even if you're only marginally interested in American music, you'll want to spend some time here absorbing the aura of these hallowed halls. Any time of day, you can also stop in at **Tootsie's Orchid Lounge,** around the corner from the Ryman Auditorium, and hear a bit of live country music. While you're downtown, you might as well drop by the **Wildhorse Saloon,** Nashville's hottest country dance hall. In the evening, check to see which up-and-coming singer-songwriters will be performing at the Bluebird Café, which, oddly enough, is located in the suburbs a short drive from downtown.

If You Have 2 Days

On your second day, view world-class touring exhibitions and explore the interactive arts education programs at the Frist Center for the Visual Arts. For a simpler but no less sublime art history lesson, visit the historic campus of Fisk University, where you can admire more than 100 masterpieces by such artists as **Picasso, Renoir, Toulouse-Lautrec,** and **Georgia O'Keeffe** at the Van Vechten Art Gallery.

From here, head out to the Music Valley area and wander the tropical gardens of the **Opryland Hotel.** If it's a Friday or Saturday, by all means finish your day by catching a performance of the *Grand Ole Opry.* This is the definitive Nashville experience.

If You Have 3 Days

On your third day, it's time to learn a bit more about Nashville history.

If you have an interest in art, old mansions, or botanical gardens, you'll find more than enough to fill your day. Start out on the east side of town at the **Hermitage, the former home of President Andrew Jackson.** Next, head into the city to the Parthenon, then take a tour of **Belmont Mansion,** Cheekwood Botanical Gardens and Museum, or **Belle Meade Plantation.** In the evening, hop from bar to bar on lower Broadway, or scoot a boot at the **Wildhorse Saloon.**

If You Have 4 Days or More

If you have more time, and if you're a history buff, head south to **Franklin,** a charmingly restored small town full of antiques malls and historic homes. You could also spend the better part of a day visiting Lynchburg, Tennessee, home of the **Jack Daniel's Distillery.** If you have the kids along, visit **Nashville's zoo** or the **Adventure Science Center.** You might also find one or more of the city's small specialty museums of interest.

1 On the Music Trail

For information on the *Grand Ole Opry* and other country music performance halls, theaters, and clubs, see chapter 8, "Nashville After Dark." For information on country music gift shops, see chapter 7, "Shopping in Nashville." If you want to drive by some homes of the country stars, pick up a copy of the "Homes of the Stars" map, sold at the **Ernest Tubb Record Shop,** 417 Broadway (© **615/255-7503**), and other country music souvenir shops around town. At the **Visitors Center** in the **Gaylord Entertainment Center,** you can also get a booklet with more information on the homes of the stars. With celebrity books all the rage these days, it's not surprising that **Davis-Kidd Booksellers,** 4007 Hillsboro Rd. (© **615/385-2645**), brings in country music stars for book signings several times a year. Call them for a schedule.

Country Music Hall of Fame and Museum ★★

If you're a fan of country music, this is *the* museum in Nashville. Even if you aren't, almost anyone with an appreciation for American popular music will thrill to such sights as Bob Dylan's barely legible inscription scrawled across a lyric sheet; Emmylou Harris' petite, bejeweled cowboy boots; and Elvis' gold-leafed Cadillac (a gift from Priscilla). Savvy multimedia exhibits let visitors explore displays on bluegrass, cowboy music (a la Roy Rogers), country swing, rockabilly, Cajun, honky-tonk, and contemporary country music through personalized CD listening posts, interactive jukeboxes, and computer stations. The *Grand Ole Opry* gets its due with a mind-boggling array of memorabilia, enhanced by vintage *Opry* recordings. And, as if all of this wasn't more than a visitor could stand, the museum also showcases such down-home *objects d'art* as Naomi Judd's rusted wringer-and-tub-style washing machine, and the kitschy cornfield from TV's *Hee Haw*—complete with Junior Samples' denim overalls and Lulu Roman's plus-size gingham dress.

Even if you've visited the museum before, there's always a reason to return for special exhibitions and events. Looking ahead, *Night Train to Nashville: Music City Rhythm & Blues 1945–1970* will examine the connections between country music and rhythm-and-blues with archival video footage and previously unpublished photographs. The exhibition opened in March 2004 and runs through December 2005. Meanwhile, lucky visitors at any time of year might catch a glimpse of a country great: Nashville resident Vince Gill is said to be a regular

Nashville Attractions: Downtown & Music Row

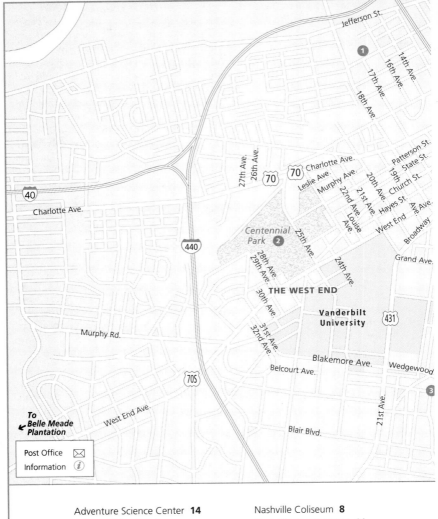

Adventure Science Center **14**
Belmont Mansion **3**
Bicentennial Capitol Mall State Park **4**
Country Music Hall of Fame and Museum **13**
Fort Nashborough **7**
The Frist Center for the Visual Arts **12**
Gaylord Entertainment Center **10**

Nashville Coliseum **8**
Nashville Toy Museum **11**
The Parthenon **2**
Ryman Auditorium & Museum **9**
Tennessee State Capitol **5**
The Tennessee State Museum **6**
Van Vechten Gallery **1**

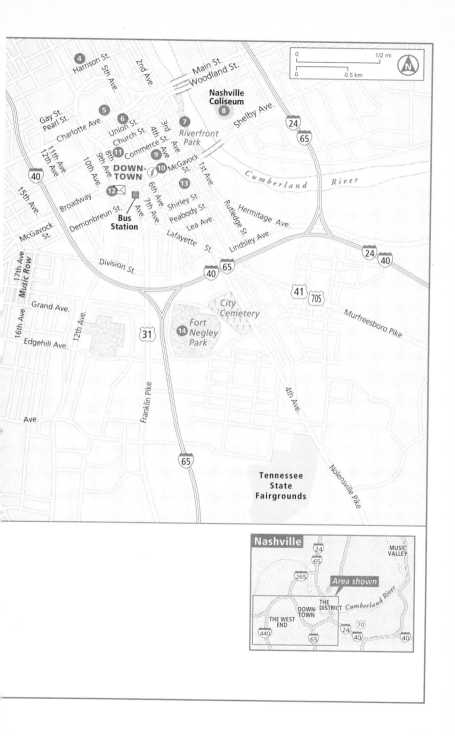

> ### Fun Fact Symbolism in the Architecture of the Country Music Hall of Fame & Museum
>
> | Architecture | Symbol |
> | --- | --- |
> | Dark windows | Piano keys |
> | Upward arch of roof | Fin of a 1950s Cadillac |
> | Spire | Country's WSM radio tower |
> | Tiered rotunda | Vinyl 78s, 45s, and CDs |
> | From overhead | Museum resembles a bass clef |

here, and legends such as Merle Haggard have been known to drop by for impromptu concerts.

If you want to arrange a visit to the old RCA recording studio, where Elvis laid down a few hits, you'll need to sign up here at the Hall of Fame. The studio itself is located in Music Row area of Nashville. Allow 2 to 3 hours.

222 5th Ave. S. (at Demonbreun) ℂ 800/852-6437 or 615/416-2001. www.countrymusichalloffame.com. Admission $16 adults, $7.95 children 6–15. Daily 10am–6pm.

Grand Ole Opry Museum ✭   Adjacent to the Grand Ole Opry House, these exhibits are tributes to the performers who have appeared on the famous radio show over the years: Patsy Cline, Hank Snow, George Jones, Jim Reeves, Marty Robbins, and other longtime stars of the show. There are also about a dozen other exhibits on more recent performers. These museums are best visited in conjunction with a night at the *Opry*, so you might want to arrive early. Allow 20 to 30 minutes (just right for browsing prior to attending a performance of the *Grand Ole Opry*).

2804 Opryland Dr. ℂ 615/871-OPRY (6779). www.gaylordopryland.com. Free admission. Daily 10am to varied closing hours depending on performance schedule. Closes for special events; call ahead. At the Grand Ole Opry House (it's within the same complex).

Music Valley Wax Museum *Overrated*   If you haven't spotted any country stars in Nashville yet, this wax museum offers the next best thing. Here you'll find wax figures of more than 50 famous stars, most of which are wearing original stage costumes. Out in front of the museum, more than 200 stars have left their footprints, handprints, and signatures in concrete. Allow 20 to 30 minutes.

2515 McGavock Pike. ℂ 615/883-3612. Admission $3.50 adults, $3 seniors, $1.50 children 6–12, free for children under 6. Memorial Day to Labor Day daily 9am–9pm; Labor Day to Memorial Day daily 9am–5pm (closing time sometimes varies). Closed Thanksgiving, Dec 25, and Jan 1. Take McGavock Parkway to Music Valley Dr.

Opryland Hotel ✭ *Moments*   Hotels aren't usually tourist attractions, but this one is an exception. With 2,883 rooms, the place is beyond big, but what makes it worth a visit are the three massive atria that form the hotel's three main courtyards. Together these atria are covered by more than 8 acres of glass to form vast greenhouses full of tropical plants. There are rushing streams, roaring waterfalls, bridges, pathways, ponds, and fountains. There are also plenty of places to stop for a drink or a meal. In the evenings, live music and a laser light show can be seen in the Cascades Atrium.

The largest of the three atriums here is the Delta, which covers 4½ acres and has a quarter-mile-long "river," a 110-foot-wide waterfall, an 85-foot-tall fountain, and an island modeled after the French Quarter in New Orleans. On this

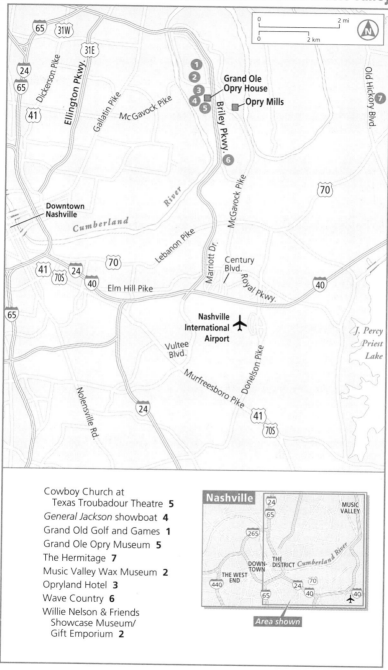

Cowboy Church at
  Texas Troubadour Theatre **5**
General Jackson showboat **4**
Grand Old Golf and Games **1**
Grand Ole Opry Museum **5**
The Hermitage **7**
Music Valley Wax Museum **2**
Opryland Hotel **3**
Wave Country **6**
Willie Nelson & Friends
  Showcase Museum/
  Gift Emporium **2**

Traveling to & Around Music Valley

To reach Music Valley from downtown, take bus no. 6 (Donelson/Opryland). A cab ride from downtown to the Opryland Hotel costs about 20 bucks. A trolley serves Music Valley attractions, but a car is really the best way to get around.

island are numerous shops and restaurants, which give the hotel the air of an elaborate shopping mall. You can take boat rides on the river and, at night, catch live music in a nightclub on the island. Allow 20 to 30 minutes.

2800 Opryland Dr. ⒸⒻ 615/889-1000. www.gaylordopryland.com. Free admission. Daily 24 hours. Parking $7; valet and overnight parking, $16). Take Interstate 40 to Exit 215 and take Briley Parkway (155 North) to Exit 12. Turn left at the second traffic light into the Gaylord Opryland complex.

Willie Nelson & Friends Showcase Museum/Gift Emporium *Overrated*
Less a museum than a souvenir shop with a few exhibits in a back room, this tourist site features some of Willie's guitars, gold and platinum records, and even his pool table. The museum is inside the Music Valley Gift Emporium. Allow 20 to 30 minutes if you're shopping for souvenirs.

2613A McGavock Pike. ⒸⒻ 615/885-1515. Admission $3.50 adults, $3 seniors, $1.50 children 6–12, free for children under 6. Memorial Day to Labor Day daily 9am–9pm; Labor Day to Memorial Day daily 9am–7pm (closing hours sometimes vary). Closed Thanksgiving, Dec 25, and Jan 1. Take McGavock Parkway to Music Valley Dr.; next door to the wax museum.

IN THE DISTRICT

All downtown attractions are accessible from the Downtown trolley.

Ryman Auditorium & Museum ★★   If you're as enamored with music history as I am, you could devote several hours to a self-guided tour of this National Historic Landmark where you're free to stand onstage—even belt out a few bars if the spirit moves you—or sit in the hardwood "pews," and wander the halls upstairs and down, looking at memorabilia in glass showcases. However, the typical tourist may be satisfied with a quick walk through the stately redbrick building. In either case, the best way to experience the Ryman is to attend a performance here.

The site of the *Grand Ole Opry* from 1943 to 1974, the Ryman Auditorium is known as the "Mother Church of Country Music," the single most historic site in the world of country music. Originally built in 1892 as the Union Gospel Tabernacle by riverboat captain Tom Ryman, this building served as an evangelical hall for many years. By the early 1900s, the building's name had been changed to honor its builder and a stage had been added. That stage, over the years, saw the likes of Enrico Caruso, Katharine Hepburn, Will Rogers, and Elvis Presley. The *Grand Ole Opry* began broadcasting from here in 1943. For the next 31 years, the Ryman Auditorium was host to the most famous country music radio show in the world. However, in 1974, the *Opry* moved to the then-new Grand Ole Opry House in the Music Valley area. Since its meticulous renovation in 1994, the Ryman has regained its prominence as a temple of bluegrass and country music. Its peerless acoustics make it a favored venue of rock's best singer-songwriters and classical musicians, as well. Allow at least an hour for a self-guided tour.

116 5th Ave. N. (between Commerce and Broadway) ⒸⒻ 615/254-1445 or 615/889-3060. www.ryman.com. Admission $8 adults, $4 children 4–11, free for children under 4. Daily 9am–4pm. Closed Thanksgiving, Dec 25, and Jan 1.

2 More Attractions

HISTORIC BUILDINGS

Belle Meade Plantation ★★ Belle Meade was built in 1853 after this plantation had become famous as a stud farm that produced some of the best racehorses in the South. Today, the Greek Revival mansion is the centerpiece of the affluent Belle Meade region of Nashville and is surrounded by 30 acres of manicured lawns and shade trees. A long driveway leads uphill to the mansion, which is fronted by six columns and a wide veranda. Inside, the restored building has been furnished with 19th-century antiques that hint at the elegance and wealth that the Southern gentility enjoyed in the late 1800s.

Tours led by costumed guides follow a theme that changes every 3 months (i.e. holidays, aspects of plantation life, etc.). These themed tours provide fascinating glimpses into the lives of the people who once lived at Belle Meade. Also on the grounds are a large carriage house and stable that were built in 1890 and that now house a large collection of antique carriages. During your visit, you can also have a look inside a log cabin, a smokehouse, and a creamery that are here on the grounds. Belle Meade's parklike grounds make it a popular site for festivals throughout the year.

In addition, Martha's at the Plantation (© **615/353-2828**), a simple yet stylish restaurant above the gift shop, is drawing raves for chef Martha Stamp's American/Southern dishes such as chicken salad, crawfish, quiches, and caramel cakes. A best-selling cookbook author, Stamp has also been featured in *Southern Living* and *Victorian* magazines, as well as on the TV show *Martha Stewart Living*. Sunday brunch is among the locals' favorites at Martha's at the Plantation, open daily 11am to 2pm. Allow a full morning or afternoon to soak up everything here.

5025 Harding Rd. © **800/270-3991** or 615/356-0501. www.bellemeadeplantation.com. Admission $10 adults, $8.50 seniors, $4 children 6–12, free for children under 6. Mon–Sat 9am–5pm; Sun 11am–5pm. Closed Thanksgiving, Dec 25, and Jan 1. Take 70 South to Belle Meade Blvd., to Deer Park Dr. and follow the signs.

Belmont Mansion ★ Built in the 1850s by Adelicia Acklen, then one of the wealthiest women in the country (see appendix B, "Nashville in Depth"), this Italianate villa is the city's most elegant historic home open to the public, and its grand salon is one of the most elaborately decorated rooms in any antebellum home in Tennessee. Belmont Mansion was originally built as a summer home, yet no expense was spared in its construction. On your tour of the mansion, you'll see rooms filled with period antiques, artwork, and marble statues. This museum also has an excellent gift shop full of reproduction period pieces. Allow at least 90 minutes to tour the mansion.

1900 Belmont Blvd. © **615/460-5459**. www.belmontmansion.com. Admission $7 adults, $3 children 6–12, free for children under 6. June–Aug Mon–Sat 10am–4pm, Sun 1–4pm; Sept–May Tues–Sat 10am–4pm. Take Wedgewood Ave. off 21st Ave. S. (an extension of Broadway), turn right on Magnolia Ave., left on 18th Ave. S., then left on Acklen.

(*Fun Fact* **Make Mine a Shower**

Portly President Howard Taft once got stuck in a bathtub at Belle Meade Plantation while visiting Nashville. The subsequent installation of a shower at Belle Meade prompted Taft to have a shower installed at the White House.

Tip

Shutterbugs, take note: Unlike many museums and historic mansions, photography *is* permitted inside the Belmont Mansion. So stock up on film or digital-camera cartridges, and click away!

Fort Nashborough   Though it's much smaller than the original, this reconstruction of Nashville's first settlement includes several buildings that faithfully reproduce what life in this frontier outpost was like in the late 18th century. The current fort looks oddly out of place in modern downtown Nashville, but if you're interested in Tennessee's early settlers, this site is worth a brief look. Allow 30 minutes or more if you've got kids who want to play here.

170 1st Ave. N. (between Church and Commerce) No phone. Free admission. Daily 9am–5pm. On the edge of Riverfront Park. on the banks of the Cumberland River.

The Hermitage ⭐   Though you may not know it, you probably see an image of one of Nashville's most famous citizens dozens of times every week. Whose face pops up so frequently? It's Andrew Jackson, whose visage graces the $20 bill, and who is the man who built the Hermitage, a stately Southern plantation home. Jackson moved to Tennessee in 1788 and became a prosecuting attorney. He served as the state's first congressman and later as a senator and judge. However, it was during the War of 1812 that he gained his greatest public acclaim as the general who led American troops in the Battle of New Orleans. His role in that battle helped Jackson win the presidency in 1828 and again in 1832.

Though the Hermitage now displays a classic Greek Revival facade, this is its third incarnation. Originally built in the Federal style in 1821, it was expanded and remodeled in 1831, and acquired its current appearance in 1836. Recordings that describe each room and section of the grounds accompany tours through the mansion and around it. In addition to the main house, you'll also visit the kitchen, the smokehouse, the garden, Jackson's tomb, an original log cabin, the spring house (a cool storage house built over a spring), and, nearby, the Old Hermitage Church and Tulip Grove mansion. You can tour the museum and grounds in a few hours.

Old Hickory Blvd., Nashville. ✆ 615/889-2941. www.thehermitage.com. Admission $12 adults, $11 seniors, $5 children 6–12, free for children under 6. Daily 9am–5pm. Closed Thanksgiving, Dec 25, Jan. 1, and 3rd week of Jan. Take I-40 east to exit 221, then head north 4 miles (6.5km).

Historic Manskers Station Frontier Life Center   Tennessee's earliest pioneer history comes to life here in a reconstruction of a fort built in 1779 by Kasper Mansker and settlers whom he had led to this spot. Today, costumed interpreters who demonstrate the skills and activities of those 18th-century settlers people the fort. Cooking fires send smoke curling from the chimneys of log cabins while weavers spin wool into yarn and woodworkers build rough-hewn furniture. Throughout the year, living-history camps are held on various weekends. During these camps, costumed camp participants live in the style of the pioneers for a few days. In addition to the fort, Historic Manskers Station also includes the Bowen Plantation house. Built between 1785 and 1787, this is the oldest brick house in middle Tennessee and is furnished with 18th-century antiques. Allow 1 hour.

Moss-Wright Park, 705 Caldwell Dr., Goodlettsville. ℭ **615/859-FORT (3678)**. Admission $5 adults, $4 for seniors, $3 for students. Tue–Sat 9am–4pm; Sun 1–5pm. Closed Jan–Feb. Take I-65 north to Exit 97, go east on Long Hollow Pike and watch for signs.

The Parthenon   Centennial Park, as the name implies, was built for the Tennessee Centennial Exposition of 1897, and this full-size replica of the Athens Parthenon was the exposition's centerpiece. The original structure was only meant to be temporary, however, and by 1921 the building, which had become a Nashville landmark, was in an advanced state of deterioration. In that year, the city undertook reconstruction of its Parthenon and by 1931 a new, permanent building stood in Centennial Park. The building now duplicates the floor plan of the original Parthenon in Greece. Inside stands the 42-foot-tall statue of Athena Parthenos, the goddess of wisdom, prudent warfare, and the arts. Newly gilded with eight pounds of gold leaf, she is the tallest indoor sculpture in the country.

In addition to this impressive statue, there are original plaster castings of the famous Elgin marbles—bas-reliefs that once decorated the pediment of the Parthenon. Down in the basement galleries of the Parthenon, you'll find an excellent collection of 19th- and 20th-century American art. The Parthenon's two pairs of bronze doors, which weigh in at 7½ tons per door, are considered the largest matching bronze doors in the world. A recent renovation of the building included air conditioning, which should make for pleasant viewing on muggy summer days. Allow about 30 minutes.

Centennial Park, West End Ave. (at West End and 25th aves.). ℭ **615/862-8431**. www.parthenon.org. Admission $3.50 adults, $2 seniors and children. Oct–Mar Tues–Sat 9am–4:30pm; Apr–Sept Tues–Sat 9am–4:30pm, Sun 12:30–4:30pm. Bus: No. 3 (West End).

Tennessee State Capitol   The Tennessee State Capitol, completed in 1859, is a classically proportioned Greek Revival building that sits on a hill on the north side of downtown Nashville. The capitol is constructed of local Tennessee limestone and marble that slaves and convict laborers quarried and cut. Other notable features include the 19th-century style and furnishings of several rooms in the building, a handful of ceiling frescoes, and many ornate details. President and Mrs. James K. Polk are both buried on the capitol's east lawn. You can pick up a guide to the capitol at the Tennessee State Museum. It won't take long to admire it from the outside.

❨Value Everybody Loves a Bargain

The Nashville Visitors Center has made it fun and easy to get the most out of a trip to Music City. The **Pick 3** and **Take 2** programs work like this: Buy a Pick 3 ticket for $25 plus tax and choose one adult or child admission to any three of 13 participating attractions, including the Frist Center for the Visual Arts and Belle Meade Plantation. Turn in one ticket stub at each of the three attractions you visit for another free adult or child admission. For $45 plus tax, the Take 2 ticket is good for one adult or child admission at any of the 9 higher-end participating venues, including the *Grand Ole Opry* and Gray Line's "Homes of the Stars" Sightseeing Tour. Turn in your ticket stubs for another free adult or child admission. Buy both the Pick 3 and Take 2 for $70—a $108 value! For more information, call ℭ **800/657-6910** or 615/259-4700.

Charlotte Ave. (between 6th and 7th Aves.). © 615/741-2692. Free admission. Mon–Fri 9am–4pm. Closed all state holidays.

Travellers Rest Historic House Museum   Built in 1799, Travellers Rest, as its name implies, once offered gracious Southern hospitality to travelers passing through a land that had only recently been settled. Judge John Overton (who, along with Andrew Jackson and Gen. James Winchester, founded the city of Memphis) built Travellers Rest. Overton also served as a political advisor to Jackson when he ran for president. Among the period furnishings you'll see in this restored Federal-style farmhouse is the state's largest public collection of pre-1840 Tennessee-made furniture. Allow an hour to tour the museum, and more if you want to wander the grounds and outbuildings.

636 Farrell Pkwy. © 615/832-8197. www.travellersrestplantation.org. Admission $8 adults, $7 seniors, $3 children 6–12, free for children under 6. Tues–Sat 10am–5pm; Sun 1–5pm. Closed Thanksgiving, Dec 25, and Jan 1. Take I-65 to exit 78B (Harding Place West), go west to Franklin Pike, turn left, and then follow the signs.

MUSEUMS

Cheekwood Botanical Garden & Museum of Art ★★ *Kids*   Once a private estate, Cheekwood today has much to offer both art lovers and garden enthusiasts. The museum and gardens are situated in a 55-acre park that's divided into several formal gardens and naturally landscaped areas. The museum itself is housed in the original Cheek family mansion, which was built in the Georgian style with many architectural details brought over from Europe. Among the mansion's most outstanding features is a lapis lazuli fireplace mantel. Within the building are collections of 19th- and 20th-century American art, Worcester porcelains, antique silver serving pieces, Asian snuff bottles, and a good deal of period furniture.

The grounds are designed for strolling, and there are numerous gardens, including: Japanese, herb, perennial, dogwood, magnolia, iris, peony, rose, azalea; and there are greenhouses full of orchids. Kids will enjoy romping around the grassy meadows on the museum grounds. Don't miss the glass bridge that awards hikers along the wooded sculpture trail. You'll also find a gift shop and good restaurant, The Pineapple Room, on the grounds. Allow a couple of hours to tour the museum, or up to a full day if you plan to explore the grounds and garden as well.

1200 Forrest Park Dr. (8 miles/13km southwest of downtown). © 615/356-8000. www.cheekwood.org. Admission $25 family, $10 adults, $8 seniors, $5 college students and children 6–17, free for children under 6. (Half-price after 3pm.) Mon–Sat 9am–5pm; Sun 11am–5pm. Closed Thanksgiving, Dec 25, Jan 1, and 3rd Sat in Apr. Take West End Ave. and continue on Tenn. 100 almost to Percy Warner Park.

Adventure Science Center *Kids*   It's hard to say which exhibit kids like the most at the Center. There are just so many fun interactive displays from which

---

Tips Take the Arts Trolley

From Tuesday through Saturday, the Frist operates an Arts Trolley that allows visitors to view the Parthenon, Fisk University Galleries, Cheekwood, Belle Meade Plantation, Vanderbilt University, Nashville Public Library, Tennessee State Museum, and the Country Music Hall of Fame. You can board at any of these locations and then leave the driving to them. Times are approximate, so call for an updated schedule, © 615/244-3340.

> **Fun Fact Planes, Trains & Automobiles**
>
> Constructed during the Depression, Nashville's main post office is home to the Frist Center for the Arts. Classical and Art Deco architectural styles are prominent within the marble and gray-pink granite building, which is on the National Register of Historic Places. Intricate grillwork celebrates icons of American progress: an airplane, a locomotive, a ship, and an automobile. Among other achievements represented in the icons: scientific research (a microscope, test tube, and flask), harvesting (a sheaf of wheat and sickle), industry (cogwheels), publishing (a book press), sowing (a hand plow), metalwork (a hammer and anvil), the pursuit of knowledge (the lamp of learning resting on books), and nautical endeavors (a dolphin and propeller).

to choose in this modern, hands-on museum. Though the museum is primarily meant to be an entertaining way to introduce children to science, it can also be fun for adults. Kids of all ages can learn about technology, the environment, physics, and health as they roam the museum pushing buttons and turning knobs. On weekends there are almost always special shows and demonstrations, and throughout the year the museum schedules special exhibits. In the **Sudekum Planetarium,** there are regular shows that take you exploring through the universe. Allow 2 hours.

800 Ft. Negley Blvd. © 615/862-5160. www.adventuresci.com. Admission $7.95 adults, $5.95 seniors and children 3–12, free for children under 3. Tue–Sat 10am–5pm; Sun 12:30–5:30pm. Closed Thanksgiving, Dec 25, and Jan 1. Bus: No. 1 (Vine Hill). 4th Ave. S. to Oak St., to Bass St. to Fort Negley.

The Frist Center for the Visual Arts ★★★ *Kids*   Opened in April 2001, the Frist Center for the Visual Arts brings world-class art exhibits to the historic downtown post office building. The nonprofit center does not maintain a permanent collection but rather presents exhibitions from around the globe. Upstairs, the **ArtQuest Gallery** ★ encourages visitors to explore a range of art experiences through more than 30 interactive multimedia stations. Creative kids and likeminded adults could spend hours here.

In addition to the high quality of its exhibitions, the Frist is free to visitors 18 and under, making it an excellent value as well. Coming exhibitions in 2004: *Jacob Lawrence: The Migration Series from the Phillips Collection,* featuring the 20th-century American artist's works tracing the movement of blacks from the rural South to the industrial North between the first and second world wars. Running concurrently will be an exhibition of European masterworks from the same collection, by artists including Cézanne, Monet, Degas, Picasso, and Gauguin. Looking farther ahead, the Frist's next blockbuster exhibition is slated for June to early October 2006. *Quest for Immortality: Treasures of Ancient Egypt* is being billed as the largest group of antiquities ever on loan from Egypt for North America.

919 Broadway. © 615/244-3340. www.fristcenter.org. Admission $8.50 adults, $7.50 seniors, free for children under 18. (Admission prices may be charged for special exhibitions.) Mon–Wed and Fri–Sat 10am–5:30pm; Thurs 10am–8pm; Sun 1–5pm. Closed Thanksgiving, Dec 25, and Jan 1. Between 9th and 10th aves. next to the Union Station Hotel.

The Tennessee State Museum *Kids*   To gain an understanding of Tennessee history, stop by this modern museum in the basement of the Tennessee

Fun Fact **African-American Heritage**

Fisk University was founded in 1866 as a liberal arts institution committed to educating newly freed slaves. Prominent 20th-century cultural figures such as educator W. E. B. Du Bois, artist Aaron Douglas, and poet Nikki Giovanni attended the school. Fisk is perhaps best known for its Jubilee Singers, an African-American singing group that preserved spirituals, or slave songs, from extinction. The choir's 1873 tour of the U.S. and Europe helped finance the construction of Fisk University. **Jubilee Hall,** one of the oldest structures on the campus, is a Victorian Gothic gem listed on the register of National Historic Landmarks. Now used as a dormitory, the building houses a floor-to-ceiling portrait of the original Jubilee Singers, commissioned by Queen Victoria of England as a gift to Fisk. To see the Hall make arrangements ahead of time (© **615/329-8500**).

Performing Arts Center. The museum houses a large display of Native American artifacts from the Mississippian period. The first whites to visit this region were long hunters (named for their long hunting trips west of the Appalachian Mountains) who arrived in the 18th century. The most famous long hunter was Daniel Boone; you'll see a rifle that once belonged to him on display here. There is also a powder horn that once belonged to Davy Crockett. Other displays focus on presidents Andrew Jackson and James K. Polk, as well as Sam Houston, another Tennessean who went on to fame elsewhere.

At press time, much of the museum's permanent collection was closed to the public due to the recent renovation of the convention center. Nonetheless, visitors may still view pre-Civil War artifacts including full-scale replicas of old buildings and period rooms, a log cabin, a water-driven mill, a woodworking shop, an 18th-century print shop, and an 1855 parlor. The lower level of the museum is devoted mostly to the Civil War and Reconstruction. (Visitors are advised to call ahead to see what is currently on display.) One block west on Union Street, you'll find the museum's Military Branch, which houses displays on Tennessee's military activity from the Spanish-American War through World War II. Allow 2 to 3 hours.

5th Ave. (between Union and Deaderick Sts.). © **800/407-4324** or 615/741-2692. www.tnmuseum.org. Free admission; donations encouraged. Tues–Sat 10am–5pm; Sun 1–5pm. Closed Easter, Thanksgiving, Dec 25, and Jan 1.

Van Vechten Gallery ★★ *Finds* If you're an art lover, don't miss a visit to this small, often overlooked treasure of a museum at Fisk University. Housed in an historic, redbrick building at the edge of the campus, it showcases part of famed photographer Alfred Stieglitz's art collection, which was donated by the photographer's widow, renowned artist Georgia O'Keeffe. Marvel at the evocative, black-and-white photos by Stieglitz and colorful abstract paintings by O'Keeffe. Rounding out this impressive collection are pieces by Diego Rivera as well as such European masters as Picasso, Cézanne, Toulouse-Lautrec, and Renoir. Allow 1 to 2 hours.

On the campus of Fisk University, Jackson St. and 18th Ave. N. (D. B. Todd Blvd.). © **615/329-8720.** www. fisk.edu. Free admission; donations encouraged. Tues–Fri 10am–5pm; Sat–Sun 1–5pm. Bus: No. 19 (Herman) or no. 29 (Jefferson).

PARKS, PLAZAS & BOTANICAL GARDENS

To celebrate the 200th anniversary of Tennessee statehood, Nashville constructed the impressive **Bicentennial Capitol Mall State Park** (© 615/741-5280), north of the state capitol. The mall, which begins just north of James Robertson Parkway and extends (again, north) to Jefferson Street between Sixth and Seventh Avenues, is a beautifully landscaped open space that conjures up the countryside with its limestone rockeries and plantings of native plants. As such, it is a very pleasant place for a leisurely stroll. The western edge of the park offers fantastic views of the Capitol.

However, this mall is far more than just a park. It is also a 19-acre open-air exhibition of Tennessee history and geography and a frame for the capitol, which sits atop the hill at the south end of the mall. Also at the south end of the mall is a 200-foot-long granite map of the state, and behind this are a gift shop/visitor center, a Tennessee rivers fountain, and an amphitheater used for summer concerts. Along Sixth Avenue, you'll find a walkway of Tennessee counties, with information on each county (beneath the plaques, believe it or not, are time capsules). Along Seventh Avenue is the Pathway of History, a wall outlining the state's 200-year history. Within the mall, there are also several memorials.

Out in the Belle Meade area, **Percy Warner Park** (2500 Old Hickory Blvd. © **615/370-8051;** www.nashville.org/parks/warnerpark) is the crown jewel of Nashville green spaces. Named for Percy Warner, a local businessman and avid outdoorsman, the wooded hills and rolling meadows extend for more than 2,000 acres. Hiking and equestrian trails draw nature enthusiasts. Though popular with bicyclists, be aware that they must share the winding, paved roads with vehicular traffic. Perfect for picnics and other outdoor pursuits, the park offers clean shelters, restrooms, and even a 27-hole golf course.

After visiting this park, it seems appropriate to take a stroll around **Centennial Park,** located on West End Avenue at 25th Avenue. This park, built for the 1896 centennial celebration, is best known as the site of the Parthenon, but also has many acres of lawns, 100-year-old shade trees, and a small lake.

See also the entry for Cheekwood Botanical Garden & Museum of Art on p. 94.

NEIGHBORHOODS
THE DISTRICT

The District, encompassing several streets of restored downtown warehouses and other old buildings, is ground zero for the Nashville nightlife scene. It's divided into three areas. Second Avenue between Broadway and Union Street, the heart of The District, was originally Nashville's warehouse area and served riverboats on the Cumberland River. Today, most of the old warehouses have been renovated and now house a variety of restaurants, nightclubs, souvenir shops, and other shops. Anchoring Second Avenue at the corner of Broadway is the **Hard Rock Cafe,** and a few doors up the street is the **Wildhorse Saloon,** a massive country music dance hall. Along Broadway between the Cumberland River and Fifth Avenue, you'll find several of country music's most important sites, including the **Ryman Auditorium** (home of the *Grand Ole Opry* for many years), **Tootsie's Orchid Lounge** (where Opry performers often dropped by for a drink), **Gruhn Guitars,** and the **Ernest Tubb Record Shop.** Along this stretch of Broadway, you'll also find **Robert's Western World,** the entrance to the **Gaylord Entertainment Center,** and the **Nashville Convention & Visitors Bureau** visitor center. The third area of The District is Printer's Alley, which is off Church Street between Third and Fourth avenues. Though not as lively as it once was during the days of Prohibition and speakeasies, the alley is an interesting place for an afternoon or early-evening stroll. At night, a few clubs still offer live music.

MUSIC ROW

Located along 16th and 17th avenues between Demonbreun Street and Grand Avenue, Music Row is the very heart of the country music recording industry and is home to dozens of recording studios and record-company offices. Demonbreun, which suffered a few years ago when the old country music museum closed (and the new Hall of Fame opened downtown), is enjoying a resurgence as shops, pubs, and restaurants begin to fill the void. The neighborhood is a combination of old restored homes and modern buildings that hint at the vast amounts of money generated by the country music industry. This is one of the best areas in town for spotting country music stars, so keep your eyes peeled. Anchoring the Music Row "turnaround" (a circular roadway at the entrance to the area) is *Musica.* The 40-foot-tall bronze sculpture of six nude figures was considered a bit shocking when it was unveiled in the fall of 2003. After all, Nashville is located in the buckle of the Bible Belt.

12TH SOUTH

If you want to get off the tourist trail for the afternoon, head south a few miles from downtown to the funky little neighborhood known as 12th Avenue South. Twentysomethings have been buying and refurbishing the area bungalows. The area, roughly bounded by Linden and Kirkwood avenues, is also home to some of Nashville's hippest new restaurants and boutiques. There are a couple of clothing stores, including **Serendipity Emporium** and **Katy K's Ranch Dressing,** as well as a cool unisex hair salon called **Trim.** Start your sojourn with a bite to eat at **Mirror** or **Mafiaoza's,** browse the boutiques, and end the trip with a gourmet Popsicle from **Las Paletas.**

A DAY AT THE ZOO

Nashville Zoo at Grassmere *(Kids)*   This 200-acre park just south of downtown is in the midst of an expansion. In the naturalistic habitats, you'll see river otters, bison, elk, black bear, gray wolves, bald eagles, and cougars, as well as other smaller animals. In the park's aviary, you can walk among many of the state's songbirds, and at the Cumberland River exhibit expect to see fish, reptiles, and amphibians. Allow 2 to 3 hours.

3777 Nolensville Pike ⓒ 615/833-1534. www.nashvillezoo.org. Admission $6 adults, $4 seniors and children 3–12, free for children under 3. Parking $2. Apr–Oct daily 9am–6pm; Nov–Mar daily 9am–4pm. Closed Dec 25 and Jan 1. Bus: No. 12 (Nolensville Rd./Harding Place). Follow 4th Ave. south to Nolensville Pike to U.S. 11 and turn on Zoo Rd.

3 Especially for Kids

Even if your child is not a little Tim McGraw or Faith Hill in training, Nashville is full of things for kids to see and do. In addition to the attractions listed below, see also the listings in this chapter for Cheekwood Botanical Garden & Museum of Art (p. 94), Adventure Science Center (p. 94), the Frist Center for the Visual Arts (p. 95), Nashville Zoo at Grassmere (see above), and the Tennessee State Museum (p. 95).

Grand Old Golf and Games and Valley Park Go-Karts With three miniature-golf courses, go-kart track and a video arcade, this place, located near the Opryland Hotel, is sure to be a hit with your kids. You can easily spend the whole day here.

2444 Music Valley Dr. ℂ **615/871-4701**. Fees 1 course $6.50, 2 courses $7.50, 3 courses $8.50; half-price for children 10 and under. Fees for Go-Karts $5 for single seat, $8 for double seat. Sun–Thurs noon–midnight; Fri–Sat noon–midnight. Take Briley Parkway to McGavock Pike to Music Valley Dr.

Nashville Toy Museum Railroad buffs, toy-train enthusiasts, and children of all ages will enjoy the huge collection of antique toys. The emphasis is on toy trains, and there are two large model train layouts that can keep kids and adults fascinated for hours. Among the several large collections in the museum are shelves full of old toy trains, antique model cars, miniature boats and ships, dolls, and teddy bears.

162 8th Ave. N. (between 1st and 2nd Sts.) ℂ **615/742-5678**. At press time, this unique store was still closed following a relocation from Music Valley to downtown. Call for admission prices and hours.

Wave Country This water park is located just off Briley Parkway about a mile from the old Opryland USA and is a summertime must for kids of all ages. There's a huge wave pool and plenty of water slides. Kids will have no objection to spending the entire day here.

Two Rivers Pkwy. (off Briley Pkwy.). ℂ **615/885-1052**. Admission $5 adults, $4 children 5–12, free for children under 5; half price for everyone after 4pm. Memorial Day to Labor Day daily 10am–8pm.

4 Strolling Around Nashville

If you'd like a bit more information on some of these sites or would like to do a slightly different downtown walk, pick up a copy of the *Nashville City Walk* brochure at the Visitors Center in the Gaylord Entertainment Center. This brochure, produced by the Metropolitan Historical Commission, outlines a walk marked with a green line painted on downtown sidewalks. Along the route are informational plaques and green metal silhouettes of various characters from history.

WALKING TOUR   DOWNTOWN NASHVILLE

Start:	Riverfront Park at the intersection of Broadway and First Avenue. (There's a public parking lot here.)
Finish:	Printer's Alley.
Time:	Anywhere from 3 to 8 hours, depending on how much time you spend in the museums, shopping, or dining.
Best Times:	Tuesday through Friday, when both the Tennessee State Museum and the Tennessee State Capitol are open to the public.
Worst Times:	Sunday, Monday, and holidays, when a number of places are closed. Or anytime the Titans have a home football game, which makes traffic and parking a mess.

Though Nashville is a city of the New South and sprawls in all directions with suburbs full of office parks and shopping malls, it still has a downtown where you can do a bit of exploring on foot. Within the downtown area are the three distinct areas that comprise The District, a historic area containing many late-19th-century commercial buildings that have been preserved and now house restaurants, clubs, and interesting shops. Because Nashville is the state capital, the downtown area also has many impressive government office buildings.

Start your tour at the intersection of Broadway and First Avenue, on the banks of the Cumberland River, at:

❶ Riverfront Park

The park was built as part of Nashville's bicentennial celebration, and is where the Nashville Trolleys start their circuits around downtown and out to Music Row. If you should grow tired of walking at any time during your walk, just look for a trolley stop and ride the trolley back to the park.

Walk north along the river to:

❷ Fort Nashborough

This is a reconstruction of the 1780 fort that served as the first white settlement in this area.

Continue up First Avenue to Union Street and turn left. Across the street is the:

❸ Metropolitan Courthouse

This imposing building, which also houses the Nashville City Hall, was built in 1937. It incorporates many classic Greek architectural details. Of particular interest are the bronze doors, the etched-glass panels above the doors, and the lobby murals. At the information booth in the lobby, you can pick up a brochure detailing the building's many design elements.

If you now head back down Second Avenue, you'll find yourself in the:

❹ Second Avenue Historic District

Between Union Avenue and Broadway are numerous Victorian commercial buildings, most of which have now been restored. Much of the architectural detail is near the tops of the buildings, so keep your eyes trained upward.

 TAKE A BREAK
Second Avenue has several excellent restaurants where you can stop for lunch or a drink. **The Old Spaghetti Factory,** 160 Second Ave. N. (*☎* 615/254-9010), is a cavernous place filled with Victorian antiques. There's even a trolley car parked in the middle of the main dining room. A couple of doors down is the new **B.B. King's Blues Club & Grill,** at 152 Second Ave. N. (*☎* 615/256-2727), a bluesy bar with a juke joint atmosphere where you can sample Southern food or grab a burger.

There are several interesting antiques and crafts stores along Second Avenue, but first take note of a couple of Nashville's best watering holes. A few doors down from the Old Spaghetti Factory you'll find:

❺ Market Street Brewery

Nashville's first microbrewery hosts tours of the brewery and tastings of its beer and ale.

Farther down the street, keep an eye out for:

❻ Wildhorse Saloon

This is Nashville's hottest country nightspot. In the daylight hours you can snap a picture of the comical, cowboy-booted horse statue near the front entrance.

Also along this stretch of the street is the:

❼ Market Street Emporium

The emporium holds a collection of specialty shops.

At the corner of Second Avenue and Broadway, turn right. Between Third and Fourth Avenues, watch for:

❽ Hatch Show Print

The oldest poster shop in the United States still prints its posters on an old-fashioned letterpress printer. The most popular posters are those advertising the *Grand Ole Opry.*

Walking Tour: Downtown Nashville

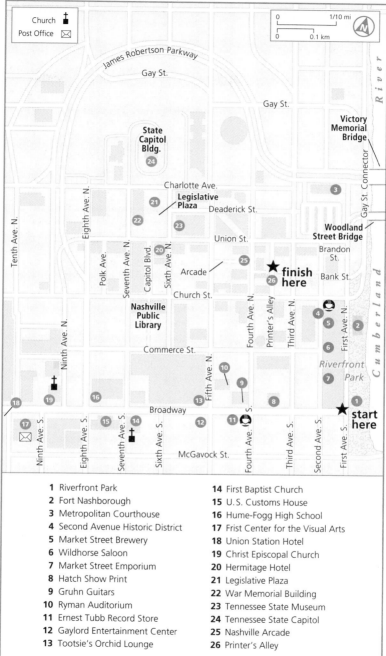

Church ⊕
Post Office ✉

0   1/10 mi
0   0.1 km

James Robertson Parkway
Gay St.
Gay St.

River

State
Capitol
Bldg.
24

Victory
Memorial
Bridge

Charlotte Ave.

21 Legislative
Plaza
Deaderick St.

22
23

Union St.

Woodland
Street Bridge

Brandon
St.

20
25

Arcade

★ **finish
here**

Bank St.

26

Church St.

Nashville
Public
Library

Commerce St.

10

9

Riverfront
Park

8

13

Broadway

★ **start
here**

16
19
18
17

15
14
12
11

McGavock St.

Tenth Ave. N.
Eighth Ave. N.
Polk Ave.
Seventh Ave. N.
Capitol Blvd.
Sixth Ave. N.
Ninth Ave. N.
Fifth Ave. N.
Fourth Ave. N.
Printer's Alley
Third Ave. N.
First Ave. N.
Ninth Ave. S.
Eighth Ave. S.
Seventh Ave. S.
Sixth Ave. S.
Fourth Ave. S.
Third Ave. S.
Second Ave. S.
First Ave. S.

Gay St. Connector
Cumberland

1 Riverfront Park	**14** First Baptist Church
2 Fort Nashborough	**15** U.S. Customs House
3 Metropolitan Courthouse	**16** Hume-Fogg High School
4 Second Avenue Historic District	**17** Frist Center for the Visual Arts
5 Market Street Brewery	**18** Union Station Hotel
6 Wildhorse Saloon	**19** Christ Episcopal Church
7 Market Street Emporium	**20** Hermitage Hotel
8 Hatch Show Print	**21** Legislative Plaza
9 Gruhn Guitars	**22** War Memorial Building
10 Ryman Auditorium	**23** Tennessee State Museum
11 Ernest Tubb Record Store	**24** Tennessee State Capitol
12 Gaylord Entertainment Center	**25** Nashville Arcade
13 Tootsie's Orchid Lounge	**26** Printer's Alley

Cross Fourth Avenue and you'll come to:

⑨ Gruhn Guitars

This is the most famous guitar shop in Nashville; it specializes in used and vintage guitars.

Walk up Fourth Avenue less than a block and you will come to the new main entrance of:

⑩ Ryman Auditorium

The *Grand Ole Opry* was held here from 1943 to 1974. The building was originally built as a tabernacle to host evangelical revival meetings, but because of its good acoustics and large seating capacity, it became a popular setting for theater and music performances.

After leaving the Ryman Auditorium, walk back down to the corner of Broadway and Fourth Avenue.

TAKE A BREAK
If you didn't stop for lunch on Second Avenue, now would be a good time. Directly across the street is **The Merchants** restaurant, at 401 Broadway (② 615/254-1892), a favorite Nashville power-lunch spot. The atmosphere is sophisticated and the cuisine is New American.
In the same block as The Merchants, you'll find the:

---

⑪ Ernest Tubb Record Shop

This store was once the home of the *Midnite Jamboree*, a country music radio show that took place after the *Grand Ole Opry* was over on Saturday nights.

Continue up the block to the corner of Fifth Avenue and you'll come to the main entrance to the new:

⑫ Gaylord Entertainment Center

Right at the corner (inside what used to be known as the Nashville Arena) is the Gaylord Entertainment Center. Inside is the Nashville Convention & Visitors Bureau Visitors Center. If you haven't already stopped in for information or

to check out the gift shop, now would be a good time.

Back across Broadway, you'll find:

⑬ Tootsie's Orchid Lounge

Grand Ole Opry musicians used to duck in here, one of the most famous bars in Nashville, before, during, and after the show at the Ryman. There's live country music all day long at Tootsie's.

From this corner, head up Broadway, and at the corner of Seventh Avenue, you'll find the:

⑭ First Baptist Church

This modern building incorporates a Victorian Gothic church tower built between 1884 and 1886. The church's congregation wanted a new church, but didn't want to give up the beautiful old tower. This is the compromise that was reached.

Across Seventh Avenue is the:

⑮ U.S. Customs House

Now leased as private office space, this Victorian Gothic building was built in 1877 and displays fine stonework and friezes. The imposing structure, with its soaring tower and arched windows, could be in any European city.

Directly across the street is:

⑯ Hume-Fogg High School

Built between 1912 and 1916, the building incorporates elements of English Tudor and Gothic design.

Two blocks farther up Broadway, you'll see a decidedly different style of architecture, the:

⑰ Frist Center for the Visual Arts

This breathtaking new art museum is housed in the historic U.S. Post Office building, designed with elements of both neoclassical and Art Deco architectural styling.

The post office shares a parking lot with:

⑱ Union Station Hotel

This Victorian Romanesque Revival building was built in 1900 as Nashville's main passenger railroad station, but in 1986 it was renovated and reopened as a luxury hotel. The exterior stone walls incorporate many fine carvings, and the lobby is one of the most elegant historic spaces in Nashville.

Head back the way you came and cross over to the opposite side of Broadway at Ninth Avenue. Here you'll find:

⓳ Christ Episcopal Church

Constructed between 1887 and 1892, the building is in the Victorian Gothic style and is complete with gargoyles. This church also has Tiffany stained-glass windows.

Continue back down Broadway and at Seventh Avenue, turn left and walk up to Union Street and turn right. In 1 block, you'll come to the:

⓴ Hermitage Hotel

This is Nashville's last grand old hotel; newly renovated and lovingly restored in 2002, the lobby exudes beaux arts extravagance, with a stained-glass skylight and marble columns and floor.

Across Union Street from the Hermitage Hotel is:

㉑ Legislative Plaza

This large public plaza is a popular lunch spot for downtown office workers.

Fronting onto this plaza is the:

㉒ War Memorial Building

This neoclassical building was built in 1925 to honor soldiers who died in World War I. The centerpiece is an atrium holding a large statue titled *Victory.* This building also houses the Tennessee State Museum Military Branch.

On the opposite side of the plaza is the:

㉓ Tennessee State Museum

In the basement of the same building that houses the Tennessee Performing Arts Center, this museum contains an extensive and well-displayed collection of artifacts pertaining to Tennessee history.

Returning to the Legislative Plaza and continuing to the north across Charlotte Street will bring you to the:

㉔ Tennessee State Capitol

This Greek Revival building was built between 1845 and 1859. Be sure to take a look inside, where you'll find many beautiful architectural details and artworks.

If you walk back across the Legislative Plaza and take a left on Union Street and then a right on Fifth Avenue (cross to the far side of the street), you'll come to the west entrance of the:

㉕ Nashville Arcade

This covered shopping arcade was built in 1903 and is modeled after an arcade in Italy. Only a few such arcades remain in the United States, and unfortunately, no one has yet breathed new life into this one. Still, you can mail a letter here or buy a bag of fresh-roasted peanuts.

Walk through the arcade and continue across Fourth Avenue. The alley in front of you leads to:

㉖ Printer's Alley

For more than a century, this has been a center for evening entertainment. Today, things are much tamer than they once were, but you can still find several nightclubs featuring live music.

5 Organized Tours

CITY & HOMES-OF-THE-STARS TOURS

Gray Line of Nashville, 2416 Music Valley Dr. (© **800/251-1864** or 615/883-5555; www.graylinenashville.com), offers more than half a dozen different tours ranging in length from 3½ hours to a full day. On the popular, 3-hour tour of the stars' homes, you'll ride past the current or former houses and mansions of such chart-toppers as Hank Williams Sr., Dolly Parton, Kix Brooks and Ronnie Dunn (separate homes), Trisha Yearwood, Martina McBride and Alan Jackson. Other

For Travelers Interested in African-American History

African Americans constitute one-quarter of Nashville's population, and for more than 200 years have played important roles in the shaping of this city. To learn more about African-American historic sites around Nashville, pick up a copy of the *African-American Guide to Cultural & Historic Sites* brochure at the Visitors Center in the Gaylord Entertainment Center.

If you'd like to take a tour to learn more about the African-American history of Nashville, contact Bill Daniel at **Nashville Black Heritage Tours,** 5188 Almaville Rd., Smyrna, TN 37167 (© **615/890-8173**). Call for rates.

themed tours focus exclusively on historical sites, honky-tonks and nightlife, and other specialty areas. Tour prices range from $10 to $69 for adults.

Grand Ole Opry Tours (© **615/883-2211;** www.gaylordhotels.com) is the official tour company of the Opryland Hotel; it offers tours similar to those of Gray Line. One of this company's more popular offerings is the Grand Old Nashville City Tour, a three-hour excursion that takes you past the homes of country legends and also includes a self-guided tour of the Ryman Auditorium and several other points of interest throughout the city. The cost is $29.

Johnny Walker Tours, 2416 Music Valley Dr. (© **800/722-1524** or 615/834-8585), has merged with Gray Line Tours. However, the company still sells group tours and individual vacation packages.

Forget the stars' homes. For a fun and campy tour of Nashville aboard a gaudy pink bus, try **Nash Trash Tours** (© **800/342-2132** or 615/226-7300; www.nashtrash.com), narrated by the spandex-clad "Jugg" sisters. Sheri Lynn and Brenda Kay dish the dirt on all your favorite country stars. Throw in a few risqué jokes, plenty of music and a policy that allows passengers to bring aboard coolers (with alcohol, if desired), and it all makes for a trashy good time in Music City. Because the tours can become rowdy, they're not advised for young children (those under 6 are not allowed.) Hours vary, but generally speaking, tours are offered Wednesdays through Saturdays, and some Sundays. Call in advance for current times and to make reservations, which are required. Tickets cost $25 for adults, $22 for seniors, and $18 for youth ages 6 to 18.

RIVERBOAT TOURS

The Opryland Hotel, 2800 Opryland Dr. (© **615/883-2211;** www.opryland hotel.com), operates the paddle-wheeler—the *General Jackson*—on the Cumberland River. Tours depart from a dock near the Opryland Hotel. At 300 feet long, the *General Jackson* showboat hearkens back to the days when riverboats were the most sophisticated way to travel. You go on this cruise for the paddle-wheeler experience, not necessarily for the food (not so great) and entertainment that go along with it. During the summer, the Southern Nights Cruise offers a three-course dinner and dancing under the stars to live bands. Fares for this trip cost $66. Mid-day cruises are also available year-round and cost $40 (includes a lunch and entertainment).

6 Outdoor Activities

BOAT RENTALS In the summer, a wide variety of boats, from canoes and paddleboats to personal watercraft and pontoon boats, can be rented at **Four Corners Marina** on Percy Priest Lake, 4027 Lavergne Couchville Pike, Antioch (℃ **615/641-9523**). This grocery store sells bait, tackle, and fishing licenses year-round. The gorgeous lake, only a few miles east of downtown, is surrounded by a series of parks, trees, and natural beauty rather than commercial and residential development.

At Kingston Springs, about 20 miles (32km) west of Nashville off I-40, you can rent canoes from **Tip-a-Canoe**, 1279 U.S. 70, at Harpeth River Bridge (℃ **800/550-5810** or **615/254-0836;** www.tip-a-canoe.com), or bring your own. The Harpeth River, a designated State Scenic River, includes a 7-mile loop that allows canoers the freedom of going it alone without having to be picked up. This section, called "The Narrows of the Harpeth," begins and ends in roughly the same area. Canoe trips of varying lengths, from a couple of hours up to 5 days, can be arranged. Rates start at $18 per canoe, which includes the shuttle upriver to your chosen put-in point. Trips lasting 2 days cost $50, while 5-day trips cost $125. The river is mostly Class I water with some Class II and a few spots where you'll have to carry the canoe.

GOLF Three area resort courses consistently get praised by Nashville golfers. The **Hermitage Golf Course,** 3939 Old Hickory Blvd. (℃ **615/847-4001;** www.hermitagegolf.com), is a challenging course on the bank of the Cumberland River. Greens fees are $47 to $55. The **Legend's Club of Tennessee,** 1500 Legends Club Lane, Franklin (℃ **615/791-8100;** www.legendsclub.com), is a bit farther out of town but offers a 36-hole course designed by Tom Kite and Bob Cupp. Greens fees for the Legend's Club are $65 to $75. For many golfing visitors, however, the **Opryland's Springhouse Golf Club,** 18 Springhouse Lane (℃ **615/871-7759;** www.gaylordhotels.com), is most convenient. This par-72, 18-hole course is set on the bank of the Cumberland River and is the site of the BellSouth Senior Classic on the PGA Senior Tour. The course boasts not only challenging links, but also an antebellum-style clubhouse that would have made Rhett Butler feel right at home. Greens fees are $55 to $69.

HORSEBACK RIDING If you want to go for a ride through the Tennessee hills, there are a couple of nearby places where you can rent a horse. The **Ramblin' Breeze Ranch,** 3665 Knight Rd., Whites Creek (℃ **615/876-1029**), 7 miles (11km) north of downtown Nashville, rents horses for $20 an hour ($15 for children ages 7–12). **Ju-Ro Stables,** 735 Carver Lane, Mt. Juliet (℃ **615/773-7433**), is located about 15 minutes from Nashville on I-40 east, at the Mt. Juliet exit, and charges $15 an hour for rides around Old Hickory Lake ($30 for moonlight rides).

SWIMMING Though most of the hotels and motels listed in this book have pools, if you'd rather go jump in a lake, head for **Percy Priest Lake.** You'll find this large man-made reservoir just east of downtown Nashville at Exit 219 off I-40. Stop by the information center to get a map showing the three designated swimming areas.

7 Spectator Sports

AUTO RACING NASCAR racing is a Southern institution, and every Saturday aspiring stock-car drivers race their cars at the **Nashville Speedway USA**

(© 615/726-1818; www.nashvillespeedway.com) on the Tennessee State Fairgrounds. The race season, which runs from April through September, also includes several pro series races, as well as a celebrity charity race. Saturday admission is $15, while tickets to the pro races run $35 to $45.

The **Music City Raceway,** 3302 Ivy Point Rd., Goodlettsville (© **615/876-0981;** www.musiccityraceway.com), is the place to catch National Hot Rod Association (NHRA) drag-racing action. The drag strip, known as Nashville's "Playground of Power," has races on Tuesday, Friday, Saturday, and some Sundays between March and October. Admission is $5 to $10 for adults; children 12 and under enter free.

BASEBALL The **Nashville Sounds** (© **615/242-4371;** www.nashville sounds.com), a triple-A team affiliate of the Pittsburgh Pirates, play at Greer Stadium, 534 Chestnut St., off Eighth Avenue South. Admission ranges from $6 general to $10 for reserved box seats ($5–$9 for children).

FOOTBALL Ever since moving to Nashville (from Houston, where they were the Oilers) in 1999, the **Tennessee Titans** have drawn loyal crowds to the 68,000-seat Nashville Coliseum on the banks of the Cumberland River. AFC champions in 2000, the Titans are perennial favorites for the playoffs. The stadium is at 1 Titans Way, Nashville, TN 37213 (© **615/565-4200;** www.titans online.com).

GOLF TOURNAMENTS The **BellSouth Senior Classic** (© **615/871-PUTT [7888]**) brings in the top players on the PGA Senior Tour and is held each year in June at the Springhouse Golf Club near the Opryland Hotel. Call for ticket prices and dates.

HOCKEY Nashville's own NHL hockey team, the **Nashville Predators** (© **615/770-PUCK [7825];** www.nashvillepredators.com), plays at the Gaylord Entertainment Center on lower Broadway in downtown Nashville. Ticket prices range from $10 to $95.

HORSE SHOWS Horse shows are important events on the Nashville area's calendar. The biggest and most important horse show of the year is the **Annual Tennessee Walking-Horse National Celebration** (© **931/684-5915**). This show takes place 40 miles (64km) southeast of Nashville in the town of Shelbyville and is held each year in late August. Advance reserved ticket prices range from $7 to $15, while general-admission tickets are $5 to $10.

The city's other big horse event is the annual running of the **Iroquois Steeplechase** (© **615/322-7284**) on the second Saturday in May. This is one of the oldest steeplechase races in the country and is held in Percy Warner Park in the Belle Meade area. Proceeds from the race benefit the Vanderbilt Children's Hospital. Tickets are $12 at the gate or $10 in advance.

Shopping in Nashville

Nashville is a great shopping city, so be sure to bring your credit cards. Whether you're looking for handmade stage outfits costing thousands of dollars or a good deal on a pair of shoes at a factory-outlet store, you'll find plenty of spending opportunities in Nashville.

1 The Nashville Shopping Scene

As in most cities of the South, the shopping scene in Nashville is spread out over the width and breadth of the city. Most of the city's best shopping can be found in the many large new shopping malls scattered around the newer suburbs. However, there are also many interesting and exclusive shops in the West End area. In downtown Nashville, you'll find gift and souvenir shops, antiques stores, and musical instrument and record stores that cater to country musicians and fans. Second Avenue North, in the historic downtown area known as The District, is becoming a souvenir and gallery district, though it still has a few antiques stores.

Country music fans will appreciate plenty of opportunities to shop for Western wear. There are dozens of shops specializing in the de rigueur attire of country music. You probably can't find a better selection of cowboy boots anywhere outside Texas, and if your tastes run to sequined denim shirts or skirts, you'll find lots to choose from.

2 Nashville Shopping A to Z

ANTIQUES

A good place to look for antiques is the corner of Eighth Avenue South and Douglas Street, where several large antiques stores are located.

Downtown Antique Mall   Among the many stalls in this historic warehouse building you'll find lots of Civil War memorabilia. There are plenty of other antiques and collectibles as well. 612 8th Ave. S. ℂ 615/256-6616.

Made in France   Though not everything here is antique, you will find quite a few European antiques. The store is an interior design shop specializing in traditional and contemporary European accent pieces such as handmade throw pillows, lamps, candlesticks, and many other small and large decorative items. 3001 West End Ave. ℂ 615/329-9300.

ART AND HOME FURNISHINGS

Cinemonde   If you are a collector of old movie posters, you won't want to miss this shop tucked away in an arcade on busy Second Avenue. They also sell collectible country music memorabilia. 138 2nd Ave. N. ℂ 615/832-1997.

Nashville Shopping

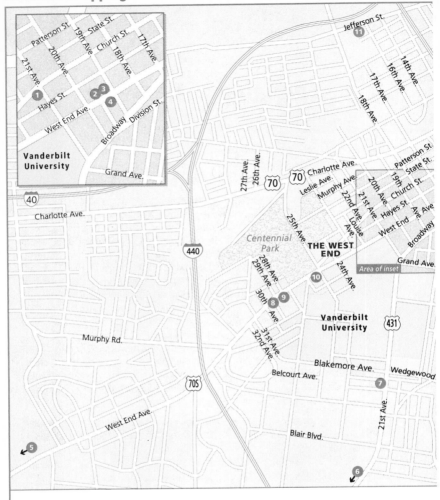

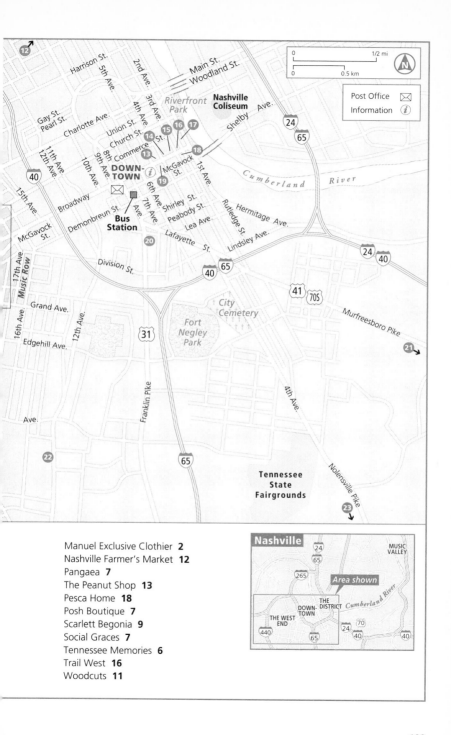

Manuel Exclusive Clothier **2**
Nashville Farmer's Market **12**
Pangaea **7**
The Peanut Shop **13**
Pesca Home **18**
Posh Boutique **7**
Scarlett Begonia **9**
Social Graces **7**
Tennessee Memories **6**
Trail West **16**
Woodcuts **11**

Cumberland Art Gallery With an emphasis on regional artists, this well-regarded gallery deals in sculptures, paintings, photographs, and works on paper in a wide variety of styles. 4107 Hillsboro Circle. © 615/297-0296.

Finer Things If you have an appreciation of unusual and highly imaginative fine contemporary crafts and art, don't miss an opportunity to drop by this eclectic gallery. 1898 Nolensville Rd. © 615/244-3003.

Hatch Show Print This is the oldest letterpress poster print shop in the country and not only does it still design and print posters for shows, but it also sells posters to the public. Reprints of old circus, vaudeville, and *Grand Ole Opry* posters are the most popular. 316 Broadway © 615/256-2805. www.halloffame. org/hatch.

Local Color Gallery This gallery specializes in works by Tennessee artists. Watercolors and other paintings comprise the largest portion of the works on sale here, but you'll also find ceramics and sculptures. 1912 Broadway. © 615/321-3141.

Pesca Home Anchoring the bustling new SoBro (South of Broadway) Design District downtown is this gorgeous store showcasing chandeliers, textiles, lamps and other accessories and fine home furnishings. 120 Third Ave. S. © 615/254-3900. www.pescainternational.com.

Woodcuts If you're interested in artworks by African-American artists, this is the place to visit in Nashville. Prints, posters, note cards, and greeting cards make up the majority of the offerings here, though they also do framing. The shop is adjacent to Fisk University. 1613 Jefferson St. © 615/321-5357.

BOOKS

Borders This multi-level bookstore, part of a national chain, dominates a busy intersection near the Vanderbilt University campus. Thousands of books, CDs, and an extensive selection of DVDs draw shoppers, as do frequent author book signings. 2525 West End Ave. © 615/327-9656. www.bordersstores.com.

Davis-Kidd Booksellers ★ For the best and biggest selection of books in Nashville, go to the Green Hills area, where you'll find this welcoming, well-stocked store. With an active roster of book signings and other community-oriented events, a good second-floor cafe, and an array of unique gift items, Davis-Kidd gets my pick as the best bookstore chain in Tennessee. (Other locations are in Memphis and Jackson.) 4007 Hillsboro Rd. © 615/385-2645. www.daviskidd.com.

Elder's Book Store This dusty old shop looks as if some of the antiquarian books on sale were stocked back when they were new. Every square inch of shelf space is jammed full of books, and there are more stacks of books seemingly everywhere you turn. This place is a book collector's dream come true. And who needs a fancy, in-store Starbucks cafe when you've got the retro Elliston Soda Shop right next door? 2115 Elliston Place © 615/327-1867. www.eldersbookstore.com.

BookMan BookWoman ★ Widely regarded (and rightfully so) as Nashville's best used bookstore, this Vandy-area favorite has tens of thousands of books, including hardcover and collectors' editions. Their inexpensive paperbacks encompass nearly every genre, including mysteries, science fiction, photography, and children's books. 1713 21st Ave. S. © 615/383-6555. www.bookmanbookwoman.com.

CRAFTS

The American Artisan   Stocking only the finest of contemporary American handicrafts from around the country, American Artisan is Nashville's best place to shop for original fine crafts. These include intricate baskets, elaborate ceramic pieces, colorful kaleidoscopes, one-of-a-kind jewelry, and beautiful wood furniture. All exhibit the artist's eye for creativity. 4231 Harding Rd. ℂ **615/298-4691.**

Pangaea ⋆⋆   From hand-carved soaps and South American textiles to one-of-a-kind Elvis icons, this eclectic boutique in Nashville's trendy Hillsboro Village area has interesting gifts to suit a variety of tastes, if not budgets. (They also sell cool clothes.) Items are on the pricey side, but for a unique shopping experience adjacent to scores of hip coffee shops and galleries, even window-shopping at Pangaea is time well spent. 1721 21st Ave. S. ℂ **615/269-9665.** www. pangaeanashville.com.

Tennessee Memories   Located in the Fashion Square shopping plaza next to the Mall at Green Hills, this small store is filled with crafts (including pottery and baskets) and gourmet food products from around the state. 2182 Bandywood Dr. ℂ **615/298-3253.** www.tennesseememories.com.

DEPARTMENT STORES

Hecht's   This is one of Nashville's two upscale department stores and is well known for its personable employees and wide selection of fine lines. **Cool Springs Galleria,** 1790 Galleria Blvd. (ℂ 615/771-2100); **Bellevue Center,** 7616 U.S. 70 S. (ℂ 615/646-5500); **Hickory Hollow Mall,** 917 Bell Rd. (ℂ 615/731-5050); and **Rivergate Mall,** 1000 Two Mile Pkwy., Goodlettsville (ℂ 615/859-5251).

Dillard's   Dillard's is recognized as one of the nation's leading department stores. They carry many leading brands and have stores at several malls around Nashville. **Bellevue Center Mall,** 7624 U.S. 70 S. (ℂ 615/662-1515); **Mall at Green Hills,** 3855 Green Hills Village Dr. (ℂ 615/297-0971); **Harding Mall,** 4070 Nolensville Rd. (ℂ 615/832-6890); **Hickory Hollow Mall,** 5248 Hickory Hollow Pkwy. (ℂ 615/731-6600); **Rivergate Mall,** Two Mile Pkwy., Goodlettsville (ℂ 615/859-2811); and **Cool Springs Galleria,** 1796 Galleria Blvd. (ℂ 615/771-7101.)

DISCOUNT SHOPPING

Johnston & Murphy Outlet   Located across the road from the airport, this outlet mall offers good shopping for all kinds of discounted shoes. Genesco Park, 1415 Murfreesboro Pike, ℂ **615/367-7413.**

Opry Mills   For bargains on everything from Bibles to fine crystal, look no farther than this mammoth "shoppertainment" venue in the Music Valley. Among the dozens of factory/outlet stores here are those by such well-known apparel retailers as Ann Taylor, Banana Republic, Gap, Guess, Levi's, and Tommy Hilfiger. Bargain shoes and handbags can be found at the Dexter, Etienne Aigner, G. H. Bass, Off Broadway Shoe Warehouse, Reebok, and Nike stores. Jewelry merchant Zales also has an outlet here, as does Mikasa and the Children's Place. The mall is open Monday through Saturday from 10am to 9:30pm, and Sunday from 11am to 7pm. 433 Opry Mills Dr. ℂ **615/514-1000.** www.oprymills.com.

> (*Fun Fact* Big Attraction
>
> Opened in May 2000, **Opry Mills** attracted more than 8 million visitors to the shopping and entertainment complex within its first 6 months. The mega-mall is in an area that was once home to the defunct Opryland amusement park.

FASHIONS
See also "Western Wear" below.

WOMEN'S
Coco   This ladies' boutique sells designer sportswear, dresses, and accessories, and features such lines as Ellen Tracy and Emmanuel. Both the fashions and the clientele tend to be upscale. 4239 Harding Rd. *C* 615/292-0362.

Posh Boutique   Trendy clothes and footwear by the likes of Diesel, Chinese Laundry, and Miss Sixty attract a young, affluent clientele. That's not to say you can't scour the place for occasional bargains. 1809 21st Ave. S. *C* 615/383-9840.

Scarlett Begonia   Ethnic fashions, jewelry, and fine crafts from around the world prove that there is life beyond country Nashville. The emphasis here is on South American clothing, and the quality is much higher than you'll find in the average import store. 2805 West End Ave. *C* 615/329-1272.

CHILDREN'S
Chocolate Soup   Kids love the name and parents love the clothes. Colorful play clothes with hand-sewn appliqués, mostly easy care, are the specialty here, and designs are created to grow with the child. 330 Franklin, Brentwood. *C* 615/370-1426.

FLEA MARKETS
Tennessee State Fairgrounds Flea Market   This huge flea market is held the fourth weekend of every month (except Dec, when it's the third weekend), attracting more than 1,000 vendors selling everything from cheap jeans to handmade crafts to antiques and collectibles. You'll find the fairgrounds just a few minutes south of downtown. Tennessee State Fairgrounds, 4th Ave. *C* 615/862-5016. www.tennesseestatefair.org.

FOOD
Nashville Farmer's Market *★*   Located across the street from the Bicentennial Mall, this large indoor farmer's market has 100 farm stalls, as well as 100 flea-market stalls. There are also more than a dozen prepared food vendors and gourmet- and imported-food stalls, selling everything from Jamaican meat patties to hundreds of different hot sauces. The market is open daily 8am to 7pm in summer; 9am to 6pm the rest of the year. 900 8th Ave. N. *C* 615/880-2001.

The Peanut Shop   If you've been trudging around downtown Nashville all day and need a quick snack, consider a bag of fresh roasted peanuts. This tiny shop in the Arcade (connecting 4th Ave. N. and 5th Ave. N.) has been in business since 1927 and still roasts its own peanuts. In fact, there are more styles of peanuts sold here than you've probably ever seen in one place. A true Nashville institution. 19 Arcade. *C* 615/256-3394.

FINE GIFTS/SOUVENIRS

Nashville abounds in shops purveying every manner of country-themed souvenirs. The greatest concentrations of these shops are in the Music Row and Music Valley (Opryland Hotel) areas, where several of the stores specialize in particular country music performers. Several of the gift shops, including the Willie Nelson & Friends Showcase Museum on McGavock Pike (Music Valley), also have backroom museums where you can see personal belongings or memorabilia of a particular star. These museums are, however, really just an excuse to get you into the big souvenir shop out front, but if you're a fan, you'll enjoy touring the exhibits and maybe picking up a souvenir. See "On the Music Trail" in chapter 6 for further information.

A Thousand Faces ⭐   Beautifully crafted one-of-a-kind gifts including jewelry, artwork, and home decor are packed inside every square inch of this vibrant West End boutique that's perfect for leisurely browsing. 1720 21st Ave. S. © 615/298-3304.

Fire Finch   Eclectic, primitive-style artwork and other interesting, upscale gift items are sold in this atmospheric store. And yes, you might see a finch or two, too. 1818 21st Ave. S. © 615/385-5090. www.firefinch.net.

Social Graces   Designer stationery sets, invitations, hand-made paper, and an assortment of luxurious writing gifts and accessories are lavishly displayed here. As part of a full day of shopping, the relatively quiet, contemplative atmosphere at this store makes a nice change of pace from some of the West End's livelier shops. 1704 21st Ave. S. © 615/383-1911. www.socialgracesonline.com.

MALLS/SHOPPING CENTERS

Bellevue Center   Though this isn't Nashville's largest shopping mall, it is considered one of the best places to shop in the city. Department stores include Dillard's, Sears, and Hecht's. There are also more than 115 specialty shops, including Abercrombie & Fitch, Banana Republic, and Godiva Chocolatier. 7620 U.S. 70 S. © 615/646-8690.

Cool Springs Galleria   South of Nashville off I-65 (at the Moore's Lane exit) is one of the city's newest shopping malls. Here you'll find four major department stores, including the upscale Parisian store, and more than 100 specialty stores, such as Yankee Candle. This mall is a 10 to 15 minute drive from downtown Nashville. 1800 Galleria Blvd. © 615/771-2128.

Hickory Hollow Mall   More than 180 specialty shops, a food court, Ruby Tuesday's restaurant as well as four department stores—Hecht's, Sears, JC Penney, and Dillard's—make this the largest shopping mall in the Nashville area. You'll find the mall south of downtown at Exit 60 off I-24 East. 5252 Hickory Hollow Pkwy., Antioch © 615/731-MALL [6255].

The Mall at Green Hills   Closer to downtown than the Bellevue Center mall, the Mall at Green Hills is almost equally exclusive and is one of Nashville's busiest malls. Among its shops are Brooks Brothers, Ann Taylor, and Pottery Barn, along with anchor stores Hecht's and Dillard's. Surrounding the mall are several more small plazas full of interesting shops and restaurants. Hillsboro and Abbott Martin rds. © 615/298-5478.

Opry Mills *Kids*   Miles of retail sales, not to mention live music around every turn, await customers at Nashville's premier shopping mall, a vast extravaganza of department stores, specialty boutiques, restaurants, and entertainment venues that's laid out in an oval, racetrack formation. At this mall, you can try your hand at rock climbing, see a first-run movie or visit the IMAX 3-D Theatre, test-drive CDs at Tower Records, and top it all off with a chocolate soda at Ghiradelli's old-time ice cream parlor. Among Opry Mill's 200 tenants are anchors Bass Pro Shops Outdoor World, Barnes & Noble, Apple Barn Cider Bar and General Store, Off Broadway Shoe Warehouse, Old Navy Clothing Co., and Rainforest Café. If you want to shop 'til you drop, this is the place to do it. 433 Opry Mills Dr. ✆ **615/514-1000.**

Rivergate Mall If you're looking for shopping in northern Nashville, head up I-65 North to Exit 95 or 96. The Rivergate Mall includes four department stores and more than 155 boutiques, specialty shops, and restaurants. 1000 Two Mile Pkwy. ✆ **615/859-3456.**

MUSIC

The Great Escape This old store adjacent to the Vanderbilt campus caters to the record and comic book needs of college students and other collectors and bargain-seekers. The used records section has a distinct country bent, but you can also find other types of music as well. This is a big place with a great selection, including records, CDs, comic books, video games, and so on. An outlet store a few blocks away, open only on Friday and Saturday, is at 1907 Broadway (no phone). Another Great Escape can be found at 111 Gallatin Rd. N. (✆ **615/865-8052**). 1925 Broadway ✆ **615/327-0646.**

Ernest Tubb Record Shop ✪ *Moments* Whether you're looking for a reissue of an early Johnny Cash album or the latest from Garth Brooks, you'll find it at Ernest Tubb. These shops sell exclusively country music recordings on CD, cassette, and a handful of vinyl records by the likes of Loretta Lynn and Jimmie Davis. There's another location out near Opryland, at 2416 Music Valley Dr. (✆ **615/889-2474**); this is where the *Midnite Jamborees* are held each Saturday night at midnight. 417 Broadway ✆ **615/255-7503.** www.etrecordshop.com.

Tower Records ✪ A music lover's paradise, this chain outlet is one of the best reasons I know to visit the Opry Mills shopping mall. Aisle after aisle of CDs offer an extensive selection of country, blues, reggae, gospel, rap, and every kind of music in between. The depth and breadth of the classical music section makes it a must for anyone looking for specific operas, oratorios, or hard-to-find titles. Cushy easy chairs and scores of headphones and mounted CD players throughout the store make browsing a pleasurable and personalized experience.

Fun Fact **The One & Only**

So just who was Ernest Tubb, anyway? One of Nashville's earliest country recording stars, this native Texan known to friends as "E. T." scored a big hit with "Walkin' the Floor Over You" in 1941. The beloved entertainer, who in gratitude to his audiences had the word "Thanks" emblazoned on the back of his guitar, earned a slew of industry awards, played Carnegie Hall, and was inducted into the Country Music Hall of Fame. After a long and successful career as one of the pioneers in country music, he died in Nashville in 1984.

DVDs, videos, T-shirts, posters, and other merchandise are also for sale. An older Tower Records location is near the Vanderbilt University campus, at 2400 West End Ave. (© 615/327-3722). 504 Opry Mills Dr. © 615/514-5800. www.tower records.com.

MUSICAL INSTRUMENTS

Gruhn Guitars   Nashville's biggest guitar dealer (and one of the largest in the world) stocks classic used and collectible guitars as well as reissues of musicians' favorite instruments. If you're serious about your guitar pickin,' this is the place to shop. Where else can you find a 1953 Les Paul or a 1938 Martin D-28? 400 Broadway. © 615/256-2033. www.gruhn.com.

Gibson Bluegrass Showcase   Nightly music is offered at this combination performance stage and retail store, where Gibson-brand guitars are sold, and where the company's bluegrass stringed instruments including Dobros, mandolins, and banjos are crafted and shipped worldwide. Free bluegrass jams are open to all comers beginning at 7pm Mondays and Wednesdays. Tuesday is Songwriters' Night. Local bands usually perform Thursdays and Fridays. Call for schedule. In Opry Mills, 161 Opry Mills Dr. © 615/514-2233.

WESTERN WEAR

In addition to places listed below, you can pick up clothing at the Wildhorse Saloon and other shops in The District. There are also clothing stores in Music Valley and on Music Row.

Boot Country   Cowboy boots, more cowboy boots, and still more cowboy boots. That's what you'll find at this boot store. Whether you want a basic pair of work boots or some fancy python-skin show boots, you'll find them here. There are other locations in Cold Springs Mall and Rivergate Mall. 304 Broadway © 615-259-1691.

Katy K's Ranch Dressing ★★ *Finds*   Can't afford a custom-made rhinestone blazer from Manuel's, that well-known tailor to the country stars? Then head south of downtown to find this one-of-a-kind boutique (look for the shapely cowgirl cutout on the building's stone facade), where you can pick up some vintage Manuel suits and spangled gowns by Nudie's of Hollywood. It's all here, from Western wear, including designer boots, belt buckles, hats and shirts— what the owners cleverly call "Ranch Dressing"—to rockabilly and punk fashions. It's a kick. 2407 12th Ave. S. © 615/297-4242. www.katyk.com.

Manuel Exclusive Clothier ★   This is where the stars get their threads. If you're a fan of country music, you've already seen plenty of Manuel's work, though you probably didn't know it at the time. Manuel has dressed Johnny Cash, Merle Haggard, Lorrie Morgan, Bob Dylan, the Rolling Stones, Emmylou Harris, Dolly Parton, Trisha Yearwood, and Pam Tillis. Unless you're an established performer, you probably won't be able to afford anything here, but it's still great fun to have a look at the pricey duds Manuel creates. Everything is impeccably tailored, with the one-of-a-kind pieces often covered with rhinestones. 1922 Broadway. © 615/321-5444.

Trail West   For all your Western-wear needs, this store is hard to beat. They handle the Brooks & Dunn Collection plus all the usual brands of hats, boots, and denim. There are other locations across from the Opryland Hotel at 2416 Music Valley Dr. (© 615/883-5933), and 312 Broadway (© 615/251-1711). 214 Broadway. © 615-255-7030.

8

Nashville After Dark

Live music surrounds you in Nashville. Not only are there dozens of clubs featuring live country and bluegrass music, as you'd expect, but there's also a very lively rock scene. Jazz, blues, and folk clubs are also part of the mix, as are nightclubs featuring dinner shows, songwriters' showcases, and family-oriented musical comedy. And, of course, there's the Grand-daddy of them all, the long-running country music radio broadcast known as the *Grand Ole Opry.*

Some of this music can be found in some rather unexpected places in Nashville. You can catch a show before you even make it out of the Nashville International Airport, where there are regularly scheduled performances by country bands. Street corners, parking lots, Riverfront Park, closed-off streets, hotel lounges, shopping malls, bars—there's no telling where you might run into great live music. Like Memphis, the city overflows with talented musicians who play where they can, much to the benefit of visitors to Nashville.

If we've given you the impression that Nashville is a city of live popular music only, let us point out the city's well-rounded, if lesser known, performing arts organizations. Nashville boasts a vibrant symphony orchestra, opera company, ballet company, the state's largest professional theater company, and several smaller community theaters.

The *Nashville Scene* is the city's arts-and-entertainment weekly. It comes out on Thursday and is available at restaurants, clubs, convenience stores, and other locations. Just keep your eyes peeled. Every Friday, the *Tennessean,* Nashville's morning daily, publishes the *Opry* lineup, and on Sunday it publishes a guide to the coming week's entertainment. *Jazz & Blues News* is a free monthly newsletter featuring news and event listings of interest to music buffs of these genres. It can be found at local bookstores and cafes such as Café One Two Three.

Nashville nightlife happens all around town but predominates in two main entertainment areas—The District and Music Valley. **The District,** an area of renovated warehouses and old bars, is the livelier of the two. Here you'll find the Wildhorse Saloon and two dozen other clubs showcasing two to three times that many bands on any given weekend night. On the sidewalks, people are shoulder to shoulder as they parade from one club to the next, and in the streets, stretch limos vie for space with tricked out pickup trucks. Within The District, Second Avenue is currently the main drag—where you'll find the most impressive of the area's clubs. However, there was a time shortly after the Civil War when Printer's Alley was the center of downtown Nashville nightlife.

Nightclubs in the alley between Church and Union streets have in the past regularly hosted top-name performances but today the alley has lost its luster. Within a few blocks of The District, you'll also find the **Tennessee Performing Arts Center** and several other clubs.

Music Valley, on the other hand, offers a more family-oriented, suburban nightlife scene. This area on the east side of Nashville is where you'll find the *Grand Ole Opry,* the Acuff Theater, the seasonal Stardust Theatre, the Nashville Nightlife theater, the Nashville Palace, the Texas Troubadour Theatre and Ernest Tubb Record Shop's *Midnite Jamboree,* as well as the Opryland Hotel, which has several bars and features plenty of live music.

Tickets to major concerts and sporting events can be purchased through **Ticketmaster** (© 615/255-9600), which maintains a desk at the Tennessee Performing Arts Center box office. A service charge is added to all ticket sales.

1 The Country Music Scene

IN MUSIC VALLEY

Cowboy Church at Texas Troubadour Theatre ★★ *Kids*   If you're looking for a down-home dose of gospel music ministry, make it to the Cowboy Church on time: The old-timey, non-denominational services kick off Sundays at 10am sharp (© **615/859-1001;** www.nashvillecowboychurch.org). Come as you are or don your best Stetson and bolo tie. Either way, you'll fit right in with the eclectic, all-ages congregation of locals and tourists alike that packs the pews every week for a patriotic praise-and-worship service. Located in a shopping plaza across the street from the Opryland Hotel, this theater is also home to the **Ernest Tubb** *Midnite Jamboree.* Recent Jamboree headliners have included Bill Anderson, Porter Wagoner, the Osborne Brothers and Connie Smith, but to find out who's scheduled during your visit, log onto the Ernest Tubb Record Shop's website at www.etrecordshop.com. Music Valley Village, 2416 Music Valley Dr. © 615/889-2474.

Grand Ole Opry ★★★ *Moments*   The show that made Nashville famous, the *Grand Ole Opry* is the country's longest continuously running radio show and airs every weekend from a theater adjacent to the Opryland Hotel. Over the years the Opry has had several homes, including the Ryman Auditorium in downtown Nashville. In late 2003 the 4,400-seat Grand Ole Opry House got its first major refurbishment since 1974, when the program was moved from the Ryman to its current home in the Music Valley. Through it all, the *Opry* remains a comforting mix of country music and gentle humor that has endured for nearly three-quarters of a century. Over the decades the program has featured nearly all the greats of country music. Nearly all *Grand Ole Opry* performances

---

(**Fun Fact** **You Don't Have to Shave Your Legs for This**

If you can't make it to the *Grand Ole Opry* in person, catch it on cable TV or even your car radio. Broadcasts of *Grand Ole Opry Live* recently moved from Country Music Television (CMT) to the Great American Country (GAC) network, where the program can be seen at 8pm (EST) Saturdays.

Just as it has been since 1925, the *Opry* can still be heard on 650 WSM-AM radio. It's also available to 200 radio stations across the country through syndication of *America's Grand Ole Opry Weekend,* which is distributed by Westwood One; Sirius Satellite Radio's Stream 132; www.gaylordopryland.com and www.wsmonline.com; and the Armed Forces Radio Network.

Nashville After Dark

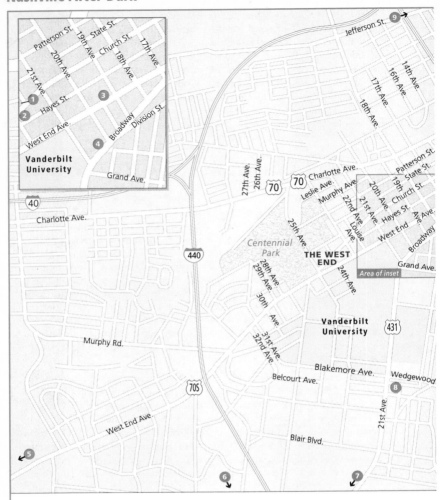

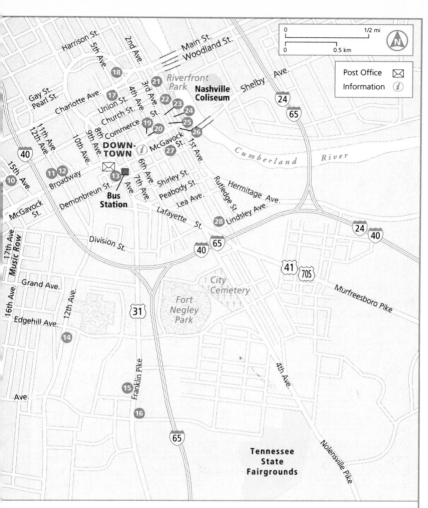

Tootsie's Orchid Lounge **20**
Tribe **10**
12th & Porter **12**
The Wild Boar **4**
Wildhorse Saloon **24**
Zanies Comedy Showplace **15**

sell out, and though it's often possible to get last-minute tickets, you should try to order tickets as far in advance as possible. The *Opry's* line-up of performers for Friday and Saturday nights are announced each Wednesday prior to the shows, which are staged at the Opry House in Music Valley from March through October, and at the Ryman Auditorium from November through February. 2804 Opryland Dr. © 615/889-6611 or 615/889-3060; www.opry.com. Tickets $24–$45 for adults and $14–$45 for children 4–11. Children 3 and under are free if they can sit in your lap.

General Jackson Showboat ⭐ If you'd like to combine some evening entertainment with a cruise on the Cumberland River, try the *General Jackson*. This huge reproduction paddle-wheeler brings back the glory days of river travel. Cruises include plenty of entertainment, including country music and comedy routines on daytime cruises and a musical stage show during the evening dinner cruises. During the summer, the Southern Nights Cruise offers dancing under the stars to live bands; dinner is optional. 2812 Opryland Dr. © 615/889-6611. Tickets $20 night cruises, $52 dinner cruises.

Gibson Bluegrass Showcase Gibson guitars are known the world over, and here's where the company's stringed bluegrass instruments including Dobros, mandolins, and banjos, are crafted. Live music can be heard most nights in the 500-seat showcase room. Free bluegrass jams are open to all comers beginning at 7pm Mondays and Wednesdays. Tuesday is Songwriters' Night. Local bands usually perform Thursdays and Fridays. There is a small bar here, but mostly the entertainment is geared toward the all-ages, family-oriented crowd. Best of all, the music is free. In Opry Mills shopping center, 433 Opry Mills Dr. © 615/514-2233. http://cafes.gibson.com/bluegrass.

Nashville Nightlife This restaurant/club features live country music along with a nightly country-dinner buffet. Shows begin at 5:30pm. A country music revue takes place center stage Tuesday through Sunday nights, while "Elvis Through the Years" is featured Monday evenings. Free karaoke happens Saturdays 8:30pm to midnight. 2620 Music Valley Dr. © 800/308-5779 or 615/885-5201. Cover $32.95.

Nashville Palace Open nightly from 5pm to 1:30am for live country-and-western music, a dance floor, and a full restaurant, this venue features acts familiar to fans of the Grand Ole Opry. Tuesday and Wednesday are Talent Nights (winners from both nights compete on Thursday nights), so be on the lookout for the next Randy Travis, who got his start here. The Palace is easy to find, located directly opposite the Opryland Hotel entrance. 2400 Music Valley Dr. © 615/885-1540. Cover $5.

⌒ *Tips* **I Want My CMT!**

Want to be on TV? Stop by the **Wildhorse Saloon** on Second Street downtown, where each Wednesday night from 7:30pm to 9pm (CST) cable TV's interactive *CMT: Most Wanted Live* is taped. Music news, artist appearances and performances, and video premieres are part of the mix—a country music version of MTV's NYC-based *TRL* program. Call ahead to get a confirmation number that will save your spot (© 615/831-0338), or arrive two hours early to put your name on a back-up list to become part of the audience. Either way, you can get your kicks for free.

Tips **Sitting Pretty**

What's the difference between the *Grand Ole Opry* at Opryland and The Ryman Auditorium? Plenty, but the most practical piece of information is this: The long pews at the Opry are padded, while the ones at the Ryman are hard, well-worn wood. But don't despair over your derriere; personal seat cushions can be 'rented' at the Ryman's refreshment stands in the lobby.

IN THE DISTRICT

In addition to the clubs mentioned here, you'll find several small bars along lower Broadway, in an area long known as **Honky-tonk Row** or **Honky-tonk Highway.** The teeming, 2-block strip between Fourth and Fifth avenues is a nostalgic neon hootenanny of country-music sights, sounds, and occasionally some good old-fashioned rabble-rousing.

Legends Corner *Value*   Today's starving artists are tomorrow's country music superstars, and this beloved dive in The District sets the stage for such happily-ever-after scenarios. Die-hard bar-hoppers insist that Legends Corner has downtown's best live local music and one of the friendliest staffs in all of Music City. Nostalgic memorabilia on the walls adds a quaint, down-home charm. And you can't beat the price: The tip jar gets passed around the room like a collection plate, enabling the rowdy crowds to help support the struggling pickers and grinners who've put Nashville on the map. 428 Broadway. ℂ **615/248-6334.** No cover.

Robert's Western World ⭐   Located just a couple of doors down from the famous Tootsie's, this former Western-wear store helped launch the career of BR5-49. These days, Brazilbilly rocks the house most Friday and Saturday nights. Also look for the up-and-coming Don Kelley Band, which has developed quite a loyal following around town. 416 Broadway. ℂ **615/244-9552.** www.roberts westernworld.com. No cover.

Ryman Auditorium ⭐⭐ *Moments*   Once the home of the *Grand Ole Opry,* this historic theater was renovated a few years back and is once again hosting performances with a country and bluegrass music slant. The Ryman was showcased in the documentary *Down From the Mountain,* a film version of the all-star bluegrass concert performed there featuring music from the movie soundtrack *O Brother, Where Art Thou?* In 2003, the venue was the site of a star-studded memorial concert for the late Johnny Cash. Today, musicians of all genres revere the intimate auditorium, where the acoustics are said to be better than Carnegie Hall's. In recent years, acts as diverse as Beck, Yo-Yo Ma, Coldplay, Al Green, and India Arie have played to packed houses at this National Historic Landmark. 116 5th Ave. N. ℂ **615/254-1445** or 615/889-6611. www.ryman.com. Tickets $18–$43.

Tootsie's Orchid Lounge ⭐ *Value*   This rowdy country dive has been a Nashville tradition since the days when the *Grand Ole Opry* was still performing in the Ryman Auditorium around the corner. Back then, *Opry* stars used to duck into Tootsie's for a drink. Today, you can see signed photos of the many stars who have downed a few here. Free live country music spills out onto the sidewalks daily 10am to 3am, and celebrities still occasionally make the scene. 422 Broadway ℂ **615/726-0463.** www.tootsies.net. No cover.

A Nashville Country Music Itinerary

The following is an itinerary I've put together to help you have a memorable Nashville music experience.

Friday

Start your weekend in a couple of clubs that are favorite haunts of the people who write the songs your favorite country stars end up recording.

- **6:30 to 7:30pm: Douglas Corner Café** (p. 124). At this nondescript neighborhood bar, some of Nashville's best up-and-coming songwriters do early-evening shows.
- **7:45 to 9pm: The Bluebird Cafe** (p. 124). This is Nashville's most famous singer-songwriters' club, best known for its "Music in the Round" shows during which several musicians take turns playing their own songs.
- **9:30 to 10:30pm: Tootsie's Orchid Lounge** (p. 121). Located out the side door of the Ryman Auditorium, this bar was long a favorite haunt of Grand Ole Opry performers. On any given day, there are likely to be three to five bands performing here over the course of a very long day (and night).
- **11pm to 1am: Wildhorse Saloon** (p. 124). Currently the place in Nashville to go line dancing, this massive dance hall has been the site of frequent television broadcasts and music video tapings. The Wildhorse is familiar to people all over the country.

Saturday

Today is a Music Valley day; you'll have to get an early start to get the most out of Music City.

- **11:30am to 2pm: A Lunch Cruise on the *General Jackson* Showboat** (p. 120). For lunch, cruise the Cumberland River while listening to strolling musicians and comedy shows. You can't do any gambling on board, but otherwise, this 300-foot-long showboat conjures up the grand old days of paddle-wheel travel.
- **1:30 to 4:30pm: "Homes of the Stars."** Play the tourist that you are and take a sightseeing bus to size up a cross-section of country music cribs. They come in all shapes and sizes, from Opry octogenarian Little Jimmy Dickens' modest two-story house to Martina McBride's suburban mansion. The wealth is obvious, yet contrasts abound.
- **6 to 9:30pm: *Grand Ole Opry*** (p. 117). This is the granddaddy of country music, a down-home blend of corny humor, country music, and an ever-changing roster of guest hosts and hostesses bringing in their own friends as accompaniment. Throw in few square-dancing interludes and the spontaneity of being part of a live radio broadcast, and no matter what your musical preferences, you can expect to be thoroughly entertained.
- **9:30 to 11:30pm: Nashville Palace** (p. 120). The stage of this nightclub just up the street from the Grand Ole Opry House has seen the likes of Ricky Van Shelton, Randy Travis, Lorrie Morgan, and Alan Jackson. Who knows who might show up when you're in town?

- **11:30pm to 1am: Ernest Tubb *Midnite Jamboree*** (p. 117). Back when the Grand Ole Opry was at the Ryman Auditorium, performers used to drop by the Ernest Tubb Record Shop for impromptu shows. This tradition continues here at the Music Valley store near the Opryland Hotel.

Sunday

Today entails a bit more driving than the previous 2 days, but the music makes the trip worthwhile.

- **9am: Opryland Hotel Brunch.** If you're not in a hurry, you might opt for a leisurely brunch inside the lush Garden Conservatory Atrium. Breakfast dishes and a full buffet of carved meats, salads, vegetables and desserts are served until 2pm at Ristorante Volare. Reservations are suggested (*©* 615/871-6848).
- **10 to 11:30am: Texas Troubadour Theatre** (p. 117). Or start your Sunday at Nashville Cowboy Church. It's a little bit country and a whole lotta gospel.
- **12 to 2pm: Opryland Hotel and the Music Valley Museums.** If you did brunch, you can walk off that "all-you-can-eat" excess and wander through the other amazing atriums of the Opryland Hotel (p. 88). Across the street from the hotel, pick up a tacky souvenir or two while visiting the Music Valley Wax Museum or the Willie Nelson & Friends Showcase Museum.
- **3 to 6pm: The Country Music Hall of Fame and Museum** (p. 85). Cap the afternoon soaking up the history of country music at this spectacular new museum. If you have time for only one country-music attraction while you're in town, make sure to make time for this.
- **6:30 to 7:30pm: Bluebird Cafe.** If you're like us, you'll want to head back to the Bluebird before you call it quits for the weekend. This early show usually showcases a single musician. If you still haven't gotten your fill, stick around after 8pm for the Writer's Showcase, which is usually a good time to catch some of Nashville's best new songwriters.
- **7:30 to 9pm: Ryman Auditorium** (p. 121). If Cowboy Church at the Texas Troubadour Theatre just didn't give you your fill of gospel music (or you couldn't get out of bed in time), see if there's a gospel show scheduled at the former home of the Grand Ole Opry. In fact, the Ryman was originally built as a church.
- **9 to 11pm: Robert's Western World** (p. 121). Catch one of Nashville's currently hot country bands, or whatever band happens to be playing in this funky lower-Broadway bar. If you don't like the band playing here, wander up and down Broadway until you find one that you do like.
- **11pm to 1am: Your choice.** If you're still on your feet, there's still plenty to do. Keep checking out the lower Broadway bars with live music or head over to the Wildhorse Saloon for one last dance.

> **Tips Shhh!**
>
> That's the slogan of **The Bluebird Cafe**. So save your hell-raising for else-where. Once the audition-winning songwriters step onstage, the Bluebird becomes pin-drop quiet. For musicians the world over, playing here is the country music equivalent of Carnegie Hall. Reserving one of the venue's 21 tables takes persistence. Weekend shows often sell out days in advance. The Bluebird advises patrons to start calling on Monday "and keep hitting the redial button until you get through!" If you can't get reservations, there's usually standing-room-only (on a first-come, first-served basis) at the bar or at benches.

Wildhorse Saloon   Run by the same company that gave Nashville the Opry-land Hotel and stages the *Grand Ole Opry,* this massive dance hall is ground zero for boot scooters. Attracting everyone from country music stars to line-dancing senior citizen groups, the Wildhorse is the scene to make these days in Nashville. There's live music most nights by both new bands and the big names in contemporary country. If you sashay up an appetite, it's worth noting that bar-becue is served 11am to midnight. The saloon is open until 1am Mondays through Thursdays, and until 3am on Fridays and Saturdays. 120 2nd Ave. N. ✆ 615/251-1000. www.wildhorsesaloon.com. Cover $4–$6 ($10–$15 for special events).

ELSEWHERE AROUND NASHVILLE

The Bluebird Cafe ★★ *Moments*   For a quintessential Nashville experience, visit this unassuming 100-seat club that remains one of the nation's premiere venues for up-and-coming as well as established songwriters. Surprisingly, you'll find the Bluebird not in The District or on Music Row but in a suburban shop-ping plaza across the road from the Mall at Green Hills. There are usually two shows a night. Between 6 and 7pm, there is frequently music in the round, dur-ing which four singer-songwriters play some of their latest works. After 9pm, when more established acts take the stage, there's a cover charge. This is the place in Nashville to catch the music of people you'll be hearing from in coming years. Because the club is so small, reservations (taken noon–5pm) are recommended. 4104 Hillsboro Rd. ✆ 615/383-1461. www.bluebirdcafe.com. No cover for early shows, but there is a minimum $7 order per person at tables. Cover fees vary for late (9pm) shows.

Douglas Corner Café   Though it has the look and feel of a neighborhood bar, this is one of Nashville's top places for songwriters trying to break into the big time—it's the city's main competition for the Bluebird Cafe. The club also has occasional shows by performers already established. It's located a few min-utes south of downtown. 2106 8th Ave. S. ✆ 615/298-1688. www.musicdigest.com/douglascorner. Cover free–$5.

Station Inn ★   Widely regarded as one of the best bluegrass venues around, this club lies in the warehouse district south of Broadway in downtown. The large stone building is nondescript, but keep looking and you'll find it. 402 12th Ave. S. ✆ 615/255-3307. www.stationinn.com. Cover $7 Tues–Sat; free Sun.

2 The Rest of the Club & Music Scene: Rock, Blues & Jazz

Exit/In   This place has none of the glitz of the bigger nightspots in The Dis-trict; it's just a beat-up club that has long been a local favorite of alternative-rock and even the fast-growing alternative country genre. Music ranges from rock to blues to reggae and a little country; there's usually live music 6 nights a week. 2208 Elliston Place. © 615/321-3340. www.exit-in.com. Cover varies.

Graham Central Station   Tucked in the middle of all the action on Second Avenue North, this entertainment complex includes four floors of music and six different clubs under one roof (in fact, there is even a party on the roof when the weather's good). Disco and Top 40 get their own dance floors, but there's also a karaoke bar, and a sports bar, as well as pool tables. Basically, this place covers all the bases. 128 N. 2nd Ave. © 615/251-9593. www.grahamcentralstationnashville. com. Cover free–$10.

12th & Porter   Located just off Broadway behind the offices of the *Tennessean,* Nashville's daily newspaper, 12th & Porter is impossible to miss. It's that turquoise-and-black building with the retro look. This place has a hip, urban feel and books alternative-rock bands. Songwriter's Night is Monday, when there's no cover. 114 12th Ave. N. © 615/254-7236. www.faisons.com. Cover free–$10.

JAZZ & BLUES

If you're here in the summer, check to see who's playing at the **Tennessee Jazz & Blues Concert Series** at Belle Meade Plantation (© **615/356-0501**).

B.B. King's Blues Club ⭐⭐   Nashville can consider itself lucky to have landed one of the legendary blues guitarist's few clubs. The original, launched in Memphis more than a decade ago, has become Beale Street's crown jewel (satellite locations are in Los Angeles and New York City). B.B. himself inaugurated the Music City spot with a sold-out, standing-room-only show in September 2003. Since then, locals and tourists craving another alternative to Nashville's pervasive country music bars have ensured this authentic blues bar has a solid future in the District. 152 Second Ave. © 615/256-2727. Cover $5–$7 (usually $50–$170 for B.B.'s increasingly infrequent, but always sold-out, concerts).

Bourbon Street Blues and Boogie Bar   If you're wandering around in The District wishing you could hear some wailing blues guitar, head over to Printer's Alley and check out the action at this smoky club. 220 Printers Alley. © 615/242-5837. www.bourbonstreetblues.com. Cover $5–$10.

Café One Two Three   Late-night and Sunday-afternoon jazz are the main musical attractions at this venerable coffeehouse and cafe. You won't easily forget the street address, either. 123 12th Ave. N. © 615/255-2233. www.faisons.com.

F. Scott's Restaurant   Live jazz is presented nightly at this suburban outpost of chic. An extensive wine list and upscale dinner menu enhance its appeal for culture vultures. Free valet parking is an added perk at this classy establishment, located a stone's throw from the Mall at Green Hills. 2210 Crestmoor Rd. © 615/269-5861. No cover.

3rd & Lindsley Bar & Grill   Eight blocks south of Broadway, in a new office complex surrounded by old warehouses, you'll find Nashville's premier blues club. The atmosphere may lack the rough edges and smoke that you'd expect of a real blues club, but the music is true blues, with some rock and Top 40. 818 3rd Ave. S. © 615/259-9891. Cover free–$10.

FOLK & CELTIC

Mulligan's Pub   This small pub in the heart of The District is always packed at night and definitely has the feel of an Irish pub. There's good Irish food, cold pints, and live Irish and American folk music Thursday to Saturday nights. 117 2nd Ave. N. ℂ 615/242-8010. No cover.

GAY & LESBIAN DANCE CLUBS AND BARS

Nashville's gay nightlife district lies to the south of Broadway (south of The District); along 4th Avenue South, you'll find no fewer than three gay bars.

The Chute Complex Whether you're in the mood for some boot scootin', some karaoke, a drag show, or relaxing in a piano bar, this men's entertainment complex has it all. There's even a restaurant and a leather bar. 2535 Franklin Rd. ℂ 615/297-4571. Cover $2–$5.

The Connection With dancing Tuesday to Sunday 8pm to 3am, this club is the largest (50,000 sq. ft.) and reigning fave among Nashville's gay clubs. With a main dance floor and a separate lounge, you can usually choose between high-energy dance music and country. There's also a patio, cafe, and even a gift shop. You'll find the club north of the Spring Street Bridge just off I-65 in the industrial area on the east side of the Cumberland River from downtown. 901 Cowan St. ℂ 615/742-1166. Cover $5.

Gas Lite Lounge A discreet downtown hideaway that caters primarily to middle-aged men, this gay and lesbian club is known for its cozy, at-home appeal. Think chandeliers and soft lighting, and a friendly staff. 1671/2 8th Ave. S. 615/254-1278. No cover.

Tribe ⋆ An energized crowd of Nashville's most beautiful dancing queens/kings congregates nightly at this SoHo-slick club. Straight or gay, it doesn't matter—as long as you're confidently hip and ready for a good time. Martinis, a full menu full of munchies, music videos and a silver and granite decor cast a shimmering spell on partygoers until the wee hours of the morning. 1517A Church St. ℂ 615/329-2912. www.tribenashville.com. No cover.

A COMEDY CLUB

Zanies Comedy Showplace This is Nashville's oldest, if not only, comedy club and has shows Wednesday through Sunday nights. Most weekend headliners have TV and movie track records. Cover is sometimes slightly higher for big-name comedians. 2025 8th Ave. S. ℂ 615/269-0221. www.zanies.com. Cover $10–$20 (plus minimum of two drink or food orders).

3 The Bar & Pub Scene

The Nashville bar scene is for the most part synonymous with the Nashville restaurant scene; an establishment has to serve food in order to serve liquor. So, in addition to the places listed below, if you want a cocktail, step into almost any moderately priced or expensive restaurant. The first thing you're likely to see is a bar.

BARS

The Beer Sellar As the name implies, this downtown landmark is all about the brew. By the bottle or on tap, there's a vast selection of beers that draws a rowdy crowd of fun-loving types. The dark but homey basement bar has a good jukebox, too. 107 Church St. ℂ 615/254-9464.

The Gerst Haus Though ostensibly a German restaurant, this place is more like a lively beer hall than anything else. They serve their own amber lager, and on weekends there is a live polka band in the evenings. 228 Woodland St. ℂ 615/244-8886.

Havana Lounge   On the second floor of an old warehouse in the middle of The District, this bar oozes tropical hipness—a la Havana or Miami in the glory days of Art Deco nightclubs. Buy a cigar, order a martini, and sit back for some serious scene making. 154 2nd Ave. N. ✆ 615/313-7665.

Jimmy Kelly's   This place is straight out of the Old South and might have you thinking that you've stepped onto the set of a Tennessee Williams play. Jimmy Kelly's is primarily a restaurant and the bar isn't very large, but you'll feel as though you're part of a Nashville tradition when you have a drink here. The place is always lively, and the clientele tends to be older and well-to-do. 217 Louise Ave. ✆ 615/329-4349. www.jimmykellys.com.

The Old Spaghetti Factory   Sure it's touristy, but the drinks are cheap. If you think Victoriana is the height of romance, you won't want to miss out on bringing a date here. It's hard to believe that this elegant room was once a warehouse. 160 2nd Ave. N. ✆ 615/254-9010.

The Wild Boar   The Wild Boar is Nashville's most expensive and exclusive restaurant, but it also has a great piano bar where you won't have to spend $80 to enjoy the atmosphere. It's always a good idea to dress as if you were coming to dinner. Jackets, like reservations for dinner, are recommended. 2014 Broadway. ✆ 615/329-1313.

BREW PUBS

Big River Grille & Brewing Works   With a more contemporary atmosphere than the Market Street Brewery (see below), this pub does a brisk food business and serves up handcrafted "boutique" beers, including lagers, pilsners and stouts, along with a seasonal brew that changes throughout the year. On a weekend night, this place stays packed. 111 Broadway. ✆ 615/251-4677.

Blackstone Restaurant & Brewery   Nashville's most upscale brew pub draws a lot of business travelers who are staying in nearby hotels. Elegantly inviting are the cushioned chairs, fireplace and a long, marbled bar. The food, including wood-fired pizzas and pretzels, is consistently good. But the beer is the main focus. Choose from a variety of brews including several that change with the seasons. There's also a six-pack sampler. 1918 West End Ave. ✆ 615/327-9969.

Bosco's ✦   With locations in Memphis and Nashville, Tennessee-based Bosco's has built a reputation as the best brew pub around. Here in Music City, Bosco's occupies a cavernous but congenial space in Hillsboro Village. Patrons can wash down fresh fish dishes, gourmet pizzas, and stuffed mushrooms with a choice of more than half a dozen beers on tap. The bar sometimes serves cask-conditioned ales. 1805 21st Ave. S. ✆ 615/385-0050.

Market Street Brewery & Public House   This dark, oaky pub is housed in a renovated warehouse in the heart of The District and has by far the most character of any microbrewery in Nashville. Most of the wide variety of brews served here are fairly light, with wheat beer a specialty. 134 2nd Ave. N. ✆ 615/259-9611.

4 The Performing Arts

THE TENNESSEE PERFORMING ARTS CENTER (TPAC)

A major renovation completed in fall 2003 gave the drab, utilitarian **Tennessee Performing Arts Center (TPAC),** 505 Deaderick St. (✆ **615/782-4000;** www.tpac.org), a much-needed makeover. Glass walls and an electronic marquee now illuminate the formerly nondescript, concrete exterior of Nashville's premier performance facility. The center houses three theaters: the Andrew

---

Tips **Ticket Tips**

If you plan to peruse the performing arts, consider calling the concierge
before you arrive. Offer a tip in exchange for having your tickets ready
and waiting for you.

Johnson, the James K. Polk, and the Andrew Jackson, whose expanded lobby
now dazzles patrons with a 30-foot waterfall and other aesthetic touches. The
three spaces can accommodate large and small productions (ticket prices range
$10–$45). Resident companies based here include the **Nashville Ballet**
(© 615/244-7233; www.nashvilleballet.com), which each year stages two full-
length ballets and two programs of selected pieces; the **Nashville Symphony**
(© 615/255-5600; www.nashvillesymphony.org), which presents a mix of
classical and pops concerts, as well as a children's series; and the **Nashville
Opera** (© 615/292-5710; www.nashvilleopera.org), which mounts four lavish
productions annually.

TPAC, as locals know it, is also home to two theater companies. The **Tennessee Repertory Theatre** (© 615/244-4878; www.tnrep.org) is the state's
largest professional theater company. Its five seasonal productions run from
September to May and include dramas, musicals, and comedies. TPAC's other
resident theater company is **Circle Players** (© 615/255-9600, a community
group nearing its 50th anniversary. This company does six productions per season and seems to take more chances on lesser-known works than the Rep does.

In addition to productions by Nashville's main performing-arts companies,
TPAC also hosts various acts such as Blue Man Group, which kicked off the fall
2003 season, and an annual **"Broadway Series"** (© 615/782-4000) that brings
first-rate touring productions to Nashville between October and June. Tickets to
TPAC performances are available either at the TPAC box office or through
Ticketmaster (© 615/255-9600).

OTHER VENUES & SERIES AROUND THE CITY

Looking beyond TPAC, you'll find a wide array of performances in the **Great
Performances at Vanderbilt** series (© 615/322-2471; www.vanderbilt.edu),
which is staged at Vanderbilt University's Langford Auditorium, 21st Avenue
South (tickets $10–$30). Each year, this series includes more than a dozen internationally acclaimed performing-arts companies from around the world. The
emphasis is on chamber music and modern dance, but touring theater productions and classical ballet companies are also scheduled. To reach Langford
Auditorium, take 25th Avenue South off West End Avenue, and then turn left
on Garland Avenue. The **Nashville Municipal Auditorium,** 417 Fourth Ave.
N. (© 615/862-6390), was for many years the site of everything from circuses
to revivals. Today the aging, dome-roofed venue plays host to everything from
rock icons like Bob Dylan to children's shows fronted by Bob the Builder. Plus,
there's always the occasional rodeo, boxing match, or "monster-truck" mash.
A stone's throw away, the **Gaylord Entertainment Center,** 501 Broadway
(© 615/770-2000; www.gaylordentertainmentcenter.com), is now the venue of
choice for major rock and country music concerts, ice shows, and, of course,
NHL hockey courtesy of the Nashville Predators.

During the summer months, outdoor performances enliven many venues
around the city. The busiest of these is the **AmSouth Amphitheatre,** 3839

Murfreesboro Pike (© 615/641-5800; www.amsouthamphitheatre.com), which hosts numerous name performers (tickets $16–$40). Pop, country, jazz, rock, ethnic, and classical music all take the stage under the stars here. Reserve a seat or spread out with a blanket and have a picnic on the grassy slopes.

The "Dancin' in The District" series brings free concerts by national acts (usually rock) to downtown Nashville's **Coliseum** every Thursday night from June to August. Admission is $3. Performances (by bands such as Hootie and the Blowfish and the Indigo Girls) take place between 5 and 10pm. For more information, call © 615/329-2556. The **Frist Center for the Arts** offers Frist Fridays on the last Friday of every month (May–Sept). Free admission includes live music and appetizers outside on the courtyard, along with entry into the Frist's galleries. For more information, call © 615/244- 3340.

Check the *Nashville Scene* to see who's performing at these concerts during your visit. Farther away, the verdant grounds of **Cheekwood Botanical Gardens and Museum of Art,** 1200 Forrest Park Dr. (© 615/353-2163; www.cheekwood.org), are the site of annual summer concerts by the Nashville Symphony each June.

If you enjoy dinner theater, you may want to check out **Chaffin's Barn Dinner Theatre,** 8204 Tenn. 100 (© 800/282-BARN [2276] or 615/646-9977; www.dinnertheatre.com), housed in a big old Dutch-colonial barn 20 minutes outside of Nashville (tickets, dinner, and show $40 adults, $20 children 12 and under; show only, $28 adults, $20 children). The dinner is an all-you-can-eat country buffet (think fried catfish, slabs of ham, green beans, and fruit cobblers and berry shortcakes) and plays are generally time-tested musicals and contemporary comedies. Shows run the gamut from *Cabaret* and *Annie Get Your Gun* to *Arsenic and Old Lace.* Performances are Tuesday through Saturday (dinner 6–7:30pm; shows 8pm) and Sunday (buffet is served noon–1:30pm; show

---

Tips **Know Before You Go**

Opry bound? Be aware that not all country stars are members of the grand ol' gang. So if you're hoping to see, say, George Strait, Wynonna, or the Dixie Chicks, look elsewhere. Many fans might not realize that *Opry* members are invited performers who must agree to a certain number of *Opry* appearances. Consequently, due to scheduling conflicts or other concerns, not every country singer who's a household name is represented.

But plenty of them are. At press time, the *Opry*'s stellar roster included: Trace Adkins, Bill Anderson, Clint Black, Garth Brooks, Jim Ed Brown, Roy Clark, John Conlee, Skeeter Davis, Diamond Rio, Little Jimmy Dickens, Joe Diffie, Holly Dunn, The Gatlin Brothers, Vince Gill, Billy Grammer, Tom T. Hall, Emmylou Harris, Jan Howard, Stonewall Jackson, Alan Jackson, George Jones, Hal Ketchum, Alison Krauss, Patty Loveless, Loretta Lynn, Martina McBride, Del McCoury, Reba McEntire, Lorrie Morgan, The Osborne Brothers, Brad Paisley, Dolly Parton, Charley Pride, Jeanne Pruett, Del Reeves, Riders In The Sky, Ricky Van Shelton, Jean Shepard, Ricky Skaggs, Ralph Stanley, Marty Stuart, Pam Tillis, Randy Travis, Travis Tritt, Ricky Van Shelton, Porter Wagoner, Steve Wariner, The Whites, and Trisha Yearwood.

2pm). Reservations are required and must be paid for 24 hours in advance. Senior and children's matinees are also offered at discounted prices. To reach Chaffin's Barn, take I-40 west to Exit 199 (Old Hickory Blvd.) and head south to Old Harding Road (Tenn. 100), turn right, and continue for 4 miles (6.5km).

And then, of course, there's the **Belcourt Theatre,** 2102 Belcourt Ave. (© **615/383-9140;** www.belcourt.org), where you can catch the latest art-house film releases and other cinematic fare that's all but ignored by today's modern multiplexes. Live entertainment is staged here occasionally as well (fitting, as the venue was one of the early homes of the *Grand Ole Opry*).

Side Trips from Nashville

After you've had your fill of Nashville's country music scene, it may be time for a change of scenery—and a taste of the real country. Heading out in any direction from Nashville, you'll hit the Tennessee hills. These are the hills famous for their walking horses and sour-mash whiskey. They also hold historic towns and Civil War battlefields that are well worth visiting.

1 Franklin, Columbia & Scenic U.S. 31

Franklin is 20 miles S of Nashville; Columbia is 46 miles S of Nashville

South of Nashville, U.S. 31 leads through the rolling Tennessee hills to the historic towns of Franklin and Columbia. This area was the heart of the middle Tennessee plantation country, and there are still many antebellum mansions along this route. Between Nashville and Franklin, you'll pass by more than a dozen old plantation homes, with still more to the south of Franklin.

ESSENTIALS
GETTING THERE The start of the scenic section of U.S. 31 is in Brentwood at Exit 74 off I-65. Alternatively, you can take I-65 straight to Franklin (Exit 65) and then take U.S. 31 back north to Nashville. From Columbia, you can head back north on U.S. 31, take U.S. 412/Tenn. 99 east to I-65, or head west on Tenn. 50 to the **Natchez Trace Parkway.** This latter road is a scenic highway administered by the National Park Service.

VISITOR INFORMATION In Franklin, stop in at the tiny **Williamson County Visitor Information Center,** 209 E. Main St. (© **615/591-8514**), open daily except holidays.

EXPLORING HISTORIC FRANKLIN
At the visitor center—housed in a former doctor's office built in 1839—you can pick up information about various historic sites around the area, including a map to the historic homes along U.S. 31 and a self-guided walking-tour map of Franklin. A 15-block area of downtown and quite a few other buildings around town have been listed on the National Register of Historic Places. Today, nearly the entire town has been restored—both commercial buildings around the central square and residential buildings in surrounding blocks—giving the town a charming 19th-century air. The best thing to do in Franklin is just stroll around admiring the restored buildings, browsing through the many antiques stores and malls. In addition to downtown antiques malls, there are others at the I-65 interchange.

Franklin is best known in Tennessee as the site of the bloody Battle of Franklin during the Civil War. During this battle, which took place on November 30, 1864, more than 6,000 Confederate and 2,000 Union soldiers were killed. Each year on November 30, there are special activities here to commemorate the battle. Among the events are costumed actors marching through town and, after dark, a bonfire. Contact the Visitor Information Center for details.

To learn more about the town's Civil War history, visit the following historic homes.

Carnton Plantation ★   Built in 1826 by Randal McGavock, a former mayor of Nashville, Carnton Plantation is a beautiful neoclassical antebellum mansion with a Greek Revival portico. During the Battle of Franklin, one of the bloodiest battles of the Civil War, this plantation home served as a Confederate hospital, and today you can still see the blood stains on floors throughout the house. The interior of the stately old home is almost completely restored and houses many McGavock family pieces and other period furnishings. Two years after the battle, the McGavock family donated 2 acres of land to be used as a cemetery for Confederate soldiers who had died during the Battle of Franklin. There are almost 1,500 graves in the McGavock Confederate Cemetery, which makes this the largest private Confederate cemetery in the country.

1345 Carnton Lane. (𝄞 **615/794-0903**. www.carnton.org. Admission $8 adults, $7 seniors, $3 children 4–12. Mon–Sat 9am–5pm, Sun 1–5pm; Closed major holidays.

Carter House   Built in 1830, the Carter House served as the Union army command post during the Battle of Franklin. Throughout the bloody fight, which raged all around the house, the Carter family and friends hid in the cellar. Today, you can still see many bullet holes in the main house and various outbuildings on the property. In addition to getting a tour of the restored home, you can spend time in the museum, which contains many Civil War artifacts. A video presentation about the battle that took place here will provide you with a perspective for touring the town of Franklin.

1140 Columbia Ave. (𝄞 **615/791-1861**. Admission $8 adults, $6 seniors, $3 children. Apr–Oct Mon–Sat 9am–5pm, Sun 1–5pm; Nov–Mar Mon–Fri 9am–4pm, Sun 1–4pm. Closed major holidays.

Lotz House   Located directly across the street from the Carter House, this restored 1858 home was built by Albert Lotz, a German woodworker. Today, the house contains a large private collection of Civil War and Old West artifacts. Several rooms in the house have also been decorated with period furnishings. This house, too, was used as a hospital after the Battle of Franklin.

1111 Columbia Ave. (𝄞 **615/794-1850**. Admission $5 adults, $4 seniors, $1.50 children 12 and under. Apr–Oct Mon–Sat 9am–5pm, Sun noon–5pm; Nov–Mar Mon–Sat 9am–4pm, Sun noon–4pm. Closed major holidays.

CONTINUING ON TO COLUMBIA

Heading south from Franklin on U.S. 31 for about 26 miles will bring you to the town of Columbia. Along the way, you'll see a dozen or so historic antebellum homes, and in Columbia itself, more old homes and three districts listed on the National Register of Historic Places.

James K. Polk House   This modest home was where James K. Polk, the 11th president of the United States, grew up and where he lived when he began his legal and political career. Though Polk may not be as familiar a name as those of some other early presidents, he did achieve two very important goals while in office: Polk negotiated the purchase of California and settled the long-standing dispute between the United States and England over where to draw the border of the Oregon Territory. The house is filled with antiques that belonged to Polk's parents when they lived here and to Polk and his family during their time in the

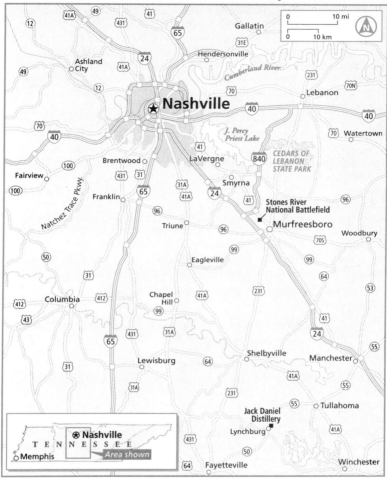

White House. In a separate building there is an exhibit of political and Mexican War memorabilia.

301 W. 7th St., Columbia. (**931/388-2354.** Admission $7 adults, $6 seniors and $4 students (maximum of $20 per family). Apr–Oct Mon–Sat 9am–5pm, Sun 1–5pm; Nov–Mar Mon–Sat 9am–4pm, Sun 1–5pm. Closed major holidays.

2 Distilleries, Walking Horses & a Civil War Battlefield

Though Tennessee was last to secede from the Union, the Civil War came early to the state, and 3 years of being on the front lines left Tennessee with a legacy written in blood. More Civil War battles were fought here than in any other state except Virginia, and the bloodiest of these was the Battle of Stones River, which took place 30 miles south of Nashville near the city of Murfreesboro. Today this battle is commemorated at the **Stones River National Battlefield.**

In the 2 decades that followed the war, Tennessee quickly recovered and developed two of the state's most famous commodities—Tennessee sippin' whiskey and Tennessee walking horses. Another 45 miles or so south of Murfreesboro, you can learn about both of these time-honored Tennessee traditions.

For those of you who are not connoisseurs of **sour-mash whiskeys,** Tennessee whiskey is *not* bourbon. This latter whiskey, named for Bourbon County, Kentucky, where it was first distilled, is made much the same way, but it is not charcoal-mellowed the way fine Tennessee sour-mash whiskey is.

Stones River National Battlefield On New Year's Eve 1862, what would become the bloodiest Civil War battle west of the Appalachian Mountains began just north of Murfreesboro along the Stones River. Though by the end of the first day of fighting the Confederates thought they were assured a victory, Union reinforcements turned the tide against the rebels. By January 3, the Confederates were in retreat and 23,000 soldiers lay dead or injured on the battlefield. Today, 351 acres of the battlefield are preserved. The site includes a national cemetery and the Hazen Brigade Monument, which was erected in 1863 and is the oldest Civil War memorial in the United States. In the visitor center you'll find a museum full of artifacts and details of the battle.

3501 Old Nashville Hwy., Murfreesboro. ⓒ 615/478-1035. www.nps.gov/stri. Free admission. Battlefield daily 8am–5pm. Closed Dec 25. Take I-24 south from Nashville for about 30 miles to Exit 78B.

Continue on I-24 to Exit 105. Drive southwest for 10 miles to Tullahoma and follow signs to:

Jack Daniel's Distillery ⭐ Old Jack Daniel (or Mr. Jack, as he was known hereabouts) didn't waste any time setting up his whiskey distillery after the Civil War came to an end. Founded in 1866, this is the oldest registered distillery in the United States and is on the National Register of Historic Places. It's still an active distillery; you can tour the facility and see how Jack Daniel's whiskey is made and learn how it gets such a distinctive earthy flavor. There are two secrets to the manufacture of Mr. Jack's famous sour-mash whiskey. The first of these is the water that comes gushing—pure, cold, and iron-free—from Cave Spring. The other is the sugar maple that's used to make the charcoal. In fact, it is this charcoal, through which the whiskey slowly drips, that gives Jack Daniel's its renowned smoothness.

After touring the distillery, you can glance in at the office used by Mr. Jack and see the safe that did him in. Old Mr. Jack kicked that safe one day in a fit of anger and wound up getting gangrene for his troubles. One can only hope that regular doses of Tennessee sippin' whiskey helped ease the pain of his last days. If you want to take home a bottle of Jack Daniel's, they can be purchased here at the distillery, but nowhere else in this county, which is another of Tennessee's dry counties. (No tastings at the end of the tour I'm afraid.)

Tenn. 55, Lynchburg. ⓒ 931/759-4221. www.jackdaniels.com. Free admission. Daily 8am–4:30pm. Tours at regular intervals throughout the day. Reservations not accepted. Closed Thanksgiving, Dec 24–25, Dec 31, and Jan 1. Take Tenn. 55 off I-24 and drive 26 miles southwest to Lynchburg.

Tennessee Walking Horse Museum The Tennessee walking horse, named for its unusual high-stepping walking gait, is considered the world's premier breed of show horse, and it is here in the rolling hills of middle Tennessee that most of these horses are bred. Using interactive videos, hands-on exhibits, and other displays, this museum presents the history of the Tennessee walking horse.

Cruising the "Music Highway" between Nashville & Memphis

- In Nashville, tour the **Country Music Hall of Fame and Museum,** 222 Fifth Ave. S. (© 800/852-6437). In Memphis, immerse yourself in the wonderful new **Soulsville: Stax Museum of American Soul Music,** 926 E. McLemore (© 901/946-2535), as well as at the Beale Street-area **Memphis Rock 'N' Soul Museum,** 145 Lt. George Lee Ave. (© 901/543-0800). OK, you've just completed a crash course in the history of American popular music!

- Get that old-time religion at the Sunday-morning **Cowboy Church** (© 615/859-1001) at the Texas Troubadour Theater in Nashville. For a cross-cultural point of comparison, while in Memphis seek out the **Full Gospel Tabernacle,** 787 Hale Rd. (© 901/396-9192), where Grammy-winning soul legend the Reverend Al Green still regularly preaches.

- Heading west to Memphis from Nashville, take a breather from the interstate at Hurricane Mills (I-40, Exit 143), drive a few miles deep into the wooded countryside, where you can sightsee and even spend the night at **Loretta Lynn's Ranch and Family Campground.** The poor coal miner's daughter bought this Graceland-esque mansion an hour's drive from Nashville when she made it big as the Queen of Country Music. Guests may tour her **Plantation Home** and the new 18,000-square-foot **Coal Miner's Daughter Museum,** which are nestled along a leafy stream within her picturesque 3,500-acre farm. There's even a log-cabin replica of her **Butcher Holler Home Place** in eastern Kentucky. Before you get back onto the main highway, stop at **Loretta's Country Kitchen** (and gift shop) for a down-home buffet of fried chicken, mashed potatoes, biscuits, and all the trimmings. For more information or to make campground reservations, call © 931/296-7700 or visit www.lorettalynn.com.

- An hour east of Memphis, you can stop by Carl Perkins's old hometown of Jackson, Tennessee. The rockabilly pioneer (*Blue Suede Shoes*) died in 1998, but his memory lives on at the fledgling **Rockabilly Hall of Fame** in the historic downtown district. In addition to the expected Sun Records memorabilia including costumes, vinyl 78 records, photos, and instruments, there are a few eye-popping oddities on display: the "paddles" from the circa-1977 defibrillator that supposedly shocked a dying Elvis at a Memphis hospital; and a wall of fame devoted to 8-by-10 glossies and newspaper clippings of game-show host Wink Martindale, who hails from these parts. For details, contact the Jackson/Madison County Convention and Visitors Bureau (© 800/498-4748).

  While you're in Jackson, tour the train museum and sip a root beer float at **Casey Jones Village** (© 800/748-9588), an old-time country store and soda fountain in Jackson named for the legendary turn-of-the-century railroad conductor who lost his life rescuing others in a fiery train wreck. Let the kids blow off some steam (so to speak) by climbing aboard a real turn-of-the-century locomotive.

-e will appeal primarily to equine enthusiasts, there
ᴀsual visitor to learn and enjoy. The annual Tennessee
ₒnal Celebration, held each August here in Shelbyville, is
ₜnessee's most important annual events. Tennessee walkers can
ₒing through their paces at various other annual shows in the
ₐa.

ₜ., Lynchburg. ✆ **931/759-5747.** Free admission. Tues–Sat 10am–12pm and 1–4pm. Closed
ₐɩdays.

ʌ UNFORGETTABLE LUNCH STOP IN LYNCHBURG

Miss Mary Bobo's Boarding House ✫ SOUTHERN   You'll feel as if you
should be wearing a hoop skirt or top hat when you see this grand white mansion, with its columns, long front porch, and balcony over the front door (but
casual, contemporary clothes are just fine). Miss Mary Bobo's, housed in
an antebellum-style mansion built slightly postbellum (in 1866), opened for
business as a boardinghouse back in 1908, and though it no longer accepts
boarders, it does serve the best lunch for miles around. Be prepared for filling
portions of good, Southern home cooking, and remember, lunch here is actually
midday dinner. Miss Mary's is very popular, and you generally need to book a
weekday lunch 2 to 3 weeks in advance; for a Saturday lunch, you'll need to
make reservations at least 2 to 3 *months* in advance.

Main St., Lynchburg. ✆ **931/759-7394.** Reservations required well in advance. Set menu $11 adults; $5
children under 10. No credit cards. Lunch seatings Mon–Fri 1pm; Sat 11am and 1pm.

10

The Best of Memphis

Memphis spawned several of the most important musical forms of the 20th century, yet Nashville stole the Tennessee limelight with its country music. Ask the average American what makes Memphis special, and he or she *might* be able to tell you that this is the city of Graceland, Elvis Presley's mansion.

What they're less likely to know is that Memphis is also the birthplace of the blues, rock 'n' roll, and soul music. Memphis is where W. C. Handy put down on paper the first written blues music, where the King made his first recording, and where Otis Redding and Al Green expressed the music in their souls.

Many fans of American music (and they come from all over the world) know Memphis. Walking down Beale Street today, sitting in the Sun Studio Cafe, or waiting to pass through the wrought-iron gates of Graceland, you're almost as likely to hear French, German, and Japanese as you are to hear English. British, Irish, and Scottish accents are all common in a city known throughout the world as the birthplace of the most important musical styles of the 20th century. For these people, a trip to Memphis is a pilgrimage. The Irish rock band U2 came here to pay homage and wound up infusing their music with Americana on the record and movie *U2: Rattle & Hum.* Lead singer Bono, recently interviewed for the city's new Soulsville museum, calls the city's musical heritage "extraordinary."

Pilgrims come to Memphis not only because Graceland, the second most-visited home in America (after the White House), is here. They come because Beale Street was once home to Handy—and later, B.B. King, Muddy Waters, and others—who merged the gospel singing and cotton-field work songs of the Mississippi Delta into a music called the blues. They come because Sun Studio's owner, Sam Phillips, in the early 1950s began recording several young musicians who experimented with fusing the sounds of hillbilly (country) music and the blues into an entirely new sound. This uniquely American sound, first known as rockabilly, would quickly become known as rock 'n' roll, the music that has written the soundtrack for the baby-boom generation.

1 Frommer's Favorite Memphis Experiences

- **Rockin' the Night on Beale Street.** This is where the blues took shape and gained its first national following. Beale Street is, as it used to be, home to numerous nightclubs where music fans can hear everything from blues to zydeco. Sure it's touristy, but there's an amazing amount of music being played along these 2 blocks. See "Beale Street & Downtown" in chapter 17.

- **Lounging in the Lobby of The Peabody.** The Peabody Memphis, 149 Union Ave. (© **800/ PEABODY** or 901/529-4000), is one of the most elegant hotels in the South, and anyone can indulge in that elegance for the price of a drink in the lobby bar. Of course, you'll also be sharing the lobby with the famous Peabody ducks. See p. 161 and 230.

- **Standing at the Sun Studio Microphone That Elvis Used for His First Recordings.** It's worth the tour admission price just to handle the microphone in this famed recording studio at 706 Union Ave. (✆ **901/521-0664**). It launched the career of Elvis Presley and created a sound that would come to be called rock 'n' roll. See p. 200.

- **Scouring the Record Bins at Shangri-La.** Your local Tower Records may have a small rockabilly section, but here at Shangri-La Records, 1916 Madison Ave. (✆ **901/274-1916**), in the town that invented the sound, you can get your hands on a copy of Warren Smith's original version of "Ubangi Stomp" or any number of rare discs and hard-to-find reissues. Be it Bessie Smith, William Burroughs, or The Band, it can be found among the bins, 78s, LPs and CDs. See p. 222.

- **Rollin' on the Mississippi River.** For many people, paddle-wheelers are the most immediately recognizable symbol of the Mississippi, and no visit to Memphis, or any other city on Ole Man River, is complete without a cruise on the Big Muddy. See p. 211.

- **Attending an Outdoor Concert on Mud Island.** Summer sunsets over the Mississippi are best appreciated when watching a famous performer put on a show at the Mud Island Amphitheater, 125 N. Front St. (✆ **800/507-6507** or 901/576-7241). Rock, pop, and country music are the mainstays here. See p. 201 and 234.

- **Browsing at A. Schwab Dry Goods Store.** Even if you hate shopping, you may enjoy the A. Schwab Dry Goods Store, 163 Beale St. (✆ **901/523-9782**), which opened in 1876 and has changed little since then. Battered wooden floors and tables covered with an unimaginable array of stuff make this more of a museum than a store. However, everything is for sale, and you'll find some of the offerings absolutely fascinating. See p. 220.

- **Cheering the Redbirds at Auto-Zone Park.** An AAA affiliate of the St. Louis Cardinals, the Redbirds (✆ **901/721-6000**) are the pride of Memphis, playing in an old-fashioned but brand-new ballpark that has been hailed as one of the best in the nation. At the entry gates, look for the giant statue of the ballplayer known as Nostalgia Man. See p. 213.

- **Chomping on Dry Ribs at Rendezvous.** It's dark, it's noisy, and the waiters are intentionally surly, but oh, those barbecued ribs! Those served at Rendezvous, 52 S. Second St. (✆ **901/523-2746**), are what Memphis calls dry ribs, which means they're rubbed with dry spices prior to cooking; you can add "wet" sauce after they come to the table. See p. 180.

- **Remembering Rev. Martin Luther King from the Balcony of the Lorraine Motel.** Mournful gospel hymns play softly in the background as visitors approach the place where the civil rights leader was assassinated in 1968. This is the conclusion of a visit to the inspiring **National Civil Rights Museum,** 450 Mulberry St. (✆ **901/521-9699**), built on the site of this once-segregated motel. See p. 202.

- **Shopping for the Tackiest Elvis Souvenir in the World.** The hip-swinging Elvis clock has become all too familiar, so why not try some stick-on Elvis sideburns, an Elvis temporary tattoo, an Elvis Christmas ornament, Elvis playing cards, an Elvis nightlight, or a little plastic tray displaying a photo of Elvis with President Richard Nixon. See "Memphis Shopping A to Z" in chapter 16.

2 Best Hotel Bets

- **Best Historic Hotel:** Even if **The Peabody Memphis,** 149 Union Ave. (© **800/PEABODY** or 901/529-4000), weren't the *only* historic hotel in the city, it would likely still be the best. From the classically elegant lobby to the excellent restaurants, and from the renovated rooms to the horse-drawn carriages waiting at the front door, everything here spells tradition and luxury. See p. 161.

- **Best for Business Travelers:** Under the same management as the Peabody, **The Ridgeway Inn,** 5679 Poplar Ave., at I-240 (© **800/822-3360** or 901/766-4000), is convenient to East Memphis business and is geared toward the business traveler. The pastry shop is a great place to start the day. See p. 170.

- **Best for a Romantic Getaway:** The sleek new **Madison Hotel,** (79 Madison Ave. (© **901/333-1200** or 866/44-MEMPHIS) is a treasure tucked inside an historic bank building downtown. What could be more romantic than watching the sunset from the rooftop garden? See p. 160.

- **Best Trendy Hotel:** The **Talbot Heirs Guesthouse,** 99 S. Second St. (© **901/527-9772**), across the street from the Peabody, is a small B&B done in a boldly contemporary style, a first for Memphis. Each guest room conjures up the pages of *Metropolitan Home.* Automatic Slim's Tonga Club, one of the city's hippest restaurants, is just a couple of doors away. See p. 161.

- **Best for Families:** With its atrium lobby (complete with stream and resident ducks), indoor pool, and two-room suites with kitchenettes, the **Embassy Suites,** 1022 S. Shady Grove Rd. (© **800/EMBASSY** or 901/684-1777), is a good bet if you've got kids with you. See p. 168.

- **Best Moderately Priced Hotel:** Its lavish refurbishment and garden-like courtyards, as well as its proximity to the convention center and the Main Street Trolley, make the **Wyndham Garden Hotel,** 300 N. Second St. (© **901/525-1800**), especially appealing. See p. 165.

- **Best Service: The Peabody Memphis,** 149 Union Ave. (© **800/PEABODY** or 901/529-4000), offers the most consistent and professional service in town. The employees here just seem to try a little bit harder to please the guests, even when overwhelmed by hordes of duck-watching daily visitors. See p. 161.

- **Best Location:** In the heart of downtown, the **Holiday Inn Select Downtown,** 160 Union Ave. (© **901/525-9141**), offers an elegant lobby, a sushi restaurant, and a prime location near Auto-Zone Park and Beale Street. See p. 164.

- **Best Hotel Pool:** Though it isn't very large, the guitar-shaped pool at the **Days Inn at Graceland,** 3839 Elvis Presley Blvd. (© **800/329-7466** or 901/346-5500), may be the most unique hotel pool in Memphis. See p. 172.

- **Best View:** Ask for a west-side room on an upper floor of the **Marriott,** 250 N. Main St. (© **888/557-8740** or 901/527-7300), and you'll get sunsets with the Mississippi River and the Pyramid in the foreground. See p. 160.

- **Best for Elvis Fans:** You just can't get any closer to Graceland than

Elvis Presley's Heartbreak Hotel, 3677 Elvis Presley Blvd. (© **877/ 777-0606** or 901/332-1000), which has a walkway straight into the Graceland parking lot. And what romantic could resist booking

the "*Burning Love* Suite"? Here you can also make a splash in the outdoor, heart-shaped pool, and indulge in Elvis videos 24 hours a day. See p. 171.

3 Best Dining Bets

- **Best Spot for a Romantic Dinner:** If you feel like playing prince or princess for a night, there's no more romantic place to do so than amid the palatial surroundings of **Chez Philippe,** 149 Union Ave. (© **901/529-4188**), at the opulent Peabody hotel. See p. 175.

- **Best Spot for a Celebration:** Amusing decor and food as creative as the atmosphere make **Automatic Slim's Tonga Club,** 83 S. Second St. (© **901/525-7948**), a good spot for a casual celebration. See p. 175.

- **Best Decor:** Dine from the comfort of refurbished hair dryer chairs at **Beauty Shop,** 966 S. Cooper (© **901/272-7111**). Or just sit at the banquette and tables and soak up the chic blush-and-cream-colored decor and retro block-glass booth dividers. See p. 181.

- **Best Wine List: Melange,** in the Cooper Young historic district of Midtown, 948 S. Cooper, © **901/ 276-0002**), has one of the best wine selections in Memphis. See p. 181.

- **Best Value:** The abbreviated bistro menu served at **La Tourelle Restaurant,** 2146 Monroe Ave. (© **901/726-5771**), provides a chance to sample this restaurant's excellent food, but you don't have to eat as many courses and you spend a lot less money. See p. 181.

- **Best for Kids:** At the **Buntyn Restaurant,** Park Avenue at Mt. Moriah (© **901/458-8776**), the folks really like kids, and the kids really like the old-fashioned meat-and-potatoes cooking. See p. 188.

- **Best Continental Cuisine:** The decor is a cross between classic French-country-inn and baronial mansion at **Paulette's,** 2110 Madison Ave. (© **901/726-5128**). The menu combines American and Hungarian influences with continental; you will find the likes of filet mignon and veal tenderloin accented with wine and herb sauces. See p. 182.

- **Best French Cuisine:** Because both have such good reputations, I couldn't choose one above the other, so I'll leave the decision up to you. The cuisine at **Le Petit Bistro,** 5007 Black Rd. (© **901/767-7840**), is contemporary French, served in a casual bistro atmosphere, while at **La Tourelle,** 2146 Monroe Ave. (© **901/726-5771**), both classic and contemporary dishes are served in an elegant setting. See p. 181 and p. 187.

- **Best View: Joe's Crab Shack,** 263 Wagner Place (© **901/526-1966;**), a casual chain restaurant, is located in a converted warehouse overlooking the Mississippi River. Both the views and the menus conjure up images of the Gulf Coast. See p. 178.

- **Best Barbecued Ribs:** The legendary **Rendezvous,** 52 S. Second St. (© **901/523-2746**), has, hands-down, the best ribs in Memphis. Accompany these with red beans and rice and some mustard slaw, toss in a bit of attitude from the waiters, and you have the makings of a very memorable Memphis meal. See p. 180.

The Best Memphis Websites

To find out more about what's happening in the Home of the Blues, check out the following websites:

- **www.bealestreet.com**: For the low-down on what's happening on this world-famous street, check out this website that offers information on live music in the clubs and links to eateries and tourist attractions here.

- **www.cityofmemphis.org**: The city's new, official website (viewable in English and Spanish) is a gold mine of practical tidbits. Check the day's weather forecast and download maps, or find the area's best biking trails or where to pay a parking ticket. It's all here on this comprehensive, user-friendly site.

- **www.commercialappeal.com**: Memphis's daily newspaper, *The Commercial Appeal*, offers a good overview of the city and surroundings, plus special sections on the Rev. Martin Luther King, Jr., and Elvis Presley. (*Take note:* the paper's longtime pop music critic, William Lee "Bill" Ellis, is also an excellent blues guitarist. Look for his internationally acclaimed CDs in local record bins.)

- **www.memphistravel.com**: The Memphis Convention and Visitors Bureau runs this boosters'-eye view of the Bluff City, with links to the more prominent attractions, selected restaurants, and updates on what's new in Memphis.

- **www.memphisflyer.com**: The city's alternative weekly newspaper, *The Memphis Flyer,* takes an irreverent look at politics, arts, and entertainment, and provides current listings for movies, gallery openings, and live music in clubs around town.

- **www.memphismagazine.com**: An online version of the city's glossy *Memphis Magazine,* this site features a comprehensive dining guide, as well as monthly restaurant reviews and news, and a useful City Guide with links to arts, entertainment, shopping, and sports and recreation.

- **Best Japanese Cuisine: Sekisui of Japan,** Humphreys Center, 50 Humphreys Blvd. (© 901/747-0001; and two other locations), serves consistently good tempura, teriyaki, *kushiyaki, yakizakana,* and platters of the freshest sushi. See p. 188.

- **Best Steaks:** The steaks at **Folk's Folly Prime Steak House,** 551 S. Mendenhall Rd. (© 901/762-8200), are such a Memphis institution that the restaurant has its own butcher shop; restaurant patrons can also buy some of the best meat available for cooking at home. See p. 186.

- **Best Late-Night Dining:** When the urge to eat strikes late at night, you can nosh tapas with your martinis at **Melange,** 948 S. Cooper St. (© 901/276-0002), which stays open until 2am; or suck down some saucy ribs at the **Rendezvous,** 52 S. Second St. (© 901/523-2746), which stays open until midnight on Friday and Saturday. See p. 180 and p. 181.

- **Best Brunch:** Sunday brunch at **The Peabody Memphis** hotel is an elegant affair, held at the Skyway on the roof level of the hotel between 10:30am and 2pm. See p. 161.

- **Best Barbecue:** When in Memphis, you have to eat as much barbecue as you can get your hands (and mouth) on. **Corky's Bar-B-Q,** 5259 Poplar Ave. (© **901/685-9744**), makes it easy with a drive-up window. See p. 188.

11

Planning Your Trip to Memphis

Whether you're visiting Memphis combined with a trip to Nashville or heading specifically to this sprawling city on the Mississippi, you're likely to have some questions before you arrive. This chapter puts all the planning information at your fingertips.

1 Visitor Information

For information on Memphis, contact the **Memphis Convention & Visitors Bureau,** 47 Union Ave., Memphis, TN 38103 (© **800/8-MEMPHIS** or 901/543-5300). You can also get information online at **www.memphis travel.com**.

For information on other parts of Tennessee, contact the **Tennessee Department of Tourism Development,** P.O. Box 23170, Nashville, TN 37202 (© **615/741-2158**).

2 Money

What will a vacation in Memphis cost? Of course, it all depends on how much you want to spend and how comfortable you want to be. If your standards are high and you like to stay in the best hotels and eat at gourmet restaurants, you may find yourself spending upwards of $130 per person per day. However, if you'd rather spend less money, you can have a comfortable Memphis vacation for less than half of that.

When it comes time to pay your bills, you'll find that a credit card is most convenient, although traveler's checks are accepted at hotels, motels, restaurants, and most stores. If you plan to rent a car, know that you'll need a credit card at almost every rental agency for the deposit.

Automated teller machines (ATMs) are readily available and use the Cirrus, PLUS, Most, Gulfnet, Moneybelt, and Pulse networks. For more information about ATMs, traveler's checks, and credit cards, see chapter 2, "Planning Your Trip to Nashville."

3 When to Go

CLIMATE

Summer is the peak tourist season in Memphis, but this doesn't coincide with the city's best weather. During July, August, and often September, temperatures can be up around 100°F, with high humidity. Memphians say that May and October are the most pleasant months of the year. During spring and fall, days are often warm and nights cool, though the weather can be unpredictable—so bring a variety of clothes. Heavy rains, which blow up suddenly from the Gulf, can hit any time of year. Winters generally aren't very cold, but expect freezing temperatures and bring a coat.

What Things Cost in Memphis	US$
Taxi from the airport to the city center	25
Taxi from the airport to Poplar Street (East Memphis)	20
Bus ride between any two downtown points	1.25
Local telephone call	.35
Double room at the Peabody (very expensive)	199–359
Double room at the Park Vista Hotel (expensive)	109–189
Double room at the Hampton Inn-Poplar (moderate)	82–89
Double room at the La Quinta Inn (inexpensive)	61–70
Lunch for one at Cielo (expensive)	25
Lunch for one at Café Society (moderate)	19
Lunch for one at Buntyn Restaurant (inexpensive)	8
Dinner for one, without wine, at Chez Philippe (expensive)	25
Dinner for one, without wine, at Automatic Slim's Tonga Club (moderate)	20
Dinner for one, without wine, at Rendezvous (inexpensive)	12
Bottle of beer	2.50–3.50
Coca-Cola	1
Cup of coffee or iced tea	1.50
Roll of ASA 100 Kodacolor film (36 exposures)	8
Movie ticket	7.50
Theater ticket to the Orpheum Theatre	18–65

Memphis's Average Monthly Temperatures & Rainfall

	Jan	Feb	Mar	Apr	May	June	July	Aug	Sept	Oct	Nov	Dec
Temp (°F)	40	44	52	63	71	79	82	81	74	63	51	43
Temp (°C)	4	7	11	17	22	26	28	27	23	17	11	6
Days of rain	10	10	11	10	9	9	9	8	7	6	9	10

MEMPHIS CALENDAR OF EVENTS

January

Elvis Presley's Birthday Tribute, Graceland. International gathering of Presley fans to celebrate the birthday of "The King" (© 800/ 238-2000). Around January 8.

Martin Luther King, Jr.'s Birthday, citywide. Events to memorialize Dr. King take place on the nationally observed holiday (© 901/ 543-5333). Mid-January.

February

Kroger St. Jude International Tennis Championship, Racquet Club of Memphis. World-class players compete in this famous tour event (© 901/765-4400). Mid- to late February.

April

Africa in April Cultural Awareness Festival, downtown. A several-day festival centering around African music, dance, theater, exhibits, arts, and crafts (℡ **901/ 947-2133**). Third week in April.

May

Cotton Maker's Jubilee, downtown. The largest African-American parade in the country and a midway are parts of this homage to King Cotton (℡ **901/774-1118**). Early May.

Memphis in May International Festival, citywide. A month-long celebration of a different country each year with musical, cultural, and artistic festivities; business, sports, and educational programs; and food unique to the country. More than a million people come to nearly 100 sanctioned events scheduled throughout the city. The most important happenings are the Memphis in May Beale Street Music Festival, International Weekend, the World Championship Barbecue Cooking Contest, and the Sunset Symphony (which culminates in a soulful rendition of *Old Man River*). Call Memphis in May (℡ **901/525-4611**). Entire month of May.

June

Carnival Memphis, citywide. Almost half a million people join in the family activities of exhibits, music, crafts, and events (℡ **901/ 278-0243**). Early June.

Germantown Charity Horse Show, Germantown Horse Show Arena. Four-day competition for prizes (℡ **901/754-0009**). Second week in June.

Native American Pow Wow, Shelby Farms Show Place Arena. Native Americans from Canada and the United States meet to participate in dance competitions, with Native American foods and crafts (℡ **901/756-7433**). Mid-June.

Federal Express St. Jude Golf Classic, Tournament Players Club at Southwind. A benefit for St. Jude Children's Hospital, this is a PGA event (℡ **901/748-0534**). Late June.

July

WMC Star-Spangled Celebration, Shelby Farms. Fourth of July entertainment and fireworks (℡ **901/726-0469**). July 4.

August

Elvis Tribute Week, Graceland and citywide. Festival commemorating the influences of Elvis (℡ **800/238-2000**). Second week in August.

Memphis Blues Festival, Tom Lee Park. Musicians celebrate the blues (℡ **901/398-6655**). Mid-August.

September

Beale Street Labor Day Music Festival, Beale Street. Memphis musicians are featured Labor Day and night in restaurants and clubs throughout the Beale Street district (℡ **901/526-0110**). Labor Day weekend.

Memphis Music and Heritage Festival, Center for Southern Folklore. A celebration of the diversity of the South (℡ **901/525-3655**). Early September.

Mid-South Fair, Mid-South Fairgrounds. Ten days of fun-filled rides, food, games, shows, a midway, and a rodeo (℡ **901/274-8800**). Last week of September.

October

Pink Palace Crafts Fair, Audubon Park. Artists and performers in one of the largest crafts fairs in Tennessee. (℡ **901/320-6320**). First weekend in October.

Southern Festival of Books, Cook Convention Center and Civic Plaza. Readings, panel discussions, and book signings by authors from around the United States, with an emphasis on Southern writers (℡ **615/320-7001,** ext. 73; www. tn-humanities.org). October 8–10,

2004. (The festival will return to Nashville in 2005; see chapter 2.)

Memphis Arts in the Park Festival, Memphis Botanic Garden. Visual-arts competition open to artists nationwide (② **901/761-1278**). Mid-October.

November

Mid-South Arts and Crafts Show, Memphis Cook Convention Center. Artists and craftspeople from more than 20 states sell their handiwork (② **423/430-3461**). Third week in November.

International Blues Competition. Blues musicians from around the country meet for performances at various venues, with the W. C. Handy Awards and post-show jam.

For more information, call the Blues Foundation at ② **901/527-BLUE.** Throughout November.

December

Merry Christmas Memphis Parade, downtown. Christmas parade with floats and bands (② **901/526-6840**). Early December.

Liberty Bowl Football Classic, Liberty Bowl Memorial Stadium. Intercollegiate game that's nationally televised (② **901/274-4600**). Late December.

Bury Your Blues Blowout on Beale, Beale Street. New Year's Eve celebration both inside the clubs and outside on Beale Street (② **901/526-0110**). December 31.

4 Health & Insurance

If you should find yourself in need of a doctor, call the referral service at Baptist Memorial Hospital (② **901/362-8677**) or Methodist Le Bonheur Med Search Doctor Locating and Information Service (② **901/726-8686**). The Baptist Memorial Hospital Medical Center is at 899 Madison Ave.

(② **901/227-2727**), with another location in East Memphis at 6019 Walnut Grove Rd. (② **901/226-5000**). For more details about medical insurance and travel insurance see chapter 2, "Planning Your Trip to Nashville."

5 Specialized Travel Resources

For tips for seniors, families, and single travelers, see "Specialized Travel Resources" in chapter 2.

FOR TRAVELERS WITH DISABILITIES

Many hotels and motels in Memphis offer wheelchair-accessible accommodations, but when making reservations be sure to ask.

See "Specialized Travel Resources" in chapter 2 for information on transportation options for disabled travelers, including discounted bus and rail tickets, and car rentals for disabled drivers.

FOR GAY & LESBIAN TRAVELERS

Volunteers staff the **Memphis Gay and Lesbian Community Center,** 892 S. Cooper (② **901/278-4297**) between 7:30 and 11pm nightly. Call for descriptions of programs and activities. Fore more information, look for the *Memphis Triangle Journal,* a free weekly newspaper that's available at local bookstores, libraries, and other locations.

FOR STUDENTS

If you don't already have one, get an official student ID card from your school. Such an ID will entitle you to discounts at museums, theaters, and attractions around town.

There are about a dozen major colleges and universities in the Memphis area. The most prominent are **Rhodes College,** 2000 North Pkwy. (© **901/ 726-3000**), which has a Gothic-style campus located opposite Overton Park; and the **University of Memphis,** on Central Avenue between Highland and Goodlett streets (© **901/678-2000**), located on a large campus in midtown Memphis.

FOR BLACK TRAVELERS

African-American heritage is built in the fabric of Memphis, evident at such big attractions as the National Civil Rights Museum and Soulsville USA, which are obviously important sites for all visitors to the city. For general travel resources aimed at African-American travelers, see "For Black Travelers" in the "Specialized Travel Resources" section of chapter 2. For Memphis-specific information, contact the Memphis Convention and Visitors Bureau.

6 Getting There

BY PLANE

For information on getting the best airfare, see "Getting There" in chapter 2. For information on flights to the United States from other countries, see "Getting to the U.S." in appendix A, "For International Visitors."

THE MAJOR AIRLINES

Memphis is served by the following airlines: **American Airlines** (© 800/433-7300); **Delta** (© 800/221-1212); **KLM** (© 800/374-7747); **Northwest** (© 800/225-2525); **Southwest** (© 800/435-9792); **United Airlines** (© 800/241-6522); and **US Airways** (© 800/428-4322).

GETTING INTO TOWN FROM THE AIRPORT

The **Memphis International Airport** (© 901/922-8000) is located approximately 11 miles south of downtown Memphis off I-240. From the airport to East Memphis, it's about 9 miles. The route into either downtown or East Memphis is on I-240 all the way. Generally, allow about 20 minutes for the trip between the airport and downtown, and 15 minutes between the airport and East Memphis—up to an hour more during rush hour. See "Getting Around Memphis" in chapter

12 for information on car-rental facilities at the Memphis airport.

Airport Shuttle Service (© 901/274-6282) operates a shuttle service between the Memphis International Airport and select downtown hotels (Peabody, Hampton Inn, Radisson, Wyndham, Marriott, Comfort Inn, Sleep Inn, Holiday Inn-Select, and Best Western). Rates are $10 one-way and $17 round-trip per person. It operates 7 days a week. For group reservations or more information, call © **901/522-1677.**

Although there is no direct bus service from the airport to downtown Memphis, it is possible, with a change of bus en route, to make this trip on **Memphis Area Transit Authority (MATA)** buses (© **901/274-6282**). These buses, however, do not run very often and are not very convenient for visitors. The buses run every 1 to 2 hours until about 5:30pm Monday through Saturday, and until 5:15pm on Sunday, and the fare is $1.25. From the lower level at the airport, take no. 32, the East Parkway/Hollywood bus, to Airways and Lamar Avenue. Transfer to no. 10, the Lamar bus (which runs about every hour on weekdays, fewer times on Sat) or the no. 56, the Union/Kimball bus (running about every half hour on weekdays), which will take you downtown. If you want to take the bus, the best bet is to call MATA or ask a bus driver for the latest schedule information.

A taxi from the airport to downtown Memphis will cost about $23; to East Memphis it will cost about $20. There are usually plenty of taxis around, but if you can't find one, call **Yellow/Checker Cab** (② **901/577-7777**) or **City Wide Cab Company** (② **901/324-4202**). The first mile is $2.90; after that, it's $1.40 per mile. Each additional passenger is 50¢ extra.

BY CAR

Memphis is a crossroads of the South and is within an 8-hour drive of many major Southern cities. Here are some driving distances from selected cities: Nashville, 210 miles; New Orleans, 393 miles; Chicago, 544 miles; St. Louis, 311 miles; and Dallas, 466 miles.

The main routes into Memphis include **I-40,** which connects Memphis with Nashville and Raleigh to the east and Little Rock and Oklahoma City to the west. **I-55** passes through the southwestern corner of the city and connects Memphis to New Orleans in the south and to St. Louis and Chicago to the north.

If you're coming in from the east and trying to get to downtown Memphis, I-40 is slightly faster than I-240. From I-40, take Danny Thomas Boulevard, or take I-40 to I-240 and get off at Union Avenue. If you're heading to East Memphis, take I-240. Poplar Avenue is the main East Memphis exit.

If you are a member of the **American Automobile Association (AAA)** and your car breaks down, call ② **800/365-4840** or 800/AAA-HELP for 24-hour emergency road service. The AAA office in Memphis is at 5138 Park Ave., Memphis, TN 38117 (② **901/761-5371**).

BY TRAIN

Amtrak (② **800/872-7245**) serves Memphis with a route that goes from Chicago through Memphis to New Orleans on the *City of New Orleans.* The coach fare between Chicago and Memphis at press time was between $84 and $150 each way, while fares between Memphis and New Orleans were about $86. If you arrive in Memphis on an Amtrak train, you'll find yourself at **Central Station,** 545 S. Main St. (② **901/526-0052**), near Calhoun Street. This historic railway station has been completely renovated into a combination transportation center with public bus and Main Street Trolley connections and retail complex. However, the neighborhood around the station remains quite run-down. If arriving by train, you should take a cab or the Main Street Trolley to your hotel.

BY BUS

The **Greyhound bus station** is at 203 Union Ave. (② **901/523-9253**), in the heart of downtown Memphis and within 2 blocks of the Peabody Hotel. **Greyhound Lines** (② **800/231-2222**) offers service to Memphis from around the country, and, in fact, Memphis is where Greyhound got started. At press time, the walk-up fare between New York and Memphis was $92 one-way and $165 round-trip. The non-discounted fare between Chicago and Memphis was $57 one-way and $98 round-trip.

PACKAGE TOURS

The best way to find out about package tours is to contact a travel agent. See also "Package Tours for the Independent Traveler" in chapter 2.

The **Delta Queen Steamboat Company,** Robin St. Wharf, 1380 Port of

New Orleans Place, New Orleans, LA 70130-1890 (*©* **800/215-7938**), offers paddle-wheel steamboat tours that include Memphis on the itinerary. Call ahead for current information.

7 Recommended Books, Films & Music

BOOKS

GENERAL   If you're interested in the civil rights movement and the life and death of Dr. Martin Luther King, Jr., you may want to read *At the River I Stand: Memphis, the 1968 Strike and Dr. Martin Luther King, Jr.* (Carlson Publishing, 1989), by Joan Turner Beifuss. This is a rather weighty tome.

FICTION   John Grisham's novels *The Firm* (Doubleday, 1991), *The Client* (Doubleday, 1993), and *The Rainmaker* (Doubleday, 1995) provide a bit of Memphis flavor and suspenseful entertainment. All three of these books are set amid the Memphis legal world and have been made into big-budget movies.

MUSIC   A lot has been written about the blues over the years, and consequently a lot has been written about Memphis and the nearby Mississippi Delta. *Rhythm Oil: A Journey Through the Music of the American South* (Vintage, 1993), by Stanley Booth, is a collection of articles that have appeared in other publications. Over the years, Booth has traveled the world in pursuit of stories on the blues and interviews with famous blues musicians. *The Land Where the Blues Began* (Pantheon Books, 1993), by Alan Lomax, is a thick but very readable account of the Mississippi Delta's blues music. The book includes plenty of interviews and song lyrics. Beale Street is where the blues finally became a force in the world of American music, and in *Beale Black and Blue* (Louisiana State University Press, 1981) Margaret McKee and Fred Chisenhall tell the history of Beale Street and the people who made it famous.

One of those Beale Street figures was B.B. King, the reigning king of the blues. Charles Sawyer's *The Arrival of B. B. King* (Da Capo Press, 1980), though a bit dated, tells the story of the Beale Street "Blues Boy." *Woman with a Guitar: Memphis Minnie's Blues* (Da Capo Press, 1992), by Paul and Beth Garon, is a biography of another of Beale Street's early blues singers.

In the early 1950s, Sun Studio in Memphis recorded some of the world's first rock-'n'-roll music. Among the artists to record here were Jerry Lee Lewis, Roy Orbison, Carl Perkins, and Elvis Presley. *Great Balls of Fire* (Mandarin Paperbacks, 1989), by Myra Lewis with Murray Silver, is a biography of Jerry Lee Lewis, the rocker whose career died when he married his 13-year-old cousin. *Dark Star: The Roy Orbison Story* (Carol Publishing Group, 1990), by Ellis Amburn, is a biography of the enigmatic Orbison. The book is drawn from interviews with Orbison's friends and family and includes a lot on the early days at Sun Studio.

For the best overviews of Memphis music and its roots, look for the reprint of Peter Guralnick's *Sweet Soul Music* (Back Bay Books, 1999). I also urge you to read any books by one of Memphis' best music historians, Robert Gordon. Two of his most acclaimed works are *It Came from Memphis* (Faber & Faber, 1996) and the recent biography of Mississippi blues great McKinley Morganfield:

Can't Be Satisfied: The Life and Times of Muddy Waters (Little, Brown and Co., 2002).

For an in-depth history of a Memphis record label that spawned hits by the likes of Otis Redding, Aretha Franklin, Isaac Hayes, and Sam & Dave, start with Rob Bowmann's *Soulsville USA: The Story of Stax Records* (Schirmer Books, 2003).

ELVIS   There has probably been more written about Elvis Presley (and I don't just mean in the tabloids) than about any other rock star in history. Currently, Peter Guralnick is considered to be the definitive biographer of Elvis. His *Last Train to Memphis: The Rise of Elvis Presley* (Little, Brown and Company, 1994) documents the star's early life (it covers his life up to 1958), while *Careless Love: The Unmaking of Elvis Presley* (Little, Brown and Company, 1998) picks up where the first tome left off, and tracks the King's sad later years. Other good, basic biographies include Jerry Hopkins's two books *Elvis: A Biography* (Warner Books, 1971) and *Elvis: The Final Years* (Playboy Books, 1981). For those who are curious what it was like to be Mrs. Elvis, there's *Elvis and Me* (Berkley Books, 1986), by Priscilla Presley. Much controversy surrounded the death of Elvis; his adoring fans were loath to learn that the king was a drug addict. In *The Death of Elvis: What Really Happened* (Delacorte Press, 1991), authors Charles C. Thompson II and James P. Cole dig deep into the cause of Elvis's death and the putative cover-up. However, two of the most controversial Elvis books have been Albert Goldman's *Elvis* (Avon, 1981), which exposed some of Elvis's kinkier habits, and *Elvis: What Happened?* (World News Corporation, 1977), by Red West, Sonny West, and Dave Hebler as told to Steve Dunleavy,

a sleazy exposé of Elvis's drug and sex habits. In the recent *That's Alright, Elvis* (Schirmer Books, 1997), by Scotty Moore (as told to James Dickerson), the last surviving member of Elvis's first trio, the early days of Elvis and rock 'n' roll are the subject.

For a more tender novella about the man and his life, look no further than Bobbie Ann Mason's simply titled *Elvis* (Viking Books, 2002).

FILMS

The movie version of John Grisham's page-turner of a novel, *The Firm* (1993), starring Tom Cruise, was a thriller and big summer hit with a number of identifiable Memphis shots. The film adaptation of Grisham's book *The Rainmaker* also has readily identifiable Memphis settings. And Jim Jarmusch's wry *Mystery Train* prominently features the mythic, if seamy, underbelly of Memphis. After a lull of a few years, the city again returned to the spotlight as the evocative backdrop for the drama *21 Grams* (2003), starring Sean Penn and Benicio del Toro.

MUSIC

W. C. Handy got the whole American music scene rolling when he wrote down the first published blues tune, "Memphis Blues," back in 1909. At a good record store you might be able to find some collections of old W. C. Handy tunes. Other Memphis blues artists to look for are "Ma" Rainey, Memphis Minnie McCoy, Furry Lewis, Albert King, Bobby "Blue" Bland, and Alberta Hunter. Sun Studio was where blues musicians B. B. King, Muddy Waters, Howlin' Wolf, and Little Milton all got their start. The names of the Sun Studio rockabilly artists have also become familiar to people all over the world—Carl Perkins, Jerry Lee Lewis, Roy Orbison,

Johnny Cash, and Elvis Presley. The sound these musicians independently created was the foundation for rock 'n' roll, although it's another Sun Studio recording artist who is credited with releasing the first rock-'n'-roll tune. His name was Jackie Brenston, and his 1952 record was titled "Rocket 88." Many Sun Studio tunes are available on reissues.

12

Getting to Know
the Home of the Blues

When you hit town, you may be surprised and even a bit baffled by Memphis. The city is spread out, so getting around can be confusing and frustrating at first. Read this chapter, and your first hours in town should be less confusing. I've also compiled a lot of useful information that will help you throughout your stay.

1 Orientation

VISITOR INFORMATION
The city's main visitor information center, located downtown at the base of Jefferson Street, is the **Tennessee State Welcome Center,** 119 N. Riverside Dr. (© **901/543-6757**). It's open daily 24 hours but staffed only between 8am and 7pm (until 8pm in the summer months). Inside this large information center, you'll find soaring statues of both Elvis and B. B. King.

At the airport, you'll find information boards with telephone numbers for contacting hotels and numbers for other helpful services.

CITY LAYOUT
Memphis, built on the east bank of the **Mississippi River,** lies just above the Mississippi state line. Consequently, growth has proceeded primarily to the east and, to a lesser extent, to the north. The inexorable sprawl of the suburbs has pushed the limits of the metropolitan area far to the east, and today the area known as **East Memphis** is the city's business and cultural center. Despite the fact that the city has a fairly small and compact downtown area, the sprawl of recent years has made getting around difficult for both residents and visitors. Traffic congestion on main east–west avenues is bad throughout the day, so you're usually better off taking the interstate around the outskirts of the city if you're trying to cross town.

In general, the city is laid out on a grid with a north–south axis. However, there are many exceptions, including downtown, which was laid out with "streets" parallel to the river and "avenues" running perpendicular to the river. Throughout the city you'll find that, for the most part, avenues run east–west and streets run north–south.

MAIN ARTERIES & STREETS Memphis is circled by **I-40,** which loops around the north side of the city, and **I-240,** which loops around the south side. **Poplar Avenue** and **Sam Cooper Boulevard/North Parkway** are the city's main east–west arteries. Poplar, heavily lined with businesses, is narrow, congested, and accident-prone. If you don't want to take the interstate, Sam Cooper Boulevard is an alternative route into downtown, as is **Central Avenue** between Goodlett Road in the east and Lamar Avenue in the west. **Union Avenue** is the

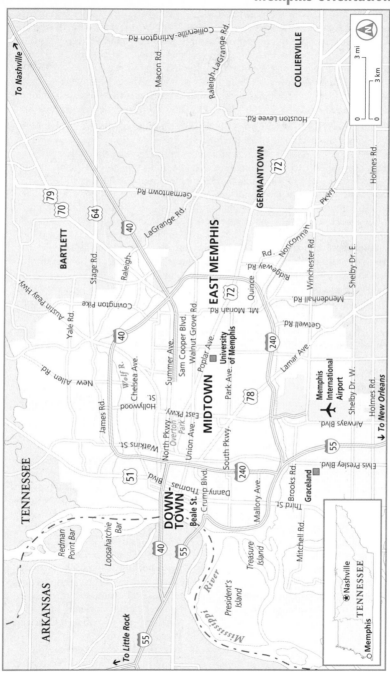

dividing line between the north and south sides of the city. Other important **east–west roads** include Summer Avenue and Park Avenue. Major **north–south arteries** include (from downtown heading eastward) Third Street/U.S. 61, I-240, Elvis Presley Boulevard/U.S. 51, Airways Boulevard/East Parkway, and Mendenhall Road. Lamar Avenue is another important road.

Out in **East Memphis,** the main east–west arteries are Poplar Avenue and Winchester Road. The main north–south arteries are Perkins Road/Perkins Road Extended, Mendenhall Road, Hickory Hill Road, and Germantown Road.

FINDING AN ADDRESS   Your best bet for finding an address in Memphis will always be to call the place first and ask for directions or the name of the nearest main cross street. Though address numbers increase the farther you get from downtown, they do not increase along each block in an orderly fashion. It is nearly impossible to determine how many blocks out an address will be. However, there are some general guidelines to get you in the vicinity of where you're going. If an address is in the hundreds or lower, you should be downtown. If the address is an avenue or other east-west road in the 2000-to-4000 range, you'll likely find it in midtown; if the number is in the 5000-to-7000 range, you should be out in East Memphis. If the address is on a street, it will likely have a north or south prefix included. Union Avenue is the dividing line between north and south.

STREET MAPS   Because the streets of Memphis can seem a bit baffling at times, you'll definitely need a good map. The **Tennessee State Welcome Center,** 119 N. Riverside Dr. (© **901/543-6757**), offers a simple map; you can also buy a more detailed one at any bookstore, pharmacy, or gas station. If you arrive at the airport and rent a car, the rental company will give you a basic map that will at least get you to your hotel or to the information center.

If you happen to be a member of **AAA,** you can get free maps of Memphis and the rest of Tennessee either from your local AAA office or from the Memphis office at 5138 Park Ave., Memphis, TN 38117 (© **901/761-5371**); it's open Monday to Friday 8:30am to 5:30pm.

THE NEIGHBORHOODS IN BRIEF

More important than neighborhoods in Memphis are the city's general divisions. These major divisions are how the city defines itself.

Downtown   The oldest part of the city, downtown is constructed on the banks of the Mississippi River. After years of efforts toward revitalization, this area has finally turned the corner to become one of the most vibrant cities in the New South. Historic **Beale Street** remains the city's main entertainment district. Elsewhere downtown, a mushrooming array of restaurants, hot night spots and cultural attractions await around every corner.

Midtown   This is primarily a residential area, though it's also known for its numerous hospitals. Though a far cry from bustling Beale Street, the **Overton Square** area is midtown's main entertainment area and is the site of several decent restaurants. South of Overton Square, you'll find the hip **Cooper-Young neighborhood**—basically a single intersection with several trendy eateries, coffeehouses, art galleries, and interesting boutiques. Midtown is also where you will find **Overton Park,** which envelops the Memphis Zoo and Aquarium, and the Memphis Brooks Museum of Art. There are many large, stately homes on park-like blocks surrounding Overton Park.

East Memphis Heading still farther east from downtown brings you to East Memphis, which lies roughly on either side of I-240 on the east side of the city. This is the city's most affluent and most newly developed region. It's characterized by multilane highways, scads of malls and shopping centers (seemingly at every major intersection), new office complexes, and a few high-rise hotels and office buildings.

2 Getting Around Memphis

BY PUBLIC TRANSPORTATION

BY BUS   The **Memphis Area Transit Authority (MATA; *C* 901/274-MATA)** operates citywide bus service. Bus stops are indicated by green-and-white signs. For schedule information, ask a bus driver or call the MATA number above. The standard fare is $1.25 and exact change is required. Transfers cost 10¢, and there's a 50% discount for travelers with disabilities and senior citizens with ID cards. (***Note:*** To qualify for the discounted fare, however, you need to show a Medicare card or obtain a MATA ID card by bringing two forms of identification to the MATA Customer Service Center at 61 S. Main St., open Mon–Fri 8am–5pm.)

BY STREETCAR   The **Main Street Trolley** (*C* **901/577-2640**) operates renovated 1920s trolley cars (and modern reproductions) on a circular route that includes Main Street from the Pyramid to the National Civil Rights Museum and Central Station and then follows Riverside Drive, passing the Tennessee State Visitors Center. It's a unique way to get around the downtown area. The fare is 60¢ each way, with a special lunch hour rate of 30¢ between 11am and 1:30pm. An all-day pass is $2.50; exact change is required, and passengers may board at any of the 20 stations along Main Street. Trolleys are wheelchair-accessible.

BY CAR

Memphis is a big sprawling city, and the best—and worst—way to get around is by car. A car is nearly indispensable for traveling between downtown and East Memphis, yet traffic congestion can make this trip take far longer than you'd expect (45 min. isn't unusual). East–west avenues and almost any road in East Memphis at rush hour are the most congested. Parking downtown is not usually a problem, but stay alert for tow-away zones and watch the time on your meter. Out in East Memphis, there is usually no parking problem. When driving between downtown and East Memphis, you'll usually do better to take the interstate.

CAR RENTALS   For tips on saving money on car rentals, see "Getting Around Nashville" in chapter 3.

   All the major car rental companies and several independent companies have offices in Memphis. Some are located near the airport only, and some have offices both near the airport and in other areas of Memphis. Be sure to leave yourself plenty of time for returning your car when you head to the airport to catch your return flight. None of the companies has an office in the airport itself, so you'll have to take a shuttle van from the car drop-off point to the airport terminal.

   Major car rental companies in Memphis include: **Alamo/National Rent-A-Car,** near the airport at 2600 Rental Rd. (*C* **800/327-9633** or 901/332-8412); **Budget Rent-A-Car,** near the airport at 2650 Rental Rd. (*C* **800/879-1227** or 901/398-8888), and at 5133 Poplar Ave. (*C* 800/879-1227 or 901/398-8888);

Dollar Rent-A-Car, near the airport at 2780 Airways Blvd. (© **800/800-4000** or 901/345-3890); **Enterprise Rent-a-Car,** near the airport at 2041 Brooks Road E. (© **800/325-8007** or 901/345-8588); **Hertz,** near the airport at 2560 Rental Rd. (© **800/654-3131** or 901/345-5680); and **Thrifty Car Rental,** near the airport at 2303 Democrat Rd. (© **800/367-2277** or 901/345-0170).

PARKING   Parking in downtown Memphis is a lot more expensive than it used to be. The best place to park in downtown is on the cobblestones between Front Street and the Mississippi River (located between Union and Poplar Aves.). This is a free public parking lot right on the river. There are also plenty of parking lots behind the Beale Street clubs; these charge big bucks for parking. Metered parking on downtown streets is fairly easy to find, but be sure to check the time limit on the meter. Also be sure to check whether or not you can park in a parking space during rush hour. Downtown parking is also available in municipal and private lots and parking garages.

In midtown, where parking is rarely a problem, there is a free lot in Overton Square between Madison Avenue and Monroe Avenue.

DRIVING RULES   A right turn at a red light is permitted after coming to a full stop, unless posted otherwise, but drivers must first yield to vehicles that have a green light or pedestrians in the walkway. Children under 4 years of age must be in a child's car seat or other approved child restraint when in the car.

Tennessee has a very strict DUI (driving under the influence of alcohol) law, and anyone caught driving under the influence with a child under 12 years of age in the car may be charged with a felony.

BY TAXI

For quick cab service, call **Checker/Yellow Cab** (© **901/577-7777**) or **City Wide Cab Company** (© **901/324-4202**), or have your hotel or motel call one for you. The first mile is $2.30; after that, it's $1.60 per mile. Each additional passenger is 50¢ extra.

ON FOOT

Downtown Memphis is walkable, though the only areas that attract many visitors are the Beale Street area and Main Street from the National Civil Rights Museum north to the Pyramid. The rest of the city is not walkable.

FAST FACTS: **Memphis**

Airport   The **Memphis International Airport** (© **901/922-8000**) serves the Memphis area; see "Getting There," in chapter 11.

American Express   There is no American Express office in Memphis, but its representative is **American and International Travel Services,** with five local offices. Two of those offices are at 2219 S. Germantown Rd. (© **901/754-6970**) and 540 S. Mendenhall Rd. (© **901/682-1595**), both open Monday to Friday 8:30am to 5pm. There is a national number for American Express (© **800/528-4800**), and for American Express travel assistance (© **800/YES-AMEX**).

Area Code   The telephone area code in Memphis is **901**.

Babysitters   Contact **Annie's Nannies** (© **901/755-1457**).

Business Hours Banks are generally open Monday to Thursday 8:30am to 4pm, with later hours on Friday. Office hours in Memphis are usually Monday to Friday 8:30am to 5pm. In general, stores located in downtown Memphis are open Monday to Saturday 10am to 5:30pm. Shops in suburban Memphis malls are generally open Monday to Saturday 10am to 9pm and on Sunday 1 to 5 or 6pm. Bars are allowed to stay open until 3am, but may close between 1 and 3am.

Car Rentals See "Getting Around Memphis," earlier in this chapter.

Climate See "When to Go," in chapter 11.

Dentists Contact **Dental Referral Service** (℃ 800/917-6453).

Doctors If you should find yourself in need of a doctor, call the referral service at **Baptist Memorial Hospital** (℃ 901/227-8428), or **Methodist/LeBonheur Healthcare** (℃ 901/726-8686).

Driving Rules See "Getting Around Memphis," earlier in this chapter.

Drugstores See "Pharmacies," below.

Embassies/Consulates See appendix A, "For International Visitors."

Emergencies For police, fire, or medical emergencies, phone ℃ 911.

Eyeglass Repair Contact **Eyemasters,** with several locations. The most convenient may be inside Oak Court Mall, at 4465 Poplar Ave. (℃ 901/683-1689).

Hospitals The **Baptist Memorial Hospital Medical Center** is at 899 Madison Ave. (℃ 901/227-2727), with another location in East Memphis at 6019 Walnut Grove Rd. (℃ 901/226-5000).

Hotlines The **Memphis hotline** (℃ 901/75-ELVIS) offers information on current music, entertainment, arts, sports, and other topics 24 hours a day. The **Crisis Counseling and Suicide Prevention** number is ℃ 901/274-7477, and the **Memphis Sexual Assault Resource Center** number is ℃ 901/272-2020.

Information See "Visitor Information," earlier in this chapter.

Libraries An impressive new main branch of the **Memphis/Shelby County Public Library** is at 3030 Poplar Avenue midtown and East Memphis. Elsewhere around town, there are more than 20 other branches (℃ 901/415-2700).

Liquor Laws The legal drinking age in Tennessee is 21. Bars are allowed to stay open until 3am every day. Beer can be purchased at a convenience, grocery, or package store, but wine and liquor are sold through package stores only.

Lost Property If you left something at the airport, call the **airport police** at ℃ 901/922-8298. If you left something on a **MATA bus,** call ℃ 901/274-6282.

Luggage Storage/Lockers There are lockers in the Greyhound station at 203 Union Ave.

Maps See "City Layout," earlier in this chapter.

Newspapers/Magazines *The Commercial Appeal* is Memphis's daily and Sunday newspaper. The arts-and-entertainment weekly is the *Memphis*

Flyer, and the monthly city magazine is *Memphis Magazine.* Out-of-town newspapers are available at Davis-Kidd Booksellers, Borders, and Bookstar.

Pharmacies (late-night) There are about 30 **Walgreen's Pharmacies** in the Memphis area ((✆ **800/925-4733** for the Walgreen's nearest you). Several have 24-hour prescription service, including the one at 1863 Union Ave. ((✆ **901/272-1141** or 901/272-2006).

Police For police emergencies, phone ✆ **911.**

Post Office The main post office is at 555 S. Third St. and there's a branch in East Memphis at 5821 Park Ave. in the White Station area. Both locations are open Monday to Friday 8:30am to 5:30pm and on Saturday 10am to 2pm. For these and other branches, dial ✆ **800/275-8777.**

Radio Memphis has more than 30 AM and FM radio stations. Some specialize in a particular style of music, including country, gospel, rhythm and blues, and jazz. WEVL at 89.9 FM plays diversified music such as alternative rock, rockabilly, blues, Cajun music, and jazz. National Public Radio (NPR) news and talk radio can be heard on 88.9 FM, and NPR classical programming can be heard at 91.1 FM.

Restrooms There are restrooms available to the public at hotels, restaurants, and shopping malls.

Safety Memphis is a large urban city, and all the normal precautions that apply in other cities hold true here. Take extra precaution with your wallet or purse when you're in a crush of people—pickpockets take advantage of crowds. At night, whenever possible, try to park your car in a garage, not on the street. When walking around town at night, stick to the busier streets, and hang with a crowd. Generally speaking, don't venture into deserted-looking areas alone at any time of day, and do not wander the streets of downtown or midtown alone after dark.

Taxes The state sales tax is 9.25%. An additional room tax of 6.7% on top of the state sales tax brings the total hotel-room tax to a whopping 15.95%.

Taxis See "Getting Around Memphis," earlier in this chapter.

Television The six local television channels are 3 (CBS), 5 (NBC), 10 (PBS), 13 (FOX), 24 (ABC), and 30 (independent).

Time Zone Tennessee is in the central time zone—Central Standard Time (CST) or Central Daylight Time, depending on the time of year—making it 2 hours ahead of the West Coast and one hour behind the East Coast.

Transit Info Call ✆ **901/274-MATA** for the MATA bus system route and schedule information. Call ✆ **901/577-2640** for information on the Main Street Trolley.

Weather For weather information, phone ✆ **901/522-8888.**

13

Where to Stay in Memphis

Persistent attempts at urban renewal have reaped big rewards for downtown Memphis, which is enjoying a long-awaited transformation into a vibrant metropolitan area. Among downtown hotels, the ultra-chic new Madison Hotel rivals the Peabody Memphis as the best in the city, but other nearby properties have been sprucing up as well. Polished newcomers include the renovated Wyndham, Marriott, Hampton Inn and Holiday-Inn Select properties, while the Talbot Heirs Guesthouse, an eight-room boutique property, remains a popular alternative for visitors seeking a more intimate lodging experience.

The city's better hotels used to be clustered in East Memphis, which is more than 20 miles by interstate highway from downtown. While these properties still attract business travelers as well as those with families wanting to avoid the drunken revelry that can sometimes consume the Beale Street area, downtown also has much to offer visitors of all budgets and backgrounds. If you book judiciously, you can avoid the rowdy after-hours crowds. Downtown Memphis also boasts an ever-increasing list of family-oriented attractions, making a stay here the best way to experience what Memphis is really all about.

The midtown area is another option, and though less convenient to Beale Street, it is near many museums and restaurants. Elvis fans may want to stay near Graceland, but beyond the mansion, the area has little to offer. Besides, you can pick up the

King's vibes no matter where you stay in Memphis. Like Waldo, he's everywhere.

Virtually all hotels now offer non-smoking rooms and others equipped for guests with disabilities. Many larger hotels are also adding special rooms for hearing-impaired travelers. When making a reservation, be sure to request the type of room you need.

If you'll be traveling with children, always check into policies regarding children. Some hotels let children under 12 stay free, while others set the cutoff age at 18. Still others charge you for the kids, but let them eat for free in the hotel's restaurant.

Almost all hotels offer special corporate and government rates. However, in this chapter I have listed only the official published rates (also known as rack rates). You may be able to get the corporate rates simply by asking; it's always worth a try. Most of the more expensive hotels have lower weekend rates, while inexpensive hotels tend to raise their rates slightly on the weekend.

If you get quoted a price that seems exorbitantly high, you might have accidentally stumbled upon a special holiday or event rate. Such rates are usually in effect for major coliseum events and college football games. If this is the case, try scheduling your visit for a different date if possible. Barring this possibility, try calling around to hotels farther out of town, where rates aren't as likely to be affected by special events. In fact, at any time, the farther you get from major business districts the less you're likely to spend on a room. If you don't mind driving 20 or 30 minutes, you can almost halve the amount you'll need to spend on a room.

For the purposes of this book, I have placed hotels in the following rate categories: **very expensive,** more than $175 for a double room; **expensive,** $125 to $175; **moderate,** $75 to $125; and **inexpensive,** less than $75. Please keep in mind, however, that the rates listed below do not include taxes, which in Memphis add up to a whopping 15.95%. (9.25% sales tax and 6.7% room tax).

1 Downtown

If you want to be where the action is, your first choice ought to be downtown. Besides Beale Street, this area is also where the majority of the city's major sporting events, concerts, and cultural performances take place. If you want to feel like you've been to Memphis, you need to experience the city's exciting revitalization.

VERY EXPENSIVE

Madison Hotel ★★★ *Moments* A member of the prestigious Small Luxury Hotels of the World, this sleek new hotel occupies the site of a former bank building. The graceful beaux arts architecture belies the bold, contemporary furnishings inside. From the elegant lobby, with its grand piano and musical instrument motif, to the rich, solid colors in the guest rooms, the Madison is a contrast between classic and modern. Whirlpool baths or jet tubs are available in many rooms. Nightly turndown and twice-daily housekeeping service keep guests feeling pampered. Take the elevator to the outdoor rooftop for breathtaking views of the Mississippi River and surrounding downtown. Every Thursday evening from April to mid-October, the hotel hosts sunset parties here, featuring live jazz.

79 Madison Ave., Memphis, TN 38103. ℭ 866/44-MEMPHIS or 901/333-1200. Fax 901/333-1297. www.madisonhotelmemphis.com. 110 units. $190–$255 doubles; $320 and up for suites. AE, DC, DISC, MC, V. Valet parking $10 (unlimited access); **Amenities:** Restaurant/lounge; indoor pool; fitness center; concierge; 24-hr. room service; lobby library. *In room:* A/C, TV, CD-player alarm clock, dataport with high-speed Internet access, minibar, coffeemaker, hair dryer, safe.

Memphis Marriott Downtown ★★ Located at the north end of downtown, on the Main Street trolley line, the 18-floor Marriott connected to the convention center is primarily a convention hotel. Recently renovated from the ground up, the hotel is a bit off the beaten track, surrounded mostly by government buildings. But the trolley will quickly take you up and down Main Street where there's more action. The lobby is built on a grand scale with soaring ceilings, marble floors, and traditional furnishings that are a welcome contrast to the stark modernity of the lobby. My favorite rooms here are the corner rooms, which have angled walls that provide a bit more character. However, the standard king rooms are also good bets. The top three floors are the hotel's concierge levels and offer extra amenities. For views of the Mississippi, ask for a room on the 10th floor or higher. The hotel's main restaurant is a casual spot serving American and international fare. Breakfast and coffee are served in a small cafe.

250 N. Main St., Memphis, TN 38103. ℭ 888/557-8740 or 901/527-7300. Fax 901/526-1561. www.marriott.com. 600 units. $129–$209 double; $349–$545 suite. AE, DC, DISC, MC, V. Valet parking $12; self-parking $7. **Amenities:** Restaurant; lounge; large indoor pool; exercise area; hot tub; sauna; concierge; room service; valet/laundry service. *In room:* A/C, TV, dataport with high-speed Internet access, coffeemaker, hair dryer, iron.

The Peabody Memphis ⭐ (Moments) For years, the Peabody enjoyed a reputation as one of the finest hotels in the South. In recent years, however, the property is showing its age. A complete renovation scheduled to begin in the spring of 2004 should rectify that. The public spaces, however, retain an air of unmatched elegance. Marble columns, gilded mezzanine railings, hand-carved and burnished woodwork, and ornate gilded plasterwork on the ceiling give the lobby the air of a palace. The lobby's most prominent feature is its Romanesque fountain. Here, the famous Peabody ducks, one of Memphis's biggest attractions, while away each day.

Chez Philippe, serving French-inspired cuisine amid palatial surroundings, has long been the best restaurant in Memphis (p. 175). Capriccio is the hotel's new lobby-level Italian restaurant for fine dining.

149 Union Ave., Memphis, TN 38103. ⓒ **800/PEABODY** or 901/529-4000. Fax 901/529-3677. www.peabody memphis.com. 468 units. $199–$359 double; $380 and up for suite. AE, DC, DISC, MC, V. Valet parking $17; self-parking $12. **Amenities:** 2 restaurants; 2 lounges; athletic facility with elegant though small pool; steam room; sauna; concierge; 24-hr. room service; massage; valet/laundry service; shoe-shine stand. *In room:* A/C, TV/VCR, 2 phone lines, dataport with high-speed Internet access, hair dryer, iron.

Talbot Heirs Guesthouse ⭐ (Finds) Trendy, contemporary styling is not something one often associates with the tradition-oriented South, which is what makes this upscale downtown B&B so unique. Each of the rooms is boldly decorated in a wide variety of styles. One room is done in bright solid colors (yellow walls and a fire engine–red tool chest for a bedside stand), while another is done in rich, subtle colors and has a neo-Victorian daybed. Most rooms have interesting modern lamps, and many have kilim rugs. The rooms vary in size from large to huge; all have full kitchens—and an unexpected amenity is complimentary in-room ice cream. Lots of interesting contemporary art further add to the hip feel of this inn. Talbot Heirs is located right across the street from The

---

The Peabody Ducks

It isn't often that you find live ducks in the lobby of a luxury hotel. However ducks are a fixture at the elegant **Peabody Memphis.** Each morning at 11am, the Peabody ducks, led by a duck-master, take the elevator down from their penthouse home, waddle down a red carpet, and hop into the hotel's Romanesque travertine-marble fountain. And each evening at 5pm they waddle back down the red carpet and take the elevator back up to the penthouse. During their entry and exit, the ducks waddle to John Philip Sousa tunes and attract large crowds of curious onlookers that press in on the fountain and red carpet from every side.

The Peabody ducks first took up residence in the lobby in the 1930s when Frank Schutt, the hotel's general manager, and friend Chip Barwick, after one too many swigs of Tennessee sippin' whiskey, put some of his live duck decoys in the hotel's fountain as a joke (such live decoys were legal at the time but have since been outlawed as unsportsmanlike). Guests at the time thought the ducks were a delightfully offbeat touch for such a staid and traditional establishment, and since then ducks have become a beloved fixture at the Peabody.

Memphis Accommodations: Downtown & Midtown

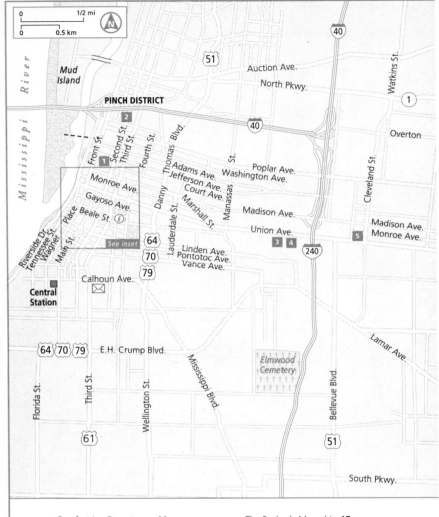

Comfort Inn Downtown **11**
French Quarter Suites Hotel **7**
Hampton Inn & Suites–Peabody Place **9**
Hampton Inn Medical Center/Midtown **5**
Holiday Inn Select Downtown **14**
La Quinta Inn **4**
Madison Hotel **13**
Memphis Marriott Downtown **2**

The Peabody Memphis **15**
Radisson Hotel Memphis **16**
Ramada Midtown/Medical Center **6**
Red Roof Inn Medical Center **3**
Sleep Inn–Downtown at Court Square **1**
SpringHill Suites by Marriott **12**
Talbot Heirs Guesthouse **10**
Wyndham Gardens Hotel **8**

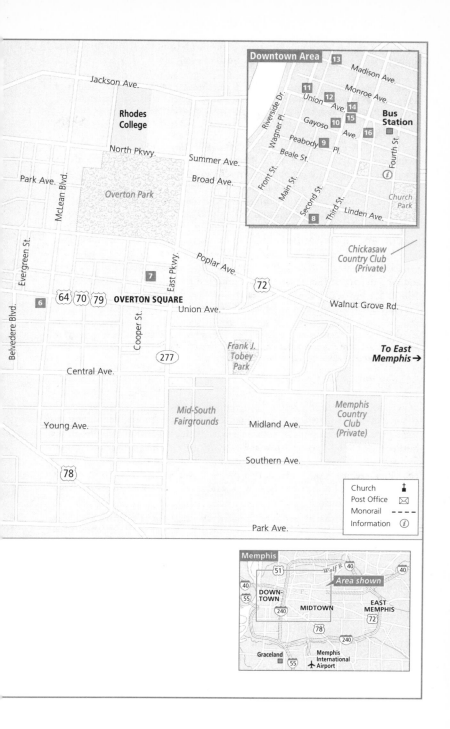

Jackson Ave.

Rhodes
College

North Pkwy.

Summer Ave.

Broad Ave.

Park Ave.

McLean Blvd.

Overton Park

Evergreen St.

Poplar Ave.

Chickasaw
Country Club
(Private)

East Pkwy.

7

(72)

Belvedere Blvd.

6

(64)(70)(79) OVERTON SQUARE

Union Ave.

Walnut Grove Rd.

Cooper St.

(277)

Frank J.
Tobey
Park

**To East
Memphis →**

Central Ave.

Memphis
Country
Club
(Private)

Young Ave.

Mid-South
Fairgrounds

Midland Ave.

(78)

Southern Ave.

Church	⛪
Post Office	✉
Monorail	- - - -
Information	ⓘ

Park Ave.

Downtown Area 13

Madison Ave.

11

Monroe Ave.

Union 12 Ave.

Riverside Dr.

14

Gayoso 10 15

**Bus
Station**

Wagner Pl.

Peabody 9

Ave. 16

Beale St.

Pl.

Fourth St.

Front St.

Main St.

Second St.

Third St.

ⓘ

Church
Park

8

Linden Ave.

Memphis

(51)

Wolf R.

(40)

(40)

Area shown

(40)

**DOWN-
TOWN**

(55)

(240)

MIDTOWN

(78)

**EAST
MEMPHIS**

(72)

(240)

Graceland

(55)

Memphis
International
✈ Airport

Peabody Memphis hotel and only a few doors down from the trendy Automatic Slim's Tonga Club, which inspired this B&B's styling.

99 S. 2nd St., Memphis, TN 38103. ℂ 800/955-3956 or 901/527-9772. Fax 901/527-3700. www.talbot house.com. 8 units. $125–$250 double. Rates include continental breakfast. AE, DC, DISC, MC, V. Nearby valet parking $17; self-parking $10. **Amenities:** Concierge; massage; laundry service; dry cleaning. *In room:* A/C, cable, CD player, dataport with high-speed Internet access, coffeemaker, hair dryer, iron.

EXPENSIVE

Hampton Inn & Suites–Peabody Place ★★ *Value* You can't get closer to spending the night on Beale Street unless you pass out on the pavement after a blues-soaked binge of bar-hopping. This award-winning property is not your typical chain hotel; in fact, it's touted by Hampton as their top hotel in the world. This stylish, curved building sits on a corner lot, jutting out into the heart of the action along Beale and Peabody Place. (Try to get a corner room with an iron balcony and watch the reverie like it's Mardi Gras.) It's just a block from the Rock 'n' Soul Museum and Gibson Showcase. Though the rooms don't have dataports, free Internet access is available 24 hours a day in the hotel's business center. Tastefully decorated rooms and public areas are immaculately clean and well-maintained, and service is among the friendliest in town. Free local calls and a breakfast cafe that serves the best beignets north of Louisiana, all combine to make this hotel an outstanding value.

175 Peabody Place, Memphis, TN 38103. ℂ 901/260-4000. Fax 901/260-4050. www.hampton-inn.com. 144 units. $155 doubles; $225 suites. Rates include continental breakfast. AE, DC, DISC, MC, V. Self-parking $10. **Amenities:** Restaurant; indoor pool; business center; exercise room. *In room:* A/C, TV w/pay movies, continental breakfast included in room rate, coffeemaker, iron.

Holiday Inn Select Downtown ★ This downtown Holiday Inn, across the street from the Peabody, is a good choice if you want to be in the heart of the downtown action. The guest rooms, though not large, do have comfortable chairs and big windows. But be advised that some of those windows butt up against other concrete buildings. Rooms facing south afford the best views of the bustle along Union Avenue below. Foodies may appreciate that the hotel is mere footsteps away from the city's best German (Erika's), Thai (Sawaddi) and barbecue (Rendezvous) restaurants, not to mention across the corner from Huey's, Memphis' beloved burger-and-beer joint. The hotel also houses one of the freshest sushi bars in town.

160 Union Ave., Memphis, TN 38103. ℂ 800/HOLIDAY or 901/525-5491. Fax 901/529-8950. www.hiselect. com. 192 units. $119–$149 double; $149–$169 suite. AE, DC, DISC, MC, V. Parking $6. **Amenities:** Restaurant; lounge; modest outdoor pool on rooftop terrace; fitness center; limited room service. *In room:* A/C, TV w/pay movies, dataport with high-speed Internet access, coffeemaker, hair dryer, iron.

SpringHill Suites by Marriott ★★ One of Memphis' newest downtown high-rise hotels is one of the best values for tourists who want a clean, comfortable suite at a reasonable price in a great location. In the heart of downtown, just a block from the Mississippi River, its location is far enough away from Beale Street to escape the drunken late-night revelry, but within easy walking distance (though you could simply step out the back door and hop on the trolley). A cheerful lobby and adjacent breakfast room provide guests with a welcome greeting. Suites are spacious, tastefully decorated, and include well-lighted work spaces with multi-line speaker phones, kitchenettes, and soft couches. Rooms with south-facing windows have great views of Court Square, a leafy park that dates back to before the turn of the century. On the ground floor in front of the hotel, the small outdoor pool is gated and landscaped, though not very private.

21 N. Main St., Memphis, TN 38103. © **901/522-2100.** Fax 901/522-2110. www.marriott.com. 102 units. $129–$139 double. AE, DC, DISC, MC, V. Free parking. Amenities: Outdoor pool; business center; valet and self-service laundry. *In room:* A/C, cable/satellite TV w/pay movies, dataport with high-speed Internet access, coffeemaker, fridge, hair dryer, iron, safe deposit boxes available at front desk.

MODERATE

Comfort Inn Downtown   Memphis' only rooftop swimming pool is the best boast of this otherwise lackluster hotel that has a prime location on Front Street overlooking the Mississippi River. Despite updated exterior work and new signage, the hotel's rooms are a bit blander than others in its price range. Quite often, you'll see busloads of tour groups staying at the hotel. So if you're after a more intimate setting you might want to look elsewhere first. Still the hotel is a viable option if other properties are booked.

100 N. Front St., Memphis, TN 38103. © **901/526-0583.** Fax 901/525-7512. www.choicehotels.com. 71 units. $80–$149 doubles and suites. AE, DC, DISC, MC, V. Free parking. **Amenities:** Outdoor pool. *In room:* A/C, TV, hair dryer.

Radisson Hotel Memphis ⭐   Across the street from the Memphis Redbirds' baseball stadium, the Radisson is also housed in a restored building. Though undergoing renovations, the lobby has an atrium with glass elevators and features the freestanding facade of a brick historic building that now serves as the entrance to a T.G.I. Friday's restaurant. This hotel, which stays packed with tour groups and conventions, has a very busy and rather impersonal feel. However, the location is good, and the rates are economical. Regular rooms are large and have modern furnishings and standard-size bathrooms. If you're willing to spend a bit more money, the executive rooms are particularly attractive and very luxurious.

185 Union Ave., Memphis, TN 38103. © **800/333-3333** or 901/528-1800. Fax 901/525-8509. www. radisson.com. 280 units. $109–$117 double; $179–$299 suite. AE, DC, DISC, MC, V. Valet parking $10. **Amenities:** Restaurant; lounge; outdoor pool; small exercise room; hot tub; sauna. *In room:* A/C, TV w/pay movies, dataport with high-speed Internet access, coffeemaker, hair dryer, iron.

Sleep Inn–Downtown at Court Square ⭐ *Value*   You can't beat the location of this upscale motel, which fills up quickly during weekends when there is a lot happening downtown. Wedged between nostalgic Court Square and the banks of the Mississippi River, it's also on the Main Street trolley line. At only six stories, this hotel is dwarfed by surrounding buildings. The modern design and economical rates make this a very appealing choice in downtown Memphis. Most rooms are large and comfortable, and business-class rooms come with fax machines, work desks, VCRs, and dual phone lines. The motel shares a free parking lot with the adjacent SpringHill Suites.

40 N. Front St., Memphis, TN 38103. © **800/SLEEPINN (753-3946)** or 901/522-9700. www.choicehotels. com. Fax 901/522-9710. 124 units. $64–$124 double. Rates include continental breakfast. AE, DC, DISC, MC, V. Free parking. **Amenities:** Small exercise room. *In room:* A/C, TV, dataport, coffeemaker, hair dryer, iron.

Wyndham Gardens Hotel ⭐   This property offers a lush garden setting and interior touches including plantation shutters and marble floors. Rooms are modem-ready, and equipped with easy chairs, TVs, and other modern amenities. The Wyndham offers an excellent location if your trip will take you to the nearby Convention Center, Pyramid, or St. Jude Children's Research Hospital.

300 N. 2nd St., Memphis, TN 38103. © **901/525-1800.** Fax 901/524-1859. www.wyndham.com. 230 units. $99–$129 single or double. AE, DC, DISC, MC, V. Self-parking $5. **Amenities:** Restaurant; outdoor pool; exercise room; limited room service; dry cleaning. *In room:* A/C, TV w/pay movies, fax, dataport with high-speed Internet access, coffeemaker, hair dryer, iron.

2 Midtown

A bit more off the beaten path, midtown is a good choice if you're looking for a quieter location that also offers cultural options but without the parking and traffic hassles that can sometimes snarl downtown. For locations of hotels in this section, see the "Memphis Accommodations: Downtown & Midtown" map on p. 162.

MODERATE

French Quarter Suites Hotel   Its perch in the heart of Overton Square used to be a big plus, but just as this fledgling midtown entertainment district has been upstaged by a newly revitalized downtown, so have the few hotels here. Though this hotel looks charming enough with its French Quarter-style court-yards and balconies, the guest rooms and public areas suggest that the hotel has not been as well maintained as others in town.

2144 Madison Ave., Memphis, TN 38104. (℃ **800/843-0353** or 901/728-4000. Fax 901/278-1262. www. memphisfrenchquarter.com. 103 units. $109–$119 double. AE, DC, DISC, MC, V. Free parking. **Amenities:** Outdoor pool; exercise room; room service; valet/laundry service; complimentary airport shuttle. *In room:* A/C, TV w/pay movies, wet bar, coffeemaker, hair dryer, iron.

INEXPENSIVE

In addition to the hotel listed below, national and regional chain motels in the area include the following (see also appendix D, "Useful Toll-Free Numbers & Websites," for toll-free telephone numbers): **Hampton Inn Medical Center/ Midtown,** 1180 Union Ave. (℃ **901/276-1175**), charging $64 to $84 double; **La Quinta Inn,** 42 S. Camilla St. (℃ **901/526-1050**), charging $61 to $70 double; and **Red Roof Inn Medical Center,** 210 S. Pauline St. (℃ **901/528-0650**), charging $40 to $47 double.

Ramada Midtown/Medical Center   Though not as new or as well main-tained as the East Memphis Holiday Inns, this midtown lodging is a good mod-erately priced choice if you're here on vacation and want to be close to both museums and nightclubs. Guest rooms are much nicer than the dismal parking garage would lead you to believe. Try to get a room on an upper floor so you can enjoy the views of the city at night. The king rooms are the best deal, with love seats and plenty of space. The hotel's restaurant has lots of Elvis posters and is done in a combination of Art Deco and 1950s-diner styling. The menu is suit-ably traditional with moderate prices. There's an adjacent lounge, and room service is available. There's also an outdoor pool and an exercise room.

1837 Union Ave. (at McLean Blvd.), Memphis, TN 38104. (℃ **800/HOLIDAY** or 901/278-4100. Fax 901/272-3810. www.ramada.com. 155 units. $59–$89 double; $89–$99 suite. AE, DC, DISC, MC, V. Free parking. **Amenities:** Restaurant; lounge; outdoor pool; exercise room; limited room service; coin-op and laundry service; dry cleaning. *In room:* A/C, TV, dataport, unstocked fridge, coffeemaker, hair dryer, iron, safes avail-able at front desk.

3 East Memphis

If your visit to Memphis brings you to any of the suburban business parks in the perimeter of the city, East Memphis is a smart choice. It's centrally located between downtown hot spots and outlying suburbs, where companies such as Federal Express and International Paper have their corporate headquarters.

EXPENSIVE

Doubletree Hotels Memphis ★★   Located inside the I-240 ring, this East Memphis hotel is a bit more convenient to midtown museums than other hotels

East Memphis Accommodations

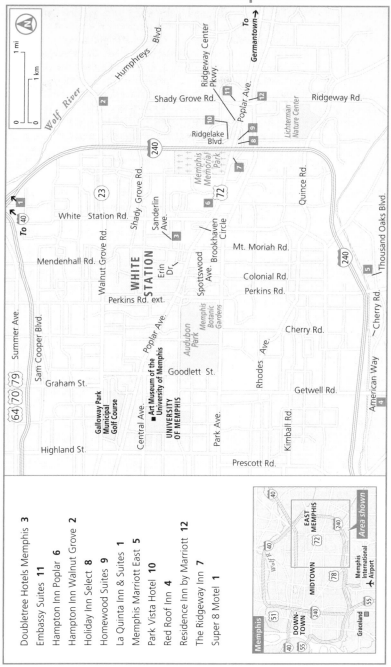

Doubletree Hotels Memphis **3**
Embassy Suites **11**
Hampton Inn Poplar **6**
Hampton Inn Walnut Grove **2**
Holiday Inn Select **8**
Homewood Suites **9**
La Quinta Inn & Suites **1**
Memphis Marriott East **5**
Park Vista Hotel **10**
Red Roof Inn **4**
Residence Inn by Marriott **12**
The Ridgeway Inn **7**
Super 8 Motel **1**

in this area. However, the hotel's real appeal is that it is within walking distance of a couple of excellent restaurants and has an indoor/outdoor pool. It's also only a very short drive to Corky's, one of the best barbecue joints in town. Built around a glass-walled atrium, the eight-floor hotel has glass elevators so you can enjoy the views. Most rooms here are designed with the business traveler in mind and have two phones, radio/television speakers in the bathrooms, and large desks. Another nice feature is large, angled windows that make the rooms seem a bit larger than standard hotel rooms. With its brass rails and potted plants, the hotel's dining room is a casual place serving moderately priced meals.

5069 Sanderlin Ave., Memphis, TN 38117. ℂ 800/445-8667 or 901/767-6666. Fax 901/683-8563. www. doubletree.com. 276 units. $119–$169 double; $199–$259 suite. AE, DC, DISC, MC, V. Free parking. **Amenities:** Restaurant; lounge; indoor/outdoor pool; exercise room; room service; valet/laundry service. *In room:* A/C, TV w/pay movies, dataport, fridge, coffeemaker, hair dryer, iron.

Embassy Suites ★★ (Kids) With its many tropical plants and artificial stream, the lobby of this modern atrium hotel looks more like a botanical conservatory than a hotel lobby. A waterfall, little beach, and giant goldfish add to the effect, and, not to be upstaged by the Peabody, this hotel even has a few resident ducks floating in its stream. Wireless Internet access is available in public areas. All the guest rooms here are spacious two-room suites that have kitchenettes, dining tables, two televisions, two phones, and sofa beds. The layouts of the rooms are good for both families and business travelers. The complete, cooked-to-order breakfast is served in the atrium, where, in the evening, there's also a complimentary manager's reception with free drinks. The moderately priced Frank Grisanti's Italian Restaurant just off the atrium serves lunch and dinner and is one of the best Italian restaurants in the city (p. 186).

1022 S. Shady Grove Rd., Memphis, TN 38120. ℂ 800/EMBASSY or 901/684-1777. Fax 901/685-8185. www.hilton.com. 220 units. $119–$189 double. Rates include full breakfast. AE, DC, DISC, MC, V. Free parking. **Amenities:** Restaurant; lounge; indoor pool; exercise room; hot tub; sauna; business center; room service; coin-op laundry; valet/laundry service; free airport transportation. *In room:* A/C, TV w/pay movies and video games, coffeemaker, hair dryer, iron.

Homewood Suites ★ (Kids) Homewood Suites offers some of the most attractive and spacious accommodations in Memphis. The suites, which are arranged around an attractively landscaped central courtyard with a swimming pool and basketball court, resemble an apartment complex rather than a hotel. The lobby has the feel of a mountain lodge and features pine furnishings, lots of natural-wood trim, and attractive decorations and artwork. Early American styling, with pine furnishings, sets the tone in the suites, many of which have wood-burning fireplaces and contemporary wrought-iron beds. There are two televisions (and a VCR) in every suite, as well as full kitchens and big bathrooms with plenty of counter space. Though there's no restaurant on the premises, you can pick up

---

⸠Fun Fact **The *Other* Ducklings**

The Peabody's ducks may be the best-known fowl around town. But few visitors realize that another upscale property, the **Embassy Suites** in East Memphis, also boasts such birds frolicking amidst its atrium's fountains and foliage. They don't get the red-carpet treatment, however. "Our ducks are from the other side of the pond," quips an Embassy Suites employee.

Kids **Family-Friendly Hotels**

Embassy Suites (_p. 168_)   The indoor pool and garden-like atrium lobby provide a place for the kids to play even on rainy or cold days, and the two-room suites give parents a private room of their own. Video games are another plus for the kids.

Homewood Suites (_p. 168_)   With a pool and basketball court and grounds that resemble an upscale apartment complex, this East Memphis hotel is a good bet for families. Plus, the evening social hour includes enough food to serve as dinner (and thus save you quite a bit on your meal budget).

microwave meals in the hotel's convenience shop. There is also a complimentary social hour on weeknights that includes enough food to pass for dinner.

5811 Poplar Ave. (just off I-240), Memphis, TN 38119. _©_ **800/CALL-HOME** or 901/763-0500. Fax 901/763-0132. www.homewood-suites.com. 140 units. $139–$169 double. Rates include cooked breakfast. AE, DC, DISC, MC, V. Free parking. **Amenities:** Outdoor pool; exercise room; passes to Gold's Gym; hot tub; basketball court; valet/laundry service; complimentary shuttle to airport, local shopping, and restaurants. _In room:_ A/C, TV w/VCR, dataport with high-speed Internet access, kitchen, coffeemaker, hair dryer, iron.

Memphis Marriott East   You'll find this hotel about midway between the airport and the Poplar Avenue exit. Catering primarily to corporate travelers, this hotel has a large courtyard garden near the lobby, with travertine and red marble floor. Though most of the rooms are a bit smaller than you might hope, the king rooms are well laid out and have large work desks with phones. Try for one of the upper floors to get a good view of the surrounding countryside. In the back of the lobby, there's an elegant piano bar. The dark-wood bar gives this lounge a classic air. High-speed Internet access is available in the lobby and at the bar.

2625 Thousand Oaks Blvd., Memphis, TN 38118. _©_ **800/627-3587** or 901/362-6200. Fax 901/360-8836. www.marriotthotels.com/memtn. 320 units. $159 double; $300 hospitality suite. AE, DC, DISC, MC, V. Free parking. **Amenities:** Restaurant; lounge; indoor and outdoor pool; exercise room; hot tub; sauna; concierge; room service; valet/laundry service; complimentary airport shuttle. _In room:_ A/C, TV w/pay movies, fax; dataport, coffeemaker, hair dryer, iron.

Park Vista Hotel   This gleaming, round high-rise dominates the skyline in an upscale East Memphis area that's also convenient to Germantown and Collierville as well as to downtown and midtown. After being acquired by the Hilton hotel group in 2003, this former Adams Mark property is undergoing extensive renovations. In addition to featuring all the modern amenities, rooms are being expanded and redecorated in cream and pastel colors. Renovations are expected to be complete by the time you read this.

939 Ridge Lake Blvd., Memphis, TN 38120. _©_ **800/774-1500** or 901/684-6664. Fax 901/762-7496. www. hilton.com. 408 units. $109–$189 double; $250–$600 suite. AE, DC, DISC, MC, V. Free parking. Located off Ridgeway Center Pkwy. at I-240 and Poplar Ave., Exit 15 East. **Amenities:** Restaurant; lounge; outdoor pool; fitness center; hot tub; business center; room service; valet/laundry service; complimentary airport shuttle. _In room:_ A/C, TV w/pay movies, dataport, coffeemaker, hair dryer, iron.

Residence Inn by Marriott _★_   Though it's not as attractively designed as the nearby Homewood Suites, this extended-stay property offers many of the same conveniences and amenities. It benefits from being within walking distance of several excellent restaurants. Some suites have rooms that open onto the lobby, while others have windows to the outside and tiny triangular balconies. You can choose a one-bedroom or two-bedroom suite, but whichever size suite you choose, you'll have plenty of space, including a full kitchen and perhaps a fireplace. The two-bedroom suites have loft sleeping areas. Be sure to ask for a room on the side away from the railroad tracks.

6141 Old Poplar Pike, Memphis, TN 38119. ℰ **800/331-3131** or 901/685-9595. Fax 901/685-1636. www. marriott.com. 105 suites. $129–$149 suite. Rates include continental breakfast as well as a light dinner from 5:30–7pm Mon–Thur. AE, DC, DISC, MC, V. Free parking. **Amenities:** Outdoor pool; sports court; valet/laundry service; complimentary social hour; grocery-shopping service. In room: A/C, TV w/pay movies, dataport with high-speed Internet access, coffeemaker, hair dryer, iron.

The Ridgeway Inn ⭐⭐   Operated by the same company that runs the Peabody, this hotel offers comparable accommodations in a modern East Memphis hotel. With its European styling, the small lobby sets a classically sophisticated tone for this popular hostelry, a favorite of business travelers. Guest rooms are comfortable and designed for the business traveler. In the king rooms you'll find a desk for working and a couch for relaxing. Furnishings are primarily reproductions of Early American pieces. Club-level rooms include a TV and hair dryer in the bathroom, continental breakfast, evening hors d'oeuvres, and evening turndown service. Terra-cotta floor tiles and gray-and-white wicker chairs give Café Expresso a traditional Italian cafe look. However, the menu features deli sandwiches, continental dishes, and a wide selection of great pastries. The adjacent Lobby Bar has a country-club feel that's more in keeping with the classic decor of the rest of the hotel. There's also an outdoor pool but, unfortunately, it's right beside busy Poplar Avenue and is usually too noisy to be relaxing.

5679 Poplar Ave. (at I-240), Memphis, TN 38119. ℰ **800/822-3360** or 901/766-4000. Fax 901/680-0248. www.ridgewayinn.com. 159 units. $89–$149 double; $150–$300 suite. AE, DC, DISC, MC, V. Free parking. **Amenities:** Restaurant; lounge; outdoor pool; exercise room; access to nearby health club; concierge; room service; valet/laundry service; complimentary airport shuttle. In room: A/C, TV w/pay movies, dataport, hair dryer, iron.

MODERATE

Hampton Inn Poplar   This Hampton Inn, conveniently located inside the I-240 ring and close to several major museums (not to mention Corky's barbecue restaurant, across the street), offers the sort of dependable accommodations that have made Hampton Inns so popular. Rooms with king-size beds, easy chairs, and a desk, are the best choice for business travelers, while those with sofa beds make a good choice for leisure travelers and families. The outdoor pool, surrounded by attractively landscaped gardens, is far enough away from the street that it isn't too noisy.

5320 Poplar Ave., Memphis, TN 38119. ℰ **800/HAMPTON** or 901/683-8500. Fax 901/763-4970. www. hamptoninn.com. 126 units. $82–$89 double. Rates include continental breakfast. AE, DC, DISC, MC, V. Free parking. **Amenities:** Outdoor pool. In room: A/C, TV w/pay movies, dataport with high-speed Internet access, coffeemaker, hair dryer, iron.

Hampton Inn Walnut Grove   Almost identical in design and level of comfort to the Hampton Inn on Poplar Avenue, this lodging is more convenient to I-240 and many newer East Memphis businesses, including the city's most upscale suburban hospital facility. One of the city's best Japanese restaurants is in a shopping center adjacent to this hotel.

33 Humphreys Center Dr., Memphis, TN 38120. (C) **800/HAMPTON** or 901/747-3700. Fax 901/747-3800. www.hamptoninn.com. 120 units. $79–$99 double. AE, DC, DISC, MC, V. Free parking. **Amenities:** Outdoor pool. *In room:* Cable TV, dataport with high-speed Internet access, hair dryer, iron.

Holiday Inn Select   This modern 10-story hotel is convenient both to east-side restaurants and to the interstate, so it is easy to get downtown to Beale Street or to Graceland. Though the hotel is geared primarily toward corporate travelers, a sunny indoor pool area makes it appealing to vacationers as well. A business center offers high-speed Internet access. Overall, the rooms are fresh and views from upper floors are pleasant. Corner king rooms are particularly spacious.

5795 Poplar Ave., Memphis, TN 38119. (C) **800/HOLIDAY** or 901/682-7881. Fax 901/682-0536. www. hiselect.com/mem-epoplar. 243 units. $69–$109 double; $89–$119 suite. AE, DC, DISC, MC, V. Free parking. **Amenities:** Indoor pool; exercise room; whirlpool; room service; valet/laundry service; complimentary airport shuttle. *In room:* A/C, cable TV, dataport, coffeemaker, hair dryer, iron.

INEXPENSIVE TO MODERATE

National and regional motel chains in the area include the following (see also appendix D for toll-free telephone numbers): **AmeriSuites,** 1220 Primacy Parkway ((C) **901/680-9700**), **La Quinta Inn & Suites,** 1236 Primacy Parkway ((C) **901/374-0330**), charging $60 to $89 double; **Red Roof Inn,** 6055 Shelby Oaks Dr. ((C) **901/388-6111**), charging $45 to $50 double; and **Super 8 Motel,** 6015 Macon Cove Rd. ((C) **901/373-4888**), charging $50 to $58 double.

4 The Airport & Graceland Areas

Obviously, if you need to be near the airport, any of these properties will suit your needs. But truthfully, the airport area encompasses neighborhoods most locals would not feel safe driving in late at night. To get a sense of what Memphis is all about, you really should try to stay in or near downtown. Besides, with the plethora of tour buses and shuttle services available, access to Graceland is as easy from downtown as it is from the airport area.

MODERATE

Courtyard Memphis Airport ★★   This clean, well-maintained property, located a few miles from the main airport terminal, has earned a reputation as the airport area's top choice among corporate road warriors. Resembling a modern, well-landscaped office park, the hotel offers rooms (and 14 suites) well equipped for business travelers. There are large work desks, daily newspaper delivery, and dinner delivery service from local restaurants.

1780 Nonconnah Blvd. Memphis, TN 38132. (C) **901/396-3600.** Fax 901/332-0706. www.marriott.com. 145 units. $64–$119 double. $109–$139 suite. AE, DC, DISC, MC, V. Free parking. **Amenities:** Outdoor pool; exercise room; whirlpool. *In room:* A/C, TV w/pay movies, dataports with high-speed Internet access, coffeemaker, iron, hair dryer, safe deposit box available at front desk.

Elvis Presley's Heartbreak Hotel–Graceland ★★ *(Moments)*   If your visit to Memphis is a pilgrimage to Graceland, there should be no question as to where to stay. This hotel has a gate right into the Graceland parking lot, with Elvis's home right across Elvis Presley Boulevard. In the lobby, you'll find two big portraits of The King, and decor that would fit right in at Graceland. Also new since being acquired by the operators of Graceland are several theme suites, including the irresistibly named *"Burning Love* Suite." (Feel your temperature rising?) If you don't want to shell out big bucks for the entire suite, ask to split it and just rent a portion (or one room) of the suite. Many guests do this, I'm told.

3677 Elvis Presley Blvd., Memphis, TN 38116. © **877/777-0606** or 901/332-1000. Fax 901/332-2107. www.elvis.com. 128 units. $90–$120 regular suite; $309–$469 for the four themed suites. AE, DC, DISC, MC, V. Free parking. **Amenities:** Heart-shaped outdoor pool. *In room:* A/C, TV w/24-hr. Elvis movies, coffeemaker, hair dryer, iron.

Holiday Inn Select Memphis Airport ★ This is one of the most attractive airport-area hotels. Step through the doors of this large property and you enter a vast, cavernous lobby with a vaguely Mediterranean feel. Inside, there's an espresso bar and lounge.

2240 Democrat Rd., Memphis, TN 38132. © **901/332-1130.** Fax 901/398-5206. www.hiselect.com. 374 units. $99–$114 double; $250–$450 suite. AE, DC, DISC, MC, V. Free parking. **Amenities:** Restaurant; outdoor pool; 2 tennis courts; exercise room; room service; complimentary airport shuttle. *In room:* A/C, TV w/pay movies, dataport, coffeemaker, hair dryer, iron.

Radisson Inn Memphis Airport ★ *(Finds)* If you're in town on a quick business meeting or plan to arrive late at night, this hotel right on the grounds of the airport is a very convenient choice. Recently renovated, all the rooms are well soundproofed so you don't have to worry about losing sleep because of overhead jets. The rooms themselves are rather dark and are not very memorable, but many are set up for business travelers with a desk and comfortable chair. The hotel's restaurant is casual with a very traditional atmosphere and menu. The outdoor pool is set in a pleasant (though sometimes noisy) sunken garden area between two wings of the hotel.

2411 Winchester Rd., Memphis, TN 38116. © **800/333-3333** or 901/332-2370. Fax 901/345-9398. www. radisson.com. 211 units. $99 double; $139 suite. AE, DC, DISC, MC, V. Free parking. **Amenities:** Restaurant; lounge; outdoor pool; 2 tennis courts; exercise room; room service; 24-hr. complimentary airport shuttle. *In room:* A/C, TV, dataport with high-speed Internet access, coffeemaker, hair dryer, iron.

INEXPENSIVE

Aside from these hotels below, visitors may search for chain motels (see appendix D for toll-free telephone numbers).

Clarion Hotel Located close to both the airport and Graceland, this may appeal to Elvis fans on a budget. The entire hotel seems to have a faded-glory feel to it, with a lobby that once might have been almost elegant but now just feels dated and dark, and likewise the restaurant. The presence of both a bar and a nightclub is an indication that people who stay here like to party. The guest rooms are adequate, though none too memorable. Some of the rooms have microwaves.

1471 E. Brooks Rd., Memphis, TN 38116. © **800424-6423** or 901/332-3500. Fax 901/346-0017. www. choicehotel.com. 249 units. $67–$77 double. AE, DC, DISC, MC, V. Free parking. **Amenities:** Outdoor pool; room service; complimentary airport shuttle. *In room:* A/C, cable TV, dataport, fridge, coffeemaker, hair dryer, iron.

Days Inn at Graceland With Graceland right across the street, it's no surprise that Elvis is king at this budget motel. Just look for the Elvis mural on the side of the building and the neon guitar sign out front, and you'll have found this unusual Days Inn. In the lobby, and on the room TVs, are around-the-clock Elvis videos.

3839 Elvis Presley Blvd., Memphis, TN 38116. © **800/329-7466** or 901/346-5500. Fax 901/345-7452. www.daysinn.com. 61 units. $70–$80 double. Rates include continental breakfast. AE, DC, DISC, MC, V. Free parking. **Amenities:** Guitar-shaped outdoor pool. *In room:* A/C, TV.

Where to Dine in Memphis

For a city most often associated with pork barbecue and Elvis's famous fried peanut-butter-and-banana sandwiches, Memphis has a surprisingly diverse restaurant scene. From escargots to etouffée, fajitas to focaccia, piroshki to pho, there's all manner of ethnic and gourmet fare around town. You'll also find plenty of barbecued ribs, fried pickles, purple-hull peas, butter beans, meat loaf, and mashed potatoes. And you might be surprised by the wealth of trendy restaurants you'd expect to encounter in any major metropolitan area. Drawing on influences from around the country and around the world, these New American and New Southern restaurants serve dishes so complex and creative that they often take a paragraph to describe on a menu.

Gourmet and ethnic foods aside, however, what Memphis can claim as its very own is slow-smoked, hand-pulled-pork-shoulder barbecue, to which you can add the spicy sauces of your choosing—chili vinegar, hot sauce, whatever. If this doesn't appeal to you, then maybe Memphis's famous ribs will. These are cooked much the same way as the pork shoulder and come dry or wet—that is, with the sauce added by you (dry) or cooked in (wet). See section 6, devoted to barbecue restaurants, at the end of this chapter.

Among the many well-known chain restaurants to be found in Memphis are **Hard Rock Cafe,** 315 Beale St. (✆ **901/529-0007**), **P.F. Chang's China Bistro,** 1181 Ridgeway Rd. (✆ **901/818-3889;** and **Ruth's Chris Steakhouse,** 6120 Poplar at Shady Grove (✆ **901/761-0055**). The newest craze to hit downtown is the hand-carved meat concept of **Texas de Brazil,** 150 Peabody Place (✆ **901/526-7600**).

For these listings, I have classified restaurants in the following categories (estimates do not include beer, wine, or tip): **expensive** if a complete dinner would cost $30 or more; **moderate,** where you can expect to pay between $15 and $30 for a complete dinner; and **inexpensive,** where a complete dinner can be had for less than $15.

1 Restaurants by Cuisine

AMERICAN
The Arcade Restaurant ⭐
(Downtown, $, p. 179)
D'Bo's Buffalo Wings 'N' Things ⭐ (South Memphis, $, p. 189)
Huey's ⭐ (Downtown, $, p. 180)
Spaghetti Warehouse (Downtown, $, p. 181)

BARBECUE
Beale St. Bar-B-Que (Downtown, $, p. 190)
Corky's Bar-B-Q ⭐ (East Memphis, $, p. 188)
Cozy Corner (Midtown, $, p. 190)
Interstate Bar-B-Q Restaurant (Barbecue, $, p. 190)

Neely's Bar-B-Q (Downtown, East
Memphis, $, p. 190)

Payne's (South of Downtown, $,
p. 190)

Rendezvous ★★ (Downtown, $,
p. 180)

CAJUN

Café 61 ★ (Downtown, $$,
p. 178)

Owen Brennan's Restaurant ★
(East Memphis, $$, p. 187)

On Teur (Midtown, $, p. 184)

CALIFORNIAN

Café Francisco (Downtown, $,
p. 191)

Napa Café (East Memphis, $$$,
p. 186)

CHINESE

Asian Palace ★★ (East Memphis,
$, p. 188)

Saigon Le ★ (Midtown, $, p. 184)

CONTINENTAL

Paulette's ★ (Midtown, $$, p. 182)

FRENCH

Chez Philippe ★★ (Downtown,
$$$, p. 175)

La Baguette ★ (East Memphis, $$,
p. 191)

La Tourelle Restaurant ★★
(Midtown, $$$, p. 181)

Le Petit Bistro ★ (East Memphis,
$$, p. 187)

GERMAN

Erika's ★★ (Downtown, $, p. 179)

ITALIAN

Elfo's Restaurant ★ (Midtown, $,
p. 183)

Frank Grisanti's Italian Restaurant
★ (East Memphis, $$$, p. 186)

Fratelli's (Downtown, $, p. 191)

Spaghetti Warehouse (Downtown,
$, p. 181)

JAPANESE

Sekisui of Japan ★★ (East Mem-
phis, Midtown, Downtown, $$,
p. 188)

MEDITERRANEAN

Melange ★★★ (Midtown, $$$,
p. 181)

Melos Taverna ★ (Midtown, $$,
p. 182)

MEXICAN/SOUTHWESTERN

Café Ole (Midtown, $, p. 183)

Salsa Cocina Mexicana ★★ (East
Memphis, $, p. 189)

Taqueria Guadalajara ★ (East
Memphis, $, p. 189)

NEW AMERICAN

Automatic Slim's Tonga Club ★★
(Downtown, $$, p. 175)

Beauty Shop ★★★ (Midtown,
$$$, p. 181)

Café Society ★ (Midtown, $$,
p. 182)

Cielo ★ (Downtown, $$, p. 178)

Glass Onion (Midtown, $$,
p. 182)

Elfo's Restaurant ★ (Midtown, $,
p. 183)

Erling Jensen–The Restaurant
★★★ (East Memphis, $$$,
p. 184)

Jarrett's ★★★ (East Memphis, $$,
p. 187)

Lulu Grille ★★ (East Memphis,
$$, p. 187)

Napa Café (East Memphis, $$$,
p. 186)

NEW SOUTHERN

Brushmark (Midtown, $$, p. 191)

Chez Philippe ★★ (Downtown,
$$$, p. 175)

The Grove Grill ★ (East
Memphis, $$, p. 186)

RUSSIAN

Café Samovar ★★ (Downtown,
$$, p. 178)

SEAFOOD

Jarrett's ★★★ (East Memphis, $$,
p. 187)

Joe's Crab Shack ★ (Downtown,
$$, p. 178)

Tsunami ★★ (Midtown, $$$,
p. 182)

SOUTHERN

Alcenia's ⭐ (Downtown, $, p. 179)

Buntyn Restaurant ⭐ (East Memphis, $, p. 188)

The Cupboard (Midtown, Downtown, $, p. 183)

Ellen's Soul Food ⭐ (Midtown, $, p. 190)

Fourway Restaurant ⭐⭐⭐ (South Memphis, $, p. 190)

Gus's World Famous Fried Chicken ⭐ (Downtown, $, p. 179)

STEAK

Folk's Folly Prime Steak House ⭐⭐ (East Memphis, $$$, p. 186)

VIETNAMESE

Pho Saigon ⭐ (Midtown, $, p. 184)

Saigon Le ⭐ (Midtown, $, p. 184)

THAI

Sawaddii (Downtown, $$, p. 179)

2 Downtown

EXPENSIVE

Chez Philippe ⭐⭐ FRENCH/NEW SOUTHERN   An opulent floral arrangement is the first thing you'll see as you step through the wrought-iron gates into this lavishly elegant restaurant in the Peabody hotel. The dining rooms are on three separate levels, with lacy New Orleans–style metalwork, wide marble columns, and sparkling chandeliers that give Chez Philippe a palatial atmosphere. On the menu, you'll find a mix of contemporary French and down-home New Southern dishes being offered by award-winning Chef José Gutier-rez. To start out your meal, you might order an appetizer of fried Roquefort with shallot vinaigrette, or a chilled mango bisque with berry ice cubes. For main course choices, you'll find such dishes as seared salmon with potato and orange beignets, filet mignon with fried veggies and chicory sauce, and roasted rack of lamb with holly-basil mashed potatoes. Soufflés are a must for dessert. Or, you could opt for refreshing sorbets or something more decadent, like the poached pear with hot chocolate sauce and roasted hazelnut ice cream. Prices are steep, but expect to be pampered.

The Peabody Memphis Hotel, 149 Union Ave. ⓒ **901/529-4188.** www.peabodymemphis.com. Reservations recommended. Main courses $21–$28. AE, DC, DISC, MC, V. Sun–Wed 11am–1pm; Thurs–Sat 11am–2pm; Tues–Sat 6–10pm.

MODERATE

Automatic Slim's Tonga Club ⭐⭐ NEW AMERICAN   For relaxed artiness and creative food in downtown Memphis, try Automatic Slim's. The name "Automatic Slim" comes from an old blues song, and the Tonga Club was a local teen hangout popular in the early 1960s. Artists from New York and Memphis created the decor (they're credited on the menu), including zebra-print uphol-stered banquettes, slag-glass wall sconces, and colorfully upholstered bar stools. Be sure to try a cocktail with some of the fruit-soaked vodka. The food here is as creative as the atmosphere. The coconut-mango shrimp with citrus *pico de gallo* is a piquant starter. Salads are adventurous plates of fresh field greens, lightly vinegared and tossed with sun-dried cherries, goat cheese, and sunflower seeds. The tasty quesadillas are cheesy tortillas topped with cilantro and onions. If you can stand the heat, try the succulent Jamaican jerk chicken, served with black beans and rice. In summer, ask for the creamy tomato basil soup. It goes great with Slim's coyote chips, crisps of potato with horseradish dipping sauce.

Memphis Dining: Downtown & Midtown

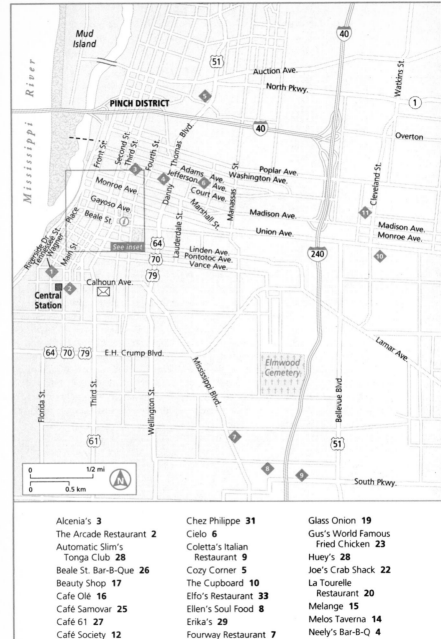

Alcenia's **3**
The Arcade Restaurant **2**
Automatic Slim's
  Tonga Club **28**
Beale St. Bar-B-Que **26**
Beauty Shop **17**
Cafe Olé **16**
Café Samovar **25**
Café 61 **27**
Café Society **12**

Chez Philippe **31**
Cielo **6**
Coletta's Italian
  Restaurant **9**
Cozy Corner **5**
The Cupboard **10**
Elfo's Restaurant **33**
Ellen's Soul Food **8**
Erika's **29**
Fourway Restaurant **7**

Glass Onion **19**
Gus's World Famous
  Fried Chicken **23**
Huey's **28**
Joe's Crab Shack **22**
La Tourelle
  Restaurant **20**
Melange **15**
Melos Taverna **14**
Neely's Bar-B-Q **4**

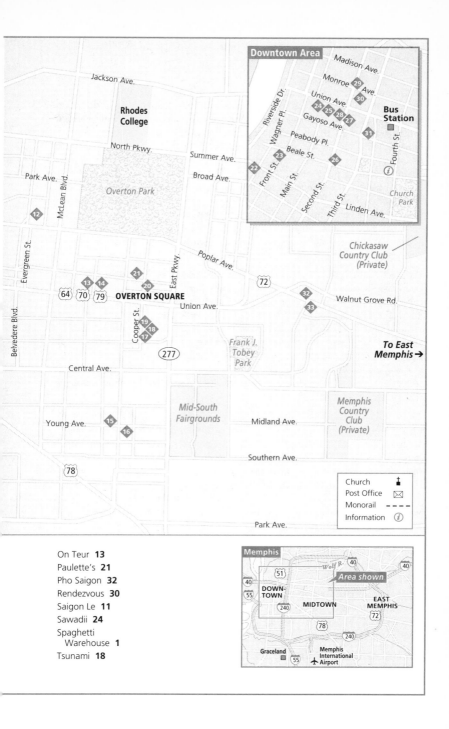

Downtown Area

Madison Ave.

Monroe 29 Ave.

Union Ave. 30

Bus Station

Gayoso Ave. 24 25 28 27

Riverside Dr.

Wagner Pl.

Peabody Pl. 31

Beale St.

23

22

Front St.

Main St.

Second St.

Third St.

26

Linden Ave.

Church Park

Rhodes College

Jackson Ave.

North Pkwy.

Summer Ave.

Broad Ave.

Park Ave.

McLean Blvd.

Overton Park

12

Evergreen St.

Poplar Ave.

East Pkwy.

Chickasaw Country Club (Private)

72

21

13 14

64 70 79 OVERTON SQUARE

20

32

33

Walnut Grove Rd.

Union Ave.

Belvedere Blvd.

Cooper St.

19 18 17

277

Frank J. Tobey Park

To East Memphis →

Central Ave.

Mid-South Fairgrounds

Memphis Country Club (Private)

Young Ave. 15

16

Midland Ave.

Southern Ave.

78

Church	⛪
Post Office	✉
Monorail	– – –
Information	ⓘ

Park Ave.

Memphis

Wolf R. 40

40

51

40

Area shown

55

DOWN-TOWN

240

MIDTOWN

EAST MEMPHIS

72

78

240

Graceland

55

Memphis International Airport

83 S. 2nd St. ⓒ **901/525-7948.** Reservations recommended. Main courses $15–$28. AE, DC, MC, V. Mon–Fri 11am–2:30pm; Mon–Thurs 5–10pm; Fri–Sat 5–11pm.

Café Samovar ★★ *Finds* RUSSIAN   Located on busy Union Avenue, the restaurant is decorated with samovars, Russian dolls, and wall murals with Russian folk themes, but it's the vodkas and Russian gypsy dancing on Friday and Saturday that really put you in the mood for the owners' authentic Russian cooking. It's tough to choose between the borscht, a heady beet-based broth bursting with cabbage and chunks of meat, and the silky seafood bisque. With a hunk of bread, this is the most delicious lunch downtown. To sample variety, begin an evening meal with *zakuska*, an appetizer plate that includes eggplant, kidney bean salad, herring, chicken-liver pâté, *pkali* (beet salad), and marinated mushrooms. Russian favorites such as beef Stroganoff, Belorussian *blinis* (crepes filled with chicken), and *piroshki* (pastries filled with chicken and vegetables) are all hearty, richly-sauced dishes that rarely disappoint.

83 Union Ave. ⓒ **901/529-9607.** Reservations not required. Main courses $9–$24. AE, DISC, MC, V. Mon–Fri 11am–2:30pm; Tues–Sat 5:30–10pm.

Café 61 ★ CAJUN   One of the best new restaurants and bars to hit the downtown area in recent months is this Cajun/American/Asian amalgam run by the folks at On Teur, another favorite eatery in Midtown. Succulent sandwiches, salads, and fish dishes are specialties. The lively decor, with its floor-to-ceiling portraits of blues greats B. B. King and W. C. Handy, is pure Delta funk—a cross between Highway 61 and Route 66. But one bite of the creamy, Cajun crawfish macaroni-and-cheese, and you'll think you've died and gone to heaven.

85 S. Second St. ⓒ **901/523-9351.** Reservations recommended for parties of 6 or more. Main courses $6–$22. AE, DC, DISC, MC, V. Sun–Thurs 11am–10:30pm; Fri–Sat 11am–11:30pm. (Bar remains open later on weekends.)

Cielo ★ NEW AMERICAN   Created by the same folks who gave you Memphis Automatic Slim's Tonga Club (not to mention the new Beauty Shop). Cielo, housed in an ornate brick Victorian mansion in the Victorian Village neighborhood just east of downtown Memphis, is a total work of art. From the lush interior design and abundance of contemporary art to the fanciful creations that appear from the kitchen, Cielo (which means "heaven" in Spanish) is a restaurant calculated to take your breath away. Some may be left breathless, while others may sense an air of pretentiousness. Consider the over-the-top salad of *mizuna* under paper-thin grilled squash and potato slices, all topped with Gorgonzola and ground, candied Brazil nuts. Among the entrees, the Napoleon made with wafers of crunchy provolone alternating with smoked eggplant, a winter vegetable puree, and goat cheese, is sumptuous, and is topped with flash-fried spinach and shiitake mushrooms and drizzled with balsamic syrup and arugula oil. Wines are pricey, but lunch is a good deal and features the same sort of culinary creativity found at dinner.

679 Adams St. ⓒ **901/524-1886.** Reservations highly recommended. Main courses $19–$30. AE, MC, V. Tues–Sat 5:30–10pm.

Joe's Crab Shack ★ SEAFOOD   This chain restaurant, located in an old warehouse, overlooks the Mississippi River and has been done up inside to conjure a New Orleans street scene. This is definitely a tourist restaurant, but the decor, fresh seafood, and especially the view of the Mississippi, make it a good downtown choice for anyone. The spicy seafood gumbo is a good way to start a meal here. After that, you could go for the deep-fried catfish filets or maybe the broiled flounder topped with etouffée or shrimp and crab sauté.

263 Wagner Place (Riverside at Beale St.). ℂ **901/526-1966.** www.joescrabshack.com. Reservations recommended. Main courses $9–$19. AE, DC, DISC, MC, V. Sun–Thurs 11am–10pm; Fri–Sat 11am–11pm.

Sawaddii THAI   Robust and spicy Thai specialties such as beef noodles, satays with spicy peanut dipping sauce, crab Rangoon, and coconut-milk-based soups are served at this new restaurant just a few blocks from the Peabody Hotel. A tastefully appointed dining room combines deep orange and black accents to nice effect. Service can be slow, and the language barrier a problem, but these quibbles shouldn't deter adventurous diners.

121 Union Ave. ℂ **901/529-1818.** Reservations accepted. Main courses $7–$18. AE, DISC, MC, V. Mon–Fri 11am–2:30pm; Sun–Thurs 5:30–9pm; Fri–Sat 5–10pm.

INEXPENSIVE

Alcenia's ⭐ SOUTHERN   This down-to-earth breakfast/lunch hangout looks like the kind of place where Stella got her groove back. The decor is shabby chic, where orange walls and purple beaded curtains blend right in with the potted plants, African artwork and tulle draped from the ceiling. Best known for its homemade preserves, Alcenia's serves up salmon croquettes, pancakes, and biscuits for breakfast. Sandwiches and Southern-style munchies are available at other hours. Call ahead to see if Alcenia's famous bread pudding is on the menu that day.

317 N. Main St. ℂ **901/523-0200.** Main courses $5–$8. AE, DC, DISC, MC, V. Tues–Fri 11am–5pm; Sat 8am–1pm.

The Arcade Restaurant ⭐ *Value* AMERICAN   Established in 1919, the Arcade stands as a reminder of the early part of the century when this was a busy neighborhood, bustling with people and commerce. Although this corner is not nearly as lively as it once was, the restaurant attracts loyal Memphians and out-of-towners who stop by for the home-style cooking and pizzas. Because the proprietors have an annoying habit of closing down when business is slow, you might want to call ahead if you're making the Arcade your destination.

540 S. Main St. ℂ **901/526-5757.** arcaderest@aol.com. Breakfast $5–$8; lunch $6–$8; pizza $7–$20. DC, DISC, MC, V. Sun–Thurs 7am–3pm; Fri–Sat 7am–9pm.

Erika's ⭐⭐ *Finds* GERMAN   The city's only German restaurant is a cozy beer hall frequented more by locals than tourists. Perhaps this is because it gets upstaged or else overlooked in favor of Rendezvous, the must-visit rib joint that shares the same building. However, if you'd rather forgo ribs in favor of a tangy sauerbraten with cooked red cabbage, give Erika's a try. Chef Erika's yeast rolls, served warm and fragrant from the oven, are huge mounds of sweet, yeasty bliss. Also excellent are the spaetzle, schnitzel, bratwurst, and fluffy dumplings.

52 S. 2nd St. ℂ **901/526-5522.** Main courses $5–$11. AE, DISC, MC, V. Tues–Sat 11am–2pm; Fri–Sat 5:30–9:30pm.

Gus's World Famous Fried Chicken ⭐ SOUTHERN   In a decidedly dingy juke-joint setting off the beaten path downtown sits this franchise of the legendary Gus's in Mason, Tennessee. Black and white, young and old, hip and square—they and every other demographic all converge here for spicy-battered chicken, beans, slaw, and pies. Service is friendly but slow, so don't go here if you're in a hurry. (If you'd like to take a road trip to the Real McCoy, the original Gus's is at 505 Highway 70 W., Mason, ℂ **901/924-2028.**)

Kids Family-Friendly Restaurants

Buntyn Restaurant (p. *188*) It's old and crowded, but always lively. This "meat-and-vegetables" restaurant will let your kids choose their poison (I mean vegetables). Meals are old-fashioned American favorites that kids love.

Corky's Bar-B-Q (p. *188*) Hand the kids barbecue sandwiches and the bottle of barbecue sauce, and they're likely to keep quiet long enough for you to enjoy your own meal.

The Cupboard (p. *183*) Wholesome comfort foods such as corn pudding, baked yams, mashed potatoes, or banana pudding for dessert are easy for kids to feed themselves.

Fourway Restaurant (p. *190)* Families fit right in at the Fourway (especially on busy Sundays after church). Fried chicken, pork chops, and turnip greens are lovingly prepared, and it shows. Service is friendly and welcoming.

Spaghetti Warehouse (p. *181*) What youngster (or young at heart adult) could resist slurping their spaghetti and meatballs from a seat in an old trolley car, or a booth made out of an antique bed frame?

---

310 S. Front St. ⓒ 901/527-4877. Main courses $6–$12 (for a large order of chicken, to go). AE, MC, V. Mon–Thurs and Sun 11am–9pm; Fri–Sat 11am–10:30pm.

Huey's ☆ AMERICAN Ask Memphians where to get the best burger in town, and you'll invariably be directed to a Huey's. This funky tavern also has one of the best beer selections in town. The original Huey's, at 1927 Madison Ave. (ⓒ **901/726-4372**), in the Overton Square area, is still in business. In recent years, suburban locations have also sprouted up in East Memphis and beyond, at 2858 Hickory Hill (ⓒ **901/375-4373**); at 1771 N. Germantown Parkway, Cordova (ⓒ **901/754-3885**); and at 2130 W. Poplar at Hacks Cross, Collierville (ⓒ **901/854-4455**).

77 S. 2nd St. ⓒ 901/527-2700. www.hueys.cc. Reservations not accepted. Main courses $6–$10. AE, DISC, MC, V. Daily 11am–2am.

Rendezvous ☆☆ *Moments* BARBECUE Rendezvous has been a downtown Memphis institution since 1948, and it has a well-deserved reputation for serving the best ribs in town. You can see the food being prepared in an old open kitchen as you walk in, but more important, your sense of smell will immediately perk up as the fragrance of hickory-smoked pork wafts past. You'll also likely be intrigued by all manner of strange objects displayed in this huge but cozy cellar. And when the waiter comes to take your order, there's no messin' around; you're expected to know what you want when you come in—an order of ribs. Also be sure to ask if they still have any of the red beans and rice that are served nightly until the pot is empty. This Memphis landmark is tucked along General Washburn Alley, across from the Peabody Hotel. Upstairs, you'll find a large bar.

52 S. 2nd St. ⓒ 901/523-2746. www.hogsfly.com. Main plates $6.50–$16. AE, DC, DISC, MC, V. Tues–Thurs 4:30–11pm; Fri 11:30am–11:30pm; Sat noon–11:30pm.

Spaghetti Warehouse (Kids) AMERICAN/ITALIAN   Families and tourists on budgets seek out this sprawling, noisy old warehouse brimming with antiques and amusing collectibles. Food is middle-of-the-road. Simple American burgers are served alongside Italian staples such as lasagna and spaghetti. Though this longtime Memphis eatery may lack the buzz of newer restaurants, it certainly has staying power.

40 W. Huling. (C) **901/521-0907.** www.meatballs.com. Main plates $6–$10. AE, MC, V. Sun–Thurs 11am–10pm; Fri–Sat 11am–11pm.

3 Midtown

For locations of restaurants in this section, see the "Memphis Dining: Down-town & Midtown" map on p. 176.

EXPENSIVE

Beauty Shop (★★★) NEW AMERICAN/GLOBAL   The first and most important thing you need to know is *not* that this hip eatery sits inside an old 1940s-style beauty shop, but that it's the latest brainchild of Karen Blockman Carrier, the creative force behind two of Memphis' coolest restaurants (Automatic Slim's and Cielo). Yes, the atmosphere is kitschy and fun. You can, indeed, dine in refurbished hair-dryer chairs. But what keeps the place packed with all the beautiful people is the fantastic food: globally inspired salads (I loved the Thai Cobb), entrees such as the whole striped bass, or the best BLTA (bacon, lettuce, tomato, and avocado sandwich) you've ever tasted.

966 S. Cooper. (C) **901/272-7111.** Reservations highly recommended. Main courses $14–$24. AE, MC, V. Mon–Fri 11am–2pm; Sat 10am–2pm; Sun 10am–3pm; Mon–Thurs 5–10pm; Fri–Sat 5–11pm.

La Tourelle Restaurant (★★) CLASSIC FRENCH   Taking its name from the turret in one corner of the turn-of-the-century house in which this Overton Square restaurant is located, La Tourelle has long been Memphis's favorite French restaurant. For those with big appetites and platinum cards, there is a six-course tasting menu; those of lesser means can, between Sunday and Thursday, opt for a very reasonably priced three-course bistro dinner menu. Dinner might begin with mesclun salad or cherrywood-smoked shrimp with saffron-horserad-ish sauce. Main dishes such as balsamic marinated swordfish are paired with wild-mushroom demiglace and roasted corn custard, while the smoked pork chop is served with sautéed sweetbreads and chanterelles in a sherry fig sauce.

2146 Monroe Ave. (C) **901/726-5771.** Reservations recommended. Main courses $22–$35; 6-course tasting menu $65; 2-course bistro menu $25. MC, V. Mon–Sat 6–10pm; Sun 11:30am–10pm.

Melange (★★★) MEDITERRANEAN   A menu as exciting as the atmosphere awaits at this hip but elegant restaurant and tapas bar. In the few years since it opened, Melange has become the toast of the town. Start with sautéed frog legs with roasted garlic, basil, and fresh tomato, and then move on to flash-fried gourmet greens splashed with vinaigrette and sprinkled with orange-yellow nas-turtiums. Entrees include an excellent *escolar,* a firm, white fish filet caramelized with a butter-wine sauce; and fork-tender honey-glazed pork tenderloins served with a sweet potato latke and ginger reduction. This is no place to skimp on dessert. Go for the Madagascar chocolate mousse timbale, or the warm blue-berry tartlet with house-made frozen vanilla custard. My favorite is the sublime trio of icy sorbets—orange blossom, rose, and violet.

948 S. Cooper. (C) **901/276-0002.** Reservations recommended. Main courses $15–$24. AE, DC, DISC, MC, V. Restaurant daily 5:30–10pm; bar open nightly until 2 or 3am.

Tsunami ★★ PACIFIC RIM/SEAFOOD Consistently ranked by locals as one of the best restaurants in Memphis, Tsunami serves creative Pacific Rim cuisine. Tropical colors over cement floors and walls enliven the otherwise uninspired setting. But the food's the thing. Appetizers run the gamut from potsticker dumplings with chile-soy dipping sauce, to shrimp satay with Thai peanut sauce. Among chef/owner Ben Smith's other specialties are roasted sea bass with black Thai rice and soy beurre blanc, wasabi-crusted tuna, and duck breast with miso-shiitake risotto. Crème brûlée fans should not miss Smith's sublime Tahitian-vanilla version of this classic. A judicious list of Australian and French wines includes champagne and a handful of ports.

928 S. Cooper. ✆ **901/274-2556.** www.tsunamimemphis.com. Reservations recommended. Main courses $18–$24. AE, MC, V. Mon–Thurs 5:30–10pm; Fri–Sat 5:30–11pm.

MODERATE

Café Society ★ NEW AMERICAN Named after a Parisian cafe, this lively bistro has a vague country-inn feel about it and is a popular ladies' lunch spot and pre-theater restaurant. As in a French cafe, you'll find convivial conversations at the small bar and outdoor seating on the street where you can sit and people-watch. Start out with some French onion soup or honey-baked brie, followed up with the likes of salmon with a sesame- and poppyseed crust or braised lamb shank with a pear brandy and walnut glaze. Lunches are reasonably priced and offer a chance to sample some of the same fine food that is served at dinner. There are also monthly four-course wine and food tastings for which reservations are required.

212 N. Evergreen St. ✆ **901/722-2177.** Reservations recommended. Main courses $13–$27. AE, DC, MC, V. Mon–Fri 11:30am–2pm; Fri–Sat 5–10:30pm.

Glass Onion *Overrated* NEW AMERICAN Despite the restaurant's intriguing name (which is the title of a John Lennon song off the Beatles' *White Album*), a great Cooper Young–area location, and its popularity with the party set, Glass Onion's food is a mixed bag. Unfortunately, I cannot recommend their signature dish, the peanut butter pork chops, but other items, such as the Gouda cheeseburger with grilled leeks, are good. Sweet-potato fries make an atypical accompaniment. Set in a renovated bungalow that has seen many restaurants come and go, Glass Onion has lovely hardwood floors and high ceilings. This, combined with a poor sound system, can make it deafening at the height of the dinner rush.

903 S. Cooper ✆ **901/274-5151.** www.glassonion.info. Reservations recommended. Main courses $7–$17. AE, DC, DISC, MC, V. Daily 11am–3am.

Melos Taverna ★ MEDITERRANEAN The Stergios family's home-style cooking has long been a mainstay at this midtown bastion of Greek cuisine. Salty feta cubes and Kalamata olives stud leafy salads. From octopus and *dolmades* (rice and beef wrapped in grape leaves) to bacon-wrapped chicken livers, and *souflaka* (charcoal-broiled shish kebab), Melos' menu is as tempting as it is tasty. Best of all are the meltingly delicious feta cheese phyllo-wrapped triangles, known as *tiropitakia*. Top it all off with ouzo, and you've got the makings of a memorable evening.

2021 Madison Ave. ✆ **901/274007.** Main courses $10–$23. AE, DISC, MC, V. Mon–Thurs 4:30–9:30pm; Fri–Sat 4:30–10:30pm.

Paulette's ★ CONTINENTAL Located in the Overton Square area, midtown's main entertainment district, Paulette's has long been one of Memphis's best and most popular restaurants. The decor is a cross between classic French-country-inn and baronial mansion. There are antiques, a high stucco ceiling with exposed beams and skylights, and traditional European paintings. In the lounge, a pianist plays soothing jazz on weekend evenings and during Sunday brunch. A few Eastern European dishes are specialties here and almost everyone begins with the Hungarian *gulyas* and *uborka salata* (cucumber salad in a sweet vinegar dressing), and then anxiously awaits the popovers with strawberry butter that accompany most entrees. Among the main courses, the beef filet is a delicious house special. However, you'll also find such dishes as pork tenderloin with cherry sauce, chicken livers bourguignon, and Louisiana crab cakes. Though the dessert list is quite extensive, you should be sure that someone at your table orders the Kahlúa-mocha pie, made with a pecan-coconut crust. Sunday brunch here is a midtown must. The proprietors also have a similar restaurant in the suburbs, the excellent **Three Oaks Grill** (2285 S. Germantown, Germantown, ℂ **901/757-8225**).

2110 Madison Ave. ℂ **901/726-5128**. Reservations recommended. Main courses $9–$25. AE, DC, DISC, MC, V. Sun–Thurs 11am–9pm; Fri–Sat 11am–10:30pm.

INEXPENSIVE

Café Ole MEXICAN/SOUTHWESTERN   Walls painted to mimic crumbling adobe, Mexican folk art, and leopard-print booths provide a casual setting for this neighborhood restaurant in the Cooper-Young area. A full bar in the back is usually crowded with neighbors toasting each other with *cervezas*, and in the summer, there's a very popular back patio. Along with the usual Southwestern standards—enchiladas, chimichangas, fajitas—there are specialties such as cowboy steak, served with beer-battered onion rings and *pico de gallo*, and shrimp diablo (shrimp sautéed in chile butter and beer).

959 S. Cooper St. ℂ **901/274-1504**. Reservations recommended. Main courses $6.50–$14. AE, DC, DISC, MC, V. Mon–Thurs 11am–10pm; Fri 11am–12am; Sat 11:30am–2am; Sun 11:30am–12am.

The Cupboard *(Kids* SOUTHERN   This place is usually packed with Memphians having a filling home-cooked meal of the Southern-style meat and vegetables variety. "Meat" includes a range of protein foods such as baked chicken, hamburger steak, or catfish filets, and the "vegetables" can be anything from turnip greens to fried green tomatoes to baked sweet potatoes to macaroni and cheese. (Yes, macaroni and cheese counts as a vegetable here.) I also like the pecan pie for dessert. There's a satellite downtown location at 149 Madison Ave. (ℂ **901/527-9111**).

1400 Union Ave. ℂ **901/276-8015**. Reservations not accepted. Meat and 2 vegetables $5.50. AE, DC, DISC, MC, V. Mon–Fri 11am–8pm; Sat–Sun 11am–3pm.

Elfo's Restaurant ✦ NEW AMERICAN/ITALIAN   In Memphis, the Grisanti family has become synonymous with Italian restaurants. That being said, the gang's latest, Elfo's, offers its lunch-only patrons a more eclectic menu than you might expect. Traditional favorites such as prosciutto-stuffed tortellini, and Elfo Pasta with garlicky shrimp and mushrooms remain in place but are augmented by American fare, including crab cakes, chicken salad, grilled salmon with asparagus, and cakes and cobblers. Like the other Grisanti restaurants, tablecloths and place settings are immaculate, service is cordial and efficient, and the food is always delicious.

3092 Poplar (inside Chickasaw Oaks). ℂ **901/888-0402**. Main courses $6–$15. AE, DC, DISC, MC, V. Mon–Sat 11am–2pm.

On Teur *(Value)* CAJUN   This funky little restaurant is on a seedy block near Overton Square, but that's part of the magic about the place—the Cajun home cooking is as satisfying as it is inexpensive. On the menu, you'll find eclectic offerings. A "samich" called the Big Easy is made with homemade New Orleans chaurice sausage, onions, and voodoo (spicy) mustard on a hoagie roll. How about an amber Jack-n-Jill? It's made with pecan-smoked amberjack and is served with a sauce of white wine, apples, and thyme. The shrimp N'awlins is spicy and comes with a satisfying Cajun sauce. You can bring your own wine or liquor for a small corkage fee, but you can't buy it here. The room can be pretty smoky, so if you don't want to suck on cigarette smoke, you might want to give this place a pass.

2015 Madison Ave. ℂ **901/725-6059.** Main courses $9–$15. AE, DISC, MC, V. Sun–Thurs 11am–10pm; Fri–Sat 11am–11pm.

Pho Saigon ★ *(Value)* VIETNAMESE   Noodle dishes, spring and egg rolls, and piquant soups are served in plentiful portions at this clean, family-run restaurant off of Poplar Avenue near Midtown. There's nothing fancy about Pho Saigon's interior, but basic chairs and tables and a few knickknacks are all that's necessary. The menu is extensive, the wait staff friendly and helpful with suggestions, and the food is fresh and utterly addictive.

2946 Poplar Ave. (ℂ **901/458-1644.** Main courses $5–$8. MC, V. Daily 10am–9pm.

Saigon Le ★ *(Finds)* VIETNAMESE/CHINESE   A popular lunch spot, Saigon Le is in an urban neighborhood close to the medical center district and is popular with hospital workers. Friendly service and generous portions of Chinese and Vietnamese dishes are the standards here. The kung pao beef is spicy, and the vegetable egg foo yung is plump with vegetables. Even though the restaurant serves good Chinese food, it's very popular for its Vietnamese food, which includes flavorful noodle, meat, fish, and vegetable dishes such as charcoal-broiled pork, spring rolls with vermicelli, and clear noodle soup with barbecued pork, shrimp, and crabmeat. At just under $6 the lunch special may be the best bargain in town.

51 N. Cleveland St. ℂ **901/276-5326.** Reservations not accepted. Main courses $6–$15. DC, DISC, MC, V. Mon–Thurs 11–9pm.

4 East Memphis

EXPENSIVE

Erling Jensen–The Restaurant ★★★ NEW AMERICAN   Chef Erling Jensen made a name for himself at the popular La Tourelle and has now ventured out on his own at this eponymous restaurant located in a converted suburban home just off Poplar Avenue near the Ridgeway Inn. Understated elegance and contemporary art set the tone for Jensen's innovative cuisine. Well grounded in the French kitchen, Jensen brings a somewhat traditional flavor to his menu. You might start a meal with crawfish mousse with penne pasta and Oregon truffles; a Parmesan, goat-cheese, and Vidalia-onion tart; or seared Sonoma foie gras with pears and sauternes. A diverse assortment of entrees make decision-making difficult, but among the options you might encounter ostrich with a ginger demiglace; vanilla-bean and Brazil nut–crusted orange roughy (a firm-fleshed white fish); or rack of lamb with a pecan, mustard, garlic, and molasses crust. There is always a wide assortment of house-made sorbets and ice creams (chocolate-marzipan-chunk ice cream, mango sorbet) available for

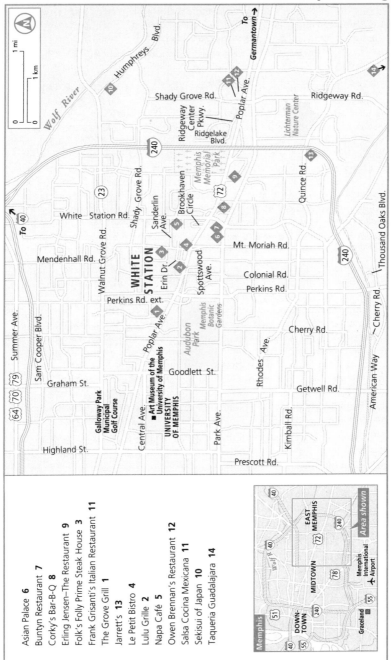

Asian Palace **6**
Buntyn Restaurant **7**
Corky's Bar-B-Q **8**
Erling Jensen–The Restaurant **9**
Folk's Folly Prime Steak House **3**
Frank Grisanti's Italian Restaurant **11**
The Grove Grill **1**
Jarrett's **13**
Le Petit Bistro **4**
Lulu Grille **2**
Napa Café **5**
Owen Brennan's Restaurant **12**
Salsa Cocina Mexicana **11**
Sekisui of Japan **10**
Taqueria Guadalajara **14**

dessert, but, of course, there are also more artistic confections, such as warm chocolate tart with roasted bananas and honey-almond-crunch ice cream. The large staff is well trained to provide impeccable service.

1044 S. Yates St. ⓒ 901/763-3700. Reservations highly recommended. Main courses $25–$32. AE, DC, MC, V. Daily 5–10pm.

Folk's Folly Prime Steak House ★★ STEAKS   Indeed, there are better-known chain steakhouses in Memphis, but there are none more beloved than this local institution. You'll find Folk's Folly just off Poplar Avenue—it's the corner building with the royal-blue awning. Just off the parking lot is a tiny butcher shop that's part of the restaurant; in the meat cases inside, you'll see the sort of top-quality meats they serve here (the likes of which you'll probably never see at your neighborhood market). Steaks are the specialty of the house, and steaks are what they do best. However, you can start your meal with anything from blackened catfish to seafood gumbo or even fried pickles. Among the prime cuts of beef are aged sirloins, filet mignons, and T-bones. Seafood offerings include Alaskan king crab legs, salmon filets, and jumbo Maine lobsters.

551 S. Mendenhall Rd. ⓒ 901/762-8200. www.folksfolly.com. Reservations recommended. Main courses $19–$40. AE, DC, MC, V. Mon–Thurs 5–10pm; Fri 5–11pm; Sat 5–11pm; Sun 5–9pm.

Frank Grisanti's Italian Restaurant ★ NORTHERN ITALIAN   Tucked into a corner of the lobby of the Embassy Suites Hotel, this classy little restaurant serves some of the best Italian food in Memphis. The atmosphere evokes the Old South far more than the trattorias of Rome, and the club-like setting attracts a well-heeled clientele. If you prefer a more casual setting, ask for a table on the atrium patio. The seafood and veal dishes are among the strong points here, and there are plenty of these to choose from. The *bistecca toscano* and *scampi portofino* are two of the most popular dishes here. If pasta is what you're after, the Elfo Special is worth considering—plenty of big shrimp and lots of garlic. There is also an elegant little bar in case you happen to arrive early.

In the Embassy Suites Hotel, 1022 S. Shady Grove Rd. ⓒ 901/761-9462. Reservations recommended weekends. Main courses $9–$25. AE, DC, DISC, MC, V. Mon–Thurs 11am–10pm; Fri–Sat 11am–11pm; Sun 5–10pm.

Napa Café CALIFORNIAN/NEW AMERICAN   In an upscale East Memphis shopping center not far from the Doubletree Hotel is this comfortable restaurant specializing in California cuisine. Favored entrees are the potato-encrusted halibut and the rack of lamb. As its name implies, Napa Café has an award-winning wine list. What's more, private dinners for parties of two or more are available in the restaurant's cozy wine cellar if you book them in advance.

5101 Sanderlin Dr. ⓒ 901/683-0441. Reservations recommended. Main courses $14–$25. AE, DC, DISC, MC, V. Mon–Fri 11am–2pm; Mon–Sat 5–9:30pm.

MODERATE

The Grove Grill ★ NEW SOUTHERN   Located in one of East Memphis's upscale shopping plazas, this big restaurant and oyster bar is a merger of contemporary and traditional decor and cuisine. The menu focuses primarily on seafood (and so does the art on the walls), with contemporary renditions of Southern favorites predominating. Three varieties of fresh oysters on the half shell are available. If you don't opt for the oysters, consider the crab and crawfish cakes with lemon-fennel remoulade or the oyster and artichoke soup. For an entree, the low-country shrimp and grits is a natural, or for a richer and less traditional dish, try the grilled pompano with crawfish beurre blanc. Entrees are served a la carte, so you'll need to pick a few dishes from the side-orders list, which reads like the veggie list in a traditional meat-and-three restaurant—warm blue-cheese slaw, grilled asparagus, and fried grit soufflé. The lunch menu is light on entrees other than sandwiches but does have plenty of interesting appetizers, soups, and salads.

Laurelwood shopping plaza, 4550 Poplar Ave. (℃) 901/818-9951. Reservations recommended. Main courses $8.50–$26. AE, DC, DISC, MC, V. Daily 11am–2:30pm and 5:30–10pm.

Jarrett's ★★★ *Finds* NEW AMERICAN/SEAFOOD   Jarrett's has the feel of a neighborhood restaurant but attracts people from all over the city. The setting may not sound auspicious—a nondescript East Memphis shopping plaza just before Quince Road crosses I-240—but the long and reasonably priced menu (fresh fish is a specialty) shows off the creativity of chef Richard Farmer, who is considered one of Memphis's finest. To start a meal, try the smoked trout ravioli with Arkansas caviar, the smoked quail spring rolls, or the prawns with macadamia-nut barbecue sauce. After such a bold opening, it is often difficult to maintain the creativity, but Jarrett's tries with such entrees as grilled yellowfin tuna with mango-jalapeño salsa, roasted pork tenderloin on onion-apple compote and applejack-sage demiglace, and filet of beef with mushroom and black-truffle Madeira sauce. At lunch, you can really indulge your indecisiveness by opting for the gourmet buffet. The small, oak-lined bar is a popular after-work hangout, and in the summer, there is a garden patio dining area wedged between two buildings and shaded by pine trees.

Yorkshire Square shopping plaza, 5689 Quince Rd. (℃) 901/763-2264. Reservations recommended for large groups. Main courses $17–$30. AE, MC, V. Mon–Sat 5–10pm.

Le Petit Bistro ★ CONTEMPORARY FRENCH   This casual bistro specializes in simple entrees such as mushroom-stuffed chicken breasts topped with white-wine cream sauce, and filet mignon au poivre (beef lightly coated with crushed pepper and topped with cognac sauce) served with sautéed mushrooms. An assortment of house-made desserts changes daily.

5007 Black Rd. (℃) 901/767-7840. Reservations recommended. Main courses $13–$22. AE, DC, DISC, MC, V. Mon–Fri 11am–2pm; Mon–Sat 5:30–10pm.

Lulu Grille ★★ NEW AMERICAN   Tucked back in a corner of an old shopping center, the Lulu Grille is surprisingly sophisticated considering its surroundings. A small bar serves as a hangout for restaurant regulars. With both sandwiches and full dinners available in the evening, this is a good bet for when you're not too hungry or members of your party have varied appetites. However, Lulu's is best known for its desserts, such as big chocolate cakes, crème brûlée, and caramel-fudge brownies. You can come for the dessert alone. But if you must, supplement your sweets with the appetizer platter, which includes smoked salmon, assorted cheeses, marinated vegetables, and olives. For a more substantial supplement, try the fat-free linguine marinara. Heartier still is the honey-cumin-glazed chicken, veal saltimbocca, or grilled jumbo shrimp.

White Station Plaza, 565 Erin Dr. (℃) 901/763-3677. Reservations accepted for 6 or more people only. Main courses $15–$25. AE, DC, DISC, MC, V. Daily 11am–10pm.

Owen Brennan's Restaurant ★ CAJUN   Located in one of East Memphis's most upscale shopping plazas and used as a set in the movie *The Firm*, Owen Brennan's has long been an East Memphis tradition, particularly for power lunches. The interior manages to conjure up the Big Easy with its Mardi Gras jesters and float decorations. Cuisine is flamboyant Cajun and Creole, from fluffy crab beignets to silky turtle soup. House specialties include the requisite blackened dishes, as well as hearty gumbos bursting with seafood. Desserts are so heavy they might make you woozy: The dense bread pudding is moistened with rum, while the caramelized Bananas Foster is drenched in it as well. A New Orleans jazz brunch is served here on Sunday with a live band and champagne on the house at noon.

Regalia Shopping Center, 6150 Poplar Ave. ✆ 901/761-0990. Reservations recommended. Main courses $13–$23. AE, DC, DISC, MC, V. Mon–Thurs 11am–9:30pm; Fri–Sat 11am–10:30pm; Sun 10am–2pm.

Sekisui of Japan ★★ JAPANESE Unlike Japanese restaurants that almost go overboard on tranquility, Sekisui is a noisy and active place, especially on weekends. The sushi bar prepares platters of assorted fish, from appetizer tidbits to a huge sushi boat that includes octopus, conch, snapper, and flying-fish-roe sushi. Fiery wasabi, a splash of soy, and shredded ginger add zing. Tempura, teriyaki, and *yakizakana* dinners come with rice, a wonderful miso soup, and salad. Some locations offer a separate *robata* grill menu. Two other Sekisui locations can be found in midtown at 25 S. Belvedere St. (✆ **901/725-0005**), and in the suburban Humphreys Center shopping center, 50 Humphreys Blvd. (at Walnut Grove Rd.; ✆ **901/747-0001**).

Inside the Holiday Inn Select downtown at 160 Union Ave. ✆ 901/523-0001. Reservations recommended on weekends. Main courses $9–$26. AE, DC, DISC, MC, V. Mon–Fri 11:30am–2pm; Sun–Thurs 5–9:30pm; Fri–Sat 5–10:30pm.

INEXPENSIVE

Asian Palace ★★ (Value CHINESE Arguably the best Chinese restaurant in the Memphis area, this large, bring-the-family eatery serves an astonishing array of authentic Chinese dishes. Yes, you can get fried rice, egg rolls, and all the expected basics. But be bold: Go for the squid with shrimp paste, or try the jellyfish. Personal favorites include the potstickers, savory won-ton dumplings fried to a delicate golden crispness; and the ginger beef with Chinese greens.

4978 Park. ✆ 901/761-7888. Main courses $4.50–$15. AE, DISC, MC, V. Daily 11am–9:30pm.

Buntyn Restaurant ★ (Kids SOUTHERN Since the 1930s, Buntyn has had a loyal clientele of regulars from the surrounding neighborhood. However, these days you'll also see people from all over the city and all over the world crammed into the crowded restaurant. What everyone comes for is the good, old-fashioned home-cookin' just like Ma used to make. Service is quick, and a basket of corn muffins and big homemade Southern-style biscuits appear on your table as soon as you sit down. Whether you order the calf's liver smothered in onions, fried chicken, homemade meatloaf, catfish steak, or maybe chicken and dumplings, you can be sure the portions will be large. Meats come with your choice of two vegetables from a long list that includes fried okra, turnip greens, purple-hull peas, and lime-cream salad. A trip to Buntyn is truly an old-fashioned Southern experience.

Park Ave. at Mt. Moriah. ✆ 901/458-8776. Main courses $4–$13. AE, DISC, MC, V. Mon–Fri 11am–8pm; Sat 4–8pm; Sun 11am–3pm.

Corky's Bar-B-Q ★ (Kids BARBECUE Corky's is good-natured and boisterous, with rock-'n'-roll tunes piped both indoors and out. Aromatic barbecue permeates the air. An argument over which is the best barbecue restaurant in Memphis persists, but this one pretty much leads the pack when it comes to pulled pork shoulder barbecue, topped with tangy coleslaw. Photographs and letters from satisfied customers line the rough-paneled lobby, where you always have to wait for a table. Corky's even has a toll-free number (© **800/9-CORKYS**) to get their delicious ribs shipped "anywhere." There's also a drive-up window for immediate barbecue gratification. A second Corky's location is at Germantown Parkway at Dexter Road in Cordova (© **901/737-1988**).

5259 Poplar Ave. © **901/685-9744**. www.corkysbbq.com. Reservations not accepted. Main courses $3–$11. AE, DC, DISC, MC, V. Sun–Thurs 10:45am–9:30pm; Fri–Sat 10:45am–10pm.

Salsa Cocina Mexicana ★★ MEXICAN/SOUTHWESTERN   Despite the location in an upscale shopping plaza, this suburban Mexican restaurant is reasonably priced. In fact, it serves the best food in the neighborhood, bar none. Mexican standards are all delicious, as are the flavorful chicken in citrus-chipotle sauce, and a sirloin steak topped with grilled poblano peppers. You can even relish the side dishes including creamy refried beans and a fabulous salsa picante. Wash it all down with an icy margarita. Service is attentive—they really care that you enjoy your meal. Mexican music plays softly in the background. When vast platters of enchiladas, guacamole, and rice show up at your table, you'll know that you've come to the right place.

Regalia Shopping Center, 6150 Poplar Ave. © **901/683-6325**. Reservations accepted only for parties of 6 or more. Main courses $8–$14. AE, DC, DISC, MC, V. Mon–Sat 11am–10pm.

Taqueria Guadalajara ★ *Finds* MEXICAN   Amidst the numbing commercial sprawl of southeastern Memphis, you'll find one of the most authentic Mexican restaurants in town. Tucked inside a colorful Mercado is this cozy taqueria specializing in (what else?) tacos, two-fisted tortillas packed with chunks of beef and a tangle of onion and cilantro, and hefty plate lunches buried under mounds of feathery rice, creamy beans, and crisp-fried tortilla chips and fiery salsa. They also make a mean menudo here.

5359 Winchester. © **901/565-8066**. Main dishes under $10. MC, V. Daily 10am–10pm.

5 South Memphis & Graceland Area

While there are not a lot of restaurants worth recommending in the Graceland or airport areas, that could change with the recent opening of the new Stax Museum of American Soul Music in South Memphis. In an effort to revitalize the area, the city also recently broke ground on a new full-service Visitors Center in the Graceland area, near Interstate 55.

D'Bo's Buffalo Wings 'N' Things ★ AMERICAN   Order a beer and a basket of wings and watch the game on TV, or call ahead and take home a couple hundred of these succulent chicken drummies and tips that are deep-fried and then slathered in mild, hot, or "suicidal" red sauces. Entrepreneur David Boyd and his wife started D'Bo's about a decade ago, selling wings out of a food trailer at area festivals. Their lip-smacking wings caught on like wildfire. Now there are D'Bo's locations throughout the city and beyond. If wings aren't your thing, the restaurant also serves great hamburgers and fries. D'Bo's' has a nice location near the Rev. Al Green's church, Full Gospel Tabernacle, but unfortunately, this particular location isn't open on Sundays. (Other locations are at 5727 Raleigh-LaGrange Rd., © **901/379-0006**; and 7050 Malco Crossing, Suite 106, © **901/363-8700**. The latter location, in southeast Memphis near Malco's Majestic movie theater complex, is also open on Sundays.)

4407 Elvis Presley Blvd. © **901/345-9464**. Main courses $5–$9. Cash only. Mon–Thurs 11am–10pm; Fri–Sat 11am–midnight.

Ellen's Soul Food ⚡ *Finds* SOUL FOOD   From turnip greens and pigs' feet to peach pie and the most mouth-watering fried chicken you're ever likely to taste in your lifetime, go find this long-treasured local landmark before the tourists catch on. Ellen's may look like a hole-in-the-wall, but once you step inside the nondescript room with its narrow lunch counter, you'll realize it's home.

601 S. Parkway E. © **901/942-4888**. Main courses $6–$8. Cash only. Tues–Sun noon–7:30pm.

Fourway Restaurant ⚡⚡⚡ *Value* *Kids* SOUTHERN   If you're looking for the legendary Fourway Grill, this is it. The beloved South Memphis landmark recently reopened with new owners and a slight name change, but the soul food remains the tastiest in town. Eat dessert first, and try the velvety sweet potato pie. Then dig into some juicy fried green tomatoes, pork chops, catfish or chicken and round it out with black eyed peas and crumbly cornbread. If he's not too busy, ask the proprietor to reminisce about the old days of this historic black neighborhood, which locals hope is poised for a comeback.

998 Mississippi Blvd. © **901/507-1519**. Reservations recommended for large groups. Main courses $5–$7. MC, V. Tues–Fri 11am–7pm; Sat 8am–7pm; Sun 11am–5pm.

6 Barbecue

Memphis claims to be the barbecue capital of the world, and with more than 100 barbecue restaurants and the annual Memphis in May World Championship Barbecue Cooking Contest, it's hard to argue the point. The standard barbecue here comes in two basic types—hand-pulled pork shoulder (pulled off the bone rather than cut off) and pork ribs. These latter can be served wet or dry (i.e., with or without sauce). The best pulled pork shoulder in town is at Corky's (p. 188) and the best ribs are served at Rendezvous (p. 180).

However, it isn't just pork shoulder and ribs that get barbecued here in Memphis. You can get barbecue spaghetti, barbecue pizza, and even barbecued bologna! Everyone in town seems to have his or her own favorite barbecue joint, and listed below are some of the ones that consistently get the best reviews.

The **Cozy Corner,** 745 North Parkway (© **901/527-9158**), is just what it sounds like and is located in midtown Memphis. **Neely's Bar-B-Q,** at 670 Jefferson Ave. (© **901/521-9798**) in downtown and at 5700 Mt. Moriah Rd. (© **901/795-4177**) in East Memphis, does the usual, but also does barbecue spaghetti and barbecued bologna. The **Beale St. Bar-B-Que,** 205 Beale St. (© **901/526-6113**), is the best place to grab some barbecue if you're doing the blues thing. Down near Graceland, there's **Payne's,** 1393 Elvis Presley Blvd. (© **901/942-7433**). And how about some barbecue pizza? This unusual fusion of two American favorites has been on the menu at **Coletta's Italian Restaurant,** 1063 South Parkway E. (© **901/948-7652**), since the 1950s. **Interstate Bar-B-Q Restaurant,** 2265 S. Third St. (© **901/775-2304**), though it isn't in the best of neighborhoods, consistently gets rave reviews for its barbecue sandwiches and ribs (and it serves barbecue spaghetti!).

7 Coffeehouses, Cafes & Pastry Shops

Sure, there's a Starbucks at practically every other intersection, but wouldn't you really rather patronize a coffee shop where you can soak up some local atmosphere? If so, your first stop should be downtown, to **The Center for Southern**

Folklore, Pembroke Square (© **901/525-3655**). It's a one-of-a-kind cafe of culture where you can belt back a cappuccino while admiring local crafts, outsider art, and hear great live music almost any time of the day. At the edge of the Cooper-Young neighborhood, you can quaff a cup o' joe and listen to live music or poetry at **Otherlands,** 641 S. Cooper St. (© **901/278-4994**). Farther down the street, you'll find **Java Cabana,** 2170 Young Ave. (© **901/272-7210**), a grungy little dive teeming with twentysomethings.

Café Francisco, 400 N. Main St. (© **901/578-8002;** www.cafefrancisco. com), is a wonderful new coffeehouse that lends a San Francisco vibe to the otherwise drab district near the Pyramid. Caffeine fiends will crave the rich coffee that's roasted here in this sophisticated cocoon. Soft couches and easy-chairs surrounded by antiques, books, and board games beckon patrons to linger. Wide booths and a long, mirrored bar are other options when grabbing a sandwich and bottled water. Number-crunchers can even check their stocks via the ticker that feeds financial stats across a screen near the bar.

Although the kitchen at **Sun Studio,** 710 Union Ave. (© **901/521-0664;** www.sunstudio.com), has recently closed (no more fried peanut-butter-and-banana 'samiches'), kids can munch a Moonpie and sip a Coke here while parents bask in the early-Elvis aura this place oozes. For more substantial fare, such as meat-and-cheese sandwiches on grilled focaccia, ride the trolley south toward **Fratelli's Market and Grill,** 513 S. Front St. (© **901/525-7777**), a cafe where you can also get tiramisu for dessert, and take home gourmet pastas, olive oils, cheeses, and imported beers.

The most bucolic view in town can be found inside the Memphis Brooks Museum of Art, where the **Brushmark Restaurant,** 1934 Poplar (© **901/544-6225;** www.brooksmuseum.org), overlooks the lush greenery of Overton Park. Indoor and outdoor seating and gourmet Southern specialties such as shrimp and grits, and spicy African peanut soup, make this bistro a special-occasion lunch spot, which is a bit dressier than a casual cafe. The restaurant is open for lunch only, and for dinner the first Wednesday of each month except January and July.

Exquisite quiche Lorraine, zesty tomato bisque and chicken salad sandwiches on chewy loaves of freshly baked French bread are delectable choices at **La Baguette,** 3088 Poplar (© **901/458-0900**). Well-to-do ladies lunch regularly at this Euro-style bistro inside tony Chickasaw Oaks shopping center adjacent to the new library. Best of all are the luscious pastries, including photo-worthy fruit tarts, croissants, and éclairs.

Farther east, be on the lookout for Davis-Kidd Booksellers. Part coffee shop, part wine bar and cafe with indoor/outdoor seating, **Bronte Bistro,** 387 Perkins Rd. Ext. (© **901/374-0881;** www.daviskidd.com), located inside the bookstore, is where the intelligentsia gather for sumptuous salads and sandwiches, conversation, and liquid refreshment.

15

Exploring Memphis

Just as in Nashville, music is the heart of Memphis, and many of the city's main attractions are related to Memphis's musical heritage. The blues first gained widespread recognition here on Beale Street, and rock 'n' roll was born at Sun Studio. W. C. Handy, the father of the blues, lived here for many years, and Elvis Presley made his Memphis home—Graceland—a household word. You'll find the history of the Memphis sound on exhibit at several museums around the city, including a couple devoted exclusively to music.

There's more to Memphis than music, however. African-American heritage, the history of the civil rights movement, and cultural opportunities abound. For example, every few years Memphis puts on an exclusive show of international importance: Wonders: The Memphis International Cultural Series presents exclusive international exhibitions. Past shows have focused on Napoleon, Catherine the Great, the Ottoman Empire, and even the *Titanic.* New for 2004 is the exhibition *Masters of Florence: Glory and Genius at the Court of the Medici,* featuring masterpieces by Michelangelo, Leonardo da Vinci, and more.

Downtown Memphis has experienced a long-awaited renaissance over the last few years, with such renovation projects as Memphis Central Station, a historic 1914 train depot. Also adding vitality is Peabody Place, one of the nation's largest mixed-use development and historic preservation projects. In addition to housing the funky Center for Southern Folklore (p. 193), it includes a 22-screen Cineplex and IMAX 3-D Theater as well as retail outlets ranging from Tower Records to Ann Taylor.

There's more. The Gibson Guitar Plant, a 75,000-square-foot guitar manufacturing facility and showcase lounge, offers visitors the chance not only to hear these instruments performed but also to see them being made. On the second floor of this complex lies *Rock 'N' Soul: Social Crossroads,* a Smithsonian Institution exhibition that traces the Memphis and Mississippi Delta's rich musical heritage.

South of downtown, Soulsville, USA is a must-see. The new Stax Museum of American Soul Music and arts academy for area youths opened in early 2003.

SUGGESTED ITINERARIES

If You Have 1 Day

Elvis fanatic or not, as long as you're here you owe it to yourself to spend part of the day at **Graceland.** After all, when will you get another chance to see the King's "Jungle Room"? Afterwards, you can tour tiny **Sun Studios,** and then head downtown for a hamburger at

Huey's or some sushi at **Sekisui.** Now walk a few blocks toward **Beale Street** to spend the afternoon immersing yourself in the sights and sounds of the awesome **Memphis Rock 'N' Soul Museum** downtown, or drive a few miles south of downtown to the brand-new **Soulsville: Stax Museum of**

American Soul. Don't lose track of time: You have to be back at **The Peabody** by 5pm if you want to catch the daily duck march. Tonight, bar hop along Beale Street.

If You Have 2 Days

Begin your second day savoring one of Memphis' most important African-American heritage sites. Allow at least 2 hours for a tour of the **National Civil Rights Museum.** Then hop on the Main Street Trolley back to Beale Street and stroll through **A. Schwab's.** Grab a bowl of gumbo at the **Rum Boogie** and go enjoy live music in the open-air **W. C. Handy Park,** before touring the great bandleader's home a few doors away. Backtrack up Beale and pause at Pembroke Square to relax with a cup of cappuccino at the **Center for Southern Folklore.** Tonight you might want to splurge on a nice dinner and then see a live theater performance in Overton Square.

If You Have 3 Days

On your third day, explore some historical homes in downtown Memphis: the restored Magevney, Mallory-Neely, and Woodruff-Fontaine houses are all within walking distance of each other. Together they comprise the area known as **Victorian Village.** Later, drive a few miles east to beautiful Overton Park, where you can visit the **Memphis Brooks Museum of Art** and the world-class **Memphis Zoo.**

1 The Roots of Memphis Music: Graceland, Beale Street & More

If you're going to Memphis, you're most likely going to Graceland, but there are also several other museums and sites here tied to the history of rock and blues music. Although the blues was born down in the Mississippi Delta south of Memphis, it was on Beale Street that this soulful music first reached an urban audience. Today, after a period of abandonment, **Beale Street** is once again Memphis's busiest entertainment district. Visitors can hear blues, rock, jazz, country, and even Irish music on Beale Street. To learn more about the various musical styles that originated along the Mississippi River, visit the **Mississippi River Museum** on Mud Island, where there are several rooms full of exhibits on New Orleans jazz, Memphis blues, rockabilly, and Elvis. All of these places are more fully described below.

In addition to being the birthplace of the blues and the city that launched Elvis and rock 'n' roll, Memphis played an important role in soul music during the 1960s. Isaac Hayes and Booker T and the MGs recorded here at **Stax Studio.** Other musicians who launched their careers from Memphis include Muddy Waters, Albert King, Al Green, Otis Redding, Sam and Dave, Sam the Sham and the Pharaohs, and the Box Tops.

Below are the sites that music fans won't want to miss while in Memphis.

Beale Street ★★ *(Moments)* To blues fans, Beale Street is the most important street in America. The musical form known as the blues—with roots that stretch

---

Impressions

The seven wonders of the world I have seen, and many are the places I have been. Take my advice, folks, and see Beale Street first.

—W. C. Handy

Memphis Attractions: Downtown & Midtown

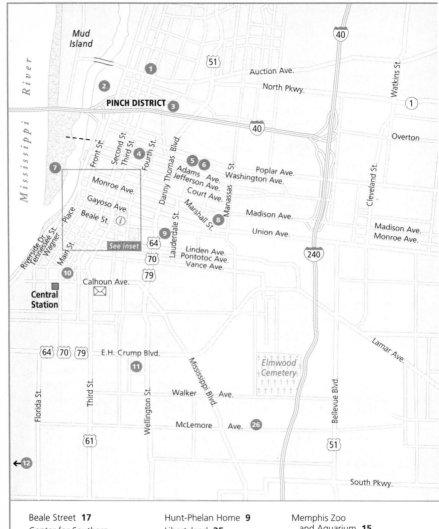

Beale Street **17**
Center for Southern
  Folklore **18**
The Children's Museum
  of Memphis **24**
Church Park **22**
Danny Thomas/
  ALSAC Pavilion **3**
Gibson Guitar Memphis
  Factory Tour, Museum,
  Café & Entertainment **20**

Hunt-Phelan Home **9**
Libertyland **25**
Magevney House **4**
Mallory-Neely House **5**
Mason Temple Church of
  God in Christ **11**
Memphis Brooks
  Museum of Art **13**
Memphis Rock 'N' Soul
  Museum **20**
Memphis Queen Line **16**

Memphis Zoo
  and Aquarium **15**
Mud Island/Mississippi
  River Museum **7**
National Civil Rights Museum **10**
National Ornamental Metal
  Museum **12**
Overton Park **14**
The Peabody Ducks **19**
Pink Palace Museum
  and Planetarium **23**

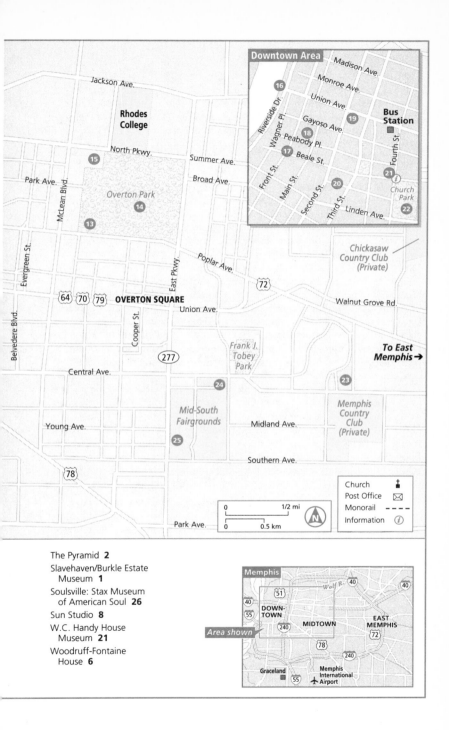

Downtown Area

Madison Ave.
Monroe Ave.
Union Ave.
Gayoso Ave.
Peabody Pl.
Beale St.
Linden Ave.

Riverside Dr.
Wagner Pl.
Front St.
Main St.
Second St.
Third St.
Fourth St.

Bus Station

Church Park

16 19 18 17 20 21 22

Jackson Ave.

Rhodes College

North Pkwy.
Summer Ave.
Broad Ave.
Park Ave.
McLean Blvd.

Overton Park

15 14 13

Evergreen St.

Chickasaw Country Club (Private)

East Pkwy.
Poplar Ave.
(72)

Walnut Grove Rd.

Belvedere Blvd.

64 70 79 **OVERTON SQUARE**

Cooper St.

Union Ave.

(277)

Central Ave.

Frank J. Tobey Park

To East Memphis →

24 23

Mid-South Fairgrounds

Memphis Country Club (Private)

Young Ave.

Midland Ave.

25

Southern Ave.

(78)

Park Ave.

Church	✝
Post Office	✉
Monorail	– – –
Information	ⓘ

0 ——— 1/2 mi
0 ——— 0.5 km

The Pyramid **2**
Slavehaven/Burkle Estate Museum **1**
Soulsville: Stax Museum of American Soul **26**
Sun Studio **8**
W.C. Handy House Museum **21**
Woodruff-Fontaine House **6**

Memphis

Wolf R.
(40) (40)
(51)
(40)
(55) **DOWN-TOWN**
Area shown (240) **MIDTOWN** **EAST MEMPHIS**
(78) (72)
(240)
Graceland Memphis International Airport
(55)

Fun Fact Elvis-in-Chief

You probably already knew that former President Bill Clinton's U.S. Secret
Service code name was "Elvis." Now it seems, The King and the Comman-
der-in-Chief will be further linked in history. Clinton's presidential library
in Little Rock, Arkansas, will feature his personal collection of Elvis memorabilia. Most of the items are gifts given to the president during his two
terms in the White House.

---

back to the African musical heritage of slaves brought to the United States—was
born here. W. C. Handy was performing on Beale Street when he penned
"Memphis Blues," the first published blues song. Shortly after the Civil War,
Beale Street became one of the most important streets in the South for African
Americans. Many of the most famous musicians in the blues world got their
starts here; besides W. C. Handy, other greats include B. B. King, Furry Lewis,
Alberta Hunter, Rufus Thomas, and Isaac Hayes.

And the blues continues to thrive here. Today, though much of downtown
Memphis has been abandoned in favor of suburban sprawl, Beale Street continues to draw fans of blues and popular music, and nightclubs line the blocks
between Second and Fourth streets. The Orpheum Theatre, once a vaudeville
palace, is now the performance hall for Broadway road shows, and the New
Daisy Theatre features performances by up-and-coming bands and once-famous
performers. Historic markers up and down the street relate the area's colorful
past, and two statues commemorate the city's two most important musicians: W.
C. Handy and Elvis Presley. In addition to the many clubs featuring nightly live
music (including B.B. King's Blues Club, and the Hard Rock Cafe), there's also
a small often overlooked museum, the W. C. Handy House—and the museum-
like A. Schwab Dry Goods store. A couple of long blocks beyond the nightlife
district of Beale Street, you'll also find the impressive (but lately neglected)
Hunt-Phelan Home, a restored antebellum mansion. For an update of events,
check out www.bealestreet.com. Allow a full afternoon to browse the shops and
restaurants, or make a night of it if you're into barhopping and live blues.

Graceland ★★   It seems hard to believe, but Graceland, the former home of
rock 'n' roll–legend Elvis Presley and annually the destination of tens of thousands
of love-struck pilgrims searching for the ghost of Elvis, is the second most visited
home in America. Only the White House receives more visitors each year. A look
around at the crowds waiting in various lines at this sprawling complex makes it
clear that Elvis, through his many recordings, numerous movie roles, and count-
less concerts, appealed to a wide spectrum of people. Today, a quarter century after
Elvis's death, Graceland draws visitors of all ages from all over the world. This is a
clear testimony to the power of a man who, if you believe the tabloids, has been
seen more since he died than he was ever seen in public when he was alive.

Purchased in the late 1950s for $100,000, Graceland today is Memphis's
biggest attraction and resembles a small theme park or shopping mall in scope
and design. There are his two personal jets (the *Lisa Marie* and the *Hound Dog
II*), the Elvis Presley Automobile Museum, the Sincerely Elvis collection of
Elvis's personal belongings, the *Walk a Mile in My Shoes* video, and, of course,
guided tours of Graceland itself. If your time here is limited to only one thing,

by all means, go for the mansion tour. It's the essence of the Big E. All the rest is just icing on Elvis' buttercream-frosted cake.

After touring the house, you get to see Elvis's office; his racquetball building; a small exhibit of personal belongings, memorabilia, and awards; a display of his many gold records; and finally, Elvis's grave (in the Meditation Garden). Then it's back across Elvis Presley Boulevard where you can watch a film about The King and visit the other Graceland attractions. True fans will want to do it all.

The Elvis Presley Automobile Museum includes not only his famous 1955 pink Cadillac, a 1956 purple Cadillac convertible, and two Stutz Blackhawks from the early 1970s, but also motorcycles and other vehicles. Accompanying this collection are videos of Elvis's home movies and a fast-paced compilation of

Elvis Trivia

- Elvis's first hit single was "Mystery Train." Recorded at Sun Studio, it made it to number one on the country charts in 1955.
- In 1956, Elvis became the second white person to have a number-one single on *Billboard's* rhythm-and-blues chart. The song was "Don't Be Cruel." The B-side was "Hound Dog."
- Elvis's first million-selling single and gold record came in 1956, when he recorded "Heartbreak Hotel" as his first release for RCA.
- During his career, Elvis won three Grammy Awards, all of which were for gospel recordings. Two of these awards were for the same song—a studio version and a live version of "How Great Thou Art."
- Elvis made 31 films and sang in all but one of these. *Charro!*, a Western released in 1969, was the only movie in which he didn't break into song at some point.
- The soundtrack to Elvis's movie *GI Blues* was on the album chart for a total of 111 weeks, 10 of which were at number one. This was his first movie after returning from service in the army.
- Highway 51 South, which runs past the gates of Graceland, was renamed Elvis Presley Boulevard in 1971, while Elvis was still alive.
- Elvis's first network-television appearance came in January of 1956 when he appeared on *Stage Show*, which was hosted by Tommy and Jimmy Dorsey.
- On a night in 1975, Bruce Springsteen, hoping to meet Elvis, jumped the fence at Graceland and ran up to the house. Unfortunately, Elvis wasn't at home, and the guards escorted Springsteen off the property.
- The King holds the record for sold-out shows in Vegas: 837 performances at the Las Vegas Hilton over a 10-year period.
- In 2003, an Elvis CD featuring his 30 No. 1 hits is released and becomes an international success. To date, sales have reached triple platinum.
- Elvis has sold more than a billion records worldwide, according to some industry estimates. That's more than any other act in recorded history.

car-scene clips from dozens of Elvis movies, which are shown in a sort of drive-in–theater setting.

A re-creation of an airport terminal serves as the entrance to the *Lisa Marie* and *Hound Dog II* private jets. The former was once a regular Delta Airlines passenger jet that was customized (at a cost of $800,000) after Elvis purchased it in 1975 for $250,000. The *Hound Dog II* is much smaller and was purchased after the *Lisa Marie* was acquired.

Sincerely Elvis is Graceland's most revealing exhibit. This is a collection of many of Elvis's personal belongings. Here you'll see everything from some of Elvis's personal record collection (including albums by Tom Jones and Ray Charles) to a pair of his sneakers. One exhibit displays gifts sent to Elvis by fans. Included are quilts, needlepoint, and even a plaque made from woven chewing gum wrappers.

The Graceland exhibits strive to reveal Elvis the man and Elvis the star. Some of the surprising facts passed on to visitors include: Elvis was an avid reader and always traveled with lots of books; Elvis didn't like the taste of alcohol; among his favorite movies were *Blazing Saddles* and the films of Monty Python.

Throughout the year there are several special events at Graceland. Elvis's birthday (Jan 8, 1935) is celebrated each year with several days of festivities. However, mid-August's Elvis Week, commemorating his death on August 16, 1977, boasts the greatest Elvis celebrations both here at Graceland and throughout Memphis. Each year from Thanksgiving until January 8, Graceland is decorated with Elvis's original Christmas lights and lawn decorations.

Devoted fans who are early risers should be aware that most mornings it is possible to visit Elvis's grave before Graceland officially opens. This special free walk-up period lasts for 90 minutes and ends 30 minutes before the mansion opens. Allow 2 to 3 hours or more (depending upon one's devotion to the King).

3734 Elvis Presley Blvd. ⓒ **800/238-2000** or 901/332-3322. www.elvis.com. Graceland Mansion Tour $16 adults, $15 seniors and students, $6.25 children 7–12. The Platinum Tour (includes admission to all Graceland attractions, including Elvis' Automobile Museum, tours of Elvis' custom jets (the *Lisa Marie* and *Hound Dog II*), and Sincerely Elvis film presentation) $25 adults, $23 seniors, $12 children 7–12. Tour reservations can be made 24 hours in advance and are recommended if you have a tight schedule. Mon–Sat 9am–5pm; Sun 10am–4pm. (Nov–Feb mansion tour does not operate Tues). Closed Thanksgiving, Dec 25, and Jan 1. Take Bellevue South (which turns into Elvis Presley Blvd.) south a few miles of downtown, past Winchester Ave. Graceland is on the left.

Memphis Rock 'N' Soul Museum ⭐⭐ With rare recordings and videos, archival photographs and interactive multimedia displays, the past century of American popular music is presented in "Social Crossroads," the first exhibition ever presented by the Smithsonian Institution outside of Washington, D.C. From field hollers and gospel hymns to the turn-of-the-century blues of W. C. Handy, it's all here. And with each new artist, from Otis Redding and Al Green to Earth, Wind & Fire, Memphis shines. Extensive displays on Sun and Stax recording studios are among the exhibition's most impressive. Allow 2 to 3 hours.

145 Lt. George Lee St. ⓒ **901/543-0800**. www.memphisrocknsoul.org. Admission $8.50 adults, $7.50 seniors, $5 children. Daily 10am–6pm. Downtown near Beale St., on S. 3rd St. (between Lee and Linden); and next to the new FedEx Forum arena. Take Beale St. to Third St. and park in the area. The museum is located in the Gibson Guitar Factory, 1½ blocks south of the intersection of Beale and 3rd sts.

Soulsville: Stax Museum of American Soul Music ⭐⭐ *(Moments* Groove on down to Soulsville, the city's newest attraction, which celebrates Memphis soul music. Opened in spring 2003, the museum sits near the site of the original (sadly,

Elvis Beyond the Gates of Graceland

You've come to Memphis on a pilgrimage and spent the entire day at Graceland. You've cried, you've laughed, you've bought a whole suitcase full of Elvis souvenirs, but still you want more of Elvis. No problem. Elvis is everywhere in Memphis.

If you're a hard-core Elvis fan and plan to visit his grave during the early-morning free visitation period at Graceland, you'll want to find a hotel as close to the mansion as possible. Directly across the street from Graceland are two properties that cater specifically to Elvis fans. Both the **Heartbreak Hotel–Graceland** and the **Days Inn at Graceland** offer round-the-clock, free, in-room Elvis videos. The former hotel actually has a pathway into the Graceland parking lot, while the latter motel has a guitar-shaped swimming pool.

Also, if you can, plan your visit for dates around Elvis's January 8 birthday festivities or during **Elvis Week,** which commemorates his death on August 16. During these festivities, you might catch an all-Elvis concert by the Memphis Symphony Orchestra, the *Taking Care of Business* Elvis-tribute ballet by Ballet Memphis, or the Elvis laser-light show at the Sharpe Planetarium in the **Pink Palace Museum.**

Any time of year, you can visit **Sun Studio,** the recording studio that discovered Elvis and where he made his first recordings. Though the studio isn't very large, its musical history is enough to give people goose bumps and bring tears to their eyes. A highlight of a visit here is a chance to actually touch the microphone that Elvis used to make his first recordings. The late Sam Phillips (who died in 2003), once brought his new musicians here to sign contracts, and this is where Elvis most certainly whiled away many hours. For a tongue-in-cheek tribute to Elvis, check out the coin-operated shrine to the King at the **Center for Southern Folklore** (p. 225) in Pembroke Square downtown.

To visit the spots around town where Elvis once walked, book a tour with **American Dream Safari** (© 901/527-8870), which tools guests around town in a 1955 Cadillac to see such Elvis haunts as Humes High School, Poplar Tunes, Sun Studio, and the Tennessee Brewery Company.

long-ago demolished) Stax recording studio, which during the 1960s and 1970s cranked out world-famous hits by Otis Redding, Booker T. and the MGs, the Bar-Kays, Al Green, Aretha Franklin, Earth, Wind & Fire, and others. Don't miss Isaac Hayes's (of *Shaft* and *South Park* fame) gold-plated, shag-carpeted Cadillac, which is on display. First-rate multi-media exhibitions, beginning with a thrilling video introduction in a darkened theater, take visitors back to a place and time when racial divisions deeply divided the South. Stax, however, was an anomaly, a virtually colorblind collaborative where black and white musicians, staff, and studio executives worked together in a shared musical passion. Allow at least 90 minutes—or an entire afternoon, if you're a true soul sister—to tour the museum. At interactive kiosks, you'll get a chance to hear hundreds of songs and watch archival video. Stax ties to Elvis, the Beatles, and Elton John are mentioned. Elsewhere,

Aerosmith, Elvis Costello, U2's Bono and scores of others offer heartfelt tributes to the lasting legacy of Stax (and Memphis's Sun) recording studios.

926 E. McLemore. ⓒ 901/946-2535. www.soulsvilleusa.com. Admission $9 adults, $8 seniors, $6 youths ages 9–12, free for children 8 and under. Mar–Oct: Mon–Sat 9am–5pm, Sun 1–5pm; Nov–Feb: Mon–Sat 10am–5pm, Sun 1–5pm. Closed major holidays. Take Danny Thomas Blvd. south to Mississippi Blvd. Turn left onto Mississippi Blvd., then left on E. McLemore Ave.

Sun Studio ★   If Elvis Aaron Presley hadn't come to Sun Studio in the early 1950s to record a song as a birthday present for his mother (so the story goes), musical history today might be very different. Owner and recording engineer Sam Phillips first recorded, in the early 1950s, such local artists as Elvis Presley, Jerry Lee Lewis, Roy Orbison, and Carl Perkins, who together created a sound that would shortly become known as rock 'n' roll. Over the years Phillips also helped start the recording careers of the blues greats B.B. King and Howlin' Wolf and country giant Johnny Cash. By night, Sun Studio is still an active recording studio and has been used by such artists as U2, Spin Doctors, The Tractors, and Bonnie Raitt. The place has great vibes, and for those who know their music history, touching Elvis' microphone will be a thrill beyond measure. However, if you aren't well-versed in this particular area of pop culture, a visit to this one-theme Sun Studio may leave you wondering what all the fuss is about. Next door is the Sun Studio cafe, a 1950s-style former diner that has long been a musicians' hangout. Allow an hour.

706 Union Ave. (at Marshall Ave.) ⓒ **800/441-6249** or 901/521-0664. www.sunstudio.com. Admission $9.50 adults, free for children under 12 accompanied by parents. Daily 10am–6pm; closed some holidays.

W. C. Handy House Museum *(Finds)*   A far cry from the opulence of Graceland, this tiny clapboard shotgun shack was once the Memphis home of the bluesman W. C. Handy—"the father of the blues"—and was where he was living when he wrote "Beale Street Blues" and "Memphis Blues." Although the house has only a small collection of Handy memorabilia and artifacts, there are numerous evocative old photos displayed, and the commentary provided by the museum guide is always highly informative. The tour lasts about 20 minutes.

352 Beale St. (at 4th Ave.) ⓒ **901/527-3427.** Admission $2 adults, $1 children. Summer Tues–Sat 10am–5pm; winter Tues–Sat 11am–4pm.

2 Nonmusical Memphis Attractions

MUSEUMS

Art Museum of the University of Memphis   Memphis takes its name from the ancient capital of Egypt, and here in the Art Museum of the University of Memphis you can view artifacts from ancient Memphis. An outstanding little collection of Egyptian art and artifacts makes this one of the most interesting museums in Memphis. Among the items on display is a loaf of bread dating from between 2134 and 1786 B.C. A hieroglyph-covered sarcophagus contains the mummy of Iret-Iruw, who died around 2,200 years ago. Numerous works of art and funerary objects show the high level of skill achieved by ancient Egyptian artists. In addition to the Egyptian exhibit, there is a small collection of West African masks and woodcarvings, and changing exhibitions in the main gallery. Allow 30 minutes to an hour.

3750 Norriswood St., CFA Building, Room 142. ⓒ **800/669-2678** or 901/678-2224. www.amum.org. Free admission. Mon–Sat 9am–5pm. Closed university holidays and for changing exhibitions. Turn south off of Central Ave. onto Deloach St. (between Patterson and Zach Curlin sts.) to Norriswood.

Dixon Gallery & Gardens ⚹ The South's finest collection of French and American impressionist and post-impressionist artworks is the highlight of this exquisite little museum. The museum, art collection, and surrounding 17 acres of formal and informal gardens once belonged to Margaret and Hugo Dixon, who were avid art collectors. After the deaths of the Dixons, their estate opened to the public as an art museum and has since become one of Memphis's most important museums. The permanent collection includes works by Henri Matisse, Pierre Auguste Renoir, Edgar Degas, Paul Gauguin, Mary Cassatt, J. M. W. Turner, and John Constable. With strong local support, the museum frequently hosts temporary exhibits of international caliber. Twice a year the Memphis Symphony Orchestra performs outdoor concerts in the Dixon's formal gardens. You'll find the Dixon Gallery and Gardens across the street from the Memphis Botanic Garden. Allow an hour for the museum, and more time for the gardens.

4339 Park Ave. ℂ 901/761-5250. www.dixon.org. Admission $5 adults, $4 seniors, $3 students, $1 children ages 5–11; gardens are only open Mon 10am–5pm (admission half-price). Tues–Sat 10am–5pm; Sun 1–5pm. Located adjacent to Audubon Park, off of Park Ave. at Cherry Rd. (between Getwell and Perkins).

Memphis Brooks Museum of Art   First opened in 1916 as the Brooks Memorial Art Gallery, this is the oldest art museum in Tennessee; it contains one of the largest art collections of any museum in the mid-South. With more than 7,000 pieces in the permanent collection, the Brooks frequently rotates works on display. The museum's emphasis is on European and American art of the 18th through the 20th centuries, with a very respectable collection of Italian Renaissance and baroque paintings and sculptures as well. Some of the museum's more important works include pieces by Auguste Rodin, Pierre Auguste Renoir, Thomas Hart Benton, and Frank Lloyd Wright. Take a break from strolling through the museum with a stop in the Brushmark Restaurant. Allow an hour to 90 minutes.

Overton Park, 1934 Poplar Ave. (between McLean and East Parkway). ℂ 901/544-6200. www.brooks museum.org. Admission $6 adults, $5 seniors, $2 students, free for children under 6; Tues–Sat 10am–4pm; Sun 11:30am–5pm.

Mud Island River Park *Kids*   Mud Island is more than just a museum. The 52-acre park on Mud Island is home to several attractions, including the **River Walk** and the **Mississippi River Museum.** If you have seen any pre-1900 photos of the Memphis waterfront, you may have noticed that Mud Island is missing from the photos. This island first appeared in 1900 and became permanent in 1913. In 1916, the island joined with the mainland just north of the mouth of the Wolf River, but a diversion canal was dug through the island to maintain a free channel in the Wolf River. To learn all about the river, you can follow a 5-block-long scale model of 900 miles of the Mississippi River. Called the **River Walk,** the model is complete with flowing water, street plans of cities and towns along the river, and informative panels that include information on the river and its history.

World War II historians won't want to miss a visit to the ***Memphis Belle,*** one of the most famous B-17s to fight in World War II. After having a look at the famous plane, you can watch a documentary about it. On the first Sunday of each month, there are guided tours of the plane's interior. On a hot day, kids of all ages will enjoy the island's huge **swimming pool** in the shape of the Gulf of Mexico. Evenings during the summer, the **Mud Island Amphitheater** (www.

mudisland.com) hosts touring acts along the likes of James Taylor and Jimmy Buffet. Allow an hour.

125 N. Front St. (at Adams Ave.). ⓒ 800/507-6507 or 901/576-7241. www.mudisland.com. Mississippi River Museum $8 adults, $6 seniors, $5 children 5–12; grounds only free. Summer daily 10am–8pm; spring and fall daily 10am–5pm; closed Mon. Parking $3–$4. To reach Mud Island, take the monorail from Front St. at Adams Ave.

National Civil Rights Museum ★★ (Moments   Dr. Martin Luther King, Jr., came to Memphis in early April of 1968 in support of the city's striking garbage collectors. He checked into the Lorraine Motel as he always did when visiting Memphis. On April 4, he stepped out onto the balcony outside his room and was shot dead by James Earl Ray. The assassination of King struck a horrible blow to the American civil rights movement and incited riots in cities across the country. However, despite the murder of the movement's most important leader, African Americans continued to struggle for the equal rights that were guaranteed to them under the U.S. Constitution.

Saved from demolition, the Lorraine Motel was remodeled and today serves as the nation's memorial to the civil rights movement. In evocative displays, the museum chronicles the struggle of African Americans from the time of slavery to the present. Multimedia presentations and life-size, walk-through tableaux include historic exhibits: a Montgomery, Alabama, public bus like the one on which Rosa Parks was riding when she refused to move to the back of the bus; a Greensboro, North Carolina, lunch counter; and the burned shell of a freedom-ride Greyhound bus. Allow 2 to 3 hours.

450 Mulberry St. (at Huling Ave.). ⓒ 901/521-9699. www.civilrightsmuseum.org. Admission $10 adults, $8 seniors and students; $6.50 children 4–17, free for children under 4. Mon, Wed–Sat 9am–5pm; Sun 1–5pm. From May–Aug, open until 6pm).

National Ornamental Metal Museum ★ (Finds   Set on park-like grounds on a bluff overlooking the Mississippi, this small museum is dedicated to ornamental metalworking in all its forms. There are sculptures displayed around the museum's gardens, a working blacksmith shop, and examples of ornamental wrought-iron grillwork such as that seen on balconies in New Orleans. Sculptural metal pieces and jewelry are also prominently featured both in the museum's permanent collection and in temporary exhibits. Be sure to take a look at the ornate museum gates. They were created by 160 metalsmiths from 17 countries and feature a fascinating array of imaginative rosettes. Just across the street is a community park that includes an ancient Native American mound. Allow 1 hour or more.

374 Metal Museum Dr. ⓒ 877/881-2326 or 901/774-6380. www.metalmuseum.org. Admission $4 adults, $3 seniors, $2 students and children 5–18, free for children under 5. Tues–Sat 10am–5pm; Sun noon–5pm. Closed 1 week between exhibit changes and the week between Christmas and New Year's. Take Crump Blvd. or I-55 toward the Memphis–Arkansas Bridge and get off at Exit 12-C (Metal Museum Dr.), which is the last exit in Tenn.; the museum is 2 blocks south.

Pink Palace Museum ★ (Kids   "The Pink Palace" was the name locals gave to the ostentatious pink-marble mansion that grocery store magnate Clarence Saunders built shortly after World War I. It was Saunders who had revolutionized grocery shopping with the opening of the first Piggly Wiggly self-service market in 1916. Unfortunately, Saunders went bankrupt before he ever finished his "Pink Palace," and the building was acquired by the city of Memphis for use as a museum of cultural and natural history.

Among the exhibits here is a full-scale reproduction of the maze of aisles that constituted an original Piggly Wiggly. Other walk-through exhibits include a pre–Piggly Wiggly general store and an old-fashioned pharmacy with a soda fountain. Memphis is a major medical center; accordingly, this museum has an extensive medical-history exhibit. On the lighter side, kids enjoy such exhibits as a life-size mechanical triceratops, a real mastodon skeleton, and a hand-carved miniature circus that goes into animated action. In the planetarium, there are frequently changing astronomy programs as well as rock-'n'-roll laser shows (the annual August Elvis laser show is the most popular). There is also an IMAX movie theater here. Allow 1 to 2 hours.

3050 Central Ave. (between Hollywood and Highland). ℂ **901/320-6320,** or 901/763-IMAX for IMAX schedule. www.memphismuseums.org. Museum $8 adults, $7.50 seniors, $5.50 children 3–12, free for children under 3; and for everyone Thurs 5–8pm. IMAX $7.25 adults, $6.75 seniors, $5.75 children 3–12. Combination tickets available. Call for IMAX showtimes. Museum hours Mon–Thurs 9am–4pm, Fri–Sat 9am–9pm, Sun noon–6pm.

HISTORIC BUILDINGS

Hunt-Phelan Home   At press time, Hunt-Phelan Home was still on the auction block, with tentative plans to convert it into a bed-and-breakfast. Built of red bricks made on the spot by slave labor between 1828 and 1832, the Hunt-Phelan home was designed by Robert Mills, who also designed the Washington Monument and part of the White House. Saved from destruction in the name of urban renewal, the house was placed on the National Register of Historic Places in 1970; today it is Memphis's only antebellum home open to the public. Continuously owned by the same family for 150 years, the home is filled with original furnishings that evoke pre–Civil War glory days. During the Civil War, the home served as headquarters for General Ulysses S. Grant, and after the war was over, teachers from the North used the home as a school for former slaves. The recorded tours of the historic building provide glimpses both into the history of the Hunt-Phelan Home and into the history of Memphis. Just a walk-by.

533 Beale St.

Magevney House   This diminutive wooden house not far from the skyscrapers of downtown Memphis is one of the oldest buildings in the city. It was here that the first Catholic Mass in Memphis was held. Purchased by Irish immigrant Eugene Magevney in 1837, the house today is furnished as it might have been in the 1850s. Among the furniture on display in the house are several pieces that belonged to the Magevneys. Allow 30 minutes.

198 Adams Ave. (between 3rd and 4th sts.). (ℂ **901/526-4464.** www.memphismuseums.org. Donations accepted. Tues–Sat 10am–2pm. Closed Jan–Feb.

Mallory-Neely House ✰   The centerpiece of the historic area known as Victorian Village (which also encompasses Magevney and Woodruff-Fontaine), the Mallory-Neely House is an imposing Italianate mansion built in 1852. Remodeled shortly before 1900, the three-story, 25-room home is an example of how wealthy Memphians lived in the latter half of the 19th century. Elaborate plasterwork moldings, ornate ceiling paintings, and a classically Victorian excess of decoration serve as a visually stunning backdrop for rooms full of original furnishings. Allow 30 minutes.

ns Ave. (between Neely and Orleans). © **901/523-1484**. www.memphismuseums.org. Admission $5 adults, $4 seniors, $3.50 students. Tues–Sat 10am–4pm; Sun 1–4pm. Guided tours every 30 min. Closed Thanksgiving, Jan–Feb.

Slavehaven Underground Railroad Museum/Burkle Estate *(Finds* Secret tunnels and trap doors evoke a period before the Civil War when this house was a stop on the underground railroad used by runaway slaves in their quest for freedom. The house is filled with 19th-century furnishings and has displays of artifacts from slavery days. Takes about an hour to get through the house.

826 N. 2nd Ave. (between Chelsea and Bicknell aves.). © **901/527-3427**. Admission $6 adults, $4 students. Summer Mon–Sat 10am–4pm; Winter Wed–Sat 10am–4pm.

Woodruff-Fontaine House Located adjacent to the Mallory-Neely House, the Woodruff-Fontaine House displays an equally elaborate Victorian aesthetic, in this case influenced by French architectural styles. Built in 1870, the fully restored 16-room home houses period furnishings. Mannequins throughout the house display the fashions of the late 19th century. Allow 30 minutes.

Victorian Village, 680 Adams Ave. © **901/526-1469**. www.memphismuseums.org. Admission $5 adults, $4 seniors, $3.50 students. Mon and Wed–Sat 10am–4pm; Sun 1–4pm. Guided tours every 30 min. Between Neely and New Orleans sts., next to Mallory-Neely House.

OTHER MEMPHIS ATTRACTIONS

Chucalissa Archaeological Museum *(Kids* The Chucalissa Archaeological Museum is built on the site of a Mississippian-period (A.D. 900–1600) Native American village. Dioramas and displays of artifacts discovered in the area provide a cultural history of Mississippi River Valley Native Americans. These people reached their highest level of cultural development during the Mississippian period, when large villages were constructed on bluffs above the Mississippi. This culture was characterized by sun worship, mound building, and a distinctive artistic style that can be seen in many of the artifacts displayed here. The reconstructed village includes several family dwellings, a shaman's hut, and a chief's temple atop a mound in the center of the village compound. The chance to walk through a real archaeologist's trench and to explore a Native American village thrills most children. Allow 1 to 2 hours.

1987 Indian Village Dr. © **901/785-3160**. www.chucalissa.org. Admission $5 adults, $3 seniors and children 4–11, free for children under 4. Tues–Sat 9am–4:30pm; Sun 1–4:30pm. South of Memphis off U.S. 61 and adjacent to the T. O. Fuller State Park.

Danny Thomas/ALSAC Pavilion This pavilion, reminiscent of a mosque, serves as both a tribute to comic actor Danny Thomas's career and to the history of the St. Jude Children's Research Hospital, which Thomas and the American Lebanese Syrian Associated Charities (ALSAC) founded to treat children with catastrophic illnesses. Over the years, Thomas helped raise millions of dollars for the hospital and is now buried in a crypt to one side of the pavilion. Allow 30 minutes.

St. Jude Children's Research Hospital, 332 N. Lauderdale St. © **901/495-3661** or 901/495-2111. Free admission. Sun–Fri 8am–4pm; Sat 10am–4pm. North of I-40 at Jackson Ave.

Memphis Zoo & Aquarium ★ *(Kids* A pair of adorable panda bears from China are the top draw these days at this underrated tourist attraction. Memphis's Egyptian heritage is once again called upon in the imposing and unusual entranceway. Built to resemble an ancient Egyptian temple, the zoo's entry is covered with traditional and contemporary hieroglyphics. Leading up to this grand entry is a wide pedestrian avenue flanked by statues of some of the animals that reside at the zoo. The zoo has recently completed a $25-million renovation that has added a 5-acre, realistic primate habitat, an exhibit of nocturnal animals, and an extensive big-cat area with habitats that are both realistic and highly imaginative. These new areas are among the best zoo exhibits in the country. In addition to the regular admission, there is a nominal fee to see the pandas in the China exhibit. Allow 2 hours or more.

Overton Park, 2000 Prentiss Place. ℂ **901/276-WILD.** www.memphiszoo.org. Admission $10 adults, $9 seniors, $6 children 2–11. Parking $2 during summer season. Mar 1 to last Sat in Oct daily 9am–6pm; last Sun in Oct to Feb daily 9am–5pm. Located inside Overton Park off of Poplar Ave. (2000 block) between McLean and East Parkway.

The Pyramid   Since its founding, Memphis, named for the ancient capital of Egypt, has evoked its namesake in various buildings and public artworks. The city's most recent reflection of its adopted Egyptian character is the 32-story, stainless-steel Pyramid, Memphis's answer to the sports domes that have been built in so many cities across the country. With a base the size of six football fields and a height greater than that of the Astrodome or the Superdome, the Pyramid seats 22,500 people. The Pyramid hosts University of Memphis college basketball, not to mention the NBA's Memphis Grizzlies, and rock and country concerts.

1 Auction Ave. ℂ **901/521-9675.** Located downtown, on N. Riverside Dr., just north of the Hernando-Desoto Bridge.

Wonders: The Memphis International Cultural Series 🚶   In 2004, visitors to Memphis will get a taste of the Italian Renaissance when *Masters of Florence: The Glory and Genius at the Court of the Medici* is on view from April 23 to October 3 at The Pyramid (1 Auction Ave.; ℂ **901/521-7909** for events; www.pyramidarena.com). The rare exhibition will include art masterpieces by Michelangelo, Leonardo da Vinci, Raphael, and Botticelli, many of which have never traveled outside of Italy. Established in 1989, Wonders is a not-for-profit organization that has spawned 10 blockbuster exhibitions, including those devoted to Catherine the Great, Napoleon, the imperial tombs of China, the Incas, and the ill-fated ship *Titanic,* among others.

Mailing address: P.O. Box 3371, Memphis, TN 38173. ℂ **901/312-9161.** www.wonders.org. Call for exhibition hours and ticket prices.

PARKS & GARDENS

In downtown Memphis, between Main Street and Second Avenue and between Madison and Jefferson Avenues, you'll find **Court Square,** the oldest park in Memphis. With its classically designed central fountain and stately old shade trees, this park was long a favored gathering spot of Memphians. Numerous historic plaques around the park relate the many important events that have taken place in Court Square. A block to the west, you'll find **Jefferson Davis Park,** which overlooks Mud Island and Riverside Drive. Several Civil War cannons face out toward the river from this small park. Below Jefferson Davis Park, along Riverside Drive, you'll find **Tom Lee Park,** which stretches for 1½ miles south along the bank of the Mississippi and is named after a local African-American hero who died saving 32 people when a steamer sank in the Mississippi in 1925—even though he, himself, could not swim. This park is a favorite of joggers and is the site of various festivals, including the big Memphis in May celebration. A parallel park called **Riverbluff Walkway** is the newest development atop the bluff on the east side of Riverside Drive.

Located in midtown and bounded by Poplar Avenue, East Parkway, North Parkway, and McLean Boulevard, **Overton Park** is one of Memphis's largest parks and includes not only the Memphis Zoo and Aquarium, but the Memphis Brooks Museum of Art, the Memphis College of Art, and the Overton Park Municipal Golf Course, as well as tennis courts, hiking and biking trails, and an open-air theater. The park's large, old shade trees make this a cool place to spend an afternoon in the summer, and the surrounding residential neighborhoods are some of the wealthiest in the city.

Farther east, **Audubon Park,** bounded by Park Avenue, Perkins Road, Southern Avenue, and Goodlett Street, is slightly larger and contains the W. C. Paul Arboretum, the Memphis Botanic Garden, Theatre Memphis, and the Audubon Park golf course.

Memphis Botanic Garden 🖈 With 20 formal gardens covering 96 acres, this rather large botanical garden requires a bit of time to visit properly. You'll find something in bloom at almost any time of year, and even in winter the Japanese garden offers a tranquil setting for a quiet stroll. In April and May the Ketchum Memorial Iris Garden, one of the largest in the country, is in bloom, and during May, June, and September the Municipal Rose Garden is alive with color. A special Sensory Garden is designed for people with disabilities and has plantings that stimulate all five senses. Other gardens include azalea and dogwood gardens, a cactus and herb garden, an organic vegetable garden, a daylily garden, and a tropical conservatory. Allow at least an hour.

Audubon Park, 750 Cherry Rd. ⓒ **901/685-1566.** www.memphisbotanicgarden.com. Admission $5 adults, $4 seniors and students, $3 children, free for everyone Tues 12:30pm–close. Mar–Oct Mon–Sat 9am–6pm, Sun 11am–6pm; Nov–Feb Mon–Sat 9am–4:30pm, Sun 11am–4:30pm. Located across from Audubon Park Golf Course on Cherry Rd., between Southern and Park aves.

3 African-American Heritage in Memphis

For many people, the city of Memphis is synonymous with one of the most significant, and saddest, events in recent American history—the assassination of Dr. Martin Luther King, Jr. The Lorraine Motel, where King was staying when he was shot, has in the years since the assassination become the **National Civil Rights Museum** (p. 202).

Long before the civil rights movement brought King to Memphis, the city had already become one of the most important cities in the South for blacks. After the Civil War and the abolition of slavery, Memphis became a magnet for African Americans, who came here seeking economic opportunities. **Beale Street** (p. 193) was where they headed to start their search. Beale Street's most famous citizen was W. C. Handy, the father of the blues, who first put down on paper the blues born in the cotton fields of the Mississippi Delta. **W. C. Handy Park,** with its statue of the famous blues musician, is about halfway down Beale Street, and Handy's small house, now the **W. C. Handy House Museum** (p. 200), is also now on Beale Street. At the **Memphis Rock 'N' Soul Museum** (p. 198), just a block off Beale Street, you can learn more about Handy and other famous African-American blues musicians who found a place for their music. Another museum with exhibits on famous black musicians is the **Pink Palace Museum and Planetarium** (p. 202).

Church Park, on the corner of Beale and Fourth streets—once the site of a large auditorium—was established by Robert R. Church, a former slave and Memphis businessman who became the city's first black millionaire. The park was a gathering place for African Americans in the early 1900s when restrictive Jim Crow laws segregated city parks.

Gospel music was part of the inspiration for the blues that W. C. Handy wrote, and that music came from the churches of the black community. The tradition of rousing musical accompaniment in church continues at many of the city's churches, but none is more famous than the **Full Gospel Tabernacle,** 787 Hale Rd. (© **901/396-9192**), which is where one-time soul-music star Al Green now takes to the pulpit as a minister. Sunday service is at 11am. **Mason Temple Church of God in Christ,** 930 Mason St. (© **901/947-9300**), is the international headquarters of the Church of God in Christ and was where Dr. Martin Luther King, Jr., gave his "I've been to the mountaintop" speech shortly before his death.

If you'd like a guide to lead you through the most important sites in Memphis's African-American heritage, contact **Heritage Tours** (© **901/527-3427;** www.heritagetoursmemphis.com), which offers both a 1-hour Beale Street Walking Tour ($8 adults, $5 youths) and 3- to 4-hour Memphis Black Heritage Tours ($20–$25 adults, $15–$20 youths). Heritage Tours also operates both the W. C. Handy House Museum and the Slavehaven/Burkle Estate Museum.

Another worthwhile attraction is the **Alex Haley House Museum** (© **731/ 738-2240**), located in the small town of Henning about 45 miles north of downtown Memphis on U.S. 51. The home place is now a museum containing memorabilia and old portraits of the Haley family. Nearby is the family burial site, where Haley and many of his ancestors, including Chicken George, are buried. The museum is open Tuesday through Saturday 10am to 5pm and on Sunday 1 to 5pm. Admission is $2.50 for adults and $1 for students.

4 Especially for Kids

Many of Memphis's main attractions will appeal to children as well as to adults, but there are also places that are specifically geared toward kids. In addition to the attractions listed below, see also the Pink Palace Museum and Planetarium (p. 202), Memphis Zoo and Aquarium (p. 204), Chucalissa Archaeological Museum (p. 204), Mud Island/Mississippi River Museum (p. 201), and The Peabody Ducks (p. 210).

A MUSEUM FOR KIDS

Children's Museum of Memphis   Located adjacent to the Liberty Bowl Memorial Stadium, the children's museum recently underwent a major expansion. The new galleries include "Going Places," "Growing Healthy," "Art Smart," and "WaterWORKS!," in addition to a parent resource center and improved gift shop. In addition, old standbys at the museum are a real fire engine for them to climb on and a kid-size city where your children can act like little grown-ups: They can go shopping for groceries, stop by the bank to cash a check, or climb up through a 22-foot-tall skyscraper. Special traveling exhibitions, such as a recent one featuring a kid-sized, fairytale castle, are also well worth a visit. Call to find out what special programs are being offered during your stay. Allow 2 to 3 hours.

2525 Central Ave. © **901/458-2678**. www.cmom.com. Admission $7 adults, $6 seniors and children 1–12. Tues–Sat 9am–5pm; Sun noon–5pm. Closed some holidays. Between Airways and Hollywood; next to Libertyland.

AMUSEMENT PARKS & FAMILY FUN CENTERS

Bogey's Golf and Family Entertainment Center 🎯   Out in the sprawling suburbs of Cordova (not far from Wolfchase Galleria) awaits Memphis' best and most well-maintained family fun attraction. Batting cages, go-karts, bumper boats and kiddie rides, and a 2-story, 3,000-square-foot arcade please all ages. Golfing options include 36 holes of mini-golf and a 100-tee driving range. Allow 2 to 3 hours.

7800 Fisher Steel Rd. © 901/757-2649. www.bogeys.com. All-day pass (excluding batting cages and driving range) $18 adults; $8.95 children 58 inches and shorter. Batting cages $20 per hour. Daily 8am–10pm (until 11pm June–July). Fisher Steel Rd. is off of Germantown Parkway (between Walnut Grove and I-40).

Libertyland   Although this amusement park has seen better days, kids will enjoy the rides at this midtown Memphis landmark next to the fairgrounds. There's the Revolution roller-coaster that does a 360-degree loop, a water slide, the giant Sea Dragon, and of course a Ferris wheel. There are also live song-and-dance performances at several different theaters. The smallest kids have their own special play areas at Tom Sawyer Island and the Kids' Korner. There's even a historic 1909 Grand Carousel. Allow 3 to 4 hours for kids to get in everything.

Mid-South Fairgrounds, 940 Early Maxwell Blvd. © **800/552-PARK** or 901/274-1776. www.libertyland.com. Admission $18 visitors 48 inches and taller (includes all shows and unlimited thrill rides), $10 visitors under 48 inches tall (includes all shows, kiddie rides, carousel, train, and antique cars), free for children 3 and under and adults 55 and older. May to mid-June and mid-Aug to Labor Day Sat 10am–8pm, Sun noon–8pm; mid-June to mid-Aug Wed–Fri and Sun noon–8pm, Sat 10am–8pm. Also open during Mid-South Fair late Sept–early Oct. Closed early Oct–Apr.

Putt-Putt Family Park   Located on the east side of town just off I-40 at Exit 12A, this miniature golf and games complex claims to be the largest of its kind in the world; whether or not that claim is true, your kids will find plenty to do. There are more than 50 holes of miniature golf, a driving range, baseball batting cages, a go-kart track, swimming pool, video game room, and picnic tables. A laser-tag arena is now open for business. Allow 2 to 3 hours.

5484 Summer Ave. (at Pleasant View). © **901/386-2992**. www.puttputtmemphis.com. All-day wristband $20. All prices subject to tax. Sun–Thurs 8am–midnight; Fri–Sat 8am–1am. (Closes 1 hr. earlier during school year).

WALKING TOUR   **DOWNTOWN MEMPHIS**

Start:	The Peabody Memphis hotel, on the corner of Union Avenue and Second Street.
Finish:	The cobblestones on the bank of the Mississippi at the foot of Monroe Street.
Time:	Approximately 2 hours, not including time spent at museums, shopping, meals, and other stops. It's best to plan on spending the whole day doing this walking tour.
Best Times:	Spring and fall, when the weather isn't so muggy, and Friday and Saturday, when Rendezvous is open for lunch.
Worst Times:	Summer days, when the weather is just too muggy for doing this much walking.

Walking Tour: Downtown Memphis

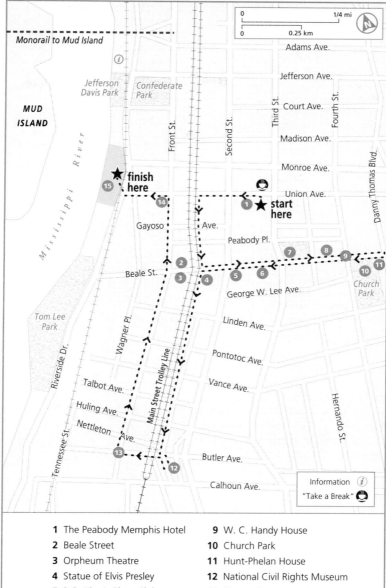

1 The Peabody Memphis Hotel
2 Beale Street
3 Orpheum Theatre
4 Statue of Elvis Presley
5 B.B. King's Blues Club
6 A. Schwab Dry Goods Store
7 W. C. Handy Park
8 New Daisy Theatre
9 W. C. Handy House
10 Church Park
11 Hunt-Phelan House
12 National Civil Rights Museum
13 Cotton Row
14 Carter Seed Store
15 "The Cobblestones"

Start your tour of Memphis's main historic districts at the posh:

❶ The Peabody Memphis hotel

This is the home of the famous Peabody ducks, which spend their days contentedly floating on the water of a marble fountain in the hotel's lobby. The ducks make their grand, red-carpet entrance each morning at 11am (and the crowds of onlookers begin assembling before 10:30am).

TAKE A BREAK
By the time the crowds thin out and you've had a chance to ogle the Peabody's elegant lobby, you may already be thinking about lunch. If it's a Friday or Saturday, you can fortify yourself at **Rendezvous,** 52 S. Second St., one of Memphis's favorite barbecue spots.

From the Peabody, walk 1 block west to Main Street, which is a pedestrian mall down which runs an old-fashioned trolley. Turn left, and in 2 blocks you'll come to:

❷ Beale Street

Which is where W. C. Handy made the blues the first original American music when he committed "Memphis Blues" to paper. Today, this street of restored buildings is Memphis's main evening-entertainment district.

On the corner of Main and Beale, you can't miss the:

❸ Orpheum Theatre

Originally built as a vaudeville theater in 1928, the Orpheum features a classic theater marquee and beautiful interior decor. Today, it's Memphis's main performing-arts center.

Across Main Street from the theater stands a:

❹ Statue of Elvis Presley

A visit to this statue is a must for Elvis fans. Bring your camera.

Continuing east on Beale Street to the corner of Second Street will bring you to:

❺ B.B. King's Blues Club

Named for the Beale Street Blues Boy himself, this is the most popular club on the street, and though B.B. King only plays here twice a year, there is still great live blues here almost every night.

A few doors down the street, you'll come to the:

❻ A. Schwab Dry Goods Store

This store has been in business at this location since 1876, and once inside, you may think that nothing has changed since the day the store opened. You'll find an amazing array of the odd and the unusual.

At Beale and Third streets, you can take a breather in:

❼ W. C. Handy Park

There always seems to be some live music in this park, also the site of a statue of Handy.

Across Beale Street from this park you'll find the:

❽ New Daisy Theatre

This is a popular venue for contemporary music, including rock, blues, and folk.

A few doors down from the New Daisy, you'll find the restored:

❾ W. C. Handy House

Though it wasn't always on this site, this house was where Handy lived when making a name for himself on Beale Street.

Diagonally across the intersection is:

❿ Church Park

Robert Church, a former slave who became the city's first African-American millionaire, gave the African-American citizens of Memphis this park in 1899.

Continue another 2 long blocks up Beale Street and you will come to the:

⓫ Hunt-Phelan House

One of the most impressive historic homes in Memphis, this antebellum treasure has recently closed to the public (there's talk of it becoming bed-and-breakfast). But for now yo can admire it from the street.

Now head back up Beale Street and take a left on Main. This is the street down which the trolley runs, so if you're feeling tired, you can hop on the trolley and take it south for the next 7 blocks. If you walk, turn left on Butler Street, and if you ride, walk east on Calhoun Street. In a very short block, you'll come to the:

⑫ National Civil Rights Museum
Once the Lorraine Motel, it was here that Dr. Martin Luther King, Jr., was assassinated on April 4, 1968. The motel has been converted into a museum documenting the struggle for civil rights.

After visiting this museum, head west on Butler Street and turn right on Front Street. You will now be walking through:

⑬ Cotton Row
In the days before and after the Civil War, and continuing into the early part of this century, this area was the heart of the Southern cotton industry.

don't miss any important si
Memphis city tour ($25
Graceland tour ($37
Graceland and th
for children 7
Graceland 7
Blues
mem

⑭
It's
sort
The   ...tural
suppl   ...c candy counter
is strai   ...ut of the 19th century.

From the Carter Seed Store, take a left on Union Street and in 2 blocks you'll reach the banks of the Mississippi at an area known as:

⑮ "The cobblestones"
This is a free public parking area and is where the Memphis Queen Line paddle-wheelers dock. The cobblestones were once used as ballast by boats coming up the river to pick up cargoes of cotton.

5 Organized Tours

RIVER TOURS

Although the economic heart of Memphis has moved to the eastern suburbs, this is still a Mississippi River town; no visit to Memphis would be complete without spending a bit of time on Ole Man River. The **Memphis Queen Line,** 45 S. Riverside Dr. (© 800/221-6197 or 901/527-5694; www.memphis queen.com) operates several paddle-wheelers, all of which leave from a dock on "the cobblestones" at the foot of Monroe Avenue in downtown Memphis. From March through November, there are 1½-hour sightseeing cruises, and in the summer, there are sunset dinner cruises and party cruises. The dinner cruises include live Dixieland and big-band music.

The 1½-hour sightseeing cruise costs $15 for adults $11 for children 4 to 17, and is free for children under 4; the sunset dinner cruise costs $40 for adults and $30 for children; party cruises are $10 per person.

CITY TOURS

You'll find half a dozen or more horse-drawn carriages lined up in front of the Peabody Memphis hotel most evenings, operated by **Carriage Tours of Memphis** (© 888/267-9100 or 901/527-7542). The carriages hold at least four people, and you can tour the downtown area, passing by Beale Street and Cotton Row. Tours cost $30 per half hour for two people ($40 for 4 people).

If you're just in town for a short time, or if you prefer to let someone else do the planning and navigating, **Coach USA,** 5275 Raleigh-LaGrange (© **901/370-6666;** www.coachusa.com), will shuttle you around the city and make sure you

nts. Two 3-hour tours are offered, including the
dults, $22 children 7–12, $10 children 4–6) and the
dults, $10 children 4–11). A combination tour with both
city of Memphis lasts 8 hours. Prices are $58 for adults, $28
to 12, and $10 for children 4 to 6.

City Tours of Memphis, 325 Union Ave. (℃ 901/522-9229; www.
phisite.com/bluecity), offers tours similar to the Gray Line tours. There is
half-day city tour that takes you past all the city's most important attractions,
and there are also Graceland tours, Beale Street night-on-the-town tours, and a
casino tour to Mississippi. The city tour costs $18 for adults and $10 for children; the Elvis Graceland Tour, $26 for adults and $19 for children; after-dark
dinner tour, $50 for adults and $40 for children includes an evening on Beale
Street with two clubs, two shows, two drinks, two meals with a choice of barbecue, chicken, or catfish and any cover charges; the casino tour, $20 per per-
son with a minimum of 6 people.

For a thoroughly unique tour of Memphis, book a tour with **American
Dream Safari** (℃ 901/527-8870; www.americandreamsafari.com). This is your
chance to be chauffeured around town in a '55 Cadillac, with stops at such key
Elvis sites as Humes High School (where he went to school) and Poplar Tunes
(where he used to buy records). Other popular itineraries include a Sunday
morning gospel tour and brunch, or the "Walking in Memphis" tour. Really,
though, what American Dream Safari offers would be better described as
authentic experiences than mere tours. Prices vary, from the Jukejoint Full of
Blues for $75 per person (which includes admission to three Delta-area clubs),
to $225 per person for an 8-hour pilgrimage along historic Highway 61.

6 Outdoor Activities

GOLF   Memphis's public golf courses include the **Stoneridge Golf Course,**
3049 Davies Plantation Rd. (℃ 901/382-1886); **The Links at Audubon Park,**
4160 Park Ave. (℃ 901/683-6941); the **Davy Crockett Park Municipal Golf
Course,** 4380 Range Line Rd. (℃ 901/368-3374); **The Links at Fox Meadows
Park,** 3064 Clark Rd. (℃ 901/362-0232); **The Links at Galloway Park,** 3815
Walnut Grove Rd. (℃ 901/685-7805); and the **T. O. Fuller State Park Golf
Course,** 1400 Pavilion Dr. (℃ 901/543-7771).

HORSEBACK RIDING   If you'd like to do some riding, head out to the east
side of the city and **Shelby Farms Riding Stables,** 7171 Mullins Station Rd.
(℃ 901/382-4250), which is open daily 8am to 4pm (7am–7pm in summer)
and charges $15 an hour for rentals.

SWIMMING   On a hot summer day, the huge "Gulf of Mexico" swimming
pool on Mud Island is a fun place for the family to cool off. See the Mud Island
listing earlier in this chapter for details.

TENNIS   The Memphis Parks Commission operates dozens of public tennis
courts all over the city. Two of the more convenient ones are **Leftwich,** 4145
Southern Ave. (℃ **901/685-7907**), and **Wolbrecht,** 1645 Ridgeway Rd. (℃ **901/
767-2889**). Court fees for 1½ hours are $3 per person for outdoor courts and
$18 to $21 for indoor courts.

7 Spectator Sports

AUTO RACING   At the **Memphis Motorsports Park,** 5500 Taylor Forge
Dr., Millington (℃ **901/358-7223**), there is everything from drag racing to

sprint-car racing to Atlantic Formula racing. The season runs from early spring to the autumn. Call for ticket and schedule information.

BASEBALL   The **Memphis Redbirds Baseball Club** (© **901/721-6000** or 901/523-7870; www.memphisredbirds.com), an AAA affiliate of the St. Louis Cardinals, plays at the new AutoZone Park, located 2 blocks east of the Peabody Memphis Hotel on Union Avenue.

BASKETBALL   The **Memphis Grizzlies** (© **901/205-1234;** www.grizzlies. com) are the city's first NBA team, having relocated from Vancouver, British Columbia, in 2001. The Pyramid has been their temporary home. Construction on their new arena, the FedEx Forum, is slated for completion in spring of 2004.

BASKETBALL   The **University of Memphis Tigers** (© **888/867-UofM** or 901/678-2331) regularly pack in crowds of 20,000 or more people when they play at the Pyramid. The Tigers often put up a good showing against nationally ranked NCAA teams, which makes for some exciting basketball. Call for ticket and schedule information.

FOOTBALL   The **Liberty Bowl Football Classic** (© **901/729-4344**) is the biggest football event of the year in Memphis and pits two of the country's top college teams in a December postseason game. As with other postseason college bowl games, the Liberty Bowl is extremely popular and tickets go fast. This game is held at the **Liberty Bowl Memorial Stadium** (www.libertybowl.org) on the Mid-South Fairgrounds at the corner of East Parkway and Central Avenue.

GOLF TOURNAMENTS   The **Federal Express St. Jude Golf Classic** (© **901/748-0534**), a PGA charity tournament, is held each year in late June at the Tournament Players Club at Southwind.

GREYHOUND RACING   Across the river in Arkansas, greyhounds race at the **Southland Greyhound Park,** 1550 N. Ingram Blvd., West Memphis, Arkansas (© **800/467-6182** or 501/735-3670). Matinee post time is at 1pm; evening races start at 7:30pm. Admission ranges from free to $6.

HORSE SHOWS   Horse shows are popular in Memphis, and the biggest of the year is the **Germantown Charity Horse Show** (© **901/754-0009;** www. gchs.org), held each June at the Germantown Horse Show Arena, which is just off Poplar Pike at Melanie Smith Lane in Germantown.

TENNIS   The **Kroger St. Jude International Indoor Tennis Championships** (© **901/765-4401** or 901/685-ACES), a part of the ATP Tour, is held each year in February at the Racquet Club of Memphis. Call for ticket and schedule information.

Fun Fact **Chef's Salad Days**

Long before he garnered fame at Stax recording studio in Memphis, before the *Theme from Shaft* won him an Academy Award, and way before his gig as the voice of *South Park's* beloved character Chef made him a household name for a whole new generation of fans . . . Isaac Hayes was a shoeshine boy on Beale Street.

Shopping in Memphis

In the last few years, downtown has come a long way in attracting new retail tenants downtown. Gradually, the number of vacant, boarded-up buildings is diminishing. With the recent opening of new shopping/ entertainment complexes such as Pembroke Square and Peabody Place, there are now dozens of options for strolling and/or spending. In addition, there are still a few tourist-friendly Beale Street stalwarts that are great for sniffing out the perfect Memphis souvenir. Out in the trendy neighborhoods in midtown Memphis, you still find a few other stores that merit visiting. For the most part, however, Memphis shopping means shopping malls—and most of those are out in East Memphis and beyond, a region of sprawling, new, and mostly quite affluent suburbs.

1 The Memphis Shopping Scene

As in Nashville and other cities of the New South, the shopping scene in Memphis is spread out. If you want to go shopping in this city, you'll need to arm yourself with a good map, get in the car, and start driving. Most people head to the shopping malls and plazas (there are dozens) in East Memphis to find quality merchandise. However, in recent years some interesting and trendy shops have started to pop up in the South Main Historic District of downtown.

Shopping malls and department stores are generally open Monday through Saturday 10am to 9pm and on Sunday noon to 6pm.

2 Memphis Shopping A to Z

ANTIQUES

Memphis's main antiques districts are at the intersection of Central Avenue and East Parkway, on Cooper Street between Overton Square and Young Street, and along Summer Avenue in East Memphis.

Crump-Padgett Antique Gallery   Housed in the 1920s Chickasaw Motor Car Company building just a block off Union Avenue near Sun Studio, this large antiques store is filled with everything from jewelry to furniture. 645 Marshall Ave. ✆ 901/522-1155.

Flashback   With 1950s furniture becoming more collectible with each passing year, it should come as no surprise that Memphis, the birthplace of rock 'n' roll in the early 1950s, has a great vintage furniture store. In addition to 1950s furnishings and vintage clothing, this store sells stuff from the '20s, '30s, and '40s, including a large selection of European Art Deco furniture. 2304 Central Ave. ✆ 901/272-2304.

Rodgers Menzies Interior Design   The prices here reflect the clientele's means, and sumptuous antiques from Europe and England predominate.

However, there are also throw pillows made from antique fabrics, French pâté urns, and other more affordable pieces. 766 S. White Station Rd. ℂ 901/761-3161.

ART

Albers Art Gallery ⭐ Owner Kathy Albers is one of the most knowledgeable and gracious art dealers in the city. Her impeccable gallery is an always-interesting showcase of works by the region's finest painters, sculptors, and craft artisans. Look for it off a side street near Poplar Avenue and the Ridgeway Inn. 1102 Brookfield Rd. ℂ 901/683-2256.

David Lusk Gallery In the most sophisticated, upscale art gallery in town, young gallery owner David Lusk showcases the South's finest contemporary artists. A wide variety of media is represented, including glass and photography. Lively receptions, educational events, and charitable efforts make this one of the most active galleries in the city. Laurelwood Center, 4540 Poplar Ave. ℂ 901/767-3800.

Jay Etkin Gallery Artist and gallery owner Jay Etkin, a native New Yorker, has for more than a dozen years been one of Memphis' most outspoken and active advocates for local contemporary artists. His new downtown loft studio (recently relocated from the Cooper-Young district) in the South Main historic neighborhood is a must for anyone in search of affordable, often delightfully offbeat, works of art. 409 S. Main. ℂ 901/543-0035.

Joysmith Studio ⭐⭐ *Finds* Brenda Joysmith, a longtime San Francisco-area artist who trained at the Art Institute of Chicago, had earned an international reputation before she returned to her native Memphis a few years ago. Best known for her pastel portraits of African-American women and children, Joysmith's works are featured in many national museums, corporate collections, in books, and on the sets of popular television shows, such as *Cosby*. Maya Angelou, Oprah Winfrey, and Alex Haley are among her celebrity fans. There's a retail shop in her studio selling affordable prints and other merchandise. 46 Huling Ave. ℂ 901/543-0505.

Lisa Kurts Gallery Longtime gallery owner Lisa Kurts represents regional and national artists in a range of media, most often paintings and two-dimensional works. Look for her space next to an interior decorator's office just north of Poplar Avenue in East Memphis. 766 S. White Station Rd. ℂ 901/683-6200.

The Willis Gallery African-American art prints, drawings, photographs, and paintings are prominently displayed in this retail outlet that's less a fine gallery than a Beale Street tourist attraction. 156 Beale St. ℂ 901/526-3162.

BOOKS

Bookstar Housed in the converted Plaza Theatre, a big shopping plaza movie theater, this is the city's biggest discount bookstore. Many selections are marked down 20% to 30%, including the latest *New York Times'* hardcover and paperback bestsellers. 3402 Poplar Ave. ℂ 901/323-9332.

Burke's Book Store ⭐ *Finds* Firmly entrenched in a gentrifying neighborhood just west of Overton Park, Burke's specializes in used, old, and collectible books. However, they have a good selection of new books as well. Each time favorite Memphis son John Grisham pens a new bestseller this is usually where he holds his first book signing. 1719 Poplar Ave. ℂ 901/278-7484.

Davis-Kidd Booksellers ⭐⭐ *Kids* Located in the prestigious Laurelwood Center shopping plaza, this large bookstore is a perennial favorite of Memphis

Memphis Shopping: Downtown & Midtown

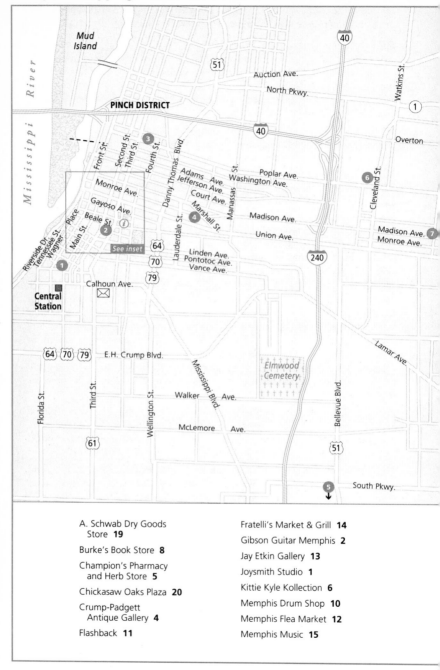

A. Schwab Dry Goods Store **19**

Burke's Book Store **8**

Champion's Pharmacy and Herb Store **5**

Chickasaw Oaks Plaza **20**

Crump-Padgett Antique Gallery **4**

Flashback **11**

Fratelli's Market & Grill **14**

Gibson Guitar Memphis **2**

Jay Etkin Gallery **13**

Joysmith Studio **1**

Kittie Kyle Kollection **6**

Memphis Drum Shop **10**

Memphis Flea Market **12**

Memphis Music **15**

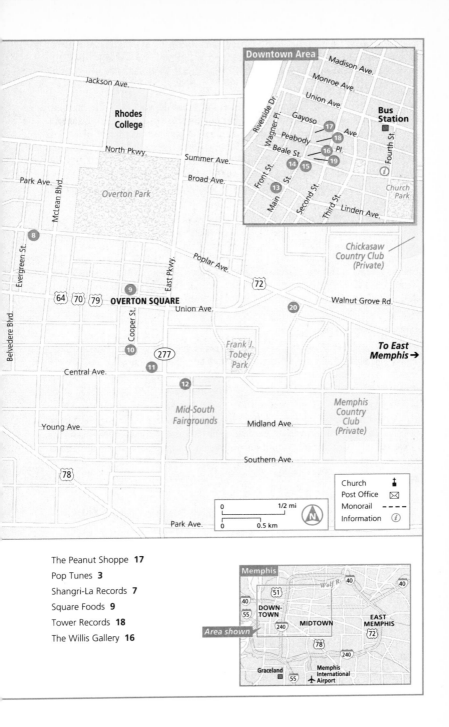

The Peanut Shoppe **17**
Pop Tunes **3**
Shangri-La Records **7**
Square Foods **9**
Tower Records **18**
The Willis Gallery **16**

readers. Books, CDs, periodicals, a cozy cafe, and a delightful assortment of unique gift items make for some of the most pleasurable browsing in the East Memphis area. Laurelwood Center, 387 Perkins Rd. Extended. ℭ **901/683-9801.**

DEPARTMENT STORES

Dillard's   Dillard's is a Little Rock, Arkansas–based department store that has expanding across the country. This is their biggest store in Tennessee, and it has a wide selection of moderately priced merchandise. Good prices and plenty of choices make this store a favorite of Memphis shoppers. You'll find other Dillard's department stores in the **Raleigh Springs Mall** (ℭ 901/377-4020), the **Oak Court Mall** (ℭ 901/685-0382), the **Hickory Ridge Mall** (ℭ 901/360-0077), and **Wolfchase Galleria** (ℭ 901/383-1029). Mall of Memphis, I-240 at Perkins Rd. ℭ **901/363-0063.**

Goldsmith's Department Store   Goldsmith's department stores are the most upscale in Memphis. The Oak Court Mall location is probably the most convenient Goldsmith's for visitors to the city. Other stores can be found in the **Hickory Ridge Mall,** 6001 Winchester Rd. (ℭ 901/369-1271); in the **Raleigh Springs Mall,** 3390 Austin Peay Hwy. (ℭ 901/377-4467); in the **Southland Mall,** 1300 E. Shelby Dr. (ℭ 901/348-1267); and in the **Wolfchase Galleria,** 2760 N. Germantown Parkway (ℭ 901/937-2600). Oak Court Mall, 4545 Poplar Ave. ℭ **901/766-4199.**

DISCOUNT SHOPPING

VF Factory Outlet World   Savings at stores such as Bugle Boy, Danskin, Bass, Nike, Van Heusen, Corning-Revere, and Old Time Pottery range up to 75% off regular retail prices. You'll find the mall just off I-40 about 30 minutes from downtown Memphis. 3536 Canada Rd., Lakeland. ℭ **901/386-3180.**

Williams-Sonoma Clearance Outlet   Williams-Sonoma, one of the country's largest mail-order companies, has a big distribution center here in the Memphis area, and this store is where they sell their discontinued lines and overstocks. If you're lucky, you just might find something that you wanted but couldn't afford when you saw it in the catalog. 4708 Spottswood Ave. ℭ **901/763-1500.**

FASHIONS

James Davis   You'll find Giorgio Armani here for both men and women. In addition, they carry more casual lines and, for women, very glamorous high-end dresses. Laurelwood Center, 400 Grove Park Rd. ℭ **901/767-4640.**

WOMEN'S

Isabella   This chic little women's boutique carries designers not usually found in other Memphis stores. There's lots of elegant evening wear, accessories, and soaps and candles for the home. Laurelwood Collection, 4615 Poplar Ave. ℭ **901/683-3538.**

Kittie Kyle Kollection   You'll find this great little shop in an older shopping center in the Medical Center neighborhood of midtown Memphis. The boutique represents small designers from around the country, with an emphasis not on current fashion trends, but personal and functional style. There's also a wide selection of jewelry and accessories. 3092 Poplar Ave. ℭ **901/452-2323.**

Pappagallo II   If you're a fan of the Pappagallo fashions and shoes, you won't want to miss this store at the corner of Poplar Avenue and Perkins Road. There's a second store at 2109 West St. in Germantown. Laurelwood Collection. 4615 Poplar Ave. ℭ **901/761-4430.**

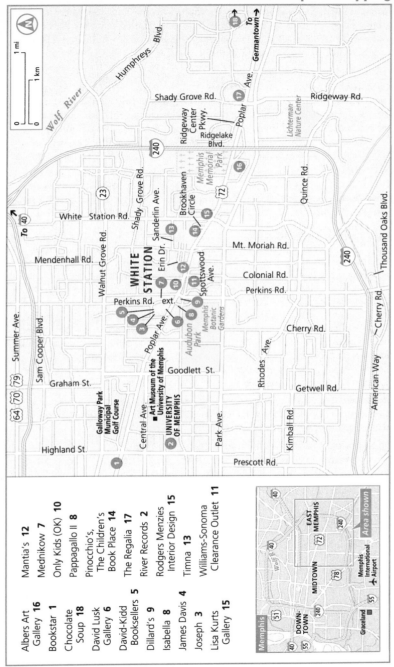

Albers Art
Gallery **16**
Bookstar **1**
Chocolate
Soup **18**
David Lusk
Gallery **6**
David-Kidd
Booksellers **5**
Dillard's **9**
Isabella **8**
James Davis **4**
Joseph **3**
Lisa Kurts
Gallery **15**

Mantia's **12**
Mednikow **7**
Only Kids (OK) **10**
Pappagallo II **8**
Pinocchio's,
The Children's
Book Place **14**
The Regalia **17**
River Records **2**
Rodgers Menzies
Interior Design **15**
Timna **13**
Williams-Sonoma
Clearance Outlet **11**

Timna   Located in a shopping center adjacent to the East Memphis Hilton, Timna features hand-woven fashions and hand-painted silks by nationally acclaimed artists. A great selection of contemporary jewelry includes both fanciful pieces and more hard-edged industrial designs. 5101 Sanderlin Centre. © 901/ 683-9369.

CHILDREN'S

Chocolate Soup   This store is practically crammed with clothes that are colorful and easy to care for. Designs that grow with the child and hand-sewn appliqués make the clothing here unique. There are also plenty of brightly colored toys and assorted things to keep kids entertained. Germantown Village Sq., Poplar Ave. and Germantown Pkwy. © 901/754-7157.

Only Kids (OK)   If you like to have the best for your children, this is the place to look. There's a wide selection of clothing and toys for infants to teenagers. Lines include Madame Alexander, Gund, Polo, Esprit de Corp, and Boston Traders. 4760 Poplar Ave. © 901/683-1234.

GIFTS & SOUVENIRS

A. Schwab Dry Goods Store ★★★ *(Kids)* *(Moments)*   This store is as much a Memphis institution and attraction as it is a place to shop. With its battered wood floors and tables covered with everything from plumbing supplies to religious paraphernalia, A. Schwab is a step back in time to the days of general stores. The offerings here are fascinating, even if you aren't in the market for a pair of size 74 men's overalls. You can still check out the 44 kinds of suspenders, the wall of voodoo love potions and powders, and the kiosk full of Elvis souvenirs. What else will you find at Schwab's? Bongo drums and crystal balls; shoeshine kits and corncob pipes; long thermal underwear and cotton petticoats; voodoo potions and praying hands and plastic back-scratchers. Don't miss this place! Open Monday through Saturday from 9am to 5pm. 163 Beale St. © 901/523-9782.

Bella Notte ★ *(Finds)*   Luscious soaps, handmade cards and one-of-a-kind gifts are gorgeously displayed in this boutique in the heart of historic Cooper Young. 2172 Young Ave. © 901/726-4131.

Champion's Pharmacy and Herb Store   Although this unusual shop is a regular pharmacy, it also sells a wide variety of herbs and old-fashioned patent medicines (Packer's Pine Tar Soap, Lydia E. Pinkham Tonic, Red Clover Salve, Old Red Barn Ointment) and has an old medicine-wagon museum. 2369 Elvis Presley Blvd. (2 miles north of Graceland). © 901/948-6622.

The Peanut Shoppe *(Kids)*   In business since 1951, this tiny peanut shop is easily spotted: Just watch for the large Mr. Peanut tapping with his cane on the front window of the shop. Inside, you'll find all kinds of peanuts, including those freshly roasted or fried on the premises. Lots of Mr. Peanut memorabilia, too. 24 S. Main St. © 901/525-1115.

Viking Culinary Arts ★   Everything and the kitchen sink await inside this spacious downtown retail store and demonstration area for Viking ranges and appliances. Top-of-the-line cookware and gadgets galore make it a great place to shop for the cooking enthusiast on your gift list. 153 S. Main. © 901/578-5822.

JEWELRY

Mednikow   This is one of the largest and most highly respected jewelry stores in Memphis, offering exquisite diamond jewelry, Rolex watches, and other beautiful baubles. 474 Perkins Rd. Extended. © 901/767-2100.

MALLS/SHOPPING CENTERS

Chickasaw Oaks Plaza ⭐ This indoor shopping center is built to resemble an 18th-century village street and houses 30 specialty shops, including gift shops, a small bookstore, and Alan Abis, a men's fashion store specializing in European styles. 3092 Poplar Ave. ℭ 901/767-0100.

Hickory Ridge Mall Located out in East Memphis, this large mall includes three department stores (Dillard's, Goldsmith's, and Sears) and more than 100 specialty shops. To keep the kids entertained, there's a carousel. Winchester Rd. at Hickory Hill Rd. ℭ 901/367-8045.

Laurelwood Tucked in behind a Sears store in an older shopping center, this newer shopping plaza houses several upscale clothing stores, Davis-Kidd Booksellers, restaurants, and Memphis's best travel agency (Regency Travel). Poplar Ave. and Perkins Rd. Extended. ℭ 901/794-6022.

Oak Court Mall With both a Goldsmith's and a Dillard's and 80 specialty shops, this mall surrounds a pretty little park full of sculptures, and the parking lot is full of big old shade trees. The attention to preserving a park-like setting makes this place stand out from most malls. 4465 Poplar Ave. at Perkins Rd. ℭ 901/682-8928.

The Regalia This small-but-elegant shopping center, next door to the Embassy Suites Hotel and just off I-240, houses clothing stores and three great restaurants. The grand architecture of this shopping center is more reminiscent of a resort than of a shopping plaza. Poplar Ave. and Ridgeway Rd. ℭ 901/767-0100.

The Shops of Saddle Creek Located out in the heart of Germantown, Memphis's most affluent bedroom community, this shopping center is home to such familiar national chain stores as Sharper Image, Banana Republic, Crabtree and Evelyn, Ann Taylor, GapKids, Brentano's, and similarly fashionable lesser-known stores. 5855 River Bend Rd. ℭ 901/761-2571.

Wolfchase Galleria ⭐ The Memphis area's newest mall is a mammoth (more than one million sq. ft.) retail center in the northeastern suburbs that boasts all the big-name department stores, including Dillard's and Goldsmith's, as well as scores of restaurants and specialty shops. From Pottery Barn finds and Godiva chocolates to Looney Tunes toys at the Warner Brothers store, this very popular (often quite crowded) mall has something for everyone. There's also a children's carousel as well as a state-of-the-art multiplex cinema with stadium seating. 2760 N. Germantown Pkwy. ℭ 901/761-5748.

MARKETS

Fratelli's Market and Grill Gourmet cheeses, olive oil, fresh-baked focaccia, and imported beers are available for take-out (or dine in) at this welcome new addition to downtown. 513 S. Front St. ℭ 901/525-7777.

Mantia's East Memphis is where you'll find this international foods market and deli. (Cheeses from throughout the world are a specialty.) It's a great place to pick up some picnic fare before heading to one of Memphis's many parks. 4856 Poplar. ℭ 901/762-8560.

Memphis Flea Market *Kids* Held on the third weekend of every month, this huge flea market has more than 2,000 spaces. Goods on sale here run the gamut from discount jeans and perfumes to antiques and other collectibles. 955 Early Maxwell Blvd., Mid-South Fairgrounds. ℭ 901/276-3532.

Square Foods ⭐ This is a complete health food store that offers groceries, produce, frozen and bulk foods as well as vitamins and herbs. The deli specializes in vegetarian fare, though fish is sometimes an option too. 2097 Madison Ave. ℭ **901/728-4371.**

MUSIC

Memphis Music This combination music and souvenir store specializes in the blues, with recordings by W. C. Handy, Leadbelly, Blind Lemon, and many of the other blues greats. There are also T-shirts with images of famous blues and jazz musicians printed on them. 149 Beale St. ℭ **901/526-5047.**

Pop Tunes This store has been around since 1946, and when Elvis lived in the neighborhood, he used to hang out here listening to the latest records. Other convenient stores are at 4195 Summer Ave. (ℭ **901/324-3855**) and 2391 Lamar Ave. (ℭ **901/744-0400**). 308 Poplar Rd. ℭ **901/525-6348.**

River Records This is the city's premier collector's record shop. They also sell baseball cards, comic books, CDs, and posters. Elvis Presley records and memorabilia are a specialty. 822 S. Highland. ℭ **901/324-1757.**

Shangri-La Records ⭐⭐ (Finds) This record store has Memphis's best selection of new and used rockabilly, as well as soul, R&B, reggae, rock, and every other kind of music for discerning tastes. Collectibles such as old concert posters, sheet music, and T-shirts are also for sale. 1916 Madison Ave. ℭ **901/274-1916.**

Tower Records ⭐ Don't miss the amazing Memphis music collection inside this bright and energetic record store that sells CDs, DVDs, magazines, books, and other cool gift items as well as Memphis souvenirs. 150 Peabody Place. ℭ **901/ 526-9210.**

MUSICAL INSTRUMENTS

Gibson Guitar Memphis Factory Tour, Museum, Cafe & Entertainment Not only can you watch Gibson guitars being manufactured, and hear them performed, you may also purchase a variety of Gibson and Epiphone stringed instruments and other merchandise at this shop located in the same building as the Memphis Rock 'N' Soul Museum. 145 Lt. George W. Lee Ave. ℭ **800/444-2766** or 901/544-7998.

Memphis Drum Shop New, used, vintage and custom drums, cymbals, hand-percussion instruments, parts, and accessories are all sold, repaired, and even rented at this great destination that's off-the-'beaten' (so to speak) path. 878 S. Cooper. ℭ **901/276-2328.**

SHOES & BOOTS

In addition to the following shoe and boot stores, you'll find an excellent selection of shoes at the **Dillard's** department store in the Mall of Memphis shopping mall.

DSW Shoe Warehouse With savings of 20% to 50% off standard retail prices and an excellent selection of major-label shoes, this store is open 7 days a week. Germantown Village Sq., Germantown Pkwy. at Poplar Ave. ℭ **901/755-2204.**

Joseph You'll find the latest in very high-end fashionable women's shoes at this shop. They also have regularly scheduled trunk shows. Laurelwood Center, 418 S. Grove Park Rd. ℭ **901/767-1609.**

Rack Room Shoes   Conveniently situated in the same mall as DSW Shoe Warehouse, this store offers good discounts on Timberland, Rockport, Nike, Reebok, and Bass shoes, among other lines. Germantown Village Sq., 7690 Poplar Ave. at Germantown Pkwy. ℂ 901/754-2565.

TOYS & KIDS' STUFF

Pinocchio's, The Children's Book Place   If you're shopping for the child who has everything, then you need to drop by this upscale children's bookstore in East Memphis (a block off Poplar Ave.). They also sell children's gifts and have an outstanding selection of puppets. 688 W. Brookhaven Circle. ℂ 901/767-6586.

WINE

Cordova Cellars   Curious to taste some Tennessee wine? Then head out east of the city (take Germantown Pkwy. south off I-40 and then turn left on Macon Rd.) to this winery, where you can tour the facility and taste some local wines. 9050 Macon Rd., Cordova (15 miles northeast of Memphis; call for directions). ℂ 901/754-3442.

17

Memphis After Dark

For a century Memphis has nurtured one of the liveliest club scenes in the South, and the heart and soul of that nightlife has always been Beale Street. Whether your interest is blues, rock, opera, ballet, or Broadway musicals, you'll probably find entertainment to your liking on this lively street. However, there is more to Memphis nightlife than just Beale Street. In downtown Memphis, at the north end of Main Street, you'll find the Pinch Historic District, which now has more than half a dozen restaurants/bars that primarily serve crowds heading to and from events at the nearby Pyramid. You'll also find several theater companies performing in midtown near Overton Square, one of the city's other entertainment districts. This area also has several popular bars, restaurants, and a few clubs. South of Overton Square, at the corner of S. Cooper Street and Young Avenue, you'll find the small Cooper-Young district, which has a funky Elvis-theme coffee-house, a few boutiques, and three good restaurants with very popular bars.

One other place to check for live music is the rooftop of the Peabody Memphis hotel. Each summer, the hotel sponsors a series called Sunset Serenades that features blues, jazz, rock, pop, and rhythm-and-blues concerts.

To find out about what's happening in the entertainment scene while you're in town, pick up a copy of the *Memphis Flyer,* Memphis's free arts-and-entertainment weekly, which comes out on Thursday. You'll find it in convenience, grocery, and music stores, some restaurants, and night-clubs. You could also pick up the Friday edition of the *Commercial Appeal,* Memphis's morning daily newspaper. The "Playbook" section of the paper has very thorough events listings.

For tickets to sporting events and performances at the Pyramid, Mud Island Amphitheatre, and Mid-South Coliseum, your best bet is to contact **Ticketmaster** (© **901/525-1515**), which accepts credit card payments for phone orders. Alternatively, you can stop by a Ticketmaster sales counter and pay cash for tickets. There are Ticketmaster counters at Cat's Compact Discs and Cassettes stores around the city.

1 Beale Street & Downtown

Beale Street is the epicenter of Memphis's nightclub scene. This street, where the blues gained widespread recognition, is now the site of more than half a dozen nightclubs, plus a few other bars, restaurants, and theaters. The sidewalks and parks of Beale Street are also alive with music nearly every day of the week and almost any hour of the day or night. For links to various clubs and other businesses along Beale, click on **www.bealestreet.com.**

Alfred's This spacious club on the corner of Third and Beale has 1950s rock 'n' roll most weekends, with a variety of bands currently packing the house. With its corner location and upstairs, outdoor patio, Alfred's also makes a great vantage point for people-watching and late night drinking and eating. The kitchen's open until 3am. 197 Beale St. © **901/525-3711.** www.alfreds-on-beale.com. Cover $3–$5.

B.B. King's Blues Club ★★ *(Moments* Yes, the "King of the Blues" does play here occasionally, though not on a regular basis. However, any night of the week you can catch blazing blues played by one of the best house bands in town. Because of the name, this club attracts famous musicians who have been known to get up and jam with whomever is on stage that night. Ruby Wilson and Little Jimmy King are two regulars here who are worth checking out. 147 Beale St. © **800/443-0972** or 901/524-5464. Cover $5–$7 (usually $50–$170 for B. B.'s increasingly infrequent, but always sold-out, concerts).

The Black Diamond Although fairly new on the Beale Street scene, this club has caught on in a big way and has attracted the likes of the Memphis Horns, Matt "Guitar" Murphy, Isaac Hayes, and The Nighthawks to get up on the stage here. The last Thursday of the month is songwriter's night. 153 Beale St. © **901/521-0800.** Cover fee–$5.

Blues City Café ★ This club across the street from B. B. King's takes up two old storefronts, with live blues wailing in one room (called the Band Box) and a restaurant serving steaks, tamales and barbecue in the other. Local rock band FreeWorld plays here regularly. 138–140 Beale St. © **901/526-3637.** Cover $4–$5.

Center for Southern Folklore ★★★ *(Finds* After bouncing between various locations on or around Beale Street for the past 10 years, this offbeat treasure that's part coffeehouse/part folk-art flea market has landed in Pembroke Square, one of downtown's prime addresses. Warm and welcoming, it's a laid-back space where you can get a meal or some munchies, sip a latte or a beer, surf the Internet, or buy anything from books, CDs, and postcards to handmade quilts, outsider-art creations, and even cornhusk dolls and corncob pipes. Best of all, you can hear the Delta's most authentic roots musicians performing at almost any time of day. Better yet, it's a nonsmoking venue. (At press time, the center was about to expand with a new retail store and cafe being added at 123 S. Main St., right along the trolley line. The Center's performance space and museum will remain farther inside Pembroke Square, at 119 S. Main St.) 119 S. Main. © **901/525-3655.** www.southernfolklore.com. No cover.

Earnestine & Hazel's ★ *(Finds* Although it's actually 4 blocks south of Beale Street, this downtown dive, which was once a sundry store that fronted for an upstairs brothel, has become one of Memphis's hottest nightspots. On Friday and Saturday nights, there's a piano bar early; and then later in the night, the best jukebox in Memphis keeps things hot. Things don't really get cookin' here until after midnight. 531 S. Main St. © **901/523-9754.** No cover.

Gibson Beale Street Showcase Lounge Sip a martini, Manhattan, champagne, or beer and enjoy music amidst this intimate setting, where low-key concerts and occasional special events are held. Through it all, you can reflect on the

Memphis After Dark

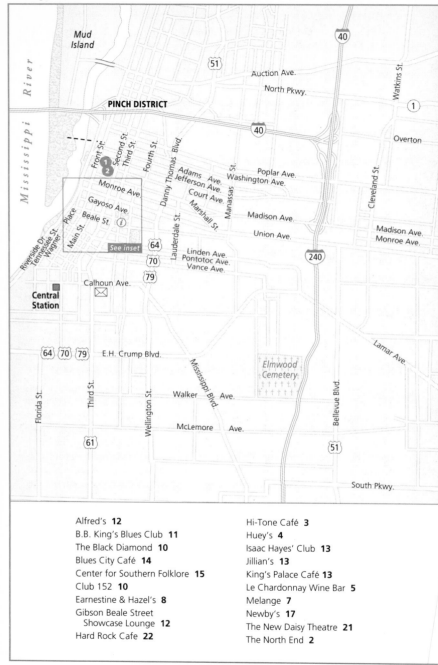

Alfred's **12**
B.B. King's Blues Club **11**
The Black Diamond **10**
Blues City Café **14**
Center for Southern Folklore **15**
Club 152 **10**
Earnestine & Hazel's **8**
Gibson Beale Street
 Showcase Lounge **12**
Hard Rock Cafe **22**

Hi-Tone Café **3**
Huey's **4**
Isaac Hayes' Club **13**
Jillian's **13**
King's Palace Café **13**
Le Chardonnay Wine Bar **5**
Melange **7**
Newby's **17**
The New Daisy Theatre **21**
The North End **2**

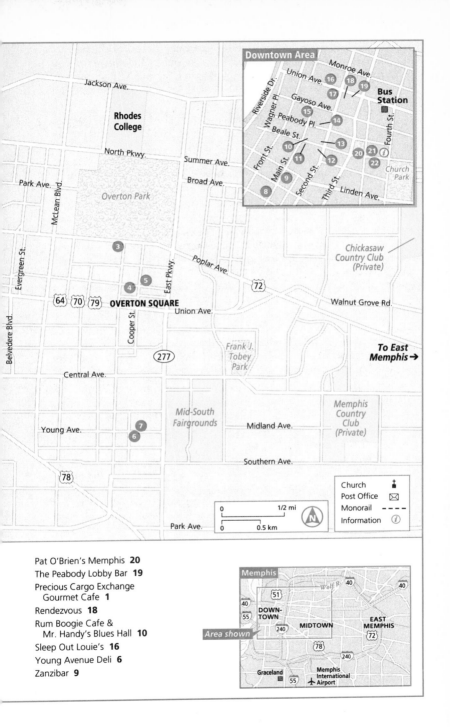

Jackson Ave.

Rhodes College

North Pkwy.

Summer Ave.

Broad Ave.

Park Ave.

McLean Blvd.

Overton Park

Evergreen St.

③

Poplar Ave.

East Pkwy.

④ ⑤

64 70 79 **OVERTON SQUARE**

Union Ave.

Cooper St.

Belvedere Blvd.

277

Frank J. Tobey Park

Central Ave.

Mid-South Fairgrounds

Midland Ave.

Young Ave.

⑦
⑥

Southern Ave.

78

0 ———— 1/2 mi
0 ———— 0.5 km

Park Ave.

Downtown Area

Monroe Ave.

Union Ave. ⑯

⑰ ⑱ ⑲

Bus Station

Riverside Dr.

Wagner Pl.

Gayoso Ave.

⑮

Peabody Pl.

⑭

Fourth St.

Beale St.

⑩

⑬

Front St.

Main St.

⑪

⑫

⑳ ㉑ ⓘ

㉒

Church Park

⑨

Second St.

Third St.

Linden Ave.

⑧

Chickasaw Country Club (Private)

Walnut Grove Rd.

To East Memphis →

Memphis Country Club (Private)

Church ✝
Post Office ✉
Monorail – – – –
Information ⓘ

Pat O'Brien's Memphis **20**
The Peabody Lobby Bar **19**
Precious Cargo Exchange
  Gourmet Cafe **1**
Rendezvous **18**
Rum Boogie Cafe &
  Mr. Handy's Blues Hall **10**
Sleep Out Louie's **16**
Young Avenue Deli **6**
Zanzibar **9**

Memphis

Wolf R. 40

51

40

55

DOWN-TOWN

240

MIDTOWN

EAST MEMPHIS

72

Area shown

78

240

Graceland

55

Memphis International Airport ✈

227

beauty of the beautiful stringed instruments made next door as you ponder the late, great George Harrison lyric (a club motto, of sorts): "I look at you all, see the love there that's sleeping, while my guitar gently weeps." Call ahead to see who's playing. 145 Lt. George Lee Ave. ℂ **901/544-7998, ext. 2.** www.gibsonmemphis.com. Cover varies.

Hard Rock Cafe   Yes, now Beale Street, too, has a Hard Rock Cafe, complete with lots of rock and blues memorabilia on the walls. This Hard Rock is the only one in the world to feature live music. Look for gold musical notes on the brick sidewalk out front that celebrate famous Memphis musicians through the years. Incidentally, the Hard Rock Cafe was founded by Isaac Tigrett, a philanthropist-entrepreneur and former Memphis resident. 315 Beale St. ℂ **901/529-0007.** www. hardrock.com. Cover usually around $5 after 9pm.

Isaac Hayes' Club 🛧 *(Moments*   Currently one of Memphis's hottest local celebs, the Grammy- and Oscar-winning songwriter and "Chef" character of *South Park* has a namesake nightclub and restaurant in Peabody Place. Guests can enjoy soul food such as ribs and nightly music in a sexy, sophisticated bar setting that considerably ups the cool quotient of Peabody Place. Hayes himself occasionally performs here. The so-called Black Moses also has an eponymous cookware store next door. 150 Peabody Place. ℂ **901/529-9222.** Cover $5–$10 (more for special events).

Jillian's   In Peabody Place, you'll find the Memphis location of this popular chain of themed entertainment complexes. From bowling and billiards to bars, video cafes, game rooms, and dancing, there's something for just about every-body. 150 Peabody Place ℂ **901/543-8800.** www.jillians.com. Fees vary by activity.

King's Palace Café 🛧   With its battered wood floor, this bar has the most authentic, old-time feel of any club on Beale Street. Though this is primarily a restaurant serving good Cajun food, including a knockout gumbo, there's live jazz and blues nightly. 162 Beale St. ℂ **901/521-1851.** No cover.

The New Daisy Theatre   The stage at the New Daisy has long been the place to see regional and national rock bands, but these days the theater books a sur-prisingly wide variety of entertainment, from boxing matches to the touring alternative-rock bands. Bob Dylan filmed a video here from his Grammy-win-ning *Time Out of Mind* CD (fitting, because Memphis musicians were featured on that work). Most recently, hometown heartthrob Justin Timberlake (who grew up just north of Memphis) headlined a sold-out show here. 330 Beale St. ℂ **901/525-8981.** www.newdaisy.com. Ticket prices vary according to event.

Pat O'Brien's Memphis   Hoist a Hurricane (a potent cocktail) at this replica of the famed New Orleans nightspot that opened on Beale a few years ago. It's been quite a hit with the Mardi Gras set. This vast brick drinking hall with the green awnings boasts a big, boozy beer hall, a posh piano bar, as well as a multi-level outdoor patio, complete with a fountain—and decent views of the Mem-phis skyline hovering a few blocks away. 310 Beale St. ℂ **901/529-0900.** www.pat obriens.com/memphis.html. Cover varies.

Impressions

I'd rather be here than any place I know.

—W. C. Handy, referring to Beale Street

Rum Boogie Cafe & Mr. Handy's Blues Hall Dozens of autographed guitars, including ones signed by Carl Perkins, Stevie Ray Vaughan, Billie Gibbons of ZZ Top, Joe Walsh, George Thorogood, and other rock and blues guitar wizards, hang from the ceiling at the Rum Boogie. There's live music nightly, with guest artists alternating with the house band, which plays everything from blues to country. 182 Beale St. © 901/528-0150. Cover $3–$5 after 9pm.

2 The Rest of the Club & Music Scene

JAZZ, ROCK, REGGAE & R&B

Newby's Located close to the University of Memphis, this cavernous club is a popular college hangout with two stages—one large, one small. There's live rock, mostly by local and regional acts, most nights of the week. Funk and alternative rock have been pretty popular here of late. 539 S. Highland St. © 901/452-8408. www.newbysmemphis.com. Cover $3–$5.

Precious Cargo Exchange Gourmet Cafe From reggae and hip-hop to DJ mixers and open-mike nights, this globally-minded bar and coffeehouse offers a refreshing diversity of entertainment. The place has plenty of atmosphere, too, with funky folk art behind the bar and colorful lighting fixtures dangling from the walls. 381 N. Main. © 901/578-8446. Cover $5–$10.

Zanzibar This new, Africa-inspired cafe in downtown's South Main arts district features occasional live jazz and other genres of music on weekends. 412 S. Main. © 901/543-9646. No cover.

> ### Impressions
> *People ask me what I miss about Memphis. And I said "Everything."*
> —Elvis

COUNTRY & FOLK

Java Cabana Located just down from the corner of Cooper and Young streets, this 1950s retro coffeehouse has poetry readings and live acoustic music on different nights of the week. Although you can't get alcohol here, you can get indulge in all manner of coffees. 2170 Young St. © 901/272-7210. No cover.

DANCE CLUBS

Club 152 Currently the hottest (but one of the few) dance clubs in town, this Beale Street newcomer is a favorite with energetic young adults who dance the night away on three floors. DJs such as Dave the Worm crank up techno, house, and alternative dance music for revelers who usually party until the early morning hours. 152 Beale St. © 901/544-7011. www.bealestreet.com. Cover fees vary.

3 The Bar & Pub Scene

BARS
DOWNTOWN

Automatic Slim's Tonga Club With hip decor, a great menu, and live music on Friday nights, Automatic Slim's Tonga Club attracts the arty and upscale thirty- and fortysomething crowd. Yummy martinis made with fruit-soaked vodka are a bar specialty. 83 S. 2nd St. © 901/525-7948.

The North End Although most people come to a bar to have a few drinks, here at The North End, in the Pinch Historic District near the Pyramid, hot fudge pie is as big a draw as cold beer. Lots of old advertising signs on the walls give this place the feel of an antiques store. There's live music several nights a week and several other bars in the neighborhood in case this place isn't happening. 346 N. Main St. ℂ **901/526-0319.** www.thenorthendonline.com.

The Peabody Lobby Bar There's no more elegant place in Memphis for a drink, but be sure you drop in well after the crowds who've gathered to watch the Peabody ducks do their daily march have dispersed, usually shortly after 5pm. Piano music is featured in the evenings. If you were to have only one drink while in Memphis, it should be here. The Peabody Memphis Hotel, 149 Union Ave. ℂ **901/529-4000.** www.peabodymemphis.com.

Rendezvous Although best known for its barbecued ribs and waiters with attitude, Rendezvous also has a big beer hall upstairs from the restaurant. It's a noisy, convivial spot, and a good place to start a night on the town or kill some time while you wait for a table in the restaurant. 52 S. 2nd St. ℂ **901/523-2746.** www. hogsfly.com.

Sleep Out Louie's For the thirtysomething downtown office crowd, this is the place for an after-work drink and a few oysters on the half shell. In the warmer months, the crowds fill the old-fashioned bar and spill out onto the alley patio. Be sure to check out the celebrity neckties on the power-tie wall. Happy hour is Monday through Friday 4:30 to 7:30pm and is one of the most popular happy hours in the city. A jazz brunch makes for a nice change of pace on Sunday mornings. 88 Union Ave. ℂ **901/527-5337.**

MIDTOWN

Hi-Tone Café ★★ Cutting-edge acts along the lines of the Disco Biscuits headline frequent late-night gigs at this ultra hip hangout, located across the street from the Memphis College of Art in Overton Park. 1913 Poplar. ℂ **901/278-8663.** www.hitonememphis.com.

Huey's This funky old dive is a midtown Memphis institution, known as the home of the best burgers in town. However, it's also a great place to sip a beer. But be warned: Spitting cocktail toothpicks at the ceiling is a favorite pastime of patrons. Sounds silly, but it's fun. Graffiti on the walls is also encouraged. 1927 Madison Ave. ℂ **901/726-4372.** www.hueys.cc.

Le Chardonnay Wine Bar Located directly behind T.G.I. Friday's in Overton Square, this is Memphis's original wine bar. With a dark wine-cellar feel, Le Chardonnay tends to attract casual young executive types, as well as people headed to the Playhouse on the Square, which is right across the parking lot. It has a great wine list. 2100 Overton Sq. Lane (at Cooper and Madison Sts.). ℂ **901/725-1375.**

Melange ★ Anchoring the Cooper-Young district, the trendiest corner in Memphis, is Melange. An upscale restaurant that's one of the best in the city, this site also offers late-night dining with savory tapas. The lively bar attracts the young and the fashionable, who gather to sip a variety of flavored martinis and other spirits. 948 S. Cooper St. ℂ **901/725-1009.** www.melangememphis.com. Free to nominal cover.

Young Avenue Deli Not so much a delicatessen as it is a cool hangout for young adults who like to eat and drink, this hot spot is also where you're likely to hear some of the best concerts by up-and-coming rock, alternative, and experimental artists. Live music is featured most nights. 2119 Young Ave. ℂ **901/278-0034.** www.youngavenuedeli.com. Cover $5–$20.

Gambling on the Mississippi

Move over Las Vegas and Atlantic City. Gamblers craving glitzy surroundings to go with their games of chance have a new option at the north end of the Mississippi Delta. Just south of Memphis, across the Mississippi state line, casinos are sprouting like cotton plants in the spring. In fact, these casinos are being built in the middle of the delta's cotton fields, rapidly replacing the region's white gold as the biggest business this neck of the delta has seen since cotton was king. For Midwestern and Southern gamblers, these Las Vegas–style casinos are an irresistible magnet. No longer is it necessary to make the long trip to Las Vegas or Atlantic City in order to play poker or roulette.

Back in the heyday of paddle-wheelers on the Mississippi, showboats and gamblers cruised the river, entertaining the masses and providing games of chance for those who felt lucky. In recent years, those days have returned to the Mississippi River as riverboats and floating casinos have opened in states bordering Tennessee. You still won't find any blackjack tables in God-fearing Tennessee, but you don't have to drive very far for a bit of Vegas-style action.

The nearest casinos are about 20 miles from downtown Memphis near the town of Robinsonville, Mississippi, while others are about 35 miles south of Memphis near Tunica, Mississippi. From Memphis, take either Tenn. 61 or I-55 south. If you take the interstate, get off at either the Miss. 304 exit or the Miss. 4 exit, and head west to the river, watching for signs as you drive.

Twelve miles south of the Mississippi state line, off U.S. 61 near the town of Robinsonville, you'll find **Goldstrike Casino,** 1010 Casino Center Dr. (© **888-24K-PLAY** or 866-245-7511), and **Sheraton Casino,** 1107 Casino Center Dr. (© **800/391-3777** or 662/363-4900). Continuing south on U.S. 61 and then west on Miss. 304, you come to **Sam's Town Hotel and Gambling Hall,** 1477 Casino Strip Blvd. (© **800/456-0711** or 662/363-0711); **Fitzgerald's Casino,** 711 Lucky Lane (© **800/766-LUCK** or 662/363-5825); **Hollywood Casino,** 1150 Commerce Landing (© **800/871-0711** or 662/357-7700); and **Harrah's,** 1100 Casino Strip Blvd. (© **800/HARRAHS** or 662/363-7777). Continuing south on U.S. 61 to Tunica and then heading west on either Mhoon Landing Road or Miss. 4, you'll come to **Bally's Saloon and Gambling Hall,** 1450 Bally's Blvd. (© **800/38-BALLY).**

Besides the casinos, the area also offers outlet mall shopping, golf, spas, and other activities. For more information, go to **www.tunica miss.com.**

EAST MEMPHIS

Belmont Grill   A great neighborhood bar, Belmont is a popular watering hole for where locals like to stop by after work to unwind. As plain as a rundown roadhouse, it's unpretentious and casual. The eatery some might call a "greasy spoon" also happens to serve terrific pub grub. Try the cheeseburgers or go for the catfish po'boys. 4970 Poplar Ave. © **901/767-0305.** No cover.

Tap House Bar & Grill   It's not that East Memphis has a dearth of good bars. It's just that most of the best ones are downtown and in Midtown. A suitable compromise is this joint, where you can grab a beer and a bite to eat. It's located near Corky's, off of Poplar Avenue 695 W. Brookhaven Circle. ℂ 901/818-2337.

BREW PUBS

Boscos Squared   Live jazz sizzles on Sundays at this popular Overton Square brew pub, known for its Famous Flaming Stone Beer. Locally owned, Boscos also boasts a terrific restaurant menu with great wood-fired-oven pizzas. An outdoor patio is perfect for large parties. If you're a cheap date (or you just like saving money), you'll appreciate that parking is free and much less hassle-free than at the downtown and Beale Street brew pubs. Plus, the food is better. 2120 Madison Ave. ℂ 901/432-2222. No cover.

Dan McGuinness' Irish Pub   With a full bar, an array of draught beers including Guinness Stout, Newcastle Brown Ale, and Bud Light, as well as premium import beers (Heineken, Corona, etc.), drink and general merriment come first at this desperate-to-be-Dublin-esque pub. A small menu offers sausages, soups, and sandwiches for munching on between pints. A large, covered patio allows drinkers to toast the passing throngs on South Main Street. 150 Peabody Place. ℂ 901/527-8500. www.danmcguinnesspub.com. No cover.

Flying Saucer Draught Emporium   When Beale Street becomes too crowded, the locals make tracks to this nearby haven for beer lovers. Frequent music, a lively pub atmosphere, and enough variety of brews to keep the blues away keep patrons satisfied—and coming back for more. 130 Peabody Place. ℂ 901/523-8536.

Gordon Biersch Brewery and Restaurant ☆   German lagers and hearty bar food (you might catch a whiff of garlic as you ride by on the Main Street Trolley) are big draws at this brewery that's a bit more upscale than the nearby Dan McGuinness' Irish Pub. Dark, polished woods and brass fixtures lend warmth to the vast dining rooms, which always seem crowded. For brunch, you can get filet mignon eggs Benedict, or nurse yourself back to health from the night before with a Hangover Pizza of scrambled eggs, Andouille sausage, and salsa fresca. 145 S. Main St. ℂ 901/543-3330. www.gordonbiersch.com. No cover.

GAY BARS

J-Wag's   Memphis's oldest gay bar is open 24 hours a day. There are nightly drink specials and regular shows, with female-impersonator shows occasionally. 1268 Madison Ave. ℂ 901/725-1909.

Lorenz/Aftershock   Weekend drag shows promise a randy good time at this neighborhood Midtown bar. Next door at Aftershock, deejays keep the gay crowd dancing until the early morning hours. 1528 Madison Ave. ℂ 901/274-8272.

Madison Flame   One of Memphis's few lesbian bars, the Madison Flame has been around for years. Located in a rundown Midtown neighborhood, the bar is male-friendly. Karaoke and disco are popular pastimes. 1588 Madison. ℂ 901/278-8272. No cover.

4 The Performing Arts

With Beale Street forming the heart of the city's nightclub scene, it seems appropriate that Memphis's main performance hall, the Orpheum Theatre, would be located here also. A night out at the theater can also include a visit to a blues club after the show.

CLASSICAL MUSIC, OPERA & BALLET

Although blues and rock 'n' roll dominate the Memphis music scene, the city also manages to support a symphony, an opera, and a ballet. The symphony performs, and big-name performers and lecturers often appear, at the brand-new, 2,100-seat **Cannon Center for the Performing Arts,** 255 N. Main St. (© **800/ 726-0915;** www.thecannoncenter.com), adjacent to the downtown center. Another of the city's premier performing-arts venues is the **Orpheum Theatre,** 203 S. Main St. (© **901/525-3000;** www.orpheum-memphis.com), which was built in 1928 as a vaudeville hall. The ornate, gilded plasterwork on the walls and ceiling give this theater the elegance of a classic opera house and make this the most spectacular performance hall in the city.

In addition to performing at the Cannon Center, the orchestra also occasionally performs at other venues, including the suburban Germantown Performing Arts Center and outdoor concerts at the lovely Dixon Gallery and Gardens. The extremely popular **Sunset Symphony,** an outdoor extravaganza held on the banks of Tom Lee Park overlooking the Mississippi River each year as part of the Memphis in May International Festival, is always a highlight of the symphony season and one of the city's definitive Memphis experiences. The **Memphis Symphony** box office is at 3100 Walnut Grove Rd. (tickets $10–$75).

Opera Memphis (© **901/678-2706;** www.operamemphis.org) also performs at both the Orpheum and Cannon Center, annually staging three or four operas (tickets $20–$70). The company, which for 50 years has been staging the best of classical opera and innovative new works for appreciative Memphis audiences, also has built a reputation for its extensive educational outreach program.

Ballet Memphis (© **901/763-0139;** www.balletmemphis.org), widely regarded as the city's crown jewel of performing arts groups, performs at both the Orpheum and Cannon Center (tickets $15–$60). For sentimentalists, the highlight of each season is the annual holiday performance of *The Nutcracker,* but exciting world premieres and contemporary dance works also rate high priority on the company's mission.

THEATER

Memphis has a relatively well-developed theater scene with numerous opportunities to attend live stage productions around the city. **Theatre Memphis,** 630 Perkins Rd. Extended (© **901/682-8323;** www.theatrememphis.org), is a commendable community theater that's been around for more than 75 years. Located on the edge of Audubon Park, it has garnered regional and national awards for excellence. There are two stages here—a 435-seat main theater that does standards, and a 100-seat, black-box theater known as Next Stage (tickets $8–$25), where less mainstream productions are staged.

Staging productions of a higher artistic caliber are two sister theaters in Midtown, **Circuit Playhouse,** 1705 Poplar Ave. (© **901/726-4656**), and the **Playhouse on the Square,** 51 S. Cooper St. (© **901/726-4656**). Another theater, **TheatreWorks,** 2085 Monroe St. (© **901/274-7139**) also puts on various productions.

These are the only professional theaters in Memphis, and between them they stage about 25 productions each year. Off-Broadway plays are the rule at the Circuit Playhouse (with the occasional premiere), while at the Playhouse on the

Square, Broadway-worthy dramas, comedies, and musicals; TheatreWorks stages more daring works, such as *Hedwig and the Angry Inch,* and *Quills* (tickets $12–$26).

OTHER VENUES

Rising 32 stories above the waters of the Mississippi River, the **Pyramid,** 1 Auction Ave., at the north end of downtown (© **901/526-5177;** www.pyramid arena.com), is far and away the most distinctive building in Memphis and one of the most distinctive arenas anywhere in the United States. For the time being it is the city's main arena and where the University of Memphis Tigers basketball team plays. It is also the site of rock concerts and other large-scale performances and events. All of that is about to change, however, when the **FedEx Forum** opens in 2004. Though the venue will be home to the NBA Memphis Grizzlies team, other big-name touring acts are likely to book the coliseum as well.

Germantown and East Memphis are the wealthiest areas of metropolitan Memphis these days, so it isn't surprising that the modern **Germantown Performing Arts Center,** 1801 Exeter Rd., Germantown (© **901/757-7256;** www. gpacweb.com), manages to schedule many of the same touring companies and performers that appear downtown at the Orpheum. The center also serves as a home base for a chamber orchestra, known as **Iris,** conducted by Michael Stern, son of the late violinist Isaac Stern.

From late spring through early fall, Memphians frequently head outdoors for their concerts, and the **Mud Island Amphitheatre,** 125 N. Front St. (© **800/ 507-6507** or 901/576-7241), is where they head most often. With the downtown Memphis skyline for a backdrop, the 5,000-seat Mud Island Amphitheatre is the city's main outdoor stage. The concert season includes many national acts with the emphasis on rock and country music concerts. Though the monorail usually runs only during the summer months, outside of summer it runs here on concerts evenings.

Impressions

Memphis ain't a bad town, for them that like city life.
          —*Light in August,* by William Faulkner

Appendix A:
For International Visitors

Country, blues, rock 'n' roll, soul—the music may be familiar, and, to a lesser extent, so too may be the cities of Nashville and Memphis. As an international visitor, you may soon find that neither Nashville nor Memphis is quite like home. This chapter will help you to prepare for some of the uniquely American situations you are likely to encounter.

1 Preparing for Your Trip

ENTRY REQUIREMENTS

Immigration laws are a hot political issue in the United States these days, and the following requirements may have changed somewhat by the time you plan your trip. Check at any U.S. embassy or consulate for current information and requirements. You can also plug into the **U.S. State Department's** Internet site at **www.travel.state.gov.**

VISAS　The U.S. State Department has a **Visa Waiver Pilot Program** allowing citizens of certain countries to enter the United States without a visa for stays of up to 90 days. At press time these included Andorra, Australia, Austria, Belgium, Brunei, Denmark, Finland, France, Germany, Iceland, Ireland, Italy, Japan, Liechtenstein, Luxembourg, Monaco, the Netherlands, New Zealand, Norway, San Marino, Slovenia, Spain, Sweden, Switzerland, and the United Kingdom. Citizens of these countries need only a valid passport and a round-trip air or cruise ticket in their possession upon arrival. Canadian citizens may enter the United States without visas; they need only proof of residence.

Citizens of all other countries must have (1) a valid passport that expires at least 6 months later than the scheduled end of their visit to the United States, and (2) a tourist visa, which may be obtained without charge from any U.S. consulate.

OBTAINING A VISA　To obtain a visa, the traveler must submit a completed application form (either in person or by mail) with a 1½-inch-square photo, and must demonstrate binding ties to a residence abroad. Usually you can obtain a visa at once or within 24 hours, but it may take longer during the summer rush from June through August. If you cannot go in person, contact the nearest U.S. embassy or consulate for directions on applying by mail. Your travel agent or airline office may also be able to provide you with visa applications and instructions. The U.S. consulate or embassy that issues your visa will determine whether you will be issued a multiple- or single-entry visa and any restrictions regarding the length of your stay.

British subjects can obtain up-to-date passport and visa information by calling the **U.S. Embassy Visa Information Line** (© 0891/200-290) or the **London Passport Office** (© 0990/210-410 for recorded information).

Irish citizens can obtain up-to-date visa information through the **Embassy of the USA Dublin,** 42 Elgin Rd., Dublin 4, Ireland (© 353/1-668-8777; or by checking the "Consular Services" section of the website at www.usembassy.ie.

Australian citizens can obtain up-to-date visa information by contacting the **U.S. Embassy Canberra,** Moonah Place, Yarralumla, ACT 2600 (© 02/ 6214-5600) or by checking the U.S. Diplomatic Mission's website at http://us embassy-australia.state.gov/consular.

Citizens of **New Zealand** can obtain up-to-date visa information by contacting the **U.S. Embassy New Zealand,** 29 Fitzherbert Terr., Thorndon, Wellington (© 644/472-2068), or get the information directly from the "Services to New Zealanders" section of the website at http://usembassy.org.nz.

IMMIGRATION QUESTIONS   Telephone operators will answer your inquiries regarding U.S. immigration policies or laws at the **Immigration and Naturalization Service's National Customer Center** (© 800/375-5283). Representatives are available from 9am to 3pm, Monday through Friday.

MEDICAL REQUIREMENTS   Unless you're arriving from an area known to be suffering from an epidemic (particularly cholera or yellow fever), inoculations or vaccinations are not required for entry into the United States. If you have a disease that requires treatment with narcotics or **syringe-administered medications,** carry a valid signed prescription from your physician to allay any suspicions that you may be smuggling narcotics (a serious offense that carries severe penalties in the U.S.).

For **HIV-positive visitors,** requirements for entering the United States are somewhat vague and change frequently. According to the latest publication of *HIV and Immigrants: A Manual for AIDS Service Providers,* although INS doesn't require a medical exam for everyone trying to come into the United States, INS officials may keep out people who they suspect are HIV positive. INS may stop people because they look sick or because they are carrying AIDS/HIV medicine.

If an HIV-positive noncitizen applies for a non-immigrant visa, the question on the application regarding communicable diseases is tricky no matter which way it's answered. If the applicant checks "no," INS may deny the visa on the grounds that the applicant committed fraud. If the applicant checks "yes" or if INS suspects the person is HIV-positive, it will deny the visa unless the applicant asks for a special waiver for visitors. This waiver is for people visiting the United States for a short time, to attend a conference, for instance, to visit close relatives, or to receive medical treatment. It can be a confusing situation.

For up-to-the-minute information, contact **AIDSinfo** (© 800/448-0440 or 301/519-6616 outside the U.S.; www.aidsinfo.nih.gov) or the **Gay Men's Health Crisis** (© 212/367-1000; www.gmhc.org).

DRIVER'S LICENSES   Foreign driver's licenses are mostly recognized in the U.S., although you may want to get an international driver's license if your home license is not written in English.

PASSPORT INFORMATION

Safeguard your passport in an inconspicuous, inaccessible place like a money belt. If you lose it, visit the nearest consulate of your native country as soon as possible for a replacement. Passport applications are downloadable from the Internet sites listed below.

FOR RESIDENTS OF CANADA   You can pick up a passport application at one of 28 regional passport offices or most travel agencies. The passport is valid for 5 years and costs C$60. Children under 16 may be included on a parent's passport but need their own to travel unaccompanied by the parent. Applications, which must be accompanied by two identical passport-sized photographs and proof of Canadian citizenship, are available at travel agencies throughout Canada or from the central **Passport Office, Department of Foreign Affairs and International Trade,** Ottawa, ON K1A 0G3 (© **800/567-6868;** www. dfait-maeci.gc.ca/passport). Processing takes 5 to 10 days if you apply in person, or about 3 weeks by mail.

FOR RESIDENTS OF THE UNITED KINGDOM   To pick up an application for a regular 10-year passport (the Visitor's Passport has been abolished), visit your nearest passport office, major post office, or travel agency. You can also contact the **United Kingdom Passport Service** at © **0870/571-0410** or visit its website at www.passport.gov.uk. Passports are £33 for adults and £19 for children under 16, with another £30 fee if you apply in person at a Passport Office. Processing takes about 2 weeks (1 week if you apply at the Passport Office).

FOR RESIDENTS OF IRELAND   You can apply for a 10-year passport, costing 57€, at the **Passport Office,** Setanta Centre, Molesworth Street, Dublin 2 (© **01/671-1633;** www.irlgov.ie/iveagh). Those under age 18 and over 65 must apply for a 12€ 3-year passport. You can also apply at 1A South Mall, Cork (© **021/272-525**) or over the counter at most main post offices.

FOR RESIDENTS OF AUSTRALIA   You can get an application from your local post office or any branch of Passports Australia, but you must schedule an interview at the passport office to present your application materials. Call the **Australian Passport Information Service** at © **131-232,** or visit the government website at www.passports.gov.au. Passports for adults are A$144 and for those under 18 are A$72.

FOR RESIDENTS OF NEW ZEALAND   You can pick up a passport application at any New Zealand Passports Office or download it from their website. Contact the **Passports Office** at © **0800/225-050** in New Zealand or 04/474-8100, or log on to www.passports.govt.nz. Passports for adults are NZ$80 and for children under 16 NZ$40.

CUSTOMS
WHAT YOU CAN BRING IN
Every visitor over 21 years of age may bring in, free of duty, the following: (1) 1 liter of wine or hard liquor; (2) 200 cigarettes, 100 cigars (but not from Cuba), or 3 pounds of smoking tobacco; and (3) $100 worth of gifts. These exemptions are offered to travelers who spend at least 72 hours in the United States and who have not claimed them within the preceding 6 months. It is altogether forbidden to bring into the country foodstuffs (particularly fruit, cooked meats, and canned goods) and plants (vegetables, seeds, tropical plants, and the like). International tourists may bring in or take out up to $10,000 in U.S. or foreign currency with no formalities; larger sums must be declared to U.S. Customs on entering or leaving, which includes filing form CM 4790. For more specific information regarding U.S. Customs, call your nearest U.S. embassy or consulate, or the **U.S. Customs** office at © **202/927-1770** or www.customs.ustreas.gov.

WHAT YOU CAN BRING HOME
U.K. citizens returning from a non-EU country have a customs allowance of: 200 cigarettes; 50 cigars; 250g of smoking tobacco; 2 liters of still table wine; 1 liter of spirits or strong liqueurs (over 22% volume); 2 liters of fortified wine, sparkling wine or other liqueurs; 60cc (ml) perfume; 250cc (ml) of toilet water; and £145 worth of all other goods, including gifts and souvenirs. People under

17 cannot have the tobacco or alcohol allowance. For more information, contact HM Customs & Excise at © **0845/010-9000** (from outside the U.K., 020/8929-0152), or consult their website at www.hmce.gov.uk.

For a clear summary of **Canadian** rules, request the booklet *I Declare,* issued by the **Canada Customs and Revenue Agency** (© **800/461-9999** in Canada, or 204/983-3500; www.ccra-adrc.gc.ca). Canada allows its citizens a C$750 exemption, and you're allowed to bring back duty-free 1 carton of cigarettes, 1 can of tobacco, 40 imperial ounces of liquor, and 50 cigars. In addition, you're allowed to mail gifts to Canada valued at less than C$60 a day, provided they're unsolicited and don't contain alcohol or tobacco (write on the package "Unsolicited gift, under $60 value"). All valuables should be declared on the Y-38 form before departure from Canada, including serial numbers of valuables you already own, such as expensive foreign cameras. *Note:* The $750 exemption can only be used once a year and only after an absence of 7 days.

The duty-free allowance in **Australia** is A$400 or, for those under 18, A$200. Citizens age 18 and over can bring in 250 cigarettes or 250 grams of loose tobacco, and 1,125 milliliters of alcohol. If you're returning with valuables you already own, such as foreign-made cameras, you should file form B263. A helpful brochure available from Australian consulates or Customs offices is *Know Before You Go.* For more information, call the **Australian Customs Service** at © **1300/363-263,** or log on to www.customs.gov.au.

The duty-free allowance for **New Zealand** is NZ$700. Citizens over 17 can bring in 200 cigarettes, 50 cigars, or 250 grams of tobacco (or a mixture of all 3 if their combined weight doesn't exceed 250g); plus 4.5 liters of wine and beer, or 1.125 liters of liquor. New Zealand currency does not carry import or export restrictions. Fill out a certificate of export, listing the valuables you are taking out of the country; that way, you can bring them back without paying duty. Most questions are answered in a free pamphlet available at New Zealand consulates and Customs offices: *New Zealand Customs Guide for Travellers, Notice no. 4.* For more information, contact **New Zealand Customs,** The Customhouse, 17–21 Whitmore St., Box 2218, Wellington (© **0800/428-786** or 04/473-6099; www.customs.govt.nz).

INSURANCE

Although it's not required of travelers, health insurance is highly recommended. Unlike many European countries, the United States does not usually offer free or low-cost medical care to its citizens or visitors. Doctors and hospitals are expensive, and in most cases will require advance payment or proof of coverage before they render their services. Policies can cover everything from the loss or theft of your baggage and trip cancellation to the guarantee of bail in case you're arrested. Good policies will also cover the costs of an accident, repatriation, or death. See "Health & Insurance" in chapter 2 for more information. Packages such as **Europ Assistance's "Worldwide Healthcare Plan"** are sold by European automobile clubs and travel agencies at attractive rates. **Worldwide Assistance Services, Inc.** (© **800/821-2828;** www.worldwideassistance.com) is the agent for Europ Assistance in the United States.

Though lack of health insurance may prevent you from being admitted to a hospital in nonemergencies, don't worry about being left on a street corner to die: The American way is to fix you now and bill the living daylights out of you later.

INSURANCE FOR BRITISH TRAVELERS   Most big travel agents offer their own insurance and will probably try to sell you their package when you book a holiday. Think before you sign. **Britain's Consumers' Association** recommends that you insist on seeing the policy and reading the fine print before buying travel insurance. **The Association of British Insurers** (© 020/7600-3333; www.abi.org.uk) gives advice by phone and publishes *Holiday Insurance,* a free guide to policy provisions and prices. You might also shop around for better deals: Try **Columbus Direct** (© 020/7375-0011; www.columbusdirect.net).

INSURANCE FOR CANADIAN TRAVELERS   Canadians should check with their provincial health plan offices or call **Health Canada** (© 613/957-2991; www.hc-sc.gc.ca) to find out the extent of their coverage and what documentation and receipts they must take home in case they are treated in the United States.

MONEY
CURRENCY   The U.S. monetary system is painfully simple: The most common bills (all green) are the $1 (colloquially, a "buck"), $5, $10, and $20 denominations. There are also $2 bills (seldom encountered), $50 bills, and $100 bills (the last two are usually not welcome as payment for small purchases). Note that a newly redesigned $100 and $50 bill were introduced in 1996, and a redesigned $20 bill in 1998. Expect to see redesigned $10 and $5 notes in the future. Despite rumors to the contrary, the old-style bills are still legal tender.

There are six denominations of coins: 1¢ (1 cent, or a penny); 5¢ (5 cents, or a nickel); 10¢ (10 cents, or a dime); 25¢ (25 cents, or a quarter); 50¢ (50 cents, or a half dollar); and the less common $1 piece.

Note: The "foreign-exchange bureaus" so common in Europe are rare even at airports in the United States, and nonexistent outside major cities. It's best not to change foreign money (or traveler's checks denominated in a currency other than U.S. dollars) at a small-town bank, or even a branch in a big city; in fact, leave any currency other than U.S. dollars at home—it may prove a greater nuisance to you than it's worth.

TRAVELER'S CHECKS   Though traveler's checks are widely accepted, make sure that they're denominated in U.S. dollars, as foreign-currency checks are often difficult to exchange. The three traveler's checks that are most widely recognized—and least likely to be denied—are **Visa, American Express,** and **Thomas Cook.** Be sure to record the numbers of the checks, and keep that information separately in case they get lost or stolen. Most businesses are pretty good about taking traveler's checks, but you're better off cashing them at a bank (in small amounts, of course) and paying in cash. *Remember:* You'll need identification, such as a driver's license or passport, to change a traveler's check.

CREDIT CARDS & ATMs   Credit cards are the most widely used form of payment in the United States: Visa (BarclayCard in Britain), **MasterCard** (Eurocard in Europe, Access in Britain, Chargex in Canada), **American Express, Diners Club, Discover,** and **Carte Blanche.** It is strongly recommended that you travel with a major credit card. You must have a credit card to rent a car, and

---

(Tips   Travel Tip

Be sure to keep a copy of all your travel papers separate from your wallet or purse, and leave a copy with someone at home should you need it faxed in an emergency.

hotels will usually require a credit card number as a deposit against an expense. There are, however, a handful of stores and restaurants that do not take credit cards, so be sure to ask in advance. Most businesses display a sticker near their entrance to let you know which cards they accept. (**Note:** Often businesses require a minimum purchase price, usually around $10, to use a credit card.)

You'll find automated teller machines (ATMs) on just about every block—at least in almost every town—across the country. Some ATMs will allow you to draw U.S. currency against your bank and credit cards. Check with your bank before leaving home, and remember that you will need your personal identification number (PIN) to do so. Most accept Visa, MasterCard, and American Express, as well as ATM cards from other U.S. banks. Expect to be charged up to $3 per transaction, however, if you're not using your own bank's ATM.

One way around these fees is to ask for cash back at grocery stores that accept ATM cards and don't charge usage fees. Of course, you'll have to purchase something first. The most commonly accepted cards are MasterCard and Visa.

SAFETY

GENERAL SAFETY SUGGESTIONS   While tourist areas are generally safe, crime is on the increase everywhere, and U.S. urban areas tend to be less safe than those in Europe or Japan. You should always stay alert. It is wise to ask your hotel front desk staff or the city's or area's tourist office if you're in doubt about which neighborhoods are safe.

Avoid deserted areas, especially at night, and don't go into public parks at night unless there's a concert or similar occasion that will attract a crowd.

Avoid carrying valuables with you on the street, and don't display expensive cameras or electronic equipment. If you are using a map, consult it inconspicuously—or better yet, try to study it before you leave your room. Hold onto your pocketbook, and place your billfold in an inside pocket. In theaters, restaurants, and other public places, keep your possessions in sight.

Remember also that hotels are open to the public, and in a large hotel, security may not be able to screen everyone entering. Always lock your room door—don't assume that once inside your hotel you are automatically safe and no longer need to be aware of your surroundings.

DRIVING SAFETY   Question your rental agency about personal safety and ask for a traveler-safety brochure when you pick up your car. Obtain written directions—or a map with the route clearly marked—from the agency showing how to get to your destination. (Many agencies now offer the option of renting a cellular phone for the duration of your car rental; check with the rental agent when you pick up the car.) And, if possible, arrive and depart during daylight hours.

Recently, more and more crime has involved cars and drivers. If you drive into a dubious neighborhood, leave the area as quickly as possible. If you have an accident, even on the highway, stay in your car with the doors locked until you assess the situation or until the police arrive. If you're hit from behind or are involved in a minor accident with no injuries and the situation appears to be suspicious, motion to the other driver to follow you. Never get out of your car in such situations. Go directly to the nearest police precinct, well-lit service station, or 24-hour store.

Always try to park in well-lit and well-traveled areas if possible. If you leave your rental car unlocked and empty of your valuables, you're probably safer than locking your car with valuables in plain view. Never leave any packages or valuables in sight. If someone attempts to rob you or steal your car, don't try to

Size Conversion Chart

Women's Clothing

American	4	6	8	10	12	14	16
French	34	36	38	40	42	44	46
British	6	8	10	12	14	16	18

Women's Shoes

American	5	6	7	8	9	10
French	36	37	38	39	40	41
British	4	5	6	7	8	9

Men's Suits

American	34	36	38	40	42	44	46	48
French	44	46	48	50	52	54	56	58
British	34	36	38	40	42	44	46	48

Men's Shirts

American	14½	15	15½	16	16 ½	17	17½
French	37	38	39	41	42	43	44
British	14½	15	15½	16	16½	17	17½

Men's Shoes

American	7	8	9	10	11	12	13
French	39½	41	42	43	44½	46	47
British	6	7	8	9	10	11	12

resist the thief/carjacker—report the incident to the police department immediately by calling © **911.**

2 Getting to the U.S.

AIRLINES From Canada, Air Canada offers service to Nashville from Toronto; and Northwest, American, and Delta all offer flights from various Canadian cities to Nashville and Memphis.

From London, you can get to Nashville and Memphis on American, Delta, Northwest, TWA, and United, or, via connecting domestic flights, on British Airways.

From New Zealand and Australia, you can fly Air New Zealand or Qantas to Los Angeles, and then take a domestic flight onward to Nashville or Memphis. United also flies to Memphis from New Zealand and Australia.

KLM flies directly to Memphis from Amsterdam.

See "Getting There" in chapters 2 (for Nashville) and 11 (for Memphis) for more information on domestic flights.

AIRLINE DISCOUNTS The idea of traveling abroad on a budget is something of an oxymoron, but travelers can reduce the price of a plane ticket by several hundred dollars if they take the time to shop around. For example, overseas visitors can take advantage of the APEX (Advance Purchase Excursion) reductions offered by all major U.S. and European carriers. For more money-saving airline advice, see "Getting There," in chapters 2 and 11. For the best rates, compare fares and be flexible with the dates and times of travel.

IMMIGRATION & CUSTOMS CLEARANCE   Visitors arriving by air, no matter what the port of entry, should cultivate patience and resignation before setting foot on U.S. soil. Getting through immigration control may take as long as 2 hours on some days, especially on summer weekends, so be sure to have this guidebook or something else to read. Add the time it takes to clear Customs, and you'll see that you should make a 2- to 3-hour allowance for delays when you plan your connections between international and domestic flights.

In contrast, for the traveler arriving by car or rail from Canada, the border-crossing formalities have been streamlined to the vanishing point. People traveling by air from Canada, Bermuda, and some places in the Caribbean can sometimes clear Customs and Immigration at the point of departure, which is much quicker.

3 Getting Around the U.S.

BY PLANE   Some large airlines (for example, Northwest and Delta) offer travelers on their transatlantic or transpacific flights special discount tickets under the name **Visit USA,** allowing mostly one-way travel from one U.S. destination to another at very low prices. These discount tickets are not on sale in the United States and must be purchased abroad in conjunction with your international ticket. This system is the best, easiest, and fastest way to see the United States at low cost. You should obtain information well in advance from your travel agent or the office of the airline concerned, since the conditions attached to these discount tickets can be changed without advance notice.

BY TRAIN   International visitors can also buy a **USA Railpass,** good for 15 or 30 days of unlimited travel on **Amtrak** (© 800/USA-RAIL). The pass is available through many international travel agents. (With an international passport, you can also buy passes at some Amtrak offices in the United States, including locations in San Francisco, Los Angeles, Chicago, New York, Miami, Boston, and Washington, D.C.) Reservations are generally required and should be made for each part of your trip as early as possible.

BY BUS   Although bus travel is often the most economical form of public transit for short hops between U.S. cities, it can also be slow and uncomfortable—certainly not an option for everyone (particularly when Amtrak, which is far more luxurious, offers similar rates). **Greyhound/Trailways** (© 800/231-2222; www.greyhound.com), the sole nationwide bus line, offers an **International Ameripass** that must be purchased before coming to the United States, or by phone through the Greyhound International Office at the Port Authority Bus Terminal in New York City (© 212/971-0492). The pass can be obtained from foreign travel agents or through Greyhound's website (order at least 21 days before your departure to the U.S.) and costs less than the domestic version. You can get more info on the pass at the website, or by calling © 402/330-8552. In addition, special rates are available for seniors and students.

BY CAR   The most cost-effective, convenient, and comfortable way to travel around the United States is by car. The interstate highway system connects cities and towns all over the country; in addition to these high-speed, limited-access roadways, there's an extensive network of federal, state, and local highways and roads. Some of the national car-rental companies include **Alamo** (© 800/462-5266; www.alamo.com), **Avis** (© 800/230-4898; www.avis.com), **Budget**

(© 800/527-0700; www.budget.com), **Dollar** (© 800/800-3665; www.dollar. com), **Hertz** (© 800/654-3131; www.hertz.com), **National** (© 800/227-7368; www.nationalcar.com), and **Thrifty** (© 800/847-4389; www.thrifty.com).

If you plan on renting a car in the United States, you probably won't need the services of an additional automobile organization. If you're planning to buy or borrow a car, automobile-association membership is recommended. The **American Automobile Association** (AAA; © **800/222-4357**) is the country's largest auto club and supplies its members with maps, insurance, and, most important, emergency road service. The cost of joining runs from $63 for singles to $87 for two members, but if you're a member of a foreign auto club with reciprocal arrangements, you can enjoy free AAA service in America.

For further information about travel to and around Nashville and Memphis, see "Getting There" in chapters 2 and 11, and "Getting Around Nashville" and "Getting Around Memphis" in chapters 3 and 12, respectively.

FAST FACTS: For the International Traveler

Automobile Organizations Auto clubs will supply maps, suggested routes, guidebooks, accident and bail-bond insurance, and emergency road service. The **American Automobile Association (AAA)** is the major auto club in the United States. If you belong to an auto club in your home country, inquire about AAA reciprocity before you leave. You may be able to join AAA even if you're not a member of a reciprocal club; to inquire, call AAA (© **800/222-4357**). AAA is actually an organization of regional auto clubs; so look under "AAA Automobile Club" in the White Pages of the telephone directory. AAA has a nationwide emergency road service telephone number (© **800/AAA-HELP**).

Business Hours Offices are usually open weekdays 9am to 5pm. Banks are open weekdays 9am to 5pm or later and sometimes Saturday mornings. Stores, especially those in shopping complexes, tend to stay open late: until about 9pm on weekdays and 6pm on weekends.

Currency & Currency Exchange See "Entry Requirements" and "Money" under "Preparing for Your Trip," earlier in this chapter.

Drinking Laws The legal age for purchase and consumption of alcoholic beverages is 21; proof of age is required and often requested at bars, nightclubs, and restaurants, so it's always a good idea to bring ID when you go out. Only beer can often be purchased in supermarkets in Tennessee.

Do not carry open containers of alcohol in your car or any public area that isn't zoned for alcohol consumption. The police can, and probably will, fine you on the spot. And nothing will ruin your trip faster than getting a citation for DUI ("driving under the influence"), so don't even think about driving while intoxicated.

Electricity Like Canada, the United States uses 110 to 120 volts AC (60 cycles), compared to 220 to 240 volts AC (50 cycles) in most of Europe, Australia, and New Zealand. If your small appliances use 220 to 240 volts, you'll need a 110-volt transformer and a plug adapter with two flat parallel pins to operate them here. Downward converters that change 220-240 volts to 110-120 volts are difficult to find in the United States, so bring one with you.

Embassies & Consulates All embassies are located in Washington, D.C. Some consulates are located in major U.S. cities, and most nations have a mission to the United Nations in New York City. If your country isn't listed below, call directory information in Washington, D.C. (© **202/555-1212**) for the number of your national embassy.

The embassy of **Australia** is at 1601 Massachusetts Ave. NW, Washington, DC 20036 (© **202/797-3000;** www.austemb.org). There are consulates in New York, Honolulu, Houston, Los Angeles, and San Francisco.

The embassy of **Canada** is at 501 Pennsylvania Ave. NW, Washington, DC 20001 (© **202/682-1740;** www.cdnemb-washdc.org). Other Canadian consulates are in Buffalo (NY), Detroit, Los Angeles, New York, and Seattle.

The embassy of **Ireland** is at 2234 Massachusetts Ave. NW, Washington, DC 20008 (© **202/462-3939**). Irish consulates are in Boston, Chicago, New York, and San Francisco.

The embassy of **Japan** is at 2520 Massachusetts Ave. NW, Washington, DC 20008 (© **202/238-6700;** www.embjapan.org). Japanese consulates are located in Atlanta, Kansas City, San Francisco, and Washington, D.C.

The embassy of **New Zealand** is at 37 Observatory Circle NW, Washington, DC 20008 (© **202/328-4800;** http://www.emb.com/nz.shtml). New Zealand consulates are in Los Angeles, Salt Lake City, San Francisco, and Seattle.

The embassy of the **United Kingdom** is at 3100 Massachusetts Ave. NW, Washington, DC 20008 (© **202/462-1340**). Other British consulates are in Atlanta, Boston, Chicago, Cleveland, Houston, Los Angeles, New York, San Francisco, and Seattle.

Emergencies Call © **911** to report a fire, call the police, or get an ambulance anywhere in the United States. This is a toll-free call (no coins are required at public telephones).

If you encounter serious problems, contact the **Traveler's Aid International** (© **202/546-1127;** www.travelersaid.org) to help direct you to a local branch. This nationwide, nonprofit, social-service organization geared to helping travelers in difficult straits offers services that might include reuniting families separated while traveling, providing food and/or shelter to people stranded without cash, or even emotional counseling. If you're in trouble, seek them out.

Gasoline (Petrol) Petrol is known as gasoline (or simply "gas") in the United States, and petrol stations are known as both gas stations and service stations. Gasoline costs about half as much here as it does in Europe (about $1.65 per gallon at press time), and taxes are already included in the printed price. One U.S. gallon equals 3.8 liters or .85 Imperial gallons.

Holidays Banks, government offices, post offices, and many stores, restaurants, and museums are closed on the following legal national holidays: January 1 (New Year's Day), the third Monday in January (Martin Luther King, Jr. Day), the third Monday in February (Presidents' Day, Washington's Birthday), the last Monday in May (Memorial Day), July 4 (Independence Day), the first Monday in September (Labor Day), the second Monday in October (Columbus Day), November 11 (Veterans' Day/ Armistice Day), the fourth Thursday in November (Thanksgiving Day), and

December 25 (Christmas). Also, the Tuesday following the first Monday in November is Election Day and is a federal government holiday in presidential-election years (held every 4 years, and next in 2004).

Legal Aid If you are "pulled over" for a minor infraction (such as speeding), never attempt to pay the fine directly to a police officer; this could be construed as attempted bribery, a much more serious crime. Pay fines by mail, or directly into the hands of the clerk of the court. If accused of a more serious offense, say and do nothing before consulting a lawyer. Here the burden is on the state to prove a person's guilt beyond a reasonable doubt, and everyone has the right to remain silent, whether he or she is suspected of a crime or actually arrested. Once arrested, a person can make one telephone call to a party of his or her choice. Call your embassy or consulate.

Mail If you aren't sure what your address will be in the United States, mail can be sent to you, in your name, c/o General Delivery at the main post office of the city or region where you expect to be (call ✆ 800/275-8777 for information on the nearest post office). The addressee must pick mail up in person and must produce proof of identity (driver's license, passport, and so on). Most post offices will hold your mail for up to 1 month, and are open Monday to Friday from 8am to 6pm, and Saturday from 9am to 3pm.

Generally found at intersections, mailboxes are blue with a red-and-white stripe and carry the inscription U.S. MAIL. If your mail is addressed to a U.S. destination, don't forget to add the five-digit postal code (or ZIP code), after the two-letter abbreviation of the state to which the mail is addressed. Tennessee's abbreviation is "TN."

At press time, domestic postage rates were 23¢ for a postcard and 37¢ for a letter. For international mail, a first-class letter of up to one-half ounce costs 80¢ (60¢ to Canada and Mexico); a first-class postcard costs 70¢ (50¢ to Canada and Mexico); and a preprinted postal aerogramme costs 70¢.

Taxes In the United States there is no value-added tax (VAT) or other indirect tax at the national level. Every state, county, and city has the right to levy its own local tax on all purchases, including hotel and restaurant checks, airline tickets, and so on.

Telephone, Telegraph, Telex & Fax The telephone system in the United States is run by private corporations, so rates, especially for long-distance service and operator-assisted calls, can vary widely. Generally, hotel surcharges on long-distance and local calls are astronomical, so you're usually better off using a **public pay telephone**, which you'll find clearly marked in most public buildings and private establishments as well as on the street. Convenience grocery stores and gas stations always have them. Many convenience groceries and packaging services sell **prepaid calling cards** in denominations up to $50; these can be the least expensive way to call home. Many public phones at airports now accept American Express, MasterCard, and Visa credit cards. **Local calls** made from public pay phones in most locales cost either 25¢ or 35¢. Pay phones do not accept pennies, and few will take anything larger than a quarter.

Most long-distance and international calls can be dialed directly from any phone. **For calls within the United States and to Canada,** dial 1 followed by the area code and the seven-digit number. **For other international calls,** dial 011 followed by the country code, city code, and the telephone number of the person you are calling.

Calls to area codes **800, 888,** and **877** are toll-free. However, calls to numbers in area codes **700** and **900** (chat lines, bulletin boards, "dating" services, and so on) can be very expensive—usually a charge of 95¢ to $3 or more per minute, and they sometimes have minimum charges that can run as high as $15 or more.

For **reversed-charge or collect calls,** and for person-to-person calls, dial 0 (zero, not the letter O) followed by the area code and number you want; an operator will then come on the line, and you should specify that you are calling collect, or person-to-person, or both. If your operator-assisted call is international, ask for the overseas operator.

For **local directory assistance** ("information"), dial 411; for long-distance information, dial 1, then the appropriate area code and 555-1212.

Telegraph and telex services are provided primarily by **Western Union.** You can bring your telegram into the nearest Western Union office (there are hundreds across the country) or dictate it over the phone (© **800/325-6000**). You can also telegraph money or have it telegraphed to you, very quickly over the Western Union system, but this service can cost as much as 15% to 20% of the amount sent.

Most hotels have **fax machines** available for guest use (be sure to ask about the charge to use it), and many hotel rooms are even wired for guests' fax machines. A less expensive way to send and receive faxes may be at stores such as the UPS Store, a national chain of packing service shops (look in the Yellow Pages directory under "Packing Services").

There are two kinds of telephone directories in the United States. The so-called **White Pages** list private households and business subscribers in alphabetical order. The inside front cover lists emergency numbers for police, fire, ambulance, the Coast Guard, poison-control center, crime-victims hotline, and so on. The first few pages will tell you how to make long-distance and international calls, complete with country codes and area codes. Government numbers are usually printed on blue paper within the White Pages. Printed on yellow paper, the so-called **Yellow Pages** list all local services, businesses, industries, and houses of worship according to activity with an index at the front or back. (Drugstores/pharmacies and restaurants are also listed by geographic location.) The Yellow Pages also include city plans or detailed area maps, postal ZIP codes, and public transportation routes.

Time   The continental United States is divided into **four time zones:** Eastern Standard Time (EST), Central Standard Time (CST), Mountain Standard Time (MST), and Pacific Standard Time (PST). Alaska and Hawaii have their own zones. For example, noon in Nashville or Memphis (CST) is 1pm in New York City (EST), 11am in Denver (MST), 10am in San Francisco (PST), 9am in Anchorage (AST), and 8am in Honolulu (HST).

Daylight saving time is in effect from 1am on the first Sunday in April through 1am the last Sunday in October, except in Arizona, Hawaii, part of Indiana, and Puerto Rico. Daylight saving time moves the clock 1 hour ahead of standard time.

Tipping Tips are a very important part of certain workers' income, and gratuities are the standard way of showing appreciation for services provided. (Tipping is certainly not compulsory if the service is poor!) In hotels, tip **bellhops** at least $1 per bag ($2–$3 if you have a lot of luggage) and tip the **chamber staff** $1 to $2 per day (more if you've left a disaster area for him or her to clean up). Tip the **doorman** or **concierge** only if he or she has provided you with some specific service (for example, calling a cab for you or obtaining difficult-to-get theater tickets). Tip the **valet-parking attendant** $1 every time you get your car.

In restaurants, bars, and nightclubs, tip **service staff** 15% to 20% of the check, tip **bartenders** 10% to 15%, tip **checkroom attendants** $1 per garment, and tip **valet-parking attendants** $1 per vehicle.

As for other service personnel, tip **cab drivers** 15% of the fare; tip **skycaps** at airports at least $1 per bag ($2–$3 if you have a lot of luggage); and tip **hairdressers** and **barbers** 15% to 20%.

Toilets You won't find public toilets or "restrooms" on the streets in most U.S. cities, but they can be found in hotel lobbies, bars, restaurants, museums, department stores, railway and bus stations, or service stations. Note, however, that restaurants and bars in resorts or heavily visited areas may reserve their restrooms for the use of their patrons. Some establishments display a notice that toilets are for the use of patrons only. You can ignore this sign or, better yet, avoid arguments by paying for a cup of coffee or a soft drink, which will qualify you as a patron. Large hotels and fast-food restaurants are probably the best bet for good, clean facilities. If possible, avoid the toilets at parks and beaches, which tend to be dirty.

Appendix B:
Nashville in Depth

Though Nashville's fortunes aren't exclusively those of the country music industry, the city is inextricably linked to its music. These days country music is enjoying greater popularity than ever before (it's now a $2-billion-a-year industry), bringing newfound importance to this city. On any given night of the week in The District, you can hear live music in two dozen clubs and bars—and not all of the music is country music. There are blues bars, jazz clubs, alternative-rock clubs, even Irish pubs showcasing Celtic music.

Nashville also has its share of shopping malls, theme restaurants, stadiums, and arenas, but it is music that drives this city. Nashville should be able to attract not only fans of country music but just about anyone who enjoys a night on the town. With all the new developments taking place around Nashville, it is obvious that Nashville is a city ascendant, rising both as a city of the New South and as Music City USA.

1 A Look at the Past

Long before the first Europeans set foot in middle Tennessee, Native Americans populated this region of rolling hills, dense forests, and plentiful grasslands. Large herds of deer and buffalo made the region an excellent hunting ground. However, by the late 18th century, when the first settlers arrived, continuing warfare over access to the area's rich hunting grounds had forced the various battling tribes to move away. Though there were no native villages in the immediate area, this did not eliminate conflicts between Native Americans and settlers.

FRONTIER DAYS The first Europeans to arrive in middle Tennessee were French fur trappers and trader Charles Charleville, who established a trading post at a salt lick, and another Frenchman named Timothy Demonbreun, who made his home in a cave on a bluff above the Cumberland River. By the middle part of the century, the area that is now Nashville came to be known as French Lick because of the salt lick.

Dateline

- 9000 B.C. Paleo-Indians inhabit area that is now Nashville.
- A.D. 1000–1400 Mississippian-period Indians develop advanced society characterized by mound-building and farming.
- 1710 French fur trader Charles Charleville establishes a trading post in the area.
- 1765 A group of long hunters camp at Mansker's Lick, north of present-day Nashville.
- 1772 The Wautauga Association becomes the first form of government west of the Appalachians.
- 1775 The Transylvania Purchase stimulates settlement in middle Tennessee.
- 1778 James Robertson scouts the area and decides to found a settlement.
- 1779 Robertson's first party of settlers arrives on Christmas Eve.
- 1780 Second of Robertson's parties of settlers, led by Col. John Donelson, arrives by boat in April; in May, the settlement of Nashborough founded.
- 1781 Battle of the Bluffs fought with Cherokee Indians.
- 1784 The small settlement's name changed from Nashborough to Nashville.

Throughout the middle part of the century, the only other whites to explore the area were so-called long hunters. These hunters got their name from the extended hunting trips, often months long, that they would make over the Appalachian Mountains. They would bring back stacks of buckskins, which at the time sold for $1. Thus, a dollar came to be called a "buck." Among the most famous of the long hunters was Daniel Boone, who may have passed through French Lick in the 1760s.

The Indian Treaty of Lochaber in 1770 and the Transylvania Purchase in 1775 opened up much of the land west of the Appalachians to settlers. Several settlements had already sprung up on Cherokee land in the Appalachians, and these settlements had formed the Watauga Association, a sort of self-government. However, it was not until the late 1770s that the first settlers began to arrive in middle Tennessee. In 1778, James Robertson, a member of the Watauga Association, brought a scouting party to the area in his search for a place to found a new settlement.

The bluffs above the Cumberland River appealed to Robertson, and the following year he returned with a party of settlers. This first group, comprised of men only, had traveled through Kentucky and arrived at French Lick on Christmas Eve 1779. The women and children, under the leadership of John Donelson, followed by flatboat, traveling 1,000 miles (1,610km) by river to reach the new settlement and arriving in April 1780. This new settlement of nearly 300 people was named Fort Nashborough after North Carolinian Gen. Francis Nash. As soon as both parties were assembled at Fort Nashborough, the settlers drew up a charter of government called the Cumberland Compact. This was the first form of government in middle Tennessee.

- 1796 Tennessee becomes the 16th state.
- 1814 Andrew Jackson, a Nashville resident, leads the Tennessee militia in the Battle of New Orleans and gains national stature.
- 1840 Belle Meade plantation home built.
- 1843 The state capital moved from Murfreesboro to Nashville.
- 1850 Nashville is site of convention held by nine Southern states that jointly assert the right to secede.
- 1862 Nashville becomes the first state capital in the South to fall to Union troops.
- 1864 Battle of Nashville, the last major battle initiated by the Confederate army.
- 1866 Fisk University, one of the nation's first African-American universities, founded.
- 1873 Vanderbilt University founded.
- 1897 The Parthenon built as part of the Nashville Centennial Exposition.
- 1920 Nashville becomes the center of the nation's attention as Tennessee becomes the 36th state to give women the vote, thus ratifying the 19th amendment to the U.S. Constitution.
- 1925 WSM-AM radio station broadcasts the first *Grand Ole Opry* program.
- 1943 *Grand Ole Opry* moves to Ryman Auditorium in downtown Nashville.
- 1944 Nashville's first recording studio begins operation at WSM-AM radio.
- 1950s Numerous national record companies open offices and recording studios in Nashville.
- Late 1950s to early 1960s Record-company competition and pressure from rock 'n' roll change the sound of country music, giving it a higher production value that comes to be known as the "Nashville sound."
- 1972 Opryland USA theme park opens in Nashville.
- 1974 *Grand Ole Opry* moves to a new theater at the Opryland USA theme park.
- 1993 Ryman Auditorium closes for a renovation that will make the *Grand Ole Opry*'s most famous home an active theater once again.

continues

Fort Nashborough was founded while the Revolutionary War was raging, and these first settlers very soon found themselves battling Cherokee, Choctaw, and Chickasaw Indians—whose attacks were incited by the British. The worst confrontation was the Battle of the Bluffs, which took place in April 1781 when settlers were attacked by a band of Cherokees.

By 1784, the situation had grown quieter, and in that year the settlement changed its name from Nashborough to Nashville. Twelve years later, in 1796, Tennessee became the 16th state in the Union. Nashville at that time was still a tiny settlement in a vast wilderness, but in less than 20 years, the nation would know of Nashville through the heroic exploits of one of its citizens.

In 1814, at the close of the War of 1812, Andrew Jackson, a Nashville lawyer, led a contingent of Tennessee militiamen in the Battle of New Orleans. The British were soundly defeated and Jackson became a hero. A political career soon followed, and in 1829, Jackson was elected the seventh president of the United States.

- 1994 With the opening of the Wild-horse Saloon and the Hard Rock Cafe and the reopening of the Ryman Auditorium, Nashville becomes one of the liveliest cities in the South.
- 1996 Nashville Arena opens in downtown Nashville.
- 1997 Bicentennial Capitol Mall State Park opens north of state capitol.
- 1999 The NFL Tennessee Titans move into the new Coliseum and the NHL Nashville Predators into the Gaylord Entertainment Center (Nashville Arena) downtown.
- 2000 The Titans take a trip to the Superbowl as the AFC champs. Opry Mills, a 1.2-million-square-foot entertainment and shopping complex, rises from the ashes of the demolished Opryland amusement park.
- 2001 Two new world-class venues open downtown: the Frist Center for the Visual Arts and Country Music Hall of Fame.

In the early part of the 19th century, the state government bounced back and forth between eastern and middle Tennessee, and was twice seated in Knoxville, once in Murfreesboro, and had once before been located in Nashville before finally staying put on the Cumberland. By 1845, work had begun on constructing a capitol building, which would not be completed until 1859.

THE CIVIL WAR & RECONSTRUCTION   By 1860, when the first rumblings of secession began to be heard across the South, Nashville was a very prosperous city, made wealthy by its importance as a river port. Tennessee reluctantly sided with the Confederacy and became the last state to secede from the Union. This decision sealed Nashville's fate. The city's significance as a shipping port was not lost on either the Union or the Confederate army, both of which coveted the city as a means of controlling important river and railroad transportation routes. In February 1862, the Union army occupied Nashville, razing many homes in the process. Thus Nashville became the first state capital to fall to the Union troops.

Throughout the Civil War, the Confederates repeatedly attempted to reclaim Nashville, but to no avail. In December 1864, the Confederate army made its last stab at retaking Nashville, but during the Battle of Nashville they were roundly rebuffed.

Though the Civil War left Nashville severely damaged and in dire economic straits, the city quickly rebounded. Within a few years, the city had reclaimed its important shipping and trading position and also developed a solid manufacturing base. The post–Civil War years of the late 19th century brought a newfound prosperity to Nashville. These healthy economic times left the city with a legacy of grand classical-style buildings, which can still be seen around the downtown area.

Fisk University, one of the nation's first African-American universities, was founded in 1866. Vanderbilt University was founded in 1873, and in 1876, Meharry Medical College, the country's foremost African-American medical school, was founded. With this proliferation of schools of higher learning, Nashville came to be known as the "Athens of the South."

THE 20TH CENTURY   At the turn of the century, Nashville was firmly established as one of the South's most important cities. This newfound significance had culminated 3 years earlier with the ambitious Tennessee Centennial Exposition of 1897, which left as its legacy to the city Nashville's single most endearing structure—a full-size reconstruction of the Parthenon. Though Nashville's Parthenon was meant to last only the duration of the exposition, it proved so popular that the city left it in place. Over the years, the building deteriorated until it was no longer safe to visit. At that point, the city was considering demolishing this last vestige of the Centennial Exposition, but public outcry brought about the reconstruction, with more permanent materials, of the Parthenon.

> **Fun Fact**
> Nashville's One Cent Savings Bank (now known as Citizen's Savings Bank and Trust) was the nation's first bank owned and operated by African Americans.

About the same time the Parthenon was built, trains began using the new Union Station, a Roman-Gothic train station. The station's grand waiting hall was roofed by a stained-glass ceiling, and, with its gilded plasterwork and bas-reliefs, was a symbol of the waning glory days of railroading in America. Today, Union Station has been restored and is one of Nashville's two historic hotels.

In 1920, Tennessee played a prominent role in the passing of the 19th Amendment to the U.S. Constitution, which gave women the right to vote in national elections. As the 36th state to ratify the 19th amendment, the Tennessee vote became the most crucial battle in the fight for women's suffrage. Surprisingly, both the pro-suffrage and the anti-suffrage organizations were headquartered in the beaux arts–style Hermitage Hotel. In 1994, this hotel was completely renovated; now known as the Westin Hermitage, it is the city's premier historic hotel.

The 20th century also brought the emergence of country music as a popular musical style. The first recordings of country music came from Tennessee, and though it took a quarter of a century for "hillbilly" music to catch on, by 1945 Nashville found itself at the center of the country music industry. The city embraced this new industry and has not looked back since.

2 The Nashville Sound: From Hillbilly Ballads to Big Business

Country music is everywhere in Nashville. You can hardly walk down a street here without hearing the strains of a country melody. In bars, in restaurants, in hotel lobbies, on trolleys, in the airport, and on the street corners, country musicians sing out in hopes that they, too, might be discovered and become the next big name. Nashville's reputation as Music City attracts thousands of hopeful musicians and songwriters every year, and though very few of them make it to the big time, they provide the music fan with myriad opportunities to hear the occasional great, undiscovered performer. Keep your ears tuned to the music that's the pulse of Nashville and one day you just might be able to say, "I heard her when she was a no-name playing at a dive bar in Nashville years ago."

As early as 1871, a Nashville musical group, the Fisk University Jubilee Singers, had traveled to Europe to sing African-American spirituals. By 1902, the city had its first music publisher, the Benson Company, and today, Nashville is still an important center for gospel music. Despite the fact that this musical tradition has long been overshadowed by country music, there are still numerous gospel-music festivals throughout the year in Nashville.

The history of Nashville in the 20th century is, for the most part and for most people, the history of country music. Though traditional fiddle music, often played at dances, had been a part of the Tennessee scene from the arrival of the very first settlers, it was not until the early 20th century that people outside the hills and mountains began to pay attention to this "hillbilly" music.

In 1925, radio station WSM-AM went on the air and began broadcasting a show called *The WSM Barn Dance,* which featured live performances of country music. Two years later, it renamed the show the *Grand Ole Opry,* a program that has been on the air ever since, and is the longest-running radio show in the country. The same year that the *Grand Ole Opry* began, Victor Records sent a recording engineer to Tennessee to record the traditional country music of the South. These recordings helped expose this music to a much wider audience than it had ever enjoyed before, and interest in country music began to grow throughout the South and across the nation.

In 1942, Nashville's first country music publishing house opened, followed by the first recording studio in 1945. By the 1960s, there were more than 100 music publishers in Nashville and dozens of recording studios. The 1950s and early 1960s saw a rapid rise in the popularity of country music, and all the major record companies eventually opened offices here. Leading the industry at this time were brothers Owen and Harold Bradley, who opened the city's first recording studio not affiliated with the *Grand Ole Opry.* CBS and RCA soon followed suit. Many of the industry's biggest and most familiar names first recorded in Nashville at this time, including Patsy Cline, Hank Williams, Brenda Lee, Dottie West, Floyd Cramer, Porter Wagoner, Dolly Parton, Loretta Lynn, George Jones, Tammy Wynette, Elvis Presley, the Everly Brothers, Perry Como, and Connie Francis.

During this period, country music evolved from its hillbilly music origins. With growing competition from rock 'n' roll, record producers developed a cleaner, more urban sound for country music. Production values went up and the music took on a new sound, the "Nashville sound."

In 1972, the country music–oriented Opryland USA theme park (now supplanted by a shopping mall) opened on the east side of Nashville. In 1974, the *Grand Ole Opry* moved from the Ryman Auditorium, its home of 31 years, to the new Grand Ole Opry House just outside the gates of Opryland.

In more recent years, country music has once again learned to adapt itself to maintain its listenership. Rock and pop influences have crept into the music, opening a rift between traditionalists (who favor the old Nashville sound) and fans of the new country music, which for the most part is faster and louder than the music of old. However, in Nashville, every type of country music, from Cajun to contemporary, bluegrass to cowboy, honky-tonk to Western swing, is heard with regularity. Turn on your car radio anywhere in America and run quickly through the AM and FM dials: You'll likely pick up a handful of country music stations playing music that got its start in Nashville.

Appendix C:
Memphis in Depth

Memphis is a city with an identity problem. Though conservative and traditional, it has spawned several of the most important musical forms of the 20th century (blues, rock 'n' roll, and soul). And although it has been unable to cash in on this musical heritage (in the profitable way Nashville has with country), Memphis is still the mecca of American music. Memphis started out as an important Mississippi River port, but urban sprawl has carried the city's business centers ever farther east—so much so that the Big Muddy has become less a reason for being than simply a way of distinguishing Tennessee from Arkansas. With a population of a million people in the metropolitan area, Memphis is reinventing itself.

Memphis is primarily known for being the city where Graceland is located, but how long can the Elvis craze sustain itself? A city needs diversity and an identity of its own. To that end, in the past few years Memphis has made considerable progress. One of the greatest hurdles to overcome has been the legacy of racial tension that came to a head with the assassination here of Martin Luther King, Jr., and the rioting that ensued. Racial tensions are still frequently named as the city's foremost civic problem, even though the casual observer or visitor may not see any signs of these difficulties. Racial tensions combined with post–World War II white flight to the suburbs of East Memphis left downtown a mere shell of a city, but today, this is changing.

These days, downtown is the most vibrant area in the metropolitan Memphis area. A new baseball stadium, the renovation of Beale Street (known as the home of the blues), and a spate of newly constructed museums, hotels, restaurants, and shops are breathing fresh life into downtown Memphis. This has succeeded not only in keeping office workers after-hours to enjoy the live music in the street's many nightclubs, but luring residents in the outlying suburban areas to flock downtown as well—a concept that was unheard of 10 years ago.

For the time being, though, Elvis is still king in Memphis. A quarter-century after the entertainer's death, Graceland remains the number-one tourist attraction in the city. Throughout the year, there are Elvis celebrations, which leave no doubt that this is still a city, and a nation, obsessed with Elvis Presley. Less popular but equally worth visiting are such attractions as Sun Studio, where Elvis made his first recording, the Rock 'n' Soul Museum, and the Memphis Music Hall of Fame, which has displays on Elvis and many other local musicians who made major contributions to rock, soul, and blues music.

1 A Look at the Past

Located at the far western end of Tennessee, Memphis sits on a bluff overlooking the Mississippi River. Directly across the river lies Arkansas, and only a few miles to the south is Mississippi. The area, which was long known as

Dateline

- 1541 Hernando de Soto views the Mississippi River from the fourth Chickasaw bluff, site of today's Memphis.

continues

the "fourth Chickasaw bluff," was chosen as a strategic site by Native Americans as well as French, Spanish, and finally American explorers and soldiers. The most important reason for choosing this site for the city was that the top of the bluff was above the high-water mark of the Mississippi, and thus was safe from floods.

Habitation of the bluffs of the Mississippi dates from nearly 15,000 years ago, but it was between A.D. 900 and 1600, during the Mississippian period, that the native peoples of this region reached a cultural zenith. During this 700-year period, people congregated in large, permanent villages. Sun worship, a distinctive style of artistic expression, and mound building were the main characteristics of this culture. The mounds, which today are the most readily evident reminders of this native heritage, were built as foundations for temples and can still be seen in places such as the Chucalissa Archaeological Museum. However, by the time the first Europeans arrived in the area, the mound builders had disappeared and been replaced by the Chickasaw Indians.

As early as 1541, Spanish explorer Hernando de Soto stood atop a 100-foot bluff and looked down on the mighty Mississippi River. More than 100 years later, in 1682, French explorer Sieur de La Salle claimed the entire Mississippi River valley for his country. However, it would be more than 50 years before the French built a permanent outpost in this region.

In 1739, the French built Fort Assumption on the fourth Chickasaw bluff. From this spot, they hoped to control the Chickasaw tribes, who had befriended the English. By the end of the 18th century, the Louisiana territory had passed into the hands of the Spanish, who erected Fort San Fernando on the bluff over the Mississippi. Within 2 years the Spanish had decamped to the far side of the river

- 1682 La Salle claims the Mississippi Valley for France.
- 1739 The French governor of Louisiana orders a fort built on the fourth Chickasaw bluff.
- 1795 Manuel Gayoso, in order to expand Spanish lands in North America, erects Fort San Fernando on the Mississippi River.
- 1797 Americans build Fort Adams on the ruins of Fort San Fernando and the Spanish flee to the far side of the river.
- 1818 The Chickasaw Nation cedes western Tennessee to the United States.
- 1819 The town of Memphis is founded.
- 1826 Memphis is incorporated.
- 1840s Cheap land makes for boom times in Memphis.
- 1857 The Memphis and Charleston Railroad is completed, linking the Atlantic and the Mississippi.
- 1862 Memphis falls to Union troops but becomes an important smuggling center.
- 1870s Several yellow-fever epidemics leave the city almost abandoned.
- 1879 Memphis declares bankruptcy and its charter is revoked.
- 1880s Memphis rebounds.
- 1890s Memphis becomes the largest hardwood market in the world, attracting African Americans seeking to share in the city's boom times.
- 1892 The first bridge across the Mississippi south of St. Louis opens in Memphis.
- 1893 Memphis regains its city charter.
- 1899 Church Park and Auditorium, the city's first park and entertainment center for African Americans, are built.
- 1909 W. C. Handy, a Beale Street bandleader, becomes the father of the blues when he writes down the first blues song for mayoral candidate E. H. "Boss" Crump.
- 1916 The nation's first self-service grocery store opens in Memphis.
- 1925 The Peabody hotel is built. Tom Lee rescues 23 people from a sinking steamboat.
- 1928 The Orpheum Theatre opens.

and the U.S. flag flew above Fort Adams, which had been built on the ruins of Fort San Fernando.

A treaty negotiated with the Chickasaw Nation in 1818 ceded all of western Tennessee to the United States, and within the year, John Overton, Gen. James Winchester, and Andrew Jackson (who would later become president of the United States) founded Memphis as a speculative land investment. The town was named for the capital of ancient Egypt, a reference to the Mississippi being the American Nile. However, it would take the better part of the century before the city began to live up to its grand name.

GROWTH OF A RIVER PORT

The town of Memphis was officially incorporated in 1826, and for the next 2 decades grew slowly. In 1845, the establishment of a naval yard in Memphis gave the town a new importance. Twelve years later, the Memphis and Charleston Railroad linked Memphis to Charleston, South Carolina, on the Atlantic coast. With the Mississippi Delta region beginning just south of Memphis, the city played an important role as the main shipping port for cotton grown in the delta. During the heyday of river transportation in the mid–19th century, Memphis became an important Mississippi River port, which it remains today. This role as river port gave the city a link and kinship with other river cities to the north. With its importance to the cotton trade of the Deep South and its river connections to the Mississippi port cities of the Midwest, Memphis

- **1940** B. B. King plays for the first time on Beale Street, at an amateur music contest.
- **1952** Jackie Brenston's "Rocket 88," considered the first rock-'n'-roll recording, is released by Memphis's Sun Studio.
- **1955** Elvis Presley records his first hit record at Sun Studio.
- **1958** Stax Records, a leader in the soul-music industry of the 1960s, is founded.
- **1968** Dr. Martin Luther King, Jr. is assassinated at the Lorraine Motel.
- **1977** Elvis Presley dies at Graceland, his home on the south side of Memphis.
- **1983** A renovated Beale Street reopens as a tourist attraction and nightlife district.
- **1991** The National Civil Rights Museum opens in the former Lorraine Motel. The Pyramid is completed.
- **1992** Memphis elects its first African-American mayor.
- **1993** Two John Grisham novels, *The Firm* and *The Client,* are filmed in Memphis.
- **1998** Memphis booms with $1.4 billion in expansion and renovation projects.
- **2000** The Memphis Redbirds baseball team play their first season in the new, $68.5 million AutoZone Park downtown.
- **2001** The Grizzlies move to Memphis, becoming the city's first, long-awaited NBA team.
- **2002** Groundbreaking begins on the FedEx Forum downtown.
- **2003** Sun Studio founder Sam Phillips dies.
- **2003** Soulsville USA: Stax Museum of American Soul Music opens in South Memphis.

developed some of the characteristics of both regions, creating a city not wholly of the South or the Midwest, but rather, a city in-between.

In the years before the outbreak of the Civil War, the people of Memphis were very much in favor of secession, but it was only a few short months after the outbreak of the war that Memphis fell to Union troops. Both the Union and the Confederacy had seen the importance of Memphis as a supply base, and yet the Confederates had been unable to defend their city—on June 6, 1862, steel-nosed ram boats easily overcame the Confederate fleet guarding Memphis. The city quickly became a major smuggling center as merchants sold to both the North and the South.

Within 2 years of the war's end, tragedy struck Memphis. Cholera and yellow fever epidemics swept through the city, killing hundreds of residents. This was only the first, and the mildest, of such epidemics to plague Memphis over the next 11 years. In 1872 and 1878, yellow fever epidemics killed thousands of people and caused nearly half the city's population to flee. In the wake of these devastating outbreaks of the mosquito-borne disease, the city was left bankrupt and nearly abandoned.

However, some people remained in Memphis and had faith that the city would one day regain its former importance. One of those individuals was Robert Church, a former slave, who bought real estate from people who were fleeing the yellow-fever plague. He later became the South's first African-American millionaire. In 1899, on a piece of land near the corner of Beale and Fourth streets, Church established a park and auditorium where African Americans could gather in public.

CIVIL RIGHTS MOVEMENT   In the years following the Civil War, freed slaves from around the South flocked to Memphis in search of jobs. Other African-American professionals, educated in the North, also came to Memphis to establish new businesses. The center for this growing community was Beale Street. With all manner of businesses, from lawyers' and doctors' offices to bars and houses of prostitution, Beale Street was a lively community. The music that played in the juke joints and honky-tonks began to take on a new sound that derived from the spirituals, field calls, and work songs of the Mississippi Delta cotton fields. By the first decade of the 20th century, this music had acquired a name—the blues.

The music that expressed itself as the blues was the expression of more than a century of struggle and suffering by African Americans. By the middle of the 20th century, that long suffering had been given another voice—the civil rights movement. One by one, school segregation and other discriminatory laws and practices of the South were challenged. Equal treatment and equal rights with whites was the goal of the civil rights movement, and the movement's greatest champion and spokesman was Dr. Martin Luther King, Jr., whose assassination in Memphis threw the city into the national limelight in April 1968.

In the early months of 1968, the sanitation workers of Memphis, most of whom were African Americans, went out on strike. In early April, Dr. King came to Memphis to lead a march by the striking workers; he stayed at the Lorraine Motel, just south of downtown. On April 4, the day the march was to be held, Dr. King stepped out onto the balcony of the motel and was gunned down by an assassin's bullet. Dr. King's murder did not, as perhaps had been hoped, end the civil rights movement. Today, the Lorraine Motel has become the National Civil Rights Museum. The museum preserves the room where Dr. King was staying the day he was assassinated and includes many evocative exhibits on the history of the civil rights movement. The museum recently received a major renovation and expansion.

By the time of Dr. King's murder, downtown Memphis was a classic example of urban decay. The city's more affluent citizens had moved to the suburbs in the post–World War II years, and the inner city had quickly become an area of abandoned buildings and empty storefronts. However, beginning in the 1970s, a growing desire to restore life to downtown Memphis saw renovation projects undertaken. By the 1980s, the renewal process was well under way, and the 1990s have seen a continuation of this slow but steady revitalization of downtown.

2 The Cradle of American Music

The blues, rock 'n' roll, and soul are sounds that defined Memphis music, and together these styles have made a name for Memphis all over the world. Never mind that the blues is no longer as popular as it once was, that Memphis long ago had its title of rock-'n'-roll capital usurped (by Cleveland, home of the Rock 'N' Roll Hall of Fame), and that soul music evolved into other styles. Memphis continues to be important to music lovers as the city from which these sounds first emanated.

The blues, the first truly American musical style, developed from work songs and spirituals common in the Mississippi Delta in the late 19th and early 20th centuries. But the roots of the blues go back even further, to traditional musical styles of Africa. During the 19th century, these musical traditions (brought to America by slaves) went through an interpretation and translation in the cotton fields and churches—the only places where African Americans could gather at that time. By the 1890s, freed slaves had brought their music of hard work and hard times into the nightclubs of Memphis.

BEALE STREET   It was here, on Beale Street, that black musicians began to fuse together the various aspects of the traditional music of the Mississippi Delta. In 1909, one of these musicians, a young bandleader named William Christopher Handy, was commissioned to write a campaign song for E. H. "Boss" Crump, who was running for mayor of Memphis. Crump won the election, and "Boss Crump's Blues" became a local hit. W. C. Handy later published his tune under the title "Memphis Blues." With the publication of this song, Handy started a musical revolution that continues to this day. The blues, which developed at about the same time that jazz was first being played down in New Orleans, would later give rise to both rock 'n' roll and soul music.

Beale Street became a center for musicians, who flocked to the area to learn the blues and showcase their own musical styles. Over the next 4 decades, Beale Street produced many of the country's most famous blues musicians. Among these was a young man named Riley King, who first won praise during an amateur music contest. In the 1940s, King became known as the Beale Street "Blues Boy," the initials of which he incorporated into his stage name when he began calling himself B. B. King. Today, B. B. King's Blues Club is Beale Street's most popular nightclub. Several times a year, King performs at the club, and the rest of the year blues bands keep up the Beale Street tradition. Other musicians to develop their style and their first followings on Beale Street include Furry Lewis, Muddy Waters, Albert King, Bobby "Blue" Bland, Alberta Hunter, and Memphis Minnie McCoy.

By the time B. B. King got his start on Beale Street, the area was beginning to lose its importance. The Great Depression shut down a lot of businesses on the street, and many never reopened. By the 1960s, there was talk of bulldozing the entire area to make way for an urban-renewal project. However, in the 1970s an interest in restoring old Beale Street developed. Beginning in 1980, the city of Memphis, together with business investors, began renovating the old buildings between Second and Fourth streets. New clubs and restaurants opened, and Beale Street once again became Memphis's main entertainment district. Today it's not just the blues, but rock, reggae, country, jazz, gospel, and folk that get played in Beale Street clubs.

HERE COMES THE KING   From the earliest days of Beale Street's musical popularity, whites visited the street's primarily black clubs. However, it wasn't until the late 1940s and early 1950s that a few adventurous white musicians began incorporating into their own music the earthy sounds and lyrics they heard on Beale Street. One of these musicians was a young man named Elvis Presley.

In the early 1950s, Sun Studio owner Sam Phillips began to record such Beale Street blues legends as B.B. King, Howlin' Wolf, Muddy Waters, and Little Milton, but his consumer market was limited to the African-American population. Phillips was searching for a way to take the blues to a mainstream (read: white) audience, and a new sound was what he needed. That new sound showed up at his door in 1954 in the form of a young delivery-truck driver named Elvis Presley, who, according to legend, had dropped in at Sun Studio to record a song as a birthday present for his mother. Phillips had already produced what many music scholars regard as the first rock-'n'-roll record when, in 1952, he recorded Jackie Brenston's "Rocket 88."

Two years later, when Elvis showed up at Sun Studio, Phillips knew that he had found what he was looking for. Within a few months of Elvis's visit to Sun Studio, three other musicians—Carl Perkins, Jerry Lee Lewis, and Johnny Cash—showed up independently of one another. Each brought his own interpretation of the crossover sound between the blues and country (or hillbilly) music. The sounds these four musicians crafted soon became known as rockabilly music, the foundation of rock 'n' roll. Roy Orbison would also get his start here at Sun Studio.

ROCK 'N' ROLL 'N' SOUL, TOO   In the early 1960s, Memphis once again entered the popular music limelight when Stax/Volt Records gave the country its first soul music. Otis Redding, Isaac Hayes, Booker T and the MGs, and Carla Thomas were among the musicians who got their start at this Memphis recording studio.

Some 10 years after Sun Studio made musical history, British bands such as The Beatles and The Rolling Stones latched onto the blues and rockabilly music and began exporting their take on this American music back across the Atlantic. With the music usurped by the British invasion, the importance of Memphis was quickly forgotten. Today, Memphis is no longer the musical innovator it once was, though in late 2003 city planners began strategizing on a bold new initiative to promote Memphis as the independent record label capital of the industry. Until that comes to pass, however, there's still an abundance of good music to be heard in its clubs. Musicians both young and old are keeping alive the music that put the city on the map.

3 Two Memphis Traditions: Pork Barbecue & the Meat-and-Three

Memphis's barbecue smoke is inescapable. It billows from chimneys all across the city, and though it is present all year long, it makes its biggest impact in those months when people have their car windows open. Drivers experience an inexplicable, almost Pavlovian response. They begin to salivate, their eyes glaze over, and they follow the smoke to its source—a down-home barbecue joint.

In a region obsessed with pork barbecue, Memphis lays claim to the title of being the pork-barbecue capital of the world. Non-Southerners may need a short barbecue primer. Southern pork barbecue is, for the most part, just exactly what its name says it is—pork that has been barbecued over a wood fire. There are several variations on barbecue, and most barbecue places offer the full gamut. Our personal favorite is hand-pulled shoulder, which is a barbecued shoulder of pork from which meat is pulled by hand after it's cooked. What you end up with on your plate is a pile of shredded pork to which you can add your favorite hot sauces.

Barbecued ribs are a particular Memphis specialty; these come either dry-cooked or wet-cooked. If you order your ribs dry-cooked, they come coated with a powdered spice mix and it's up to you to apply the sauce, but if you order it wet-cooked, the ribs will have been cooked in a sauce. Barbecue is tradition-ally served with a side of coleslaw (or mustard slaw) and perhaps baked beans or potato salad. In a pulled-pork-shoulder sandwich, the coleslaw goes in the sand-wich as a lettuce replacement. Corky's is the undisputed king of Memphis bar-becue, while the Rendezvous is famed for its dry-cooked ribs.

The city's other traditional fare is good old-fashioned American food—here, as in Nashville, known as "meat-and-three," a term that refers to the three side vegetables that you get with whatever type of meat you happen to order. While this is very simple food, in the best "meat-and-three" restaurants, your vegeta-bles are likely to be fresh (and there's always a wide variety of choices). Perhaps because of the Southern affinity for traditions, Memphians both young and old flock to "meat-and-three" restaurants for meals just like Mom used to fix.

Appendix D:
Useful Toll-Free Numbers
& Websites

AIRLINES

Air Canada
☏ 888/247-2262
www.aircanada.ca

Air New Zealand
☏ 800/262-1234 or
   800/262-2468 in the U.S.
☏ 800/663-5494 in Canada
☏ 0800/737-767 in New Zealand
www.airnewzealand.com

Alaska Airlines
☏ 800/426-0333
www.alaskaair.com

American Airlines
☏ 800/433-7300
www.aa.com

American Trans Air
☏ 800/225-2995
www.ata.com

America West Airlines
☏ 800/235-9292
www.americawest.com

British Airways
☏ 800/247-9297
☏ 0870/850-9850 in Britain
www.britishairways.com

Continental Airlines
☏ 800/525-0280
www.continental.com

Delta Air Lines
☏ 800/221-1212
www.delta.com

Midwest Express
☏ 800/452-2022
www.midwestexpress.com

Northwest Airlines
☏ 800/225-2525
www.nwa.com

Qantas
☏ 800/227-4500 or
   612/9691-3636 in Australia
www.qantas.com

Southwest Airlines
☏ 800/435-9792
www.southwest.com

United Airlines
☏ 800/241-6522
www.united.com

US Airways
☏ 800/428-4322
www.usairways.com

Virgin Atlantic Airways
☏ 800/862-8621 in continental U.S.
☏ 0293/747-747 in Britain
www.virgin-atlantic.com

CAR-RENTAL AGENCIES

Advantage
☏ 800/777-5500
www.advantagerentacar.com

Alamo
☏ 800/327-9633
www.alamo.com

Avis
☏ 800/331-1212 in continental U.S.
☏ 800/TRY-AVIS in Canada
www.avis.com

Budget
☏ 800/527-0700
www.budget.com

Dollar
© 800/800-4000
www.dollar.com

Enterprise
© 800/325-8007
www.enterprise.com

Hertz
© 800/654-3131
www.hertz.com

National
© 800/CAR-RENT
www.nationalcar.com

Payless
© 800/PAYLESS
www.paylesscarrental.com

Rent-A-Wreck
© 800/535-1391
www.rentawreck.com

Thrifty
© 800/367-2277
www.thrifty.com

MAJOR HOTEL & MOTEL CHAINS

Baymont Inns & Suites
© 800/301-0200
www.baymontinns.com

Best Western International
© 800/528-1234
www.bestwestern.com

Clarion Hotels
© 800/CLARION
www.hotelchoice.com

Comfort Inns
© 800/228-5150
www.hotelchoice.com

Courtyard by Marriott
© 800/321-2211
www.courtyard.com or
www.marriott.com

Days Inn
© 800/325-2525
www.daysinn.com

Doubletree Hotels
© 800/222-TREE
www.doubletree.com

Econo Lodges
© 800/55-ECONO
www.hotelchoice.com

Fairfield Inn by Marriott
© 800/228-2800
www.marriott.com

Hampton Inn
© 800/HAMPTON
www.hampton-inn.com

Hilton Hotels
© 800/HILTONS
www.hilton.com

Holiday Inn
© 800/HOLIDAY
www.basshotels.com

Howard Johnson
© 800/654-2000
www.hojo.com

Hyatt Hotels & Resorts
© 800/228-9000
www.hyatt.com

ITT Sheraton
© 800/325-3535
www.starwood.com

Knights Inn
© 800/843-5644
www.knightsinn.com

La Quinta Motor Inns
© 800/531-5900
www.laquinta.com

Marriott Hotels
© 800/228-9290
www.marriott.co'

Microtel Inn &
© 888/771-7'
www.microt‹

Motel 6
© 800/4·
　(800/
www.n

Quality Inns
© 800/228-5151
www.hotelchoice.com

Radisson Hotels International
© 800/333-3333
www.radisson.com

Ramada Inns
© 800/2-RAMADA
www.ramada.com

Red Carpet Inns
© 800/251-1962
www.reservahost.com

Red Lion Hotels & Inns
© 800/547-8010
www.hilton.com

Red Roof Inns
© 800/843-7663
www.redroof.com

Residence Inn by Marriott
© 800/331-3131
www.marriott.com

Rodeway Inns
© 800/228-2000
www.hotelchoice.com

Sleep Inn
© 800/753-3746
www.sleepinn.com

Super 8 Motels
© 800/800-8000
www.super8.com

Travelodge
© 800/255-3050
www.travelodge.com

Vagabond Inns
© 800/522-1555
www.vagabondinn.com

Wyndham Hotels and Resorts
© 800/822-4200 in continental U.S.
and Canada
www.wyndham.com

Index

See also Accommodations and Restaurant indexes, below.

ACCOMMODATIONS IN NASHVILLE

RESTAURANTS IN NASHVILLE

FROMMER'S® COMPLETE TRAVEL GUIDES

Alaska
Alaska Cruises & Ports of Call
Amsterdam
Argentina & Chile
Arizona
Atlanta
Australia
Austria
Bahamas
Barcelona, Madrid & Seville
Beijing
Belgium, Holland & Luxembourg
Bermuda
Boston
Brazil
British Columbia & the Canadian Rockies
Brussels & Bruges
Budapest & the Best of Hungary
California
Canada
Cancún, Cozumel & the Yucatán
Cape Cod, Nantucket & Martha's Vineyard
Caribbean
Caribbean Cruises & Ports of Call
Caribbean Ports of Call
Carolinas & Georgia
Chicago
China
Colorado
Costa Rica
Cuba
Denmark
Denver, Boulder & Colorado Springs
England
Europe
European Cruises & Ports of Call

Florida
France
Germany
Great Britain
Greece
Greek Islands
Hawaii
Hong Kong
Honolulu, Waikiki & Oahu
Ireland
Israel
Italy
Jamaica
Japan
Las Vegas
London
Los Angeles
Maryland & Delaware
Maui
Mexico
Montana & Wyoming
Montréal & Québec City
Munich & the Bavarian Alps
Nashville & Memphis
New England
New Mexico
New Orleans
New York City
New Zealand
Northern Italy
Norway
Nova Scotia, New Brunswick & Prince Edward Island
Oregon
Paris
Peru
Philadelphia & the Amish Country
Portugal

Prague & the Best of the Czech Republic
Provence & the Riviera
Puerto Rico
Rome
San Antonio & Austin
San Diego
San Francisco
Santa Fe, Taos & Albuquerque
Scandinavia
Scotland
Seattle & Portland
Shanghai
Sicily
Singapore & Malaysia
South Africa
South America
South Florida
South Pacific
Southeast Asia
Spain
Sweden
Switzerland
Texas
Thailand
Tokyo
Toronto
Tuscany & Umbria
USA
Utah
Vancouver & Victoria
Vermont, New Hampshire & Maine
Vienna & the Danube Valley
Virgin Islands
Virginia
Walt Disney World® & Orlando
Washington, D.C.
Washington State

FROMMER'S® DOLLAR-A-DAY GUIDES

Australia from $50 a Day
California from $70 a Day
England from $75 a Day
Europe from $70 a Day
Florida from $70 a Day
Hawaii from $80 a Day

Ireland from $60 a Day
Italy from $70 a Day
London from $85 a Day
New York from $90 a Day
Paris from $80 a Day

San Francisco from $70 a Day
Washington, D.C. from $80 a Day
Portable London from $85 a Day
Portable New York City from $90 a Day

FROMMER'S® PORTABLE GUIDES

Acapulco, Ixtapa & Zihuatanejo
Amsterdam
Aruba
Australia's Great Barrier Reef
Bahamas
Berlin
Big Island of Hawaii
Boston
California Wine Country
Cancún
Cayman Islands
Charleston
Chicago
Disneyland®
Dublin
Florence

Frankfurt
Hong Kong
Houston
Las Vegas
Las Vegas for Non-Gamblers
London
Los Angeles
Los Cabos & Baja
Maine Coast
Maui
Miami
Nantucket & Martha's Vineyard
New Orleans
New York City
Paris
Phoenix & Scottsdale

Portland
Puerto Rico
Puerto Vallarta, Manzanillo & Guadalajara
Rio de Janeiro
San Diego
San Francisco
Savannah
Seattle
Sydney
Tampa & St. Petersburg
Vancouver
Venice
Virgin Islands
Washington, D.C.

FROMMER'S® NATIONAL PARK GUIDES

Banff & Jasper
Family Vacations in the National Parks

Grand Canyon
National Parks of the American West
Rocky Mountain

Yellowstone & Grand Teton
Yosemite & Sequoia/Kings Canyon
Zion & Bryce Canyon

FROMMER'S® MEMORABLE WALKS

Chicago	New York	San Francisco
London	Paris	

FROMMER'S® WITH KIDS GUIDES

Chicago	Ottawa	Vancouver
Las Vegas	San Francisco	Washington, D.C.
New York City	Toronto	

SUZY GERSHMAN'S BORN TO SHOP GUIDES

Born to Shop: France	Born to Shop: Italy	Born to Shop: New York
Born to Shop: Hong Kong, Shanghai & Beijing	Born to Shop: London	Born to Shop: Paris

FROMMER'S® IRREVERENT GUIDES

Amsterdam	Los Angeles	San Francisco
Boston	Manhattan	Seattle & Portland
Chicago	New Orleans	Vancouver
Las Vegas	Paris	Walt Disney World®
London	Rome	Washington, D.C.

FROMMER'S® BEST-LOVED DRIVING TOURS

Britain	Germany	Northern Italy
California	Ireland	Scotland
Florida	Italy	Spain
France	New England	Tuscany & Umbria

HANGING OUT™ GUIDES

Hanging Out in England	Hanging Out in France	Hanging Out in Italy
Hanging Out in Europe	Hanging Out in Ireland	Hanging Out in Spain

THE UNOFFICIAL GUIDES®

Bed & Breakfasts and Country Inns in:
- California
- Great Lakes States
- Mid-Atlantic
- New England
- Northwest
- Rockies
- Southeast
- Southwest

Best RV & Tent Campgrounds in:
- California & the West
- Florida & the Southeast
- Great Lakes States
- Mid-Atlantic
- Northeast
- Northwest & Central Plains

- Southwest & South Central Plains
- U.S.A.

Beyond Disney
Branson, Missouri
California with Kids
Central Italy
Chicago
Cruises
Disneyland®
Florida with Kids
Golf Vacations in the Eastern U.S.
Great Smoky & Blue Ridge Region
Inside Disney
Hawaii
Las Vegas
London
Maui

Mexio's Best Beach Resorts
Mid-Atlantic with Kids
Mini Las Vegas
Mini-Mickey
New England & New York with Kids
New Orleans
New York City
Paris
San Francisco
Skiing & Snowboarding in the West
Southeast with Kids
Walt Disney World®
Walt Disney World® for Grown-ups
Walt Disney World® with Kids
Washington, D.C.
World's Best Diving Vacations

SPECIAL-INTEREST TITLES

Frommer's Adventure Guide to Australia & New Zealand
Frommer's Adventure Guide to Central America
Frommer's Adventure Guide to India & Pakistan
Frommer's Adventure Guide to South America
Frommer's Adventure Guide to Southeast Asia
Frommer's Adventure Guide to Southern Africa
Frommer's Britain's Best Bed & Breakfasts and Country Inns
Frommer's Caribbean Hideaways
Frommer's Exploring America by RV
Frommer's Fly Safe, Fly Smart

Frommer's France's Best Bed & Breakfasts and Country Inns
Frommer's Gay & Lesbian Europe
Frommer's Italy's Best Bed & Breakfasts and Country Inns
Frommer's Road Atlas Britain
Frommer's Road Atlas Europe
Frommer's Road Atlas France
The New York Times' Guide to Unforgettable Weekends
Places Rated Almanac
Retirement Places Rated
Rome Past & Present

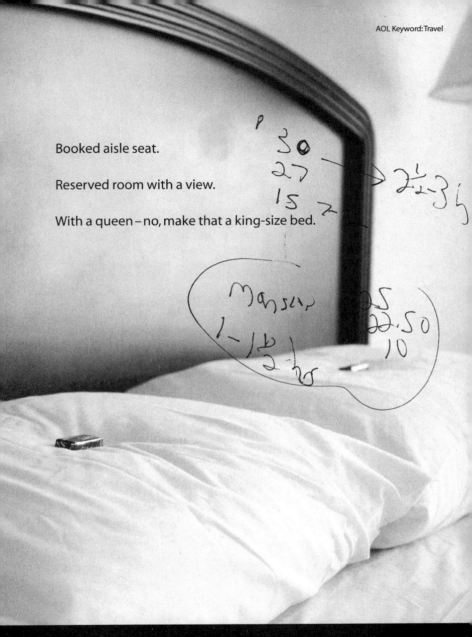

Fly.
Sleep.
Save.

Now you can book your flights and
hotels together, so you can get even better deals
than if you booked them separately.

Travelocity

**Visit www.travelocity.com
or call 1-888-TRAVELOCITY**

SHADOW
SQUADRON

STEEL HAMMER

STONE ARCH BOOKS
a capstone imprint

SHADOW
SQUADRON

STEEL
HAMMER

WRITTEN BY
CARL BOWEN

ILLUSTRATED BY
WILSON TORTOSA

AND
BENNY FUENTES

COVER ART BY
MARC LEE

2012.241

AUTHORIZING

Shadow Squadron is published by
Stone Arch Books,
A Capstone Imprint,
1710 Roe Crest Drive
North Mankato, MN 56003
www.capstonepub.com

Cataloging-in-Publication Data is available on the
Library of Congress website.

ISBN: 978-1-4965-0385-5 (library binding)
ISBN: 978-1-4965-0389-3 (paperback)

Summary: Shadow Squadron has never had an
easy mission, but under Lieutenant Commander
Ryan Cross's leadership, the team has routinely
achieved the impossible. But this time, the team
has an especially tall order: parachute onto a
moving train, secure a large cache of weapons, and
neutralize the elite ISIS soldiers on board.

Printed in China by Nordica
1116/CA21601670
102016 010084R

CONTENTS (316.98)

2012.101

SHADOW SQUADRON DOSSIER

CROSS, RYAN

RANK: Lieutenant Commander
BRANCH: Navy SEAL
PSYCH PROFILE: Cross is the team leader of Shadow Squadron. Control oriented and loyal, Cross insisted on hand-picking each member of his squad.

PHOTO NOT AVAILABLE

PAXTON, ADAM

RANK: Sergeant First Class
BRANCH: Army (Green Beret)
PSYCH PROFILE: Paxton has a knack for filling the role most needed in any team. His loyalty makes him a born second-in-command.

YAMASHITA, KIMIYO

RANK: Lieutenant
BRANCH: Army Ranger
PSYCH PROFILE: The team's sniper is an expert marksman and a true stoic. It seems his emotions are as steady as his trigger finger.

LANCASTER, MORGAN

RANK: Staff Sergeant
BRANCH: Air Force Combat Control
PSYCH PROFILE: The team's newest member is a tech expert who learns fast and has the ability to adapt to any combat situation.

PHOTO NOT AVAILABLE

JANNATI, ARAM

RANK: Second Lieutenant
BRANCH: Army Ranger
PSYCH PROFILE: Jannati serves as the team's linguist. His sharp eyes serve him well as a spotter, and he's usually paired with Yamashita on overwatch.

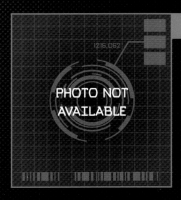

PHOTO NOT AVAILABLE

SHEPHERD, MARK

RANK: Lieutenant
BRANCH: Army (Green Beret)
PSYCH PROFILE: The heavy-weapons expert of the group, Shepherd's love of combat borders on unhealthy.

2019.681

CLASSIFIED

MISSION BRIEFING

STEEL HAMMER

012

Official orders have come down for us to travel to Iraq. The memo states we'll be training local forces to defend themselves from Islamic State insurgents, but that's just a cover story. Our actual assignment will be to sabotage ISIS equipment in order to interreupt their supply chain.

In short, we're going to be clogging the gears of their war machine. Stay sharp, people, or we'll get chewed up, too.

— Lieutenant Commander Ryan Cross

3245.98 ● ● ●

IRAQ

PRIMARY OBJECTIVE(S)

- Sabotage ISIS supply chain

- Rendezvous with Peshmerga forces

SECONDARY OBJECTIVE(S)

- Secure any munitions found

1932.789

0412.981

1624.054

INTEL

DECRYPTING
||||▬|||| ||▬||▬||||▬|||▬|||

12345

COM CHATTER

- ISIS: the terrorist organization Islamic State of Iraq and Syria. Also referred to as the Islamic State of Iraq and Levant, or the Islamic State of Iraq and al-Sham.

- KEVLAR: bullet-resistant fabric

- PESHMERGA: military force of Iraqi Kurdistan

- NEOPRENE: flexible synthetic rubber that prevents leaking

3245.98 ● ● ●

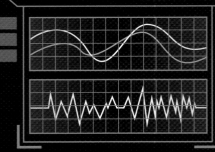

CHAPTER ONE

MOVING TARGETS

Lieutenant Commander Ryan Cross had done plenty of parachuting throughout his military career. From emergency bailouts to controlled insertions deep behind enemy lines, he'd handled jumps in all conditions under all sorts of circumstances. He'd never so much as bruised a heel on a jump. The idea that he might be scared to take the long fall was completely out of the question.

With all that said, Cross definitely had his misgivings about this particular jump.

One point against it was that he was behind enemy lines — *deep* behind enemy lines. He had no direct support from his government, only the aid of friendly local forces. Secondly, it was a night jump, which was more than a little risky over unfamiliar, unfriendly territory. Modern GPS and night-vision technology alleviated most of the foreseeable complications, but the risk was still there.

Lastly, this jump was a HALO jump — high-altitude, low-opening. Cross and his team had walked out of their MC130-J Commando II on a very precise schedule at some 30,000 feet and wouldn't open their chutes until they were only 2,500 feet off the ground. That left Cross very little time to react if his main chute's lines got tangled, or if the thing simply didn't deploy, and he had to activate his reserve chute.

But none of those factors concerned Cross too much. He'd done plenty of night jumps, HALO jumps, and jumps into enemy territory. No, his main area of concern was this mission's unusual landing zone: *the top of a moving train.*

This particular train was moving south through northern Iraq, from Mosul toward Baiji, but Cross meant to stop it well before it got to that city. The train was manned by members of the Islamic State terrorist group, ISIS. Its cargo included weapons, ammunition, and desperate prisoners all taken from central Iraq when ISIS had begun expanding its influence across that region.

ISIS's prisoners were packed into two passenger cars behind the engine. The next three boxcars were stacked high with crates of stolen war goods — much of which had come from the US in the first place. The rest of the cars were either tankers full of oil or flatbeds carrying pickup trucks, jeeps, and Humvees. Five guards rode outside the train. Mission intel suggested that at least another seven were positioned throughout the interior.

Four of the five exterior guards were positioned on top of the train in teams of two. They were placed behind heavy machine guns mounted on tripods, which were surrounded by sandbag barriers. One gun stood atop the first prisoner car. The second gun stood atop the last car full of weapons. The last exterior guard sat at ease at the very rear of the train, smoking a cigarette as he dangled his feet above

the tracks. An AK-47 lay across his lap. None of the guards outside had yet noticed Cross or his team approaching. Things were about to get ugly.

Taking a slow, calming breath, Cross tapped the touchscreen of the datapad bound to the inside of his left forearm in a Kevlar and neoprene bracer. On it was an altimeter reading at the top and a circle with the words "Go Time" written in the center. The altimeter reading turned from green to yellow to red, and then the circle turned red as well. Both began to flash.

Cross tapped the screen right in the center of the circle. That sent the message to the other three soldiers falling behind him, as well as to the overwatch team waiting on a rise about 500 yards away from the landing zone. The train was still well behind them and the jumpers were still well more than 2000 feet above the ground. But according to the math, it was now or never.

"Go time," he said into the mouthpiece of his oxygen bottle. The old thrill rose within him. It heated his blood and sharpened his senses to battle readiness as he yanked the ripcord.

* * *

The team Cross led was codenamed Shadow Squadron: a covert, black-tier, special missions unit of the US armed forces. Formed by and answering to the Joint Special Operations Command of the greater US Special Operations Command, the eight-soldier team consisted of the cream of the elite of special operations soldiers from all four branches of the military. Cross was a Navy SEAL, but he commanded Green Berets, Army Rangers, a Marine from the Special Operations Regiment, an Air Force Combat Controller, and even a former CIA operative from the agency's Special Activities Division.

Together, the team took on assignments in situations or areas where the US military had an interest but couldn't be seen taking direct action. Shadow Squadron's existence was secret, its tech was top of the line, and its budget was astronomical and well camouflaged. It was no surprise that the team's mission record was nearly spotless.

Cross had lost men to death, injury, and even a better job offer, but his team always got the job done.

They'd fought pirates off the coast of Somalia, human traffickers in Mali, drug-runners in Colombia, rogue American mercenaries in the Gulf of Mexico, Russian Spetznaz in the bitter cold of Antarctica, and a whole rogues' gallery of criminals, terrorists, and other enemies of the state all around the world.

Like avenging ghosts, the squad went where it was needed, did what it was called upon to do, and disappeared.

Cross's time with Shadow Squadron was the high mark of his career, the service he was most proud of. It didn't bother him that he earned no glory in the work due to the highly secret and sensitive nature of his assignments. That wasn't why he did the job. Knowing that he had led his team with honor, courage, and professionalism was more than enough of a reward for him.

Well, that and the times he got to feed his inner adrenaline junkie by doing something like HALO-jumping behind enemy lines onto the back of a moving train in the dead of night.

* * *

With Cross in the sky were Sergeant First Class Adam Paxton, a Green Beret, and Cross's second in command; Sergeant Mark Shepherd, another Green Beret; and Second Lieutenant Aram Jannati from the Marine Special Operations Regiment.

Upon receiving the "Go Time" signal, all four men opened their chutes at once and pitched themselves downward over the railroad tracks. Cross took the sudden kick of deceleration like a boxer taking a shot in the gut. He got his descent under control ahead of them. He didn't have much time to line up, match speed, and aim for a flat part of the train. Fortunately, the train wasn't going terribly fast, so landing on it wasn't going to feel *too* much like getting hit by a speeding car.

Unfortunately, the sound of the engine and the rumble and clack of the wheels on the tracks weren't enough to mask the sound of four parachutes popping so low overhead. As Cross craned his neck to look at the train coming up below and behind them, he saw the men at the machine gun nests bolt upright and begin looking around frantically. He couldn't spare more than a moment to take note, though, as the ground was rushing up awfully fast and the train's engine compartment was just passing below him.

No time to worry about the machine gunners, he thought. *Focus. Focus . . .*

All at once, Cross hauled backward on his jump rigging, lurched out of his breakneck dive, and swung forward beneath his parachute like a kid on a playground. Hoping he'd judged his momentum correctly, Cross cut away the parachute right at the edge of the forward swing so that all of his momentum continued to carry him forward along with the direction of the train. He'd practiced the maneuver dozens of times in preparation for the mission, but even though he now pulled it off just as he'd practiced, he hit the train an awful lot harder than he expected.

THUD!

The impact knocked the wind out of him. He wasted precious seconds gasping for air that wouldn't come. He got up to a knee with a wall of gray closing in around his vision, his hands numbly trying to unsling his M4 carbine from its rig. The landing had left him one boxcar away from the forward machine gun position. As his black silk parachute drifted away into the night, he saw one of the two ISIS men in their sandbag nest looking at him in stupefied awe. The other man awkwardly swung his M60E4 machine gun around to take aim.

* * *

Salvation came from 500 yards away in the darkness. From a blind on a rise overlooking the train tracks, Lieutenant Kimiyo Yamashita — an Army Ranger and the team's primary sniper — lay hidden on overwatch along with Staff Sergeant Morgan Lancaster — a USAF Combat Controller. Staring down the night-sights of the Leupold scope mounted atop his M110 sniper rifle, Yamashita squeezed off a single shot. His bullet neutralized the man at the forward machine gun as a threat.

From Cross's perspective, there was no muzzle flash and no sound of a shot. One moment the man was bringing his machine gun to bear, the next he'd slumped forward over it.

For her part, Lancaster neutralized the other three Islamic State men atop the train with a single touch on the tablet computer before her. The device was connected wirelessly to three extremely advanced weapons systems called autoguns. They were set up around the overwatch position, each with an M110 sniper rifle settled into a nest of servos and actuators. They could move them smoothly and quickly across a range of 45 degrees up, down, left, or right from their starting positions.

Atop each rifle was a $10,000 three-lens rifle scope that included state-of-the-art range-finding and tracking hardware and a high-definition infrared camera. All of it was connected back to Lancaster's tablet. With the device, she could mark a target in each scope's field of vision, set the autoguns to track said targets, and command them to fire with a simple tap on the screen.

As she made that tap now, the other three ISIS soldiers at the two machine gun sites fell dead at their posts. It had been only seconds after they'd realized that five armed men were parachuting onto the top of their train.

"Got my three," Lancaster said to Yamashita with a self-satisfied grin. They watched as one of the two men she'd shot off the rear machine gun nest slumped over and rolled off the side of the train. "How you doing, John Henry?"

Lancaster's playful tone annoyed Yamashita, but he kept his eyes glued to his Leupold scope, watching the Islamic State man at the rear of the train. That man hadn't noticed the four Shadow Squadron soldiers landing atop the cars, but he certainly did notice when the body of one of his comrades bounced past him on the ground and rolled away from the train. Grabbing up his rifle in a panic, the man stood and began to make his way across the last flatbed toward the front of the train to investigate. Sighting down on him, Yamashita pulled the trigger.

POP!

"Don't brag," he said softly as the last guard fell dead, leaving a gruesome smear across the back bumper of the stolen Humvee lashed to the flatbed in front of him. "Your computer's doing the hard part for you."

Lancaster let out a low, impressed whistle through her teeth. "Show-off," she whispered.

Yamashita gave her a nod and tapped the two-way canalphone nestled in his left ear.

* * *

"Clear," overwatch reported.

Cross tapped his canalphone as he climbed to his feet, finally able to take a breath. "Roger that," he said, sucking wind. "Police your gear and rendezvous with Clean-Up."

"Sir," Yamashita's voice replied in his ear. "Out."

Cross surveyed the top of the train through the lens of his AN/PSQ-20 night-vision system while unslinging his M4 and sliding a round into the chamber. Farther back he could see Paxton double-checking the two dead men at the second machine gun nest. Shepherd was climbing up on the back of the rear weapons car. Jannati was moving forward across the top of the nearest oil tanker car.

"Fireteam, we're clear," Cross said, relaying overwatch's report to the other three men. "Status report?"

"Fine, sir," Paxton said.

"I'm all right," Shepherd said. He sounded as jacked up on adrenaline as Cross felt. "Nearly missed the train, but I got a toe on it at the last second. Holy cow, man. Whose idea was this, anyway?"

Yours, you ham, Cross thought with a wry grin.

"My cutaway got stuck for a second," Jannati reported from the rear of the train. "I missed by a couple of cars, but I'm coming up now."

"Eyes open," Cross said. "No way they missed us thumping down on top of this thing. When they don't hear from their friends, they're going to send somebody up to investigate."

As if on cue, a cell phone next to the dead machine gunner lit up and started buzzing.

"Gather up," Cross said. "And get ready."

"Sir," the men responded.

Moments later, the other three soldiers joined up with Cross. Fortunately, no one from inside the train had emerged to investigate the noise they made coming together.

However, both dead machine gunners' cell phones started ringing.

"Listen up, here's the play," Cross said quickly and quietly. "I'm going forward to secure the engine. I want you —" he pointed at Shepherd "—to come down the back of this car and get ready by the door."

Shepherd nodded.

Cross looked at Paxton and Jannati, "I want you two on the second car, one on each end. On my signal, we all go in together, neutralize the IS targets, and secure the prisoners. When that's done, I'll come back and stop the train. After that, we'll sweep and clear the boxcars. When there's nobody left, we'll call for Clean-Up. Everybody got it?"

His men nodded.

"Let's do it."

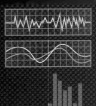

DECRYPTING

12345

COM CHATTER

- AL-QAEDA: a global terrorist organization

- CALIPH: a political and religious leader believed to be the successor to Mohammed, the Koran's prophet

- IED: Improvised Explosive Device, which is a handmade bomb

3245.98 ● ● ●

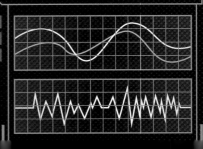

CHAPTER TWO

OIL AND RELIGION

The assignment that had given rise to Shadow Squadron's current mission in Iraq had come to them some weeks ago. Back home at the team's stateside headquarters and command center, Cross came into his mission briefing room with Paxton, his second, at his side. The other six members of the team were already there and waiting around the conference table. Paxton headed for his seat by the head of the table, dragging a finger across the tablet computer screen recessed into the table's surface. The touchscreen blinked to life, as did the computer whiteboard on the wall at the far end of the room. Both screens displayed the sword-and-globe emblem of Joint Special Operations Command.

"Morning," Cross said, moving to the head of the room to stand before the whiteboard. "Some of you have heard the rumors already, but let me be the first to confirm them for you. Orders have come down for a long-term deployment. We're going to Iraq as part of the 300."

From the opposite end of the table, Shepherd was the first to react. He sat up straight with a big grin and immediately began quoting lines from a similarly named movie he loved.

"This is where we fight," he growled in a cartoonish imitation of the main character's accent.

"This is where they die!" Jannati chimed in. He was almost as big a fan of the movie as Shepherd.

"Give them nothing," Shepherd said, nodding at Jannati.

"But take from them everything!" Jannati said.

Paxton glanced their way. "Guys, settle down," he said. Paxton didn't raise his voice or so much as frown at them. He simply let the gravity of his tone do all the work.

"Sorry," Jannati said, still grinning.

Around the table, the others' reactions were mixed. Lancaster simply nodded, accepting the news. Williams wrinkled his nose like he'd smelled something bad. Carter Howard — the team's newest member, on permanent loan from the CIA's Special Activities Division — rolled his eyes, shook his head, and smirked.

The most telling and subtle reaction came from Yamashita. For a moment, the sniper's eyes focused inward, and he clenched his jaw so hard that the muscles around it stood out in hard white knobs. His lip twitched in what might have grown into a snarl. His eyebrows drew together for just a fraction of a second. The whole expression came and went in a blink before the sniper's usual calm, professional façade returned — but not before Cross saw it play out on the stoic soldier's face.

Cross could hardly fault Yamashita for the anger and distaste. To dramatically understate the case, the United States had a complicated relationship with the nation of Iraq. From the 1960s to the 1990s,

foreign affairs between the two had swung back and forth from the US arming Kurdish rebels in their fight against Iraq's dictatorial anti-Western government to supplying Iraq with chemical weapons to use against their neighbor Iran. In the early '90s, the US even took up arms against Iraq directly when Iraq tried to annex and conquer its southern neighbor Kuwait in an attempt to seize Kuwait's oil wealth in order to pay off Iraq's vast war debts.

The short war that ensued resulted in Iraq's inferior armed forces being pushed back out of Kuwait, as well as a cease-fire agreement that called for the destruction of Iraq's chemical weapons arsenal, regular inspections by the United Nations, and a no-fly zone enforced by US air power.

Iraq's tyrannical leader, Saddam Hussein, remained in power, however. The US allowed him to do pretty much whatever he wanted within Iraq itself. While the CIA covertly funded, armed, and trained dissident groups within Iraq, the US did nothing when Hussein brutally cracked down and killed his own people to maintain his power. The prevailing attitude from the United States seemed to be that it wanted Saddam Hussein removed from power, but it would rather the Iraqis did the job themselves. The most the US did from the end of the war to the end of the century was repeatedly warn Iraq about its failure to comply with the terms of the war's cease-fire agreement.

Relations between Iraq and the US steadily worsened. Unable to deny or ignore the way Saddam Hussein ruled Iraq, American President George W. Bush decided that the time had come to remove Hussein from power. He tried to make the argument that removing Hussein made America itself safer because then Iraq wouldn't be able to use its hidden stockpile of chemical weapons or supply them to terrorists who could use them against America itself (this despite the fact that there was no conclusive evidence that Iraq had such weapons any longer).

When diplomacy finally broke down for good, the US led a coalition of allied nations against the armies of Iraq. As before, the vastly superior coalition forces quickly prevailed, toppling the Iraqi regime and capturing Iraq's capital.

In a perfect world, that would have been the

end of the matter. But rather than surrendering, forces loyal to the Iraqi regime splintered and hid throughout the nation, leading guerilla attacks against the occupying forces.

Making matters worse, certain terrorist groups — Al-Qaeda not the least among them — sent weaponry and soldiers into Iraq to aid the deposed insurgents. Its government in ruins, Iraq plunged into a state of civil war.

For the next eight years, American combat forces remained in Iraq. Their supposed mission was to help maintain the peace, see to the safe installation of a new and democratically elected Iraqi government, and train the new Iraqi army to defend itself against the lingering insurgency. That latter goal, however, largely failed thanks to the ferocity and bloody-minded determination of the insurgents.

As the US commitment in Iraq dragged on, support for it faded away back home. President Bush left office, and his successor, President Barack Obama, campaigned on the promise of ending the conflict there and bringing all the troops home at long last.

For all of the previous three Presidents' high-minded talk of the need to end Saddam Hussein's tyranny and free the people of Iraq, the American people's patience was at an end. They wanted their sons and daughters and husbands and wives back home and out of harm's way once and for all. The final withdrawal of American forces from Iraq finally came at the dawn of the 21st century's second decade. It was a welcome relief to those waiting ever so anxiously for loved ones to return home.

Cross himself had spent much of his time with the SEALs in Iraq helping to root out insurgents. Most of the members of his new team had done so as well in their various capacities with their own branches of the military.

Howard had actually been there before the fighting started, helping the SAD lay the groundwork for the invasion. They knew firsthand the drudgery and monotony of fighting an invisible guerilla army for the sake of people who viewed them as interlopers and occupiers. They had seen the worst sorts of people thriving in the postwar chaos, exploiting their own people's fear and weakness and greed and religious intolerance for their own ends. Although Cross and the others had never grown tired of doing their duty, neither had they been unwilling to see that duty come to an end.

Only it wasn't really over. Now, with combat operations and the full withdrawal in the past, US troops were returning once again to Iraq. They were intended to act only as advisors and trainers for the local forces, and there were only to be some 300 or so of them. Nevertheless, the deployment was yet one more sign that America's long and complicated relationship with Iraq was far from resolved or finished.

"Begging your pardon, Commander," Shepherd said before Cross could continue, "but advising and training isn't really our strong suit."

"True," Cross said, though it technically wasn't true. Aiding and training foreign local forces was one of the core competencies of a modern special operations soldier. What Shepherd meant was that although Shadow Squadron could ably fill that role, that wasn't the sort of assignment Command generally gave them. "The truth is, we're not going to teach the locals how to do their jobs. We're going to help them swat down some noisy troublemakers once and for all. It's outside the letter of what the President says we 300 are going for, but he's not naïve. He knows this is something that needs to get done, so he wants it done right."

He paused, watching the others around the table nod — all except Yamashita. He stared blankly at the table, quietly absorbing the information like a machine.

"The problem," Cross continued, "is the terrorist group calling itself Islamic State, formerly the Islamic State of Iraq and al-Sham (Levant), or ISIS."

Cross tapped the tactical datapad strapped to his forearm and swiped a file to the touchscreen on the tabletop. A second tap brought up a recent photo on the computer whiteboard. The team saw a man in the black robes, beard, and hat of a Muslim priest. He was standing in front of an oscillating fan on the balcony of a mosque in Iraq. A pair of microphones stood before him as he gave a speech to the cameras below.

"Islamic State is led by this man," Cross went on. "Abu Bakr al-Baghdadi. He has a list of terrorist activities going back to before the invasion in 2003. We actually had him in custody for a while in 2004, but he was released and went right back to doing what he was good at. By 2010, he was the leader of Al-Qaeda in Iraq, responsible for car bombings, kidnappings, suicide bombings, IEDs — you name it. A few years later, he tried to expand his organization into Syria to profit on the civil war going on there. Without actually asking anybody, he tried to claim that Al-Qaeda in Iraq was going to be incorporating another terrorist group, Al-Nusra Front, into one organization under his leadership."

"Rude," Williams said. "Even for a terrorist."

Cross nodded. "Al-Nusra publicly rejected him for it. In fact, his methods and theology were so extreme that *Al-Qaeda* kicked him out. Not that it did much good. He'd built up enough followers by then to form his own splinter group: ISIS. Al-Baghdadi's stated goal is to establish a caliphate — an Islamic theocracy — across Syria and Iraq. Of course, he would be the head, as caliph. His group has dug its roots in deep in Syria, pushing Al-Nusra out of most of Syria and keeping President Assad's government forces out as well."

"Isn't that what we wanted?" Jannati asked. "I thought our government wanted Assad out. Weren't we on Al-Nusra's side?"

"We were on the side of the Free Syrian Army," Paxton said. "That was before Al-Nusra infiltrated it and took it over in the name of Al-Qaeda. But even though ISIS was separate from Al-Nusra, that doesn't make it better. It's a militant, extremist Sunni cult. When it moves into an area, it kills non-Sunnis, publicly rounds up anyone who raises objections, then establishes harsh Sharia laws."

"Wait," Jannati said, a look of bitter realization dawning on his face. "Were these guys connected to our White Needle situation when we were deployed in Syria?"

Not long ago, Shadow Squadron had been in Syria trying to capture two terrorists who were fleeing justice in Afghanistan and Iraq. The pair had planned to launch a stolen chemical warhead into a civilian population. The part of the whole scenario that had baffled and infuriated Jannati at the time was that the town in the warhead's sights was controlled by rebels already. Prisoners captured after the attack was foiled had claimed that the group wanted to blame Syrian President Assad for the attack in hopes of motivating the US military to step in and help them. Of course, this was before it became common knowledge that President Assad had already been using banned chemical weapons to suppress the rebellion all along.

"We think so," Cross said. "Looking back over the evidence, our analysts have come to believe that the attack was actually planned by ISIS agents to punish Al-Nusra for defying Al-Baghdadi."

Yamashita let out a sharp sigh of disgust and scowled at the table. A few of the others glanced at him, but no one said anything.

"In any case," Cross said, "Islamic State is a bigger threat now than it's ever been. It captured and now controls half the border between Iraq and Syria. A swath of northern Syria is theirs, and they're determined to march on Baghdad. Working with Sunnis across the nation, they've already seized Fallujah, Tikrit and Mosul. They're practically running the regular Iraqi army out of town without a fight. They're extremely well organized, and their early victories have allowed them to seize a treasure-trove of weapons and vehicles."

"Weapons and vehicles we left for the Iraqis," Yamashita said softly.

Cross nodded. "Taking Mosul also gave them access to the city's banks, from which the group stole more than $400 million in cash. It was well funded before, but now they have real spending power. ISIS is all over various social media sites, putting out propaganda and recruiting newcomers from all over the world. It's got the guns to put in their hands when they show up and more than enough money to feed and take care of them. From its perspective, Islamic State has nothing to worry about — its caliphate is right around the corner."

Cross paused and took a breath. "It's our job to make sure they understand just how wrong they are. Everybody got that?"

"Hoorah!" the others around the table replied — except Yamashita. He remained silently staring at the tabletop.

"Hoorah," Cross said back. "Now get your gear. We're on a plane in two hours. You're dismissed."

The team stood, excited chatter bubbling up around the table. As the others filed out, Yamashita drifted along with them, not saying anything. Cross frowned, watching him from where he stood at the head of the table. Just before the sniper left the briefing room, Cross made a decision.

"Kim," Cross said, "hang back a second."

Yamashita waited until everyone else was gone, then shut the door. He came back to his seat and stood behind it with no expression on his face.

"Commander?" he asked.

"You've got a problem with this new assignment," Cross said.

"No, sir."

"That wasn't a question, Lieutenant. The others don't read you that well, but I do. You had a real

43

problem with our last mission in Iraq. I know you haven't forgotten our chat about it."

Yamashita clenched his jaw again and broke eye contact. It took him a moment to reply. "I did have a problem, but I got it squared away. I assumed you and I had an understanding about it."

"We do," Cross said, softening a little. "But that doesn't mean you're automatically fine. You tensed up as soon as the word Iraq came out of my mouth. Talk to me."

Yamashita took a deep breath that did little to calm him. The sniper gripped the back of his chair in white-knuckled fingers and snorted like a bull working himself up to charge.

"What is it about that place?" he said evenly. "About all those places? Why do we care so much about these deserts full of oil and religion? We keep putting weapons in the wrong people's hands, expecting them to make their lives better somehow, but they only end up hating us. It never changes. It just goes around and around forever. Are we supposed to accept that? Does Command really expect us to keep putting our lives on the line just because nobody can figure out how to get us off the treadmill of history?"

"I don't have the answers you want," Cross said, "though I wish I did. I don't know why we keep repeating our old mistakes. Maybe it's human nature."

Yamashita closed his eyes in defeat. Clearly he'd been hoping to hear something wiser or more definitive than what Cross offered.

"But there's something I do know," Cross pushed on. "People like you and me, we can't indulge ourselves with the high-minded ideals of the big picture. At our level, we don't have that luxury."

The sniper frowned, looking down at the desk once more.

"We can't obsess over what's out of our control," Cross continued. "Our job's too hard without that kind of distraction looming over us. We have to focus on the assignments in front of us. *Getting the job done, keeping each other safe.* It's up to us to play our parts and play them right. It's up to Command and the politicians to make sure those parts add up to something better than what we started with."

"But is that enough for you, Commander?" Yamashita asked. "Is that faith enough for you to keep risking your life out there?"

"That isn't why I'm willing to risk my life in the field, Lieutenant," Cross said.

Yamashita tilted his head. "So why do you?" he asked.

"Think about it," Cross said with a nod. "I'm pretty sure you already know the answer. When you figure it out, it'll answer your questions a lot better than I can."

"Let's hope so, Commander," the sniper said.

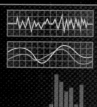

INTEL

DECRYPTING
IIIIIIIIIII IIIIIIIIIIIIIIIIIII

12345

COM CHATTER

- HUMVEE: military vehicle that combines the features of a jeep with a light truck.

- M84 GRENADE: stun grenade

- MANIFEST: list of things or people aboard a given ship

- PESHMERGA: Kurdish forces of Iraqi Kurdistan

3245.98 ● ● ●

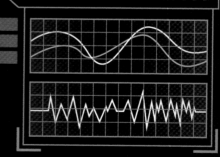

CHAPTER THREE

LOCAL FORCES

On the train . . .

Securing and stopping the train took ten tense minutes of work. Cross and his men moved quickly and with grim determination through the engine compartment and passenger cars. They caught the Islamic State militants by surprise and took them down before they had a chance to raise an alarm. The sound and flash suppressors on the team's M4 carbines kept the people in one car from knowing what was happening in the others.

Cross, Paxton, Shepherd, and Jannati entered the passenger cars, identified the enemy militants, and eliminated them fast enough to negate any risk to their prisoners.

However, the second goal — actually stopping the train — proved more diffcult than Cross was expecting. He connected the feed from his helmet camera to Lancaster's tablet, which enabled her to see what he was seeing. In short order, she was able to walk Cross through the necessary steps to shut the engine down.

That left only the last few guards remaining. They were hidden away in the boxcars, watching over the Islamic State's shipment of stolen weapons and other equipment.

Two of the guards left their posts when the train stopped, coming forward to see what the problem was. They walked right into Jannati and Shepherd's field of fire. The last guard saw what happened to his comrades and tried to barricade himself inside the boxcar. Luckily, Paxton managed to get an M84 stun grenade through the sliding door just before the guard slammed it shut.

FOOOOM!

The flashbang went off right at the militant's feet, disorienting him just long enough for the fire team to move up on him and surround him. Taking him prisoner would have been ideal, but when they burst in on him, they found him sitting on the floor at the rear of the boxcar with an open and overturned box of frag grenades on his lap. Bleeding from his nose and staring blindly in the direction he felt his enemies were coming from, he snatched up one of the grenades and rushed to yank off the safety clip.

BANG!

BANG!

BANG!

BANG!

Four shots rang out as one. The man lay still. The grenade rolled out of his limp fingers, the pin still firmly in place.

"Clear," Cross said.

Shepherd confirmed that the other boxcar was clear, too. No guards remained. The train was theirs.

"Call Clean-Up," Cross said.

"Sir," Paxton said.

"Inventory," Cross said to Shepherd as the four of them climbed back out of the train. "Look for a manifest. If not, just give me your best guess."

"Sir," Shepherd said.

"With me," Cross said to Jannati, leading him toward the passenger cars. Together, the two of them dragged the dead men out of the cars and moved them away from the tracks. Then they gathered the dazed, abused, and shell-shocked prisoners together under the stars. Jannati began trying to explain that they'd been rescued and that everything was going to be all right. Most of them simply stared at him without a word, either due to shock or mistrust.

The bravest of them turned out to be a French Iraqi woman in her early thirties who stepped forward as their representative. She explained that she'd been working with a team of investigators from Human Rights Watch. They'd been trying to document and expose the cruel abuses perpetrated by ISIS as its campaign of terror and conquest spread across Iraq. Many of the prisoners, like her, had been rounded up for speaking out against what ISIS was doing. Others were Shiites or Christians who'd been arrested for not being Sunnis but had promised to convert in order to save their lives. Still others had been branded criminals for breaking the strict tenets of sharia law that Islamic State had put into place. Some had no idea why they'd been rounded up. All of them had been detained in secret facilities in their hometowns where Islamic State was now in command, until that very morning when they'd all been loaded onto this train. Many assumed they were being transferred to an Islamic State prison in Baiji.

More likely, as the Human Rights Watch investigator quietly told Cross, they were being taken to an isolated location where they were going to be executed and their bodies hidden away in a mass grave. It wouldn't have been the first time that ISIS had rid itself of dissidents in such a way. She'd investigated and reported on two such sites herself — one in Syria, one in Iraq — before her capture. Knowing what she knew, it was nothing short of a miracle to her that she was still alive. That Cross and his soldiers had come when they did to free them was, she said, a miracle heaped on top of another miracle.

"Still working on that last part," Cross told her. "You think you can keep these people calm and focused and get them to come with us without a lot of fuss?"

"Maybe," she said. "Where will you take us?"

"Erbil," Cross told her.

She nodded, satisfied with the answer. Erbil lay in Iraqi Kurdistan, some 30 miles north and east of their current location. It was the largest city in that region and had thus far kept ISIS out while allowing refugees from the Islamic State's brutality to find safety within.

"I can do this," she said. "My name is Miriam, by the way."

"A pleasure to meet you, Ma'am," Cross said. "Now get them ready. We're leaving as soon as Clean-Up gets here."

Clean-Up referred to the unit consisting of the rest of Cross's team, as well as local Peshmerga forces helping out with the operation. The Peshmerga, literally translated as "those who confront death," were the local military of Iraqi Kurdistan. Less formally, the term also applied to any Kurd willing to take up arms to fight for Kurdish rights in Iraq.

The Peshmerga were no strangers to working with American military forces. They'd aided US troops throughout the invasion and subsequent insurgency. Their assistance had proven instrumental in the capture of Saddam Hussein. They'd even had a hand in capturing a crucial Al-Qaeda figure, which had contributed to the successful hunt for Osama bin Laden.

These days, with much of the regular Iraqi army in a shambles after a series of quick and demoralizing defeats by ISIS, it was the Peshmerga who were best able to stand up to the Islamic State and protect their citizens from its advances and abuses. Sunni, Shiite, Christian, Assyrian, Turkmen — they did what they could to protect them all, and they did it well. In fact, it was information from the Peshmerga that had enabled Cross's team to locate and intercept this train. And it would be the Peshmerga whom Cross counted on to protect these would-be prisoners from the Islamic State, assuming he could get everyone safely into Erbil.

The wait for Clean-Up was longer than Cross anticipated. Meanwhile, Shepherd finished his inventory. Cross and Miriam explained to the prisoners where they were headed and did what they could to answer questions, except when the questions had to do with Shadow Squadron itself.

Jannati kept a lookout. Paxton gathered up all the Islamic State militants' cell phones and took them into the train's engine compartment. He stayed by the radio and monitored the cells in an attempt to intercept any useful communications.

The Peshmerga soldiers and the rest of Cross's team showed up in three Russian-made military vehicles. Two of them were desert-camo Ural 5323 trucks. The third was a flat tan GAZ-66. The Urals were 8x8 troop transports with canvas shells over the backs. The GAZ was a smaller 4x4 with an open back that was full of soldiers. Most of them were locals, though Carter Howard sat back there with them, making them laugh. He'd worked with many of the men before and during the war, and he'd been Shadow Squadron's point of contact with them when the team had arrived.

Williams, the medic, was in the passenger seat. Yamashita and Lancaster emerged together from the back of one of the Urals. With everyone present, Shadow Squadron, the leaders of the Peshmerga platoon, Miriam, and a few inquisitive prisoners collected around Cross. Only Paxton stayed out of the huddle.

"The boxcars aren't full, but it's a good haul," Shepherd said, handing Cross a clipboard he'd found on the train. "It's mostly crates of assault rifles and ammunition, plus some lighter anti-armor and anti-personnel weapons."

Cross handed the clipboard to the leader of the Peshmerga, a lieutenant with a bald head and the lower half of one ear missing. The lieutenant frowned at it then looked at the prisoners and frowned at them too.

"Too much here for one trip," he said.

"We can get all the civilians in one Ural," Cross said. "Load up as much off the train as you can in the other one and the GAZ. We'll get the Humvees off the train, and my team will take those. We'll all make for Erbil and decide —"

"My men will take the Humvees," the Peshmerga lieutenant cut in. "They, the GAZ, and the cargo are going east into Kirkuk. We have brothers in arms there still fighting to push Islamic State out. They need what we have here more than those in Erbil."

"Qasem, this isn't what we agreed on," Howard said, trying to keep his voice friendly and reasonable. "You said —"

"We'll leave you the second Ural to take these here to safety," the lieutenant said to Cross, ignoring Howard. "We'll be back for it in the morning."

"Is this why you agreed to help us?" Cross asked, his voice low and even despite what he was thinking. "You just wanted the weapons? You knew there were civilians involved."

"I didn't know there were so many," the lieutenant said, looking down at the clipboard. Whether he meant prisoners or weapons, Cross couldn't tell. "Anyway, these are our vehicles. I decide how they are used."

"Those Humvees are US military equipment," Jannati said, scowling.

"True," the lieutenant said. "But there are many more of us here than there are of you, young man. And none of you are supposed to be here in the first place."

Howard flinched as if he'd been slapped. "Qasem! Are you seriously going to —"

"Sir?" Paxton cut in, joining the group in a hurry with a worried look on his face. "Problem." A tense silence fell over the others.

"What is it?" Cross asked, continuing to glare at the Peshmerga lieutenant.

"Communications from Mosul and Baiji have cut off," Paxton explained. "They stopped asking for the engineer over the radio. A whole bunch of calls and texts went out to the militants' phones from the same three numbers, asking what was going on and why nobody was answering. Then all the calls stopped, and nobody's tried again for five minutes. They know something's wrong."

"They will likely be here soon," Qasem said, a satisfied smile on his face. "Will you accept the loan of my truck, or would you and yours like to walk these people to Erbil?"

"We'll take it," Cross said through clenched teeth. "But don't think this will be forgotten."

"Was that an implied threat, Commander?" Qasem asked. "I think you would remember that this is not America's war anymore."

With that, Qasem walked away, drawing the rest of his men with him. He began giving orders, but his people had already started moving the weapons and other gear from the train to the Ural closest to it. Others leaped up onto the flatbeds and began untethering the stolen Humvees.

"What just happened?" Paxton asked.

"We got mugged," Jannati muttered.

"I got that guy's son out of Gitmo," Howard said, staring after Qasem in disbelief.

"All right, lock it down," Cross said. "We've got somewhere to be." He turned to Miriam. "Start getting your people in the back of that truck." He looked at Jannati and Williams. "Help her out."

The three of them moved off.

"Sir, were we counting on them to plot a safe route back to Erbil?" Lancaster asked.

Cross nodded. "Now it's your job. You'll ride up front with me. The rest of you will be in the rear with the civilians. Gather up all our gear off the other vehicles and let's move out. We're leaving in five."

Lancaster, Howard, Yamashita, and Shepherd moved off, leaving Paxton and Cross alone.

"We're not that far from Mosul," Paxton pointed out. "Baiji either. Islamic State's got to know something's wrong by now. They'll send people out to find out why nobody on the train's answering them. They probably have already."

"Probably," Cross agreed.

"Is five minutes enough to get ahead of them?"

"I hope so."

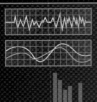

INTEL

DECRYPTING
IIIIIIIII IIIIIIIIIIIIII IIIII

12345

COM CHATTER

- MH-60: highly versatile version of the Sikorsky Black Hawk helicopter

- WILD BOAR: nickname for a Polish-made, all-terrain vehicle used by infantry

- URAL: Russian-made military vehicle that is similar to a Humvee

3245.98 ● ● ●

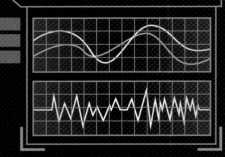

CHAPTER FOUR

1324.014

STRIKING FIRE

The Peshmerga were still loading their vehicles when Cross's people pulled away in their truck. Ten seconds later, the sound of a helicopter came rushing in from the darkness.

WHIR-WHIR-WHIR-WHIR

The aircraft, a Sikorsky MH-60 Black Hawk, thundered into view overhead. It shined a halogen searchlight out one of the side doors. The beam washed over Shadow Squadron's vehicle and passed to the Peshmerga working like ants. The helicopter wobbled, turned awkwardly in the air and pointed its nose down at the train.

SHOOOM!

A second later, a missile lanced out and tore through the top of the second passenger car. The explosion split open the train and obliterated half of the Peshmerga soldiers instantly. The others scrambled for cover and started firing back.

"That's not one of ours," Lancaster whispered, half in shock. She looked back and forth between the tactical datapad on her wrist and the rearview mirror out her window.

"The Iraqis lost one of our Black Hawks when ISIS took Mosul," Cross said through gritted teeth. He was struggling to keep the overloaded 8x8 truck under some semblance of control. "We didn't figure they had anybody who could fly it."

Fortunately, whoever that pilot was, he wasn't terribly good. The helicopter's movements in the air were anything but graceful, and he'd positioned the aircraft much closer to the attack zone than he should have. As the Peshmerga began to return fire on him, the pilot had to maneuver the Black Hawk around in a huge, ungainly half-circle.

Once it was righted again, the chopper brought its M134 miniguns into firing position. And the helicopter wasn't the only Islamic State vehicle coming to fight.

"Sir, there are three Wild Boars coming up the tracks from the south," Shepherd reported in Cross's canalphone from the rear of the truck. Each one could hold 13 people and had a powerful machine gun on top. "They have ISIS flags painted on the hoods."

"Are they on our trail?" Cross asked.

Another missile streaked down from the Black Hawk, obliterating the Kurds's vehicles. The grim whine of its miniguns soon followed.

"No, sir," Shepherd said. "They're circling what's left of the train."

"We could let Qasem deal with them," Howard suggested with cold satisfaction in his voice. "He's got plenty of weapons to keep them busy with."

"Not with that Black Hawk overhead," Lancaster murmured.

Cross ground his teeth but nodded. Even caught

by surprise, the Peshmerga were plenty tough enough to deal with either the Black Hawk or three trucks worth of Islamic State soldiers. Either, but not both.

"Yamashita," Cross said. "How far's the Black Hawk from us?"

"About 900 yards," the sniper replied.

"Too far?"

"No, sir," Yamashita replied with obvious reluctance in his voice. "But we'll need to stop."

"You've got 30 seconds. One shot."

Cross ground the truck to a halt with the engine running and silently counted the seconds. At the rear, Yamashita jumped out and dropped to one knee by the side of the road. He waited for the Black Hawk to stop and hover, then he pulled the trigger.

BANG!

Cross counted a full ten seconds after the shot, but nothing happened. The helicopter moved again and continued firing.

"No hit," Yamashita said calmly. "One more."

"Your time's up," Cross said.

"I could set up an autogun," Lancaster suggested. "It'll get the job done."

"Before I let your steam drill beat me down," Yamashita said, "I'm gonna die with a hammer in my hand."

"What?" Cross asked.

Rather than answer, Yamashita took another shot.

BANG!

"Hey, I said one shot, Lieu —"

"Wait for it," Yamashita interrupted.

As soon as the words were out of his mouth, the Black Hawk suddenly bucked in the air, and all fire from it ceased. It pitched hard to the left and began to corkscrew down out of the sky. It hit the ground, tumbled, and caught fire as it rolled. Cross saw the whole thing in the truck's side mirror.

"I'm back in," Yamashita reported.

"Lord, lord," Lancaster said with a wry smile.

"The Black Hawk's toast," Shepherd reported from the back of the truck. "But two of the Boars are breaking off and coming this way. I guess the third one's staying to deal with the remaining Kurds."

"Good luck to them," Cross said. He slammed the truck back into gear and floored the accelerator.

The 10-ton, eight-wheel vehicle didn't exactly fly away. It more lurched off and slowly chugged up to its top speed of 50 miles per hour. For the moment, Cross had to keep it on the road while Lancaster pored over satellite maps of the area in search of a path out of harm's way — assuming one even existed. Erbil was close, but not knowing the area and driving a much slower vehicle put Cross's people at a severe disadvantage. The Wild Boars were half as heavy and had a top speed that doubled the Ural's. They were going to catch up in no time.

"Can you get us air support?" Cross asked.

"I'm trying," Lancaster said. "We don't have the air presence we used to during the war. The only inbound option is prioritizing the Peshmerga . . ."

"Figures," Cross grumbled. "How about if —"

"Sir," Paxton cut in over the canalphone, "they're going to be right on us in about a minute. Can we get off this road?"

Cross didn't even need to pass the question to Lancaster. He could see that the broken, hilly terrain would only slow the Ural down without offering any hiding places. The Boars would just catch up sooner.

"Negative," Cross said. "You're going to have to brush them back as best you can."

There came a long pause before Paxton finally replied. His voice was calm and cold, tinged with resignation. "Roger that, Commander. Out."

INTEL

DECRYPTING
IIIIIIIII IIIIIIIIIIIII I

12345

COM CHATTER

- LEUPOLD: brand of telescopic site used for sniper rifles

- M240L: lightweight machine gun with a high rate of fire

- M67: fragmentation grenade with a 16-foot explosive radius

- PK: high-powered, Soviet-made machine gun

3245.98 ● ● ●

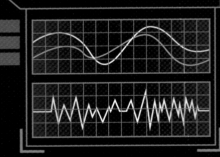

CHAPTER FIVE

1324.014

BROTHERS-IN-ARMS

"You heard the man," Paxton said to the rest of the Shadow Squadron.

"What did he say?" Miriam asked from her seat near where Paxton stood.

"Things are about to get real loud, sweetheart," Shepherd said with a slightly maniacal grin.

"I want everybody up near the cab," Paxton said to the wide-eyed civilians. "Get as close to the front of the truck as you can, pack in as tight as you can, and get down. *Move!*"

The Iraqis didn't react at first, but the last word barked at them authoritatively sent them scrambling into motion. They huddled together near the front of the cargo compartment, kneeling and wrapping their arms around one another.

As they huddled, Paxton addressed his fellow soldiers. "Mark, I need you at the rear with me. Get your 240 out."

"Yeah," was all Shepherd said. He reached for his M240L machine gun where it lay packed with the rest of his gear and exchanged his M4 for it. His eyes were wild with anticipation.

"Kim, Aram, Kyle, Carter," Paxton went on, "I want a wall between us and the civilians."

"You got it," the medic said.

"Hoo, boy . . ." Howard said.

Yamashita just nodded.

"Wait," Jannati said. "Let me get back there with you guys. I can do more good shooting than —"

Paxton didn't shake his head or raise his voice. He simply laid a hand on Jannati's shoulder and said softly, "We'll handle it, Marine."

"They're coming up in range," Shepherd said. He knelt by the truck's tailgate and propped his machine gun on it. "You ready?"

Jannati nodded at Paxton and backed off. Paxton turned to the rear of the truck and knelt beside Shepherd. Jannati, Williams, Howard, and Yamashita moved to the edge of where the Iraqis huddled. They turned around and positioned as much of themselves as they could between the unarmed civilians and what was about to come.

Paxton looked at Shepherd and gave him a nod as the two Wild Boars charged forward, cutting off a bend in the road to catch up. When they regained the road, Islamic State soldiers came up out of the armored roof of each vehicle and took up the PK machine guns on top.

"*De oppresso liber*," Paxton said solemnly.

Shepherd snorted out half a laugh and rolled his eyes. "*Semper ubi, sub ubi*," he replied.

Then a storm of bullets filled the air.

BOOM BANG BOOM BANG BOOM

Shepherd and the two PKs opened up at the same time. Paxton was just a fraction of a second slower. Shepherd let fly on full auto, spraying back and forth across the Boars' grills, hoping to disable them.

Paxton had only three-round bursts available to him, but he tried to put them to their best effect. His first two bursts went into the windshield of the nearer vehicle, covering it with a spider web of cracks. Less than half of his bullets connected, however, due to range and the motion between the target and his firing platform.

Shepherd's spray of bullets didn't do much either, as most of his shots bounced harmlessly off armor plating or punched out headlights.

The opposition's return fire was far more effective. The first burst from the two PKs tore up the ground right behind the fleeing Ural then stitched two jagged lines upward through the rear of the truck. Both of its back two tires were hit and came apart all over the road. The rear end shimmied and skidded back and forth a second before Cross could regain control.

The wooden tailgate was shredded. All three

soldiers in front of the civilians took hits on their body armor. Jannati also took a hit in the shoulder, while Williams caught one in the meat of his thigh. Howard took one in the small of his back right under the edge of his armor. Yamashita was the only one to make it through without any extra hits. Despite their efforts, one of the civilians was hit as well, and his scream rose above the chaos of battle.

Shepherd and Paxton took the worst of it. The opening barrage knocked them both back. Paxton wound up sitting down hard, clutching his M4 in one hand. He couldn't feel his legs, and his left arm lay heavy and useless at his side. His ears rang, and he was dizzy from a bullet that glanced off his helmet.

Unable to see over the tailgate, he forced his rifle up over the edge and squeezed the trigger over and over again, blind-firing at the vehicles behind. He couldn't see what happened, but one of his bursts connected with the windshield he'd already hit once, covering it with more holes and cracks. He didn't hit the driver — the windshield was evidently bullet-proof glass — but he made it so hard to see that the driver missed a curve in the road and ran into a ditch. Its gunner tried to fire again, but the Boar's erratic path made it impossible to aim straight.

When Paxton's weapon ran dry, he looked over at Shepherd. For all he could tell, Shepherd was dead. The gunfire had knocked him flat on his back with his knees up and his machine gun between them. Blood pooled on the cargo bed beneath him. Through his own haze of pain and shock, Paxton couldn't see Shepherd's chest moving.

"Mark!" Paxton barked at his fellow Green Beret. "Mark, get up!"

Somehow, from somewhere at the edge of life, Shepherd heard his name. His eyes popped open. He groaned and coughed up a mouthful of blood.

And then he got mad.

His eyes blazing, his lips pulled back from red-stained teeth in a snarl, he heaved himself back upright like a zombie lurching back to life. He couldn't lift his machine gun high enough to put it over the top of the tailgate, so he kicked out with both legs and broke the tattered, bullet-ruined panel right off the back of the truck.

RAT-A-TAT-A-TAT-A-TAT-TAT!
RAT-A-TAT-A-TAT-A-TAT-TAT!

Fire bloomed from his M240 as he clenched the trigger in a death grip. The weapon bucked in his hand, throwing bullets wildly out the back. One of them punched out the second boar's last remaining headlight. A few cracked the windshield. And some, miraculously, found the gunner behind the PK and threw him off the back of the vehicle. The boar swerved and slowed down, though it didn't leave the road.

Shepherd's ammo box ran out. He dropped the empty weapon beside him.

"That a boy," Paxton said. "Now come here."

Wild-eyed, Shepherd rolled over on one side toward Paxton, who dragged himself one-armed to meet him halfway. When they were side-by-side, Paxton unhooked an M67 fragmentation grenade from his web belt. He managed to get rid of the safety one-handed.

"Give me a hand with this," Paxton said.

Shepherd, barely aware of his surroundings, held out his good hand. Paxton hooked the ring of the pin over his finger.

"Pull," Paxton said.

Shepherd's finger flexed. Together, they managed to yank the pin out, though the effort made a gray cloud close in around the edges of Paxton's vision. Fortunately, he kept the spoon tight against the side of the grenade so it didn't go off.

Meanwhile, the boar that had gone off the road pulled off and disappeared into the darkness. The other one, however, picked up speed once more, and a new gunner climbed up behind the PK. Paxton saw the man aim the machine gun's barrel toward the rear of the truck. Over the road noise and the engines, Paxton could hear the man calling his name. But it couldn't have been his voice, could it? He didn't know his name. The voice had to be coming from somewhere else.

Doesn't matter, Paxton thought. They wouldn't be able to take another barrage of bullets. He had to do something. They only had a few seconds.

Paxton's weak, blood-slicked fingers freed the spoon. It popped off the grenade.

Five, he counted in his head.

Four . . .

Gray closed in. The machine gunner took aim. Someone said his name again.

Three . . .

With a hideous gasp, Shepherd collapsed once more and was still.

Paxton closed his eyes.

Two . . .

He threw the grenade. It bounced onto the road and disappeared in the dust.

One . . .

Paxton passed out.

* * *

"Paxton!" Cross shouted, fighting to keep the damaged truck on the narrow dirt road. Not only were the back tires out, but the thing was leaking fuel, and a dozen warning lights flickered on the dashboard. "Paxton, what's happening back —"

KABOOOOOOOOM!!

A grenade explosion cut him off. The blast sounded like it had gone off in the cab with him. For a split second he thought it had come from the boar, putting an end to their Ural truck's desperate flight.

But a glance in the side mirror showed him the truth: the blast had gone off right under the boar's front driver-side tire, blowing the wheel off and taking out the engine. Black smoke streamed from the vehicle as it skidded to a halt. For the few seconds Cross could spare to watch it, no one got out of the vehicle and no more shots came from its machine gun.

"Somebody talk to me!" Cross demanded.

"We've got wounded," Yamashita said. "One civilian took a flesh wound. Williams caught one in the leg, through-and-through. Jannati's shoulder is in pieces. Howard's hit in the back. Williams is doing what he can, but they're out of the fight. Howard might not make it."

Yamashita paused, took a deep breath, then exhaled in a hiss of pain. "Paxton and Shepherd are dead."

Lancaster clenched her teeth and whispered to herself. Cross couldn't make out the words.

"I only saw one of the boars go down," Cross said, shoving all the other information away to be processed later. "Are both of the vehicles out of commission?"

"Negative," Yamashita said. "We only slowed the first one down. It's making its way back to the road now. I can see it in my Leupold. Looks like it's heading for the wreckage of the second boar. I figure they'll take on survivors and pick up the chase again."

"Anything you can do from here?" Cross asked.

"I'm sorry, Commander," Yamashita said. "They're moving, the truck's moving, and they're too far away. Maybe when they get closer . . . I don't know. How much more road do we have left?"

Cross looked at Lancaster. "How much farther?"

"We're close," Lancaster said, her face pale and drawn. She seemed to be fighting back the urge to throw up. "We're close, but . . . they're still going to get to us before we get across into Erbil."

"A lot of road," Cross told Yamashita.

"Then stop," Yamashita said. "I'm not hurt, and there's only one boar left. I can slow it down when it comes in range."

"Too risky," Cross said. "If I stop this thing long enough for you to do that, I might not be able to get it going again. And if we have to walk our wounded from here to Erbil, we'll all be sitting ducks if anyone else comes looking for us."

"I didn't say wait, Commander," Yamashita said so softly that Cross barely heard him. "Just slow down long enough for me to get out. I'll keep them off you and watch the road for anybody else. When you get past the safe point, call me. I'll reel in."

"Kim . . ."

"Sir, this isn't a hard decision. It's the only option you've got. Besides, I've been doing a lot of thinking about the talk we had before we got here. I figured out the answer to my question. The one about why you're willing to risk your life."

Cross's stomach sank. "Tell me."

"Us," Yamashita replied. "You risk your life to keep us safe, so we can get the job done. That's your answer, isn't it, Commander?"

Cross's eyes blurred. He blinked to clear them. "That's exactly the reason, Lieutenant."

"Mine, too," Yamashita said. "Now let me out of the truck."

Cross slowed and pulled over. "Do what you have to do," he said.

"Sir," Yamashita said. A moment later, he added, "Okay, I'm out. Get moving."

"Erbil's not far now, Lieutenant," Cross told him. "I'll reel you in as soon as we get there."

"Sir," Yamashita said. "Out."

"Good luck, Kim," Cross said. "And thank you. Out."

* * *

Yamashita waited for several seconds as the Ural drove away to make sure Cross wouldn't change his mind and turn around. When he was satisfied

the Commander wasn't coming back, he dug the canalphone out of his ear, dropped it on the ground, and crushed it with his heel.

"Sorry, Commander," he whispered, smiling sadly. "I'd reel in if I could, but we both know that's not an option."

He took a deep breath, wincing due to a cracked rib under his armor vest. Then he moved off to a low hillside that offered him the best firing angle over the road. The undamaged boar was idling next to its damaged counterpart, and soldiers from the latter were climbing into the former. They were about 2,000 yards out.

Yamashita unscrewed the sound and flash suppressor from the end of his M110. Once he started firing, they'd see him, they'd hear him, and they'd come for him. He wouldn't give them a choice in the matter. They'd hunt him down, and he'd make them work for it. He'd waste their time by picking off as many of them as he could. As many as it took for Cross to get the others to safety like he'd promised.

As for himself . . .

"Well, I'm gonna die with a hammer in my hand, Lord, Lord," Yamashita sang. "I'm gonna die with a hammer in my hand."

CLASSIFIED

MISSION DEBRIEFING

OPERATION

STEEL HAMMER

012

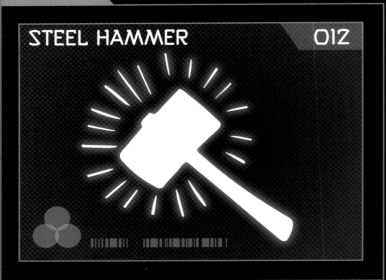

PRIMARY OBJECTIVES

- Sabotage ISIS supply chain

- Rendezvous with Peshmerga forces

SECONDARY OBJECTIVES

x Secure any munitions found

STATUS

2/3 COMPLETE

3245.98

CROSS, RYAN

RANK: Lieutenant Commander
BRANCH: Navy Seal
PSYCH PROFILE: Team leader
of Shadow Squadron. Control
oriented and loyal, Cross insisted
on hand-picking each member of
his squad.

We incurred heavy losses on this mission. We also saved many innocent lives. Adam Paxton, Mark Shepherd, Carter Howard, and Kimiyo Yamashita died the way they lived: in selfless service of the innocent and as our brothers-in-arms.

We've lost team members before. We will lose team members again. But Shadow Squadron will persevere as an ideal, as the invisible arm of liberty, as a memorial to those who sacrificed their lives for all of us.

- Lieutenant Commander Ryan Cross

2019.681

CREATOR BIO(S)

AUTHOR

CARL BOWEN

Carl Bowen is a father, husband, and writer living in Lawrenceville, Georgia. He was born in Louisiana, lived briefly in England, and was raised in Georgia where he went to school. He has published a handful of novels, short stories, and comics. For Stone Arch Books, he has retold *20,000 Leagues Under the Sea*, *The Strange Case of Dr. Jekyll and Mr. Hyde*, *The Jungle Book*, *Aladdin and the Magic Lamp*, *Julius Caesar*, and *The Murders in the Rue Morgue*. He is the original author of *BMX Breakthrough* as well as the Shadow Squadron series.

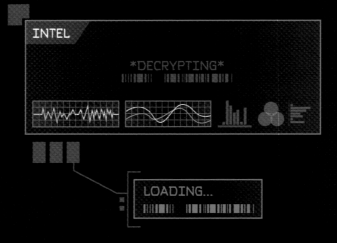

INTEL

DECRYPTING

LOADING...

ARTIST

WILSON TORTOSA

Wilson "Wunan" Tortosa is a Filipino comic book artist best known for his work on *Tomb Raider* and the American relaunch of *Battle of the Planets* for Top Cow Productions. Wilson attended Philippine Cultural High School, then went on to the University of Santo Tomas where he graduated with a Bachelor's Degree in Fine Arts, majoring in Advertising.

ARTIST

BENNY FUENTES

Benny Fuentes lives in Villahermosa, Tabasco, in Mexico, where the temperature is just as hot as the sauce. He studied graphic design in college, but now he works as a full-time illustrator in the comic book and graphic novel industry for companies like Marvel, DC Comics, and Top Cow Productions. He shares his home with two crazy cats, Chelo and Kitty, who act like they own the place.

2019.681

AUTHOR DEBRIEFING

CARL BOWEN

Q/When and why did you decide to become a writer?
A/I've enjoyed writing ever since I was in elementary
school. I wrote as much as I could, hoping to
become the next Lloyd Alexander or Stephen King,
but I didn't sell my first story until I was in college.
It had been a long wait, but the day I saw my story
in print was one of the best days of my life.

Q/What made you decide to write *Shadow Squadron*?
A/As a kid, my heroes were always brave knights or
noble loners who fought because it was their duty,
not for fame or glory. I think the special ops soldiers
of the US military embody those ideals. Their jobs
are difficult and often thankless, so I wanted to
show how cool their jobs are and also express my
gratitude for our brave warriors.

Q/What inspires you to write?
A/My biggest inspiration is my family. My wife's love
and support lifts me up when this job seems too hard
to keep going. My son is another big inspiration.

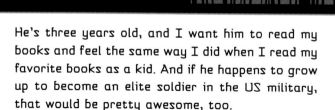

He's three years old, and I want him to read my books and feel the same way I did when I read my favorite books as a kid. And if he happens to grow up to become an elite soldier in the US military, that would be pretty awesome, too.

Q/Describe what it was like to write these books.
A/The only military experience I have is a year I spent in the Army ROTC. It gave me a great respect for the military and its soldiers, but I quickly realized I would have made a pretty awful soldier. I recently got to test out a friend's arsenal of firearms, including a combat shotgun, an AR-15 rifle, and a Barrett M82 sniper rifle. We got to blow apart an old fax machine.

Q/What is your favorite book, movie, and game?
A/My favorite book of all time is *Don Quixote*. It's crazy and it makes me laugh. My favorite movie is either *Casablanca* or *Double Indemnity*, old black-and-white movies made before I was born. My favorite game, hands down, is *Skyrim*, in which you play a heroic dragonslayer. But not even *Skyrim* can keep me from writing more *Shadow Squadron* stories, so you won't have to wait long to read more about Ryan Cross and his team. That's a promise.

INTEL

DECRYPTING

ALPHA

COM CHATTER

-MISSION PREVIEW: After an unknown aircraft crashes in Antarctica near a science facility, Shadow Squadron is deployed to recover the device. But when Russian special forces intervene, Cross gets caught between the mission's objective and the civilian scientists' safety.

3245.98 ● ● ●

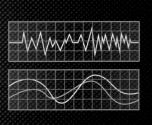

SHADOW SQUADRON

PHANTOM SUN

CARL BOWEN

PHANTOM SUN

Cross tapped his touchscreen to start the video. On the screen, a few geologists began pointing and waving frantically. The camera watched them all for another couple of seconds then lurched around in a half circle and tilted skyward. Blurry clouds wavered in and out of focus for a second before the cameraman found what the others had pointing at — a lance of white fire in the sky. The image focused, showing what appeared to be a meteorite with a trailing white plume behind it punching through a hole in the clouds. The camera zoomed out to allow the cameraman to better track the object's progress through the sky.

"Is that a meteorite?" Shepherd asked.

"Just keep watching," Brighton said, breathless with anticipation.

Right on cue, the supposed meteorite suddenly flared white, then changed directions in mid-flight by almost 45 degrees. Grunts and hisses of surprise filled the room.

"So . . . not a meteorite," Shepherd muttered.

The members of Shadow Squadron watched in awe as the falling object changed direction once again with another flare and then pitched downward. The camera angle twisted overhead and then lowered to track its earthward trajectory from below.

"And now . . . sonic boom," Brighton said.

The camera image shook violently for a second as the compression wave from the falling object broke the speed of sound and as the accompanying burst shook the cameraman's hands. A moment later, the object streaked into the distance and disappeared into the rolling hills of ice and snow. The video footage ended a few moments later with a still image of the

gawking geologists looking as excited as a bunch of kids on Christmas morning.

"This video popped up on the Internet a few hours ago," Cross began. "It's already starting to go viral."

"What is it?" Second Lieutenant Aram Jannati said. Jannati, the team's newest member, came from the Marine Special Operations Regiment. "I can't imagine we'd get involved if it was just a meteor."

"Meteorite," Staff Sergeant Adam Paxton corrected. "If it gets through the atmosphere to the ground, it's a meteorite."

"That wasn't a meteorite, man," Brighton said, hopping out of his chair. He dug his smartphone out of a cargo pocket and came around the table toward the front of the room. He laid his phone on the touchscreen Cross had used and then synced up the two devices. With that done, he used his phone as a remote control to run the video backward to the first time the object had changed directions. He used a slider to move the timer back and forth, showing the object's fairly sharp angle of deflection through the sky.

"Meteorites can't change directions like this," Brighton said. "This is 45 degrees of deflection at least, and the thing barely even slows down."

"I'm seeing a flare when it turns," Paxton said. "Meteors hold a lot of frozen water when they're in space, and it expands when it reaches the atmosphere. If those gases are venting or exploding, couldn't that cause a change of direction?"

"Not this sharply," Brighton said before Cross could reply. "Besides, if you look at this…" He used a few swipes across his phone to pause the video and zoom in on the flying object. At the new resolution, a dark, oblong shape was visible inside a wreath of fire. He then advanced through the first and second changes of direction and tracked it a few seconds forward before pausing again. "See?"

A room full of shrugs and uncomprehending looks met Brighton's eager gaze.

"It's the same size!" Brighton said, tossing his hands up in mock frustration. "If this thing had exploded twice — with enough force to push something this big in a different direction both times — it would be in

a million pieces. So those aren't explosions. They're thrusters or ramjets or something."

"Which makes this what?" Shepherd asked. "A UFO?"

"Sure," Paxton answered in a mocking tone. "It's unidentified, it's flying, and it's surely an object. It probably has little green men inside, too."

"You don't know that it doesn't," Brighton said. "I mean, this thing could be from outer space!"

"Sit down, Sergeant," Chief Walker said.

Brighton reluctantly did so, pocketing his phone.

"Don't get ahead of yourself, Ed," Cross said, retaking control of the briefing. "Phantom Cell analysts have authenticated the video and concluded that this thing isn't just a meteorite. It's some kind of metal construct, though they can't make out specifics from the quality of the video. I suppose it's possible it's from outer space, but it's much more likely it's man-made. All we know for sure is that it's not American made. Therefore, our mission is to get out to where it came down, secure it, zip it up, and bring it back for a full analysis. Anyone have any questions so far?"

"I do," Jannati said. "What is Phantom Cell?"

Cross nodded. Jannati was the newest member of the team, and as such he wasn't as familiar with all the various secret programs. "Phantom Cell is a parallel program to ours," Cross explained. "But their focus is on psy-ops, cyberwarfare, and research and development."

Jannati nodded. "Geeks, in other words," he said.

Brighton gave him a sour look but said nothing.

"What are we supposed to do about the scientists who found this thing?" Lieutenant Kimiyo Yamashita asked. True to his stoic nature, the sniper had finished his breakfast and coffee while everyone else was talking excitedly. "Do they know we're coming?"

"That's the problem," Cross said, frowning. "We haven't heard a peep out of them since this video appeared online. Attempts at contacting them have gone unanswered. Last anyone heard, the geologists who made the video were going to try to find the point of impact where this object came down. We have no idea whether they found it or not, or what happened to them."

"Isn't this how the movie *Aliens* started?" Brighton asked. "With a space colony suddenly cutting off communication after a UFO crash landing?"

Paxton rolled his eyes. "Lost Aspen, the base there, is pretty new," he said. "And it's in the middle of Antarctica. It could just be a simple technical failure."

"You have zero imagination, man," Brighton said. "You're going to be the first one the monster eats. Well... after me, anyway."

"These are our orders," Cross continued as if he had never been interrupted. "Find what crashed, bring the object back for study, figure out why the research station stopped communicating, and make sure the civilians are safe. Stealth is going to be of paramount importance on this one. Nobody has any territorial claims on Marie Byrd Land, but no country is supposed to be sending troops on missions anywhere in Antarctica, either."

"Are we expecting anyone else to be breaking that rule while we are, Commander?" Yamashita asked.

"It's possible," Cross said. "If this object is man-

made, whoever made it is probably going to come looking for it. Any other government that attached the same significance to the video that ours did could send people, too. No specific intel has been confirmed yet, but it's only a matter of time before someone takes an active interest."

"Seems like the longer the video's out there, the more likely we're going to have company," Yamashita said.

"About that," Cross said with a mischievous smile on his face. "Phantom Cell's running a psy-ops campaign in support of our efforts. They're simultaneously spreading the word that the video's a hoax and doing their best to stop it from spreading and to remove it from circulation."

"Good luck to them on that last one," Brighton snorted. "It's the Internet. Phantom Cell's good, but nobody's that good."

"Not our concern," Cross said. "We ship out in one hour. Get your gear on the Commando. We'll go over more mission specifics during the flight. Understood?"

"Sir," the men responded in unison. At a nod from Cross, they rose and gathered up the remains of their breakfast. As they left the briefing room, Walker remained behind. He gulped down the last of his coffee before standing up.

"Brighton's sure excited," Walker said.

"I knew he would be," Cross replied. "I didn't expect him to try to help out so much with the briefing, though."

"Is that what I'm like whenever I chip in from up here?" Walker asked.

Cross fought off the immediate urge to toy with his second-in-command, though he couldn't stop the mischievous smile from coming back. "Maybe a little bit," he said.

Walker returned Cross's grin. "Then I wholeheartedly apologize."

TRANSMISSION ERROR

PLEASE CONTACT YOUR LOCAL LIBRARY OR
BOOKSTORE FOR MORE DETAILS...

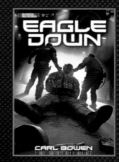

LOGGING OUT...

2012.101